THE MYTH OF JOSÉ MARTÍ

ENVISIONING CUBA

Louis A. Pérez Jr., editor

THE MYTH OF
JOSÉ MARTÍ

Conflicting Nationalisms in Early
Twentieth-Century Cuba

LILLIAN GUERRA

•

THE UNIVERSITY OF NORTH CAROLINA PRESS • CHAPEL HILL AND LONDON

Designed by April Leidig-Higgins
Set in Minion by Copperline Book Services, Inc.
Manufactured in the United States of America

The paper in this book meets the guidelines for perma-
nence and durability of the Committee on Production
Guidelines for Book Longevity of the Council on
Library Resources.

Library of Congress Cataloging-in-Publication Data
Guerra, Lillian.   The myth of José Martí: conflicting
nationalisms in early twentieth-century Cuba /
Lillian Guerra.
p. cm. — (Envisioning Cuba)
Includes bibliographical references and index.
ISBN 0-8078-2925-0 (cloth: alk. paper)
ISBN 0-8078-5590-1 (pbk.: alk. paper)
1. Martí, José, 1853–1895 — Influence.   2. Nationalism —
Cuba — History — 20th century.   3. Cuba — Politics and
government — 20th century.   I. Title.   II. Series.
F1783.M38G78 2005   813'.6 — dc22   2004062098

cloth   09 08 07 06 05   5 4 3 2 1
paper   09 08 07 06 05   5 4 3 2 1

CONTENTS

ILLUSTRATIONS, MAP, & TABLE

ACKNOWLEDGMENTS

THIS WORK REPRESENTS the fulfillment of a promise that I made to myself when I first seriously considered dedicating my life to the pursuit of scholarly knowledge. In the nearly two years I spent in Cuba researching the dissertation that formed the basis for this book, I came to realize that my own pursuit of history was as much personal as academic. In Cuba, I discovered a dynamic community of intellectuals who embraced me and my project, whatever their differences of interpretation and opinion. I also found over 200 relatives who opened their doors and hearts to me as if they had always known me and as if they had always expected that I would one day "come back," despite the fact that I was not born in Cuba but in the United States. "Technically," as one relative said to me, his eyes twinkling, "that means that you never left." This book expresses the sense of love for Cuba and commitment to its sovereignty that I found not only in all the Cubans whom I met in Cuba but that I also share.

Indeed, since that first extended and unforgettable stay from 1996 to 1998, I have never really left. Going to Cuba regularly and weaving the complex halves of my life together has become the center of my being and the well of my inspiration. Given the historic and unjust divides that separate not only Cuba from the United States but also many Cubans from one another, not a day goes by that I do not recognize how privileged I am. Unlike most Cubans, who do not have the luxury to travel back and forth or see both sides of Cuba's reality for themselves, the national and the imperial, I can count large, extended families as well as vibrant, intellectual communities of friends and colleagues on both sides of my own daily divide.

At a time when monies for research projects in Cuba were still hard to come by, the Institute for the Study of World Politics and a special fund for previous recipients of the Mellon Minority Academic Careers Fellowship provided funds for the fieldwork portion of this project. The University Fellowship of the University of Wisconsin-Madison and two further semesters of support from the John D. and Catherine T. MacArthur Foundation provided the funds that enabled me to focus on writing. I am grateful to all of these institutions. I am especially grateful to the Andrew W. Mellon Foundation for designating me a

Mellon Minority Academic Fellow when I first fell in love with history as a college sophomore at Dartmouth. Without the many years of mentorship under Professors Doug Haynes, Raúl Bueno, and Leo Spitzer that it entailed, I would never have become a scholar of Latin America or a professor of history.

I am also deeply indebted to all of my *compañeros* at the Instituto de Historia de Cuba, especially Amparo Hernández Denis and José Cantón Navarro, whose personal warmth and endless patience with my need for advice and letters of introduction can never be fully reciprocated. In the eight years that I have worked in Cuba, the Instituto de Historia has always offered consistent and enthusiastic support for my perspective and projects. Without its support, this book would not have been possible. I am deeply indebted to the staff of the Archivo Nacional de Cuba and the dedicated Cuban historians who spent as many *horas nalgas* before the documents as I did. Marial Iglesias, Francisco Pérez, Yolanda Díaz, Gloria García, and others served as models for the kind of "deep research" I wanted to do. I also thank Niurys of the Fondo de Libros Raros at the University of Havana and the staff of the Centro de Estudios Martianos, especially Pedro Pablo Rodríguez, Maylo Pajón, Renio Díaz Triana, and Ana Elena Arazoza. I also thank the archivist-historians of the Archivo Provincial de Cienfuegos "Ritica Suárez del Villar y Suárez del Villar," especially Mitsi, Mery, and Berta as well as Orlando García, its director. Together, these intellectuals not only guided me through their document collections and clarified my own interpretations of them but also helped me resurrect the ghosts of my family's past.

I also want to thank the community of historians at the University of Wisconsin-Madison that prepared me for my work in Cuba and guided its fruition so steadily upon my return. For sharing what was a challenging and at times emotionally harrowing journey toward my doctoral degree, I thank the friends and colleagues who supported me along the way, especially Ileana Rodríguez Silva, Leo Garofalo, Solsireé Del Moral, Joe Hall, Jean Weiss, Tom Green, Cindy Green, Ruthie Green, Ellie Green, Louise Pubols, Tracey Deutsch, David Chang, María Moreno, Eileen Willingham, Anne Macpherson, Nancy Appelbaum, René Reeves, Patrick McNamara, Bert Kreitlow, Thomas Andrews, and Andrés Matías Ortíz. For having opened up the horizons of my creativity and helping me to harness its energy so consistently over the years, I am most indebted to my graduate advisers, Florencia Mallon, Francisco Scarano, and Steve J. Stern. They taught me not only how to do "good history" but also how to remain emotionally engaged and politically passionate about my subject, just as they are. Perhaps most important, Florencia, Franco, and Steve never stopped believing in me. Their faith in my skills, talents, and ambition has proved unwavering, even when my own has faltered.

I owe a great deal of thanks to my students at Bates, some of whom accompanied me to Cuba on different occasions, for being my community of "Latin Americanists" in Maine and for making my efforts to fuse a passion for teaching and a love of research worthwhile, especially Michael McCarthy, Kate Marshall, Andrea Noyes, Alexa Miller, Margherita Pilato, Nate McConarty, Bill Spirer, Galen Haggerty, Trent Lierman, Eric Stanculescu, Stephen Gresham, Patrick Quirk, Charlie Henry, and Currier Stokes. I am also grateful to my former colleagues, especially Steve Hochstadt, Liz Tobin, Dennis Grafflin, Michael Jones, John Cole, and Hilmar Jensen at Bates College for always appreciating and supporting my needs as I completed revisions and drafts of this work. I also thank Sylvia Hawks, our area coordinator for the Bates history department, whose efficiency, assistance, and optimism always proved foundational to any Cuba-related project. I am especially indebted to Lisa Maurizio, an expert on ancient Greek culture, for her advice, brilliant conversation, and suggestions on theoretical approaches for interpreting the meaning and function of myths. In addition to being a constant source of personal support, Kevin Yelvington, of the University of South Florida, has offered pivotal and well-timed advice on interdisciplinary approaches to race, identity, and José Martí. I am also deeply indebted to Aline Helg, who read the original version of this book as a doctoral dissertation out of no obligation other than her passionate commitment to the subject of Cuba's internal political struggles and the kindness of her heart. Despite its exceedingly lengthy and rough form, Aline returned twelve single-spaced, handwritten pages of notes to me. Her notes became the initial guide for the revisions that led to the manuscript of this work. Louis A. Pérez and Alejandro de la Fuente, who served as readers for the University of North Carolina Press, honored me with their critical, keenly targeted, and frank remarks at an earlier stage of the publication process. Ultimately, the need to satisfy their concerns impelled me to make this a more accessible, theoretically coherent study than it might otherwise have been. Thanks also go to Elaine Maisner whose support, interest, and steady optimism about transforming this manuscript into a book proved critical. I also thank my new colleagues at Yale, especially Stuart Schwartz and Gil Joseph, for appreciating the potential of this book.

This book is dedicated to the people who have most supported the fusion and transformation of myself that coming to life in Cuba over the last few years has meant to me. In Cuba and because of Cubans, I have become whole. In this regard, I especially thank Kevin A. Lewis, who offered unwavering support and never questioned my need to go to Cuba or the benefits of my being there, even when that meant long separations and the challenges that come with them. I also thank the many other central supporters of my growth process, some of whom are both colleagues in Cuba and lifelong friends: Marial Iglesias, Marlene Ortega, Arelys Hernández Plasencia, Rolando Milián, Jorge Macle, Manuel Barcia Paz, Yolanda Díaz, Rolando Misas, Arsenio Cicero, Oílda Hevia, Reinaldo Funes, Mayra Mena Mujíca, Hernán Venegas Delgado, Jennifer Sandoval, Gretchen Schweitzer, Claudia Aburto Guzmán, and Manuel López Oliva. I thank my mother, Luisa Guerra, for offering me her prayers, steadfast support, and funny stories by phone while I was in Cuba, and my father, Tomás Guerra, for allowing me to cultivate and never questioning the independence of mind that takes me to Cuba and brings me back again. I also thank my sister, Lucy Guerra, for her strength in happily shouldering my parents' worries about me and for putting them to rest once and for all by going there (and coming back) herself.

Finally, I thank all of my family in Cuba, most especially the Amores of Cienfuegos and Havana, the Guerras of Pinar del Río, and the nine relatives of the del Castillo Sotolongo family of Centro Habana with whom I feel I share a home after so many visits and long stays. This book stands as a testament to the power of their love, laughter, and resilience, whatever the challenges and however great the hardships of over four decades of collective and personal isolation. My conversations with Norma Sotolongo Bellas, Don Luis del Castillo Trujillo, and Diego Sotolongo Bellas, as well as with Normita, Diego Angel, Luisito, Yanfiel, Patricia, and Raúl Rodríguez, surely made me into a better scholar, but more important, they made me into a better person. Since 1997, three of these wonderful people have passed away: Raúl, who was himself a historian at the Instituto Cubano de Artes e Industrias Cinematográficas and the first intellectual to introduce me to the rigors of analyzing the contradictions of the Republic; Norma, my grandmother's first cousin, who became both a second grandmother to me and my best friend; and her husband and my unofficial mentor in the political history of Cuba, Don Luis. Today, I am all the more grateful that God and the spirits granted me the privilege of getting to know and to love Norma and Don Luis so well. I often feel their spirit buoy me with the strength and passion to do my work, just as it did when I set off every morning for the Archivo Nacional in Old Havana and came home again every afternoon to trade memories and stories about the past.

It is to Norma and Don Luis's own personal and historic memories as well as to their ever-vibrant and inspiring spirit that I offer this work.

THE MYTH OF JOSÉ MARTÍ

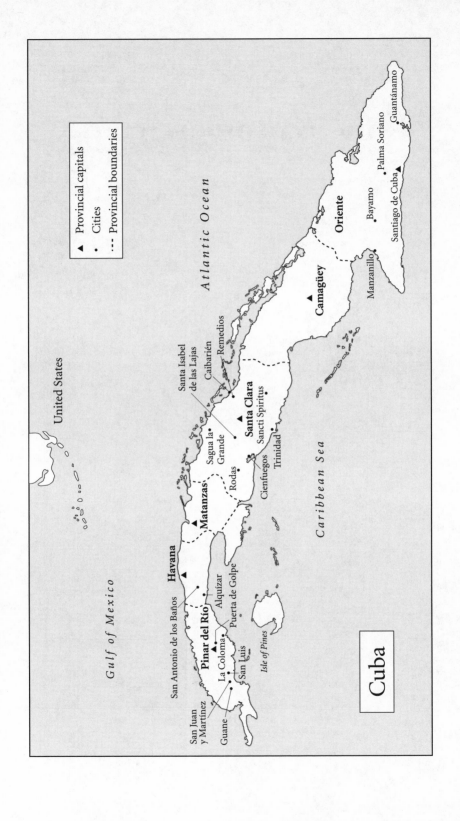

Cuba

INTRODUCTION

· ·

Multiple Nations, Multiple
Martís, 1895–1921

ON FEBRUARY 24, 1905, citizens of the Cuban Republic gathered under a thick blanket of dense, gray clouds in Havana's Central Park. They eagerly awaited the presentation of Cuba's first marble statue of José Martí. The occasion also marked the tenth anniversary of the start of Cuba's third and final war for independence from Spain. Together with General Máximo Gómez, the rebels' commander in chief, José Martí had launched the war on that very day in 1895 when he issued the Grito de Baire, the official call to arms. Killed in his first military encounter with loyalist troops less than three months later, Martí had been one of the revolutionary movement's key organizers and principal ideologues since the mid-1880s. Despite his intense activism and prolific writing on behalf of independence, Martí's long fifteen-year exile in the United States and Spain's censorship of his works had effectively limited knowledge of his work among Cubans on the island. Still, thanks in part to the return of Martí's fellow emigrés to Cuba at the end of the war in 1898, Martí's fame was growing. Although plans to erect a monument to Martí had been in the works since 1899, building of the monument had been stalled for years. A lack of funds was not the main problem; rather, it was the uncertainty of Cuba's political destiny itself.

Instead of independence and political sovereignty, the end of the war in 1898 brought a four-year U.S. military occupation followed by a pro-U.S. republican administration. The latter proved deeply reluctant to implement any revolutionary reforms. Moreover, the U.S. Congress's imposition of the Platt Amendment to the 1901 Cuban Constitution as a condition for military withdrawal effectively granted the United States the right to intervene whenever it deemed that Cuba's domestic policies were endangering its interests. Regardless of what they thought of Martí's contributions to the war or how differently they viewed the future that they hoped to build, Martí's former comrades-in-arms now faced an embarrassing reality. Commemorating the death of Martí on the anniversary of the 1895 War's original call to arms implied honoring the birth of a nation. Yet, the long-term viability and security of that nation remained dubious at best.

The uncertainty of Cuba's sovereignty and the precariousness of its internal harmony may actually help explain the basis of Martí's appeal. Two years earlier, a law had established the date of Martí's death on May 19, 1895, as a national day of mourning. Yet, the Cuban National Congress did not begin to hold "solemn sessions" in which a keynote speaker intoned the memory of Martí until after the erection of the monument in 1905. That year became pivotal. Over the next two decades, commemorations of all kinds would become commonplace, despite the fact that concerns about Cuba's sovereignty and social stability never went away. Indeed, as U.S. economic and political intervention intensified, these concerns only deepened. Reflections on the historical role and meaning of Martí, public and private, collective and personal, increased in proportion to external challenges and internal political strife as time wore on.

Passionate and tireless in his writing and strategizing on behalf of independence in the years before the war, Martí had called incessantly for social unity amidst ideological division. He prophesied the need for vigilance against U.S. pretensions and demanded the casting aside of personal interest for the sake of revolution and a just society. Cuba would be a republic "with all and for all," Martí had famously pledged. Standing in the shadow of the life-size marble Martí in Havana's Central Park, Tomás Estrada Palma, the first president of the Republic, reminded his audience of Martí's promise that February day in 1905. Yet, General Gómez remained largely silent. His silence attested to many Cubans' alienation from Estrada Palma's government as well as his own. Since taking power in 1902, Estrada Palma's administration had come to rely on violence to repress its critics and adamantly rejected any policies that might have subverted Cuba's colonial legacies. The Cuba of 1905 was becoming a nation that only a small number of independence activists might have imagined.

In his keynote address in honor of Martí, Estrada Palma noted his government's active support for Spanish immigration and foreign investment as the solutions to Cuba's historic social inequalities and economic problems. Rather than breaking up the plantation system, redistributing land to veterans, or providing native-owned businesses with state protection and the financial credit to compete with foreign firms, Estrada Palma promised greater advantages to the very groups that had long held sway in Cuba's economy and society.[1] Many former revolutionaries in the crowd must have found the president's speech appalling. After so much struggle and bloodshed, little seemed to have changed.

INTRODUCTION

Far from unique, this official, state-sponsored manipulation of José Martí in 1905 and the paradoxical celebration of his image by Cubans who had become each other's political opponents are deeply emblematic of an ingrained pattern in Cuban history. To specialists, students, and even casual observers of Cuba, the historic tendency of Cuban political activists to appropriate Martí's image and interpret his words for their own purposes is well known.[2] In fact, from his death until today, the proliferation of new works on or by Martí has increased at the rate of 140 titles per annum.[3] Although many of the works on Martí remain hagiographic, a number of scholars have begun to read Martí's actions and words with a more critical eye. Placing them in historical context, these works consider the degree to which Martí constructed his projects for the liberation of Cuba and Latin America from all forms of colonialism in ambivalent, even ambiguous terms.[4] These terms seem to have invited multiple interpretations and, as one scholar remarked, "[to have created] several Martís."[5] When I began researching this book, this was precisely the phenomenon that I wanted to explain. As I started my work, I realized that the mythification of Martí and the process of nation-building were inextricably tied. I also noticed that a proliferation of works on Martí and interpretations of his writings accompanied increasing social upheavals between 1895 and 1921, the year that marked the consolidation of U.S. neocolonialism in Cuba. Who were these multiple Martís to the first generations of Cubans who crafted their images? Why did understanding and explaining Martí to one another become so important? What did these multiple Martís signify?

This book argues that competing interpretations of José Martí represented different, conflicting interpretations of nation. It is for this reason that Martí became the principal touchstone for the expression and debate of Cuban national sentiments during the first decades of the Republic. Yet, an analysis of the evolving images of Martí is not the central story of this book. Rather, such images serve as critical guideposts that direct our understanding of how different political sectors justified and conceived their actions, ideological differences, and objectives from Martí's lifetime through 1921. By 1921, the collapse of Cuba's sugar economy and the resulting financial dependence of the Cuban state on loans, aid, and direct support from the United States illustrated at an economic level what had been apparent politically for years. That is, Cuba's revolutionary leadership of the 1895 War had presided over the demise of Martí's elusive promise of a nation with which all Cubans could identify and in which all counted themselves as principal constituents. By 1921, they had presided over the stillbirth rather than the birth of a republic. In that same year, the Cuban state formally codified the status of Martí as Cuba's principal national hero, granting him monopoly rights to the title of "Apostle" and requiring all Cuban citizens to honor Martí on the date of his birth in legally prescribed ways.[6] That the consolidation of the image of Martí as a state-controlled icon occurred in the same year that the state's legitimacy and that of its ex-revolutionary leaders reached historic lows was no coincidence. Rather, the efforts of Cuba's political elites to stake an exclusive claim to Martí's legacy and to control interpretations of Martí belied the desperation of their position and how little control they actually had. By 1921, political leaders who voiced the origin of their authority as leaders personally endowed by Martí with the right to rule faced an increasingly incredulous and hostile Cuban public, many of whom no longer cared to listen and had developed their own, alternative images of Martí.

This work offers no authoritative understanding of what Martí meant. Nor does it provide a definitive sense of the extent to which Martí's successors fulfilled his vision, because it makes no claims as to what precisely that vision entailed in terms of a political system or economy. Rather, this book focuses on the discursive and practical battles over the shape and direction of the nation following Martí's death. To do this, it begins by suggesting how and why Martí drew support for the cause of the 1895 War from ideologically and historically divided sectors through a discourse of social unity that was as much messianic as it was pragmatic. Meant to appeal to Cubans with opposing points of view before the war, this discourse became critical to how Cubans demanded the implementation of their own visions of nation and expectations for the Republic afterward. In the early Republic, references to Martí and claims to his legacy became the fundamental means by which Cuban nationalists of conflicting ideological positions discredited each other. They highlighted their differences and charged one another with betraying their respective views of nation through competing images of Martí. Over time, as conflicts and divisions grew, Martí became increasingly important. A commitment to his image and the nostalgia for a past whose future had still not been determined became the primary means through which political opponents could "talk" to each other and offer each other the basis for mutual accord. Eventually, however, the potential for reaching such an accord and the offers that political opponents extended came to seem as ethereal and symbolic as Martí himself.

In short, this work contends that the mythification of Martí through patriotic rituals and discourses became critical to the survival and articulation of distinct, ideal views of nation that emerged during the 1895 War. Yet, at the same time, it argues that conflicting views of the nation predated the myth of Martí even as they became bound up in it. Martí came to embody the requirement of social unity behind the cause of the 1895 War—independence—that lay at the heart of each of these ideal "nations." When politically active Cubans transferred their energies from the cause of independence from Spain to fulfilling the cause of their own respective ideal of nation in the state, Martí became the vehicle through which they voiced demands for conformity to their respective view. By "re-membering" Martí into their particular vision of nation, these Cubans derived contradictory lessons from Martí's life and words. Through Martí, they filtered these lessons into memories of the 1895 Revolution that served to justify current approaches to the present and future. They also demanded that others conform to the validity of those approaches.

I first visited and lived in Cuba between 1995 and 1998. Not surprisingly, the hundred-year anniversaries of Martí's death and the deaths of equally important martyrs such as the mulatto general Antonio Maceo meant that memories of the 1895 War and its culmination in a U.S. military occupation seemed very much on everyone's mind. At the time, I was researching my dissertation in Cuba and lived with my family in the turn-of-the-century neighborhood known as Centro Habana. Once the residential area of choice for the senators and congressmen of the First Republic, its buildings now sagged with the burden of history and the weight of so many generations' disillusionment. Never did the memory of Martí or the struggles of the early Republic seem very far away.

Only a few blocks down from the peasant market where I shopped lay the area of Centro Habana called Cayo Hueso, or Key West. Named for the thousands of cigarmakers (*tabaqueros*) who immigrated to Florida in the 1880s and returned to Cuba after the war, Cayo Hueso once teemed with the radicalism of organized workers in the early twentieth century. The views and labor activism of these emigré *tabaqueros* had inspired the formulation of Martí's vision of social justice and, as my own research soon revealed, triggered many of the Republic's early conflagrations. Often, I savored the irony that whether I was coming or going, relaxing or working, it always seemed that there was no way to avoid Martí. Twice a day, on my way to and from Cuba's National Archive, I walked past the Central Park monument to Martí and the house of his birth. Like many Cubans had done before me and many still do today, I began to imagine how Martí might react to events of the day and situations of the past. Constantly, I wondered whether he would have lived up to his own myth as a compromiser, radical nationalist, political savior, and social unifier had he, in fact, lived. Every day, it seemed I had a different answer to this question.

As a historian, I knew that I would never find a single answer. As a Cuban (at least by desire, if not by birth), I felt I knew the origin of the question, Would the Republic and Cuba's twentieth-century history have been different if Martí had lived? To me, the question derived from a profound sense, highly promoted in the works of Martí, that Cubans should always be united. Yet, today as yesterday, it seemed to me that we never were. Cubans in the 1895 War had not fought Spain just as Cubans in the Republic had not fought each other for the same, unified vision of nation. Rather, they had fought, sometimes in alliance across race and class, sometimes divided by race and class, for multiple visions of nation. The coexistence of conflicting, multiple images of Martí in the Republic typified the emergence and struggle among Cubans for multiple images of nation. Martí's brilliance as a political strategist and organizer lay in his recognition that Cubans had drastically, almost irreconcilably, different ideas of what Cuban society should be like after the war. These ideas ranged from a modernist, liberal version of the plantation-dominated past with little if any change in the social hierarchy to a complete subversion of that past.

In life as in death, Martí's appeal lay in the discourse of social unity that he forged in order to mitigate the immediate impact of these conflicts on preparations for war. Martí emphasized the power of the collective political will and individual self-sacrifice as the means for resolving differences. Social unity was Martí's mantra, and as such, it made him a fiercely seductive symbol whose appropriation became increasingly necessary for competing political sectors in the Republic as they became more divided. Martí had promised to found a republic for all. However, he never explained the form of government the republic should take. As he himself admitted only days before his death, Martí did not explicitly promise democracy, but the honesty and sincerity of his and other leaders' personal authority.[7] Whatever Martí may have meant, Cubans quickly discovered after the war that democracy and personal authority were not the same thing. Proponents of political democracy as well as those who favored authoritarian forms of order each found in Martí the legitimacy and authenticity of their vision of the state and the nation for which they fought.

Every time Cubans collectively honored Martí in the face of growing conflicts among themselves, they articulated their right to implement their vision of nation through the state. By invoking Martí as a the hallmark of social unity, Cubans periodically asserted that they had once all agreed on what these views and plans for the nation were and committed themselves to fighting for its fulfillment, no matter what the cost. Nonetheless, as many historians of Cuba's long and complex independence process (1868–98) have demonstrated, questions of strategy and ideology and the political objectives of independence divided rather than unified the leadership as well as the rank and file.[8] Social unity was more fiction than historical reality, but one that framed and conditioned people's actions in that reality.

In this sense, between 1895 and 1921, the "myth" that Cubans constructed of José Martí as a signifier of social unity was a fictional narrative, based on their desire for a harmonious, even utopic future as well as the need to shape and recollect the past in such terms. This book contends that just because a narrative was not necessarily born of facts does not mean that it was not "true" to those who articulated it. As William Doty argues, "Our myths are *fictional*, to be sure, but . . . fictional need not mean unreal."[9] For politically active Cubans in the early twentieth century, the myth of Martí did not make him the father of social unity but the embodiment of social unity. Ultimately, belief in this myth became as true and as real as belief in distinct ideals of nation. As mainstream political parties' efforts to claim exclusive rights to state power led to the ideological and structural decay of the republican order in the early 1920s, a new generation of Cubans would have to decide whether or not these ideals of nation they had inherited were still worth fighting for.

This study uses the term "myth" to connote the common essence or root of Cubans' nationality in the repeated narrative of self-sacrifice, collective struggle, and commitment to a "nation for all" that emerged during the War of 1895. Little by little since the time of his death, Cuban politicians, social activists, and intellectuals incarnated this narrative in the figure of José Martí. The process eventually culminated in the 1920s with a duel between opposing images of Martí that Cuban nationalists performed and ritualized. And, as with all myths, its meaning depended on the desires of myth-tellers.[10] It became the shared creation myth from which each political sector's interpretation of the nation was derived. The myth of Martí anticipated the future of Cuba, "determin[ing] and shap[ing] ideals and goals for both the individual and society."[11] With increasing intensity, it functioned in Cuban society much as foundational national myths about the Pilgrims' good intentions toward the Indians or the inevitability of the conquest of the West have functioned in U.S. society for years: it became "*both true and crucial* to those who perceive[d] it through their experienced world."[12]

As with possibly all national mythologies, myths of creation are also frequently coupled with myths of destruction.[13] Thus, this work contends that the myth of Martí as social unity connected conflicting visions of nation to each other by positing a common origin or foundation. Yet, it also connoted an apocalyptic myth that forecast the destruction of the shared foundations of Cuban nationality if people protested too vehemently or broke ranks with other Cubans for "sectoral" reasons. When Cuban activists attacked each other through discourse or armed revolt in the early Republic, they often did so in all-or-nothing terms. Opposition to a certain political position could be considered not only threatening or antithetical to the interests of Cuba but also a betrayal of the sacred standard for judging *cubanidad*: one's commitment to social unity and one's belief in José Martí.

This study seeks to track and make sense of Cubans' competing claims to define and implement the nation. It analyzes these claims through key political sectors' discourses on the nation and the actions they took that justified and illuminated those discourses in the name of Martí. I argue that Cuban supporters, participants, and leaders of the 1895 Revolution were nationalists because they conceived of what they did and their relationship to each other as intimately connected to the long-term goal of designing and building a particular, unique vision of state and society all their own. During the 1895 War and after it, each of these groups operated under a set of assumptions about the Revolution, their place within it, and the right they earned for their support of it to build a new society on their own terms. These assumptions about the past, present, and future that linked individuals and groups of Cubans into an armed social and political movement formed the nexus of different Cuban nationalisms. The goal of seeing them implemented in a new society guided by a new state motivated proponents of independence to confront and attack the colonial state in the 1890s. Very similar goals motivated activists to confront and attack the republican state from 1902 to 1921.

Explaining the Origins of Conflicting Visions of Nation in the Early Republic

The product of a slave regime predicated on the innate social worth of whites and the inherent inferiority of blacks, nineteenth-century Cuba was a society in which ideals of social hierarchy and elites' surveillance of people of color, both slave and free, permeated nearly all aspects of daily life and culture.[14] Because of this, Cubans experienced a protracted independence process that was crippled by extreme racial tensions and divided political visions of how these tensions might be held in check from the start. Until the late 1860s, white Creole elites grudgingly traded the benefits of political autonomy for the comforts of social control that Spanish colonialism provided over slaves, free blacks, and the urban and rural poor, many of whom were of mixed race. Indeed, so important had social control over these populations been to planters that they often contemplated trading one imperialism for another and, in the 1840s and 1850s, actively sought the island's annexation to the United States.[15]

Because of this history, Cubans of varying social conditions who came to favor independence in the 1860s and 1870s did so for radically different reasons and ends in mind. Begun in 1868 with the Ten Years' War (1868–78), the struggle for Cuban independence and national sovereignty came at a time when slavery and sugar remained the cornerstones of the island economy and its color-class hierarchy. Facing high prices for slaves caused by a reduced supply, increasing competition from European beet sugar, and the inefficiency of unmechanized mills, a small group of Creole planters came to consider separation from Spain beneficial in 1868 for a specific set of highly personal reasons. They saw in their own experience of menacing poverty and technological backwardness a microcosm of Cuba's future. Thus, decades after independence had been achieved in nearly every former colony of Spanish America, these Creole planters freed their slaves in order to fight a revolution that they hoped would primarily benefit the planters themselves.[16]

However, separatist planters soon found that Cuba's slaves and free people of color quickly transformed the struggle in practical and ideological terms. Casting abolition as the twin goal of independence, the overwhelming numbers of blacks and mulattoes who joined the war between 1868 and 1878 radicalized its social vision. The success of their efforts played into white social fears of a race war à la Haiti, but it also forced Spain to begin a gradual process of reforming, and eventually abolishing, slavery altogether. All along, Spain proved only too willing to exploit the racial fears of whites as a means for discrediting the movement. In the end, these efforts when coupled with slave defiance and the advancement of free blacks within the rebel army itself prompted most white revolutionaries to reach a pact with Spain in 1878. In so doing, they turned their backs on former compatriots of color who remained committed to the cause and continued it through the Guerra Chiquita, or Little War, as late as 1881. Creole leaders signed the Pact of Zanjón in 1878 for the sake of restraining the tide of social change that threatened to sweep over the color-class pyramid of colonial society. They not only feared the radical transformation of society but also that such a transformation would proceed at a pace that they could not control and from which they could not expect to benefit.[17]

Thus, the ambivalence of white separatist leaders impeded the process of transforming the social contradictions of the colony into a more egalitarian national landscape. To a certain extent, Cuba's first two wars for independence only deepened these contradictions. On the one hand, the collapse of these military efforts left open-ended the process of achieving a social consensus among separatist forces on key questions of economic justice, racial equality, and future state support for these ideals. Moreover, the failure of revolutionaries to oust the Spanish appears to have allowed Spain partially and temporarily to co-opt the spaces for greater social, political, and economic participation by marginalized groups that the wars had opened up. Indeed, Spain, rather than a victorious national state, abolished slavery in 1886. Spain, rather than a victorious national state, promulgated the first series of antidiscrimination laws in favor of black civil rights in the late 1880s and early 1890s.[18] And Spain, rather than a victorious national state, tolerated the formation of a powerful anarchist labor movement that initially channeled working-class elements away from independence as a goal and toward engagement with the colonial state for the protection of workers' rights and improved conditions.[19] In short, Spanish officials attempted to co-opt the spaces for change that their opponents and revolutionary critics had traditionally reserved for themselves.

However, the fact that Spain failed to reform the colonial system, eventually abandoned workers' rights altogether, and neglected to enforce laws that would have provided state protection for black concerns only pushed Cubans who demanded radical social change to reconsider independence as a viable political alternative. On the other hand, a number of intellectuals and middle-class professionals and a small number of Creole planters also grew increasingly alienated from Spain during this period. Many of them emigrated abroad as a result. Faced with an ever-more corrupt political system, an economy in shambles, and an outdated infrastructure, these groups of Creole elites felt increasingly marginalized from the centers of colonial power and yearned for the chance to modernize Cuba. By forging independence, they wanted to rid Cuba and themselves of the kind of caste privileges that continued to allow greater economic advantage to Spanish-born immigrants over Creoles.

Fractured and regimented, the colony offered no possibility of liberation or social growth as members of these groups defined it. They therefore began to locate the source of liberation and the meaning of their identity elsewhere, in images of an alternative political entity of communal cooperation that they perceived and articulated differently. Importantly, like the veteran and privileged Creole leaders who joined the new independence movement of the 1890s, workers and former slaves who supported independence continued to espouse a radical set of principles for changing the political, social, and economic landscape. Despite the overwhelming potential they represented to any successful revolutionary state that might have responded to them as a constituency, their enthusiasm for contesting the structural sources of power did not so much sharpen as blunt the enthusiasm of separatist leaders for doing the same. This was the case even as José Martí and the political network of emigré associations he directed from New York organized support for a new revolution in the early 1890s. This continued to be the case even after the War of 1895 broke out. As a result, multiple visions of nation emerged within the same discursive matrix of the revolutionary movement, each constructed in counterposition, if not opposition, to one another's goals. Still, ensuring that disparate visionaries of the nation did not have to surrender differences in their conceptualizations of it was the key to fostering support for a new war. They simply had to tolerate these differences, often silently, for the sake of forging an alliance. Conflicting nationalists later interpreted this tenuous alliance as evidence of having achieved social unity in the 1895 War and embodied that memory in the myth of José Martí.

In the process of preparing and experiencing the war itself, multiple understandings of the elements and ideals that constituted the future political entity of Cuba emerged. Feelings of marginality from the colonial power allowed some pro-independence Creoles of educationally or economically privileged background to identify in the struggle for independence with social groups far more marginalized than they. Others, however, retained a much more socially conservative view of their role as cultural and ideological leaders vis-à-vis the former slaves, organized workers, and intellectuals of color who constituted the Revolution's primary following. As a result, the nation for which each set of actors fought diverged from the nation for which others fought. This situation only intensified when U.S. military intervention in 1898 cut short the process of internal negotiation and consensus among revolutionary forces. This process might have otherwise laid the groundwork for a new, corporatist national state that might have mediated competing needs, interests, and views.

Founding contributors to the study of Cuban history in the United States and Cuba have tended to view U.S. imperialism as an overwhelming force that fragmented and diluted the nationalist aspirations of politically powerful Cubans who decided to accommodate to changing circumstances as best they could.[20] Thus, as Louis A. Pérez Jr. argues in his most recent work, *On Becoming Cuban*, so completely did the United States come to dictate the framework and terms of Cubans' "moral universe" that Cuban identity itself emerged as a cultural derivative of the more fixed and consciously secure imperial identity of the United States.[21] Other historians of Cuba have relied on economic and material approaches in order to demonstrate the depth of U.S. control before 1959. Seeing the Republic through a teleological lens, many have argued that the socialist outcome of Cuba's struggle for sovereignty ultimately represented the fulfillment of the kind of society proposed by José Martí.[22] More recently, revisionist historians such as Aline Helg, Ada Ferrer, Alejandro de la Fuente, and Marial Iglesias Utset have begun to analyze the course of the Republic in terms of the actions and complex changing political consciousness of local actors.[23] In particular, Helg, Ferrer, and de la Fuente focus on the role that race and racial prejudice played in shaping Cuba's independence process and its implications for the political development of the Republic. These historians question the degree to which a consensus on the role of race in relation to the political and social development of postindependence society emerged among revolutionaries in the 1895 War.

Despite their differences of approach and emphasis, both traditional and re-visionist historians of Cuba inevitably confront and explain the contradiction between political discourses of racial and social inclusion forged during the 1895 War and state practices of exclusion during the Republic. All these historians explore the relative power of the Cuban state to implement visions of nation, not only in relation to U.S. imperial mandates but also with regard to different groups of Cubans who defied its authority. In all cases, they have found the power of the Cuban state wanting, crippled by pressures for social change from within and demands for conformity from without.

In this regard, my own study is no different. It plots an analytical path be-tween the polarities of promise and betrayal inherent in the Cuban political process of the early twentieth century. And like Pérez's *On Becoming Cuban*, this book seeks to tap the political culture and consciousness of Cubans as con-tributors and participants in the building of a neocolonial society. However, it argues that, at the time of the 1895 War, Cubans had already developed a sense of themselves as "Cuban." After the United States' imposition of a neocolonial framework within which Cubans struggled to construct a nation, they asserted the historical origins of their conflicting visions of nation and policed its bound-aries through political action as well as discursive means. They reserved the right to define what being "Cuban" meant. The cult of Martí emerged because Cubans refused to surrender their memory, however nostalgic or fictional, of total unity and deployed it offensively as well as defensively in their struggles with one another. As Ernest Renan argues for all peoples engaged in a project of nation-building, Cubans recognized that "of all cults, that of the ancestors is the most legitimate, for the ancestors have made us what we are." They desired to "have common glories in the past and to have a common will in the present; to have performed great deeds together, . . . to perform still more."[24] During the first two decades of the Republic, Cubans often accused each other, rather than the United States, of representing the primary threat to building a nation.

Thus, this work demonstrates that it was Cubans' commitment to nation-building on conflicting terms rather than the subversion of nation-building by U.S. imperialism that formed the central axis of Cuba's social and political de-velopment until 1921. It argues that Cuban nationalists engaged, manipulated, and even legitimated the role of U.S. imperialists in Cuba's internal governance for two reasons. First, they sought to blunt the appeal of rival nationalisms, and second, they wanted to neutralize the authenticity of their proponents' historical claims to acquire or retain state power. Ultimately, by 1921, Cuban nationalists' efforts to gain greater power and authority over one another in the context of U.S. imperialism ensured U.S. neocolonial hegemony at all levels of Cuban society.

The following section explains the role and definition of these concepts of "nation" and "nationalism" as well as the categories of analysis that appear in this work. It also defines the elements that characterized the three central Cuban nationalisms and each group of nationalists' interpretation of the myth of José Martí.

Theorizing Nations and Nationalism:
The Case of Early Twentieth-Century Cuba

Recently, the concepts of nation and nationalism have acquired negative connotations in "the West."[25] Similarly, imperialism, arguably the manifestation of U.S. nationalism abroad, continues to be a dirty little word in the lexicon of most U.S. Americans. Few understand why Latin Americans, especially Cubans, refuse to share this view. Yet, national projects for advancing a society's economic and political interests, whether imperial or anti-imperial, have long relied on collective, society-wide validation of the idea that such plans would be good for the "nation." According to Eric Hobsbawm and Ernest Gellner, nations and nationalisms developed in the nineteenth century because these concepts bridged the ideological chasm opened up by the collapse of agrarian, monarchical societies in Europe and the development of industry, mechanical communication, and notions of modernity. Thus, elites who already wielded considerable power invented and promoted ideas of nation in order to retain control of the state.[26] Refining these earlier arguments, Benedict Anderson subsequently articulated a key idea that few scholars, if any, had been willing to recognize: that is, the location of the origins of nations and nationalism in the human imagination.[27] However, a central problem remained: Anderson and his predecessors promoted a largely Eurocentric and elite-centered standard by which to judge when and how nationalisms and nations emerge as well as the form they take. Ideas of nation always seemed to "trickle down" to the masses.

As Florencia Mallon argues, Anderson's idea that nations were "imagined communities" still relied on "the twin myths of bourgeois and Western exceptionalism."[28] Mallon challenges these myths by arguing that nationalism is an open-ended discourse, "a political and intellectual process" in which struggles for power and struggles over meaning are deeply enmeshed. Thus, Mallon explains, elites and subalterns, states and communities are never freed from each other, or even capable of existing in a stable way without each other. When a state becomes hegemonic, as in the case of Mexico, it does so through the participation of all groups. For as long as they remain committed to being parts of a historically rooted but ever-changing concept of nation, they remain connected to one another because their projects, goals, and identities are connected.[29]

In the case of early twentieth-century Cuba, efforts to build a strong nation-state based on a more equitable distribution of power and wealth failed. Eventually by the 1920s, the hegemony and sovereignty of U.S. imperialism usurped the hegemony and sovereignty of the Cuban state. How did Cuban politicians as well as workers, black activists, veterans, intellectuals, and other popular groups participate in this process? To what degree were they responsible for it? And why did Cubans who were so divided (even to the point of taking up arms against one another) nonetheless invoke the concept of social unity in its singular representative, José Martí?

My own efforts to find answers to these questions began in Cuba's national and provincial archives. Casting my net as widely as possible, I drew up a wealth of personal and public testimonies. Poring over them, breathing in the emotions that produced them, it seemed to me that they all attested to the same thing. During and after the last war for independence, Cubans consistently addressed the past even as they railed against or confirmed the present. In diaries, letters, manifestos, newspapers, secret police reports, and the like, Cubans seemed to speak past each other, toward a truth that they imagined differently and remembered differently. This truth, by their own account, was the nation. Ranging from the sublime to the palpable, the ubiquitous to the elusive, the nations that Cubans talked about were the lenses through which they justified their political activity and its relationship to their social condition. Over time, I came to believe that Cubans often talked past each other in speaking about the nation because they had, in fact, not only imagined different nations but also felt that they had begun to experience what life would be like in such nations during the 1895 War. In 1898, the process of negotiating, incorporating, and refuting differences for the sake of forming a single national project was cut short by the intrusion of a foreign power. From that moment on, the evolution of Cuban nationalisms and the development of U.S. imperialism—both processes that had been taking place simultaneously before the 1895 War—became ensnared. The contradictions between Cubans' visions of nation and the contradictions within early forms of U.S. imperialism were joined.

In preparing this work, I conceived of the nation much as my archival sources indicated they had conceived it. That is, the nation was nothing more and nothing less than the mental location of liberation in the form of a political entity and a community yet to be achieved. At one level, this meant that while the nation was a goal that its proponents cast as eminently achievable, it was also a project constantly under construction and, depending on circumstances and the reactions of others, subject to revision and modification. Implied in these projects were locally derived, historically contingent, and even personally specific definitions of liberation.

For example, some Cubans, like lower- and working-class black veterans, defined liberation as the equalization of historic injustices through the redistribution of wealth and political power. Others equated liberation with freedom from the backward policies and customs of the Spanish. For them, liberation meant being modern, prosperous, and culturally respectable in ways already idealized in countries that were "modern," such as the United States. With these definitions of liberation as their guides, Cubans located its fulfillment in visions of nation that they struggled with and against each other to achieve.

The first of these, *pro-imperialist nationalism*, was championed by white, formally educated, middle- and upper-class emigrés who left Cuba in the 1870s and early 1880s, either because they had supported previous independence wars or had suffered economically from their results. Having spent most of their adult lives in the United States and Europe before supporting the 1895 War and returning to Cuba shortly afterward, pro-imperialist nationalists hoped to bring the physical technology and cultural features of modernity to Cuban society. They envisioned a nation shaped by foreign investment, large-scale agriculture, and state-sponsored acculturation of the masses to European and American standards of "civilization." Pro-imperialist nationalists advocated and measured others by cultural standards that they believed they themselves had already achieved.

Largely citizens of the United States themselves, pro-imperialist nationalists were "imperialist." Although they did not see annexation of Cuba to the United States as necessary or even desirable, they proposed that both Cuba and the United States benefit from an intimate economic and cultural relationship that constricted the boundaries of Cuba's political sovereignty. Yet, these same groups were equally "nationalist." They saw in the Hispanic dimensions of Creole society the rudiments of a greatness that Spain had repressed and that independence would release. Moreover, they believed in U.S. benevolence and expected that U.S. influence, whether diplomatic, economic, or political, could only benefit Cuba's development by improving its chances at achieving the modernizing national liberation they envisioned. For the pro-imperialist nationalists, there was no contradiction between the emigré and Cuban halves of their identities because there was no contradiction between Cuba's national liberation and seeking a close bond with U.S. power and culture.

For example, in 1895 when pro-imperialist nationalists took over the running of the Partido Revolucionario Cubano (Cuban Revolutionary Party [PRC]) after Martí left for the war in Cuba, they reflected their understanding of nation in the reports and priorities of the PRC organ, *Patria*. As editor, Martí had given profiles of working-class or black organizations equal weight with reports on the activism of elite professional revolutionaries.[30] Martí's *Patria* also marginalized discussion of the United States and U.S. Americans in its pages, preferring to focus exclusively on the social conditions of Cubans and the task of bringing them together. By contrast, pro-imperialist nationalist editors of *Patria* published article after article on U.S. Americans' support for the war and their ties to elite Cuban revolutionary clubs. They also published essays drawing historical analogues between the United States' and Cuba's struggles for liberty. This new *Patria* included almost no reports (if any) on La Liga Antillana (Antillean League), the black mutual aid and instructional society Martí had helped to found, and no mention of Haiti.[31]

Significantly, the pro-imperialist nationalists' *Patria* did not venerate a Martí who sought to mediate social differences among Cubans but one who "purified" those he could not "change" by immersing them along with himself in the "Jordan" of patriotic self-abnegation. In this way, he made them "worthy of the redemptive task"—that is, worthy of inclusion in the Revolution.[32] Buoyed by their own material success and acculturation as one-time immigrants, pro-imperialist nationalists would later adopt a laissez-faire and increasingly repressive approach to social change in the Republic. They did so by interpreting the 1895 War and memories of Martí in terms of self-reliance and self-abnegation. Because they had supported these ideals during the war, pro-imperialist nationalists relied on the same ideals to guide policies of the state with respect to socially marginal "others" like workers and black activists afterward. When they called for social unity, they actually demanded negation of past injustices that certain groups may have suffered for the sake of a more prosperous and modern "whole."

On the other hand, veteran leaders, both white and of color, rooted their *revolutionary nationalism* in the military experience of the previous independence wars of 1868–78 and 1879–80. They conceived of a nationalism that called for social change through a top-down, state-engineered approach. Revolutionary nationalists envisioned a nation that transferred patron-client systems of social interaction that they associated with memories of the rebel army and the ideal culture of Cuba's rural life to the realm of state-society politics. They deferred to this patriarchal model and its attendant memories as they confronted issues of race or class and subsumed both dimensions of their own identities to its rubrics. Laced with authoritarian aspects, commitment to a vertically organized, electoral democracy formed the core of this revolutionary nation.

Consequently, revolutionary nationalists interpreted the nation and called other Cubans to unite around it through a Martí who promised to create a society of equals so long as the Cuban masses, those who had been "unequal" in the past, promised to respect their leaders' authority. General-in-Chief Máximo Gómez provided one of the best illustrations of this when he ordered his troops, in June 1896, to commemorate the death of Martí. When his forces passed near the place where Martí had been shot by Spanish soldiers the year before, Gómez drove a cross into the site where Martí had fallen from his horse, fatally wounded. Gómez had ordered the cross, engraved with Martí's initials, to be made for the occasion. After staking it into the ground, Gómez instructed each soldier to pick up a stone and lay it, one by one, at the foot of the cross, his voice reportedly cracking under the weight of his emotions. After Gómez had finished speaking, one of his assistants, Fermín Valdés Domínguez (who was also a childhood friend of Martí), said, "This modest monument [should] be an altar on which we all may come to sing the hymn of . . . victory, . . . to glorify Martí, dead, who was the Revolution, and Gómez, conqueror, who was the War."[33] The only role left to the soldiers was that of obedient bystanders: this nation depended on the understanding that ultimate authority and ultimate legitimacy rested not with the masses but with their leaders.

Importantly, Máximo Gómez, although the supreme leader of Cuba's rebel army, was not himself Cuban by birth but Dominican. However, Gómez's "foreign-ness" and a personal history of having served in the Spanish colonial army stand as evidence of the broad inclusiveness that defined the most explicitly radical form of Cuban nationalism articulated by the leaders of the 1895 War. Indeed, Gómez, Cuban mulatto general Antonio Maceo, and others constructed this nationalism in dialogue with the needs and demands of popular-class followers who pursued independence as a way to ensure profound social change and historic rupture. That Gómez became supreme commander despite his association with the enemy and his alien origins could only have served to strengthen the appeal of the rebel cause. Gómez and others like him typified many soldiers' desire to break cleanly with the past and forge a collective future based on new affiliations and merits derived from the war itself.

By contrast, *popular nationalism* rooted itself in an ideological amalgam of social desires and models of democracy derived from various historical experiences of marginalization. Proponents included emigré workers in Florida and New York, former soldiers and lower-ranking officers of the 1895 War, black civil rights and labor activists, as well as some popular-class and middle-class women. During the first years of the Republic, popular nationalists proposed a horizontal vision of nation in which the state prioritized the needs of its citizens and rewarded those who had suffered not only in war for its existence but also under Spanish colonialism. During the war and after it, popular nationalists who appropriated Martí depicted him as a spiritual messiah who promised an ideal but achievable society on earth. Appreciative of Martí's efforts to overcome class and racial prejudices through common morality, working-class and lower-middle-class emigrés from Florida were among the first popular nationalists to appropriate Martí in this way. In 1897, for example, Wenceslao Galvez projected a protectionist, paternal, and just nation through a messianic version of the myth of Martí:

> Where is he? In all places. Perhaps he is God? Who knows! What is certain is that he is everywhere, in homes, on the street, in the councils, [revolutionary] Clubs, newspapers, in short, everywhere. . . . His portrait is in all Cuban homes, in all the establishments. . . . In the home of the most powerful and that of the most humble, he is there, sometimes in his full person, sometimes only as a bust and of him the white and the black speak with *cariño*. . . . *The only great man who is not censured by the small!* . . . "Oh, if only he lived!" is heard in moments of anguish, because if he lived there would be no obstacles or anything in the way. Oh, if only he lived! His shadow protects us, his shadow extends itself over all things, and there is no Cuban on the face of the earth to whom he does not appear at the hour of sleep, who has him at the head of his bed, and it is because he is the Cuban soul, he is the soul of the fatherland.[34]

By the end of the 1895 War, popular nationalist soldiers in the field who had presumably never met Martí similarly extolled Martí's supernatural virtues through camp songs that also celebrated beloved generals, both living and deceased, in similar terms.[35]

In sum, nations and nationalisms may be best defined historically in terms of the relational identities that they invoked and the nature of the state that they posited. Beginning in Cuba's last anticolonial war in 1895, nationalists conceived projects for the state as extensions of their "nations." By gaining state power in the Republic, nationalists believed they could ensure not only the implementation of their visions but also the legitimacy of their own notions of identity vis-à-vis those of others. After all, if people "imagined" nations, they also "acted," with nationalist ideals and tenets in mind, to implement the nation-project in practice. Conflicts arose precisely because their visions did not coincide.

As others have shown, the presence of the United States ensured that Cuban politicians did not necessarily feel the need to negotiate their differences among themselves because they believed that they had a third, more powerful imperialist ally on which to rely.[36] This work shows that not only revolutionary and pro-imperialist nationalist members of Cuba's political elites engaged U.S. imperialism to the detriment of national sovereignty, but popular nationalists did as well. Preferring to alienate rather than incorporate the socially radical views of popular nationalists, political elites entered the Republic opposed to each other because their visions of nation and memories conflicted too much. Political elites' unresponsiveness drove popular nationalists to seek concessions from foreigners that their own native leaders would not give. The result was a paradox: neocolonial hegemony, rather than nation-state hegemony, prevailed.

Class and race consciousness were the facilitators of this process. Class identities, like racial affiliations, emerged in the Republic in ambiguous, contradictory ways that reflected their origins in Cuba's nonlinear capitalist development under slavery. Colonial capitalist development based on the combination of forced and free labor formed the foundation of Cuban society in the nineteenth century. This led to the formation of a complex and multitiered class hierarchy. Elites were divided not only by ethnic lines based on Creole versus peninsular descent but also in terms of their relation to the colonial state. Political proximity to state interests or intimacy with state agents conditioned material circumstances. For much of the second half of the nineteenth century, color divided non-elites as much as enslavement or freedom. Before and after abolition, access to education and degrees of incorporation of European-derived cultural elements differentiated individuals' status within the non-elite class. However, the fabric of social identification among non-elites was not as frayed as longstanding differences of color and culture might imply. Free and unfree workers coexisted in all productive sectors of the economy. Additionally, colonial elites of all kinds idealized slavery and total subservience as labor models. These circumstances favored a collective identification among non-elites with one another that reinforced the tendency of Creole and peninsular elites to perceive and refer to them as a communal unit from the 1880s to the 1890s. It is likely that urban and rural workers, ex-slaves, and the urban poor constituted a "popular-class" sector that perceived itself as such at the time.[37] As we shall see, the process of social upheaval and guerrilla warfare that launched Cuba's political struggles over nation in 1895 intensified these bonds among marginalized sectors.

If the popular classes developed one half of what appeared to be a class binary from the 1890s through the 1920s, Cubans who comprised the colonial elites before 1895 or comprised the new political and economic elites that resulted from the 1895 War did not necessarily follow suit. Somewhat open to racially integrated admission depending on one's approximation of white cultural standards of education and one's prominence in the 1895 War, elite status after 1898 did not, at least for the first decade and a half of the Republic, necessarily rely on the possession of great or even substantial material wealth. First and foremost, elite status implied relative proximity to the axis of power in the state and the protection that access to state power implied.

Thus, during the first fifteen years of the Republic, power was not so much materially derived as relationally conceived. Sheer wealth alone did not make any group politically powerful by default. This was especially true when the Republic was still young and politicians took the ideological differentiation of their parties seriously. After the inauguration of the Republic in 1902, a nucleus of civilian and military leaders either ascended to office in the state or formed the inner circles of political parties with direct access to and representation within the state. As a result, the majority of leaders of the 1895 War became members of competing "political elites." Those who were ostracized for their espousal of socially radical beliefs or chose to ostracize themselves in order to pressure the state formed "marginal elites." These marginal elites often allied with organized workers, black veterans of lower-class background, and peasants in the pursuit of the same popular nationalist vision of nation: one that posited participation in the Revolution of 1895 as a vehicle for social mobility and the state as the instrument for ensuring that such mobility took place.

Essentially, then, this study does not cast aside traditional historians' espousal of class analysis or the revisionists' insistence on race but proposes that the formation of race-class identities in the Republic found its roots in the process of imagining the nation. It is from the angle of nation and nationalism that the importance of racial and class differences emerge in sharpest relief. That is, by studying issues of race and class in the context of struggles over the nation, we can see more clearly how those issues affected the political outcome of neocolonial forms of rule by the 1920s. This is not to say that all Cubans were nationalists. Rather, it identifies as nationalists those groups that propelled Cuba's political development and came to do battle with each other over economic policies that they justified as beneficial to society as a whole. Seeing the nation as the lens through which many Cubans' interpreted their political realities and justified their aspirations complicates what might otherwise seem a simple tale of neocolonial collaboration. It serves to explain the longevity of what became, by the 1920s, a thoroughly corrupted political system, as well as the passion with which many Cubans defended that system and attacked each other as traitors of "nation" and the mythical figure they claimed was its highest champion, José Martí.

The following chapter explores the origins of Cuban nationalisms in the 1890s. It examines the role of José Martí in the process of combining emergent visions of nation into a discourse and a practice of social unity. It also anticipates the implications that this entanglement held for the way in which Cubans began to weave remembrances of history into the process of history-making itself between 1895 and 1921.

ONE

· ·

Mystic, Messiah, and Mediator

Interpreting Martí through Texts and Contexts

ON JUNE 8, 1899, Juan Bonilla, a cigarmaker and member of the all-black reading circle La Liga Antillana, wrote an impassioned letter to his friend and fellow
activist Juan Gualberto Gómez. Peppering his letter with direct quotes from
José Martí's writings, Bonilla recounted how Martí had personally inspired him
to pursue ideals of truth and justice, especially through the readings he recommended to La Liga, a list that included Renan's *Life of Jesus* and works by Emer-
son and Seneca. However, Bonilla's purpose in writing Gómez was more than
commemorative. He wanted him to know that despite Martí's death, Bonilla
and other Cubans could continue to receive Martí's counsel, even from beyond
the grave.

Since the early months of the U.S. military intervention of 1898, Bonilla had
been conducting an "investigation" into the spiritist movement among New York
City's Cuban emigrés. Like all spiritists, emigré adherents sought to prove the
immortality of the soul by using the "scientific" methods of spiritism's founder,
Allan Kardec. After attending countless séances, Bonilla had received several important messages from figures such as José and Antonio Maceo, as well as Martí.
Cynically, the spirit of José Maceo characterized Cubans' current attitudes toward the U.S. occupation as "identical to those of Zanjón, in '78." However, the
spirit of Martí insisted that all of Cuba's dead heroes were working ceaselessly
"to save Cuba," even if it appeared that "in the end, [the United States was] going
to take her." Bonilla concluded that Cubans' only hope was to found a political
party modeled on the PRC and the example of leadership provided by Martí, a
man who, like Jesus himself, prophesied his own immortality.[1] Bonilla insisted,
"What matters about these investigations is that all [our deceased leaders] agree
that the only way to save Cuba is through the strictest unity of all its elements.

Our dead ask only for Unity, and predict a fortuitous future for Cuba if only we can achieve this first triumph."[2]

Written four years after Martí's death, Bonilla's testimony colorfully illustrates how many popular nationalist revolutionaries closest to Martí regarded his legacy. A mystic who meditated on the meaning of liberation, Bonilla's Martí was also an earthly messiah who had managed to make the impossible possible. Through the structure of the PRC and the goal of absolute independence, Martí had united Cubans whose class interests, cultural values, and historical experience could not have been more distinct. By the time of his death in 1895, these multiple dimensions of Martí's image had already begun to fuse into a myth of social unity based on conflicting ideological meanings.

In the early 1890s, the intricate weaving of popular nationalists' support for Martí into the preparatory and governing structures of the Revolution made their demands for social justice practical and discursive foundations of Cuba's struggle for liberation. Martí's willingness to embrace the radical visions of nation that working-class emigrés imagined and the central role that themes of historic sin and future redemption for all Cubans, rich and poor, played in PRC discourse and policies were critical. Martí's strategies for achieving social unity behind the drive for war not only made the solutions to racial and class inequality in Cuba feasible but, more important, they also made the problem of inequality itself impossible for conservative nationalists to ignore. Martí's efforts to embody and perform the messianic ideals of self-abnegation, mediation of differences, and material denial for the sake of a collective end created the basis for his mythification as a national icon of unity and a symbol of Cubans' commitment to the goal of a nation, however defined. By the time of Martí's death at the outset of the revolution in Cuba, his apotheosis as a national myth of unity may have been unavoidable. Later, Martí's image would become the mantra by which many popular nationalists asserted their legitimacy and made demands within a movement that increasingly sought to channel them away from the institutional centers of power. To justify such actions and defend their own authority, pro-imperialist and revolutionary nationalist leaders had to respond to strident reminders of the mystical, messianic, and mediating Martí in order not to lose their own legitimacy in the wake of idealized memories of the past.

Most previous assessments of the appropriation of Martí have located Cubans' "discovery" of him in the 1920s, relegating it to the activities of a few intellectuals and radical activists whose excavation of Martí's writings made his ideas widely known to a national audience, ostensibly for the first time.[3] Despite a flurry of new interpretations of Martí's work and influence in the last few years, it is easy to see why this view has endured. Spanish censors, high rates of illiteracy, and the popularity of other leaders with more radical social credentials such as Antonio Maceo make it impossible to say exactly how extensive Martí's popularity or knowledge of him may have been among Cubans during and after the 1895 War. However, as we shall see, political elites and diverse social groups of Cuba's popular classes consistently appropriated Martí's image through the early Republic. Rooted in an analysis of Martí's own social reality, this chapter explores how Martí himself worked hard to make his message and his own image appeal to groups with contrary interests, different ideological sensibilities, and ultimately, distinct nationalist goals, especially among his own emigré communities in the United States. This analysis lays the groundwork for explaining why Martí's image and discourse of social unity became signifiers of conflicting visions of nation after his death and over the course of the early Republic.

This chapter argues that Martí crafted a message of liberation and revolution within his own peculiar emigré context that could be and was meant to be interpreted in more than one way. He also made conscious efforts to exemplify that message symbolically in his own life and actions. Martí's brilliance lay in his ability to convince Cubans, of opposing class interests and perspectives on questions of social equality, that they could find their "true" selfless selves and seek their country's historical redemption from a colonial, slave-holding past in the cause of independence. Central to Martí's appeal was his willingness to allow his listeners, observers, and readers to draw their own conclusions to the dilemmas that his denunciations of Spanish colonialism set up. In the process, Martí, consciously and unconsciously, confirmed the right of all Cubans to interpret the nation for themselves and to shape, consequently, their own interpretation of Martí.

Race, Class, and the Problem of Equality

In a context of divided perceptions and indeterminate outcomes, Martí's discourse and practice emerged as a product of specific needs. In practical terms, Martí needed to bring together under the leadership of a single party the thousands of emigrés who had left Cuba for economic or ideological reasons to settle in the United States. And he needed to link the emigré movement to the military enterprise of socially radical and prestigious generals such as Antonio Maceo, Enrique Collazo, and Máximo Gómez who lived in exile elsewhere. In ideological terms, Martí had to make the Revolution acceptable to both the popular-class emigré groups and those who would do the bulk of the fighting in Cuba. But he also needed to retain the support of professional and intellectual elites who would govern its finances and represent the war diplomatically. For Martí, the question of how to attract and keep the support of all groups was just as important for the short-term, for the organization of the Revolution, as for the long-term, for the organization of a Republic "with all and for the good of all." Martí recognized how easily the scale of social forces could be tipped out of balance in both the Revolution and the Republic and warned his readers, comrades, and audiences of the need to keep these forces in balance. If Cubans did not do so, the Revolution would collapse as it had done before. Worse yet, neglecting the social balance in the Republic would lead to an authoritarian government, U.S. domination, or the kind of social chaos Martí perceived as dictating the history of Cuba's sister republics in Latin America.

As laden with overt messianic images as it was riddled with silences on the question of future government policies, Martí's carefully crafted and often circuitous discourse avoided precision and practicality in discussing just how a newly founded republic might mitigate the social, class, and racial extremes that defined the colony. Through the top-down structures of the PRC and his own paternalistic leadership style, Martí ensured that ideological differences among potential constituents and the implications that these differences held for the social and political order in the Republic would be neutralized rather than aired. The discursive silencing of key differences served as temporary and symbolic sacrifices of personal and sectoral interests for the sake of unity. By articulating a collective patriotic consciousness in which all might share, Martí himself insisted that building social unity through the symbolic inclusion of all needs and interests in the war could form the basis for their negotiation in the Republic. At the center of these needs and interests stood the former breaking points for Cuba's earlier independence wars, principally, the issues of class privilege and race inequality.

Martí talked and wrote incessantly about the insignificance of race and the impossibility of racial hatred among Cubans while, at the same time, silencing the reality that issues of race and persisting racial hatred remained primary obstacles to both social unity and social peace. As Ada Ferrer points out, Martí represented a general trend among white separatist writers at the time. As a group, these writers glossed slavery as a sin for which white Cubans had already been redeemed and whose legacy black Cubans had already overcome—all because of the first struggle for independence, the Ten Years' War.[4] Ferrer asserts that revolutionaries of 1895 brought to fruition an "ideology of raceless nationality" that was long in the making. This ideology was, in part, the product of efforts to construct a viable counterdiscourse to Spanish campaigns that exploited racial fears and discredited independence as leading to a "race war." But it was also, in part, an expression of what she considers Martí's exceptional perspective on "racial equality" and his courage in fomenting that view among supporters.[5] Ferrer contends that the language and concept of "raceless nationality" allowed white revolutionaries to insist that the transcendence of race had already occurred even as black revolutionaries insisted that the contrary was still true.[6]

Most analysts of the 1895 War and readers of Martí have long insisted that Martí called for "racial equality" and that this tenet formed an ideological pillar of the Revolution of 1895.[7] And yet, Martí's efforts to attract and then balance radical and conservative forces within the movement meant that while he included socially marginal groups symbolically, he did not necessarily endow these groups with the same structural authority within the PRC that he offered their conservative, wealthier, and formally educated counterparts. Whatever his commitment to improving the condition of socially marginal sectors may have been in the long run, Martí drew his closest associates within the PRC, such as pro-imperialist nationalists Tomás Estrada Palma and Gonzalo de Quesada (both of whom were U.S. citizens), from the conservative ranks of emigré society. However, even as he denied openly radical black activists such as Rafael Serra y Montalvo from leadership in the PRC, Martí acted the part of social democrat whenever the chance presented itself. His efforts apparently succeeded. Popular nationalists recognized the value of Martí's strategy and appreciated his efforts to include them as equally valuable. Perhaps the best evidence of this came after his death, when popular nationalists increasingly referred to Martí's personal style in order to evaluate the ideological attitudes and political worth of his PRC successors.

An 1896 letter written by Nestor Carbonell, an emigré leader from Tampa, provides a case in point. Criticizing the social elitism of the PRC's national delegates, Carbonell cited Martí's contrasting actions as testament to the fact that Martí would never have tolerated such attitudes: "When Martí would arrive from his long trips from the North and from the South, the home in which he would stay was that of the black woman Paulina in Tampa. Without waiting enough time for anyone to find grounds for complaint, he would take the coach and alone or accompanied, he would go to visit those homes where he could be seen by Cubans who otherwise might not be able to visit him. . . . What politician ever more exemplary?"[8] Ignoring the fact that Martí was himself responsible for these delegates' appointments, Carbonell insinuated that if Martí had only lived, he would have appointed Carbonell to the governing council of the PRC instead.

Of course, Martí's actions acquired greatest significance in light of his words. Understanding the circuitous writing style and contradictory discourse on which Martí relied for broad and, at other times, specific political ends involves analyzing the resonance and dissonance between his public versus private correspondence. In doing so, one finds that no such terms as "racial equality" or even "social equality" ever appeared in Martí's writings, speeches, or correspondence (whether public or private). Given that black and mulatto intellectuals close to Martí did not hesitate to use such direct terminology in their own writings, and that Martí himself supported the work of their organizations, the omission is striking and revealing.

One such example of a mulatto intellectual was Juan Gualberto Gómez, a longtime friend of Martí. Gómez had known Martí since his days in the Havana law firm where Martí worked upon returning to Cuba from exile in 1878 until separatist activities prompted Martí's expulsion once again. Renowned for his successful litigation in the Spanish supreme court during the late 1880s of cases favoring the racial desegregation of public schools and nondiscrimination in public places, Gómez founded and directed newspapers committed to the "defense of the general interests of the people of color" in Cuba. The first of these, *La Fraternidad*, published in Havana, became the principal organ of La Liga Antillana, night school and literary salon for black Cuban and Puerto Rican workers in New York.

Founded in 1889 by cigarmaker and intellectual Rafael Serra y Montalvo, La Liga's instructors included José Martí and a number of black emigrés such as Juan Bonilla, all of whom were, by most accounts, fanatically devoted to Martí. One year after Martí founded the PRC in New York in 1891 to organize and coordinate dozens of emigré revolutionary societies for a last war against Spain, Gómez founded the Directorate of the Societies of Color in Cuba. The latter's purpose was to promote black civil rights and unite the political forces of black Cubans in order to acquire greater protection of their rights from local officials of the government of Spain. *La Igualdad* (Equality), as Gómez titled the directorate's official organ in Havana, counted on the support and frequent contributions of Serra, writing from New York. Indeed, *La Igualdad* and the PRC's official voicebox, *Patria*, celebrated and publicized the other's existence.[9]

While overt assertions of equality and direct references to the need to expand the rights of Cubans "of color" peppered the writings and motivated the activities of men like Gómez and Serra in the 1880s and 1890s, Martí adopted an indirect, pragmatic approach to the question of racial equality. Because the movement already counted on broad black support, both on the island and among emigrés, Martí formulated an approach to race that he hoped would co-opt the support of even the most politically and socially conservative whites. Martí thought that the cross-class, cross-racial character of PRC activities would itself serve to undermine and discredit the deepest of racial antipathies and prejudice. Wanting to spark an awakening of consciousness in favor of a system that promoted the rights of all Cubans, Martí avoided launching direct verbal attacks on the primary source of inequality in Cuba—white racism and the legacies of slavery. Rather, he focused on the redemption that forgetting the past in favor of the future could offer. Thus, in his first public speech on behalf of Cuban independence to New York's emigré community, Martí chose his words carefully, wanting to include all without alienating any. As the highly intelligent and erudite emigré Blanche Zacharie de Baralt remembered, "Martí searched for precise phrases to address each group present: he even touched on the racial issue, assuring the blacks and the mulattoes (there were a good number of them seated in the very last rows of the hall) that they were intrinsic to the triumph of Cuban arms, just as the Indians had been to the followers of Bolívar, Páez and San Martín, in the South American wars of independence."[10] But even such a cautious and apparently utilitarian inclusion of blacks in the revolutionary cause as this did not diminish Martí's image in the eyes of black activists whose own approach was comparatively more daring.

In this speech as well as in other subsequent public appearances he made in New York City on behalf of the Revolution, Martí faced an audience dominated by a majority of white Cuban exiles who had since achieved middle-class or better status in the United States. Along with their island counterparts, they shared suspicions of the long-term aspirations of blacks in Cuba, an attitude reinforced by the intensification in racism that characterized the post-Reconstruction culture of the United States at the time. Equality for blacks in Cuba amounted to a loss of power for whites. Yet, the anticolonial struggle against Spain had to be, for all involved, a process of empowerment. Seeking to avoid knee-jerk responses of rejection and alienation, Martí chose discursive and political strategies of subtle persuasion that he extended to even the most socially and politically conservative Cuban emigrés. He hoped that their disdain and racial fears would not serve the interests of Spain. Emigré coordination of financial support for the war effort from abroad proved critical to the carrying out of the war in the field. Thus, Martí shaped the potential for social revolution and the creation of a future state in the late 1880s and early 1890s by weaving together a vast complex of civilian and military alliances. To achieve these alliances, Martí relied on a multilayered discourse of identity that resonated with the conflicting, emerging nationalisms of Cubans. At the same time, he pursued a deliberate course of action meant to force Cuban patriots to interact and to acknowledge each other's importance within the organizational structures created for the Revolution.

Only one of thousands of emigrés who left the island in the 1870s and 1880s for the United States and other countries, Martí had spent the last fifteen years of his life traveling in Europe, Central America, and the Caribbean and eventually between the Florida and New York communities of emigrés in the United States. Compared with other revolutionaries, Martí's direct observation and experience of prevailing conditions on the island since the time of his youth was greatly limited. Rather, Martí shaped his understanding of Cuba through a comparative understanding that he derived from other Latin American republics. During this time, Martí lived and worked as a poet, translator, correspondent for Latin American newspapers, and consul for Argentina and Paraguay—a post he resigned in 1889 after Spanish diplomats complained of his activism in favor of Cuban independence.[11] In the early 1890s, Martí assigned himself the mandate of bringing together the diverse array of emigré communities under one organizational structure made up of working-class cigarmakers, wealthy entrepreneurs, professionals, and intellectuals. Even more critically, he courted and eventually renewed ties between middle-class emigrés and socially radical veterans of previous wars for independence such as Antonio Maceo and Máximo Gómez.

The gains Martí made in uniting Cubans for a renewed war by 1895 and that popular nationalists such as Nestor Carbonell later took for granted came at the cost of some struggle. Among the most radical and popular military leaders of the Ten Years' War, such as Máximo Gómez, Enrique Collazo, and Antonio Maceo, Martí suffered from an image problem. His refusal to support their effort for another revolution in 1884–85 had led Gómez to denounce him and other emigré leaders for forming part of the "aristocratic" rather than the "democratic" wing of the Revolution. By contrast, Gómez insisted that the Revolution would have to come from the "poor class, the people, and always the people. They are the ones who will give us powder and bullets so we can take to the field."[12] His statements testified to the origins of the revolutionary nationalism for which he and other military veterans would soon be fighting.

Indeed, Martí had failed to support Gómez's and Maceo's efforts in the mid-1880s despite the fact that they had garnered the full backing of working-class emigrés in the cigar-making communities of Tampa and Key West. Radicalized by their own labor struggles, first in Cuba and then in exile, cigarmakers espoused a combination of anarchist and socialist beliefs that guided their understandings of what an ideal future Cuban society might look like.[13] Although their contacts with and support for previous independence movements had been extensive, cigarmakers' requests to have revolutionary leaders mediate labor disputes with their emigré employers had consistently failed to work to their advantage. Moreover, many cigarmakers were affiliated with the Knights of Labor and had, especially with the failure of the Maceo-Gómez push for war in 1885, begun to associate their interests less with freeing Cuba and more with demanding freedom as full members of U.S. society.[14] At the time, Martí expressed his disdain and suspicion for Florida's workers in a letter to Enrique Trujillo, always an ardent critic of the labor movement and the radicalism that Maceo's and Gómez's support for it belied.[15]

Five years later, Martí had neither reversed course nor had come to see the poor as the anchor of the Revolution in the same way that Máximo Gómez had. Rather, his analysis of Latin America's raucous politics, near constant state of civil war, and general economic stagnation during the last century led him to believe that no group was expendable to the well-being of society. Balance of interests and mediation of differences were the keys to success. Convinced that the failure of previous wars was attributable to a lack of trust among Cubans and their social fears of each other, Martí determined to fuse their energies at all costs. Martí clarified the reasons for his unitary approach to organizing a renewed war in his analysis of three related phenomena: the experience of other Latin American republics; the inability of Cubans of radical and conservative social tendencies to find common ground; and the growing evidence of U.S. imperial ambitions with respect to Cuba.

In Martí's estimation, the greatest problems Latin American republics faced stemmed from two countervailing tendencies. The first of these was elites' habit of excluding racially and culturally distinct populations from the priorities of the state and their own understandings of national identity. The second was the propensity of marginalized groups to respond to exclusionary policies and exclusionary identities with rejection, vengeance, and violence. Thus, Martí harshly criticized the unwillingness of educated men to recognize their racially diverse populations as constituents. Significantly, however, he explained the logic for inclusion and incorporation of these historically marginalized groups in terms that were as pragmatic as they were paternal.

With few exceptions, literary scholars' focus on Martí's strident critiques of Latin American elites have led them to neglect the highly critical and quite traditional views Martí provides of Latin America's majority, whom he perceived, in such works as "Our America," as racial "Others."[16] Here, Martí depicts blacks, Indians, and peasants as obscured by ignorance, darkness, and childlike behavior, their only spark of life coming from the fires of vengeance. In each case, the cultural characterization is specific to the racial stereotype commonly associated with each category of Other: "The Indian, mute, would make circles around us and would run off to the hills to baptize his children. The black, always surveiled, sung in the night the music of his heart, alone and unknown, among the birds and the beasts. The peasant, the creator, stirred himself up, blind with indignation, against the disdainful city, against his very creation." What is unique about

Martí's vision is its paternalist insistence that Americans could do more together than apart: "The genius would have been in making brothers of . . . the Indian head-band and the scholar's robe." Invoking the trope of the indigenous Mother America who needed to be purified of a bodily disease, Martí called on her sons to stop denying her history of violation and make some effort "to know" the black and indigenous Others lurking in the background.[17] Rather than imitate Europeans, Latin American elites should embrace and acculturate the Other, argued Martí, so as to be able to govern the whole of society benevolently and without violence.

Rejecting the harshly racialized vision of Argentina's Domingo Sarmiento, Martí insisted that struggle was not between "the civilized and the barbarous," as Sarmiento claimed, but between "the false erudition" of Eurocentric lackeys and men who were ignorant of the world of letters and had been forced to remain in "nature." The "natural man" was not bad but "good, and he obeys and values superior intelligence." This was the case as long as those of superior intelligence did not mistreat or offend him, "which is something which the natural man does not forgive, disposed to recover his respect by force." In order to avoid the tyranny and violence that dismissing and ignoring such members of society had provoked in the past, Martí advised his fellow elites to get to know and include *elementos incultos*, that is, the uncultured elements of their societies in their respective national projects. Otherwise, predicted Martí, countries comprised of both "cultured and uncultured elements" would descend into social chaos and violence: "The uncultured masses are lazy and timid in the ways of intelligence, and want to be governed well; but if the government hurts them, they shake it off and govern themselves."[18]

This example demonstrates a paradoxical theme in Martí's thought and writings that reemerged later with regard to his analysis of Cuba. On one hand, Martí openly rejects Latin America's new bourgeoisie, a product of late nineteenth-century liberal economic policies, yet he simultaneously appropriates their bourgeois standards for judging the Latin American "masses." However, as Susana Rotker argues, Martí's attitude was neither entirely unique nor illogical; it was a product of the times. Martí, like other late nineteenth-century Latin American writers, "suffered the displacement and vertigo" that modernity produced.[19] As a newspaper chronicler of both the technological triumphs and social turbulence of late nineteenth-century U.S. society for Latin American readers, Martí counted himself among the new intermediary sector of urban intellectuals who, like European writers, found themselves living a moment of transition in the social order. Rationalism, urbanization, the apotheosis of science, social Darwinism, materialism, and positivism comprised a complex of ideas and experiences whose outcome was supposed to be nothing less than humanity's methodical march toward perfection. Nonetheless, Martí's admiration for the United States, a country that represented the quintessential model of "progress," had given way to disillusion and disdain. Increasing class tensions, political corruption, corporate monopolies, rising racial hostilities, xenophobia, and a utilitarian approach to humanistic pursuits in the arts marked Martí's worldview.[20] Like other modernist writers, Martí's "classless position" provoked a creativity that was self-consciously directed and "isolated between the uneducated classes and the bourgeoisie."[21]

Physically distant from Cuba and structurally isolated within the emerging modernity of American societies, Martí's experience of multiple marginalities led him to reject the United States as a center of falsity and artificiality.[22] Yet, he could side neither with the racial Others, who desired liberation whatever the cost, nor with their oppressors, whose values he abhorred. As Latin American liberal elites and many of his fellow emigrés strove to imitate the U.S. model, Martí saw the struggle in Cuba as a crucible of the times. If any Latin American country were to succeed, Cuba's struggle had to defy the inauthentic values of the false social progress of the United States and the colonized mentalities of Latin American elites. Cuba had to represent in its search for collective truth and liberty the ultimate authenticity.

Consequently, Martí wrote carefully when he approached the concepts of "race" and "racial equality" with regard to Cuba, where slavery had only officially ended in 1886. He attempted to silence race-specific understandings of social difference among Cubans for two reasons. First, he desperately wanted to change the terms of the debate then dominating intellectual and political circles. Breaking with the conventions of the time, Martí reoriented this debate away from rigid biological definitions of race to notions rooted in the malleability of culture. Thus, Martí's "othering" of blacks and Indians in "Our America" represented an effort to view these groups as potential citizens whose cultural impediments (compared to whites) he readily admitted did exist. Yet, Martí argued that their social condition could be remedied if only elites would recognize the real cause of the *incultos'* tendency to violence and cultural backwardness. Structural injustice, not innate racial instincts, lay at the heart of social difference, Martí contended.

An 1893 edition of *Patria*, written and edited by Martí, illustrates a similar approach with regard to Cuba. Under the title "War of the Races," Martí wrote that on one occasion, in the city of Santiago in Cuba, a man invited members of an elite black society to join him in organizing a political party for blacks alone. The president of the society then responded, "Well, we apologize, Sir, that we cannot help you. *Here all of us are white.*" Martí followed this story with an essay in which he celebrated the decision of a secret African society of black Cubans in Key West to rescind their use of drums in rituals and to adopt literacy standards as requirements for advancing to higher status within the organization. Tomás Surí, an ex-slave and veteran of previous independence wars, not only learned to read because of this, reported Martí, but was inspired to demand that his three sons make his example the foundation for a new Cuba by agreeing to fight in the next independence war.[23] In this way, Martí asserted the idea that whiteness, as the president of the Santiago black society stated, was a matter of culture, not color. Anyone might acquire that culture, if only they were willing to try. As in the case of Surí, one step in the right direction (toward the acquisition of literacy rather than drumming) led to another (consciousness of the collective cause of making a free Cuba).

Through parables such as these, Martí clearly asserted a scale of admission to the ranks of equality with educated Cubans (who were mostly white) that was based on acculturation. Carefully, Martí confirmed the continuing superiority of educated white Cubans and invited black Cubans to feel included in a multilayered vision of nation that could accommodate and nurture the virtues of both groups. When speaking to an exclusively black audience in La Liga, Martí reiterated the same ideas, analyzing "the unfortunate social gradation of the races [*los grados sociales y funestos de las razas*]; the sources of blame or reasons for this level or another; the causes of culture and the insufficiencies of a merely literary culture, as well as the inviability of a natural politics in accord with the conditions of the country . . . , informed by primitive or lettered ire, of one or the other [race]."[24]

Importantly, many Cuban black leaders who were already well educated, such as Juan Gualberto Gómez or Martí's co-instructors at La Liga, seem to have shared this view. Like many middle-class black U.S. Americans of their day, Cuban black activists were concerned with divesting their communities of the legacies of slavery and "uplifting the race" through greater access to education, the acquisition of valuable skills, and better jobs. But in Cuba and the circum-Caribbean region more broadly, the pursuit of cultural attributes that wealthy whites acquired without effort had a deeper social meaning. "Whitening" was the process through which individuals and families had adapted the religious practices of Catholicism and the speech styles and cultural mores of the educated and wealthier classes in order to improve their social standing by becoming culturally more acceptable to white society and therefore *racially* whiter. Over the course of the nineteenth century, this generated a spectrum of intermediate racial categories, largely used to describe free people of African descent who were not enslaved and who occupied professions in petty commerce or lucrative positions as skilled tradesmen that serviced all sectors of society, including whites.[25] However, in Cuba, the flexibility of intermediate racial categories and the advantages of whitening had diminished considerably as Creole whites and Spaniards struggled to maintain a society based on slavery that, for internal and external reasons, was collapsing from within.

By Martí's time, black mutual aid societies in Cuba, under the direction of Gómez, sought not only equal access to education but also the elimination of state discrimination in record-keeping, legal treatment, and the judicial system.[26] Indeed, their insistence that the Spanish colonial state eliminate any discursive distinction by race belied the idea that, with slavery now ended, there was no structural reason and therefore no ideological reason to repress black advancement. In the Cuba of the 1890s, racial tensions ran particularly high, in part because the Spanish government found itself in a peculiar position. For decades, Spain had discouraged independence sympathies among Cuba's Creole planters through the fueling of racial fears and successfully discrediting black participation in the independence wars of the 1870s and early 1880s on the same basis.[27] Suddenly, Spain now had to respond to an increasingly organized constituency of free black subjects.

In works such as his 1892 article "Enough" published in *Patria*, Martí saw the uncertainty about what this meant for both blacks and whites as a cause to be exploited in arguing the case for Cuba's freedom. While Spanish Autonomists on the island debated whether blacks should have the right to vote in future colonial elections, Martí contended that references to color ought to cease entirely.[28] Although he admitted that it was "more difficult to allude to virtue [in a black person] for his having lived closer to slavery," ultimately color was not a marker of worth, only an accidental caprice of nature. He who was worthy enough to die for the sake of a free Cuba in earlier wars, insisted Martí, was more than worthy enough to vote.[29] In the 1894 article "The Plate of Lentils," Martí argued this point even more forcefully, criticizing Gómez's Directorate of the Societies of Color for wasting its time attempting to gain greater rights from Spain. Attributing abolition to Cuban revolutionaries of the Ten Years' War who had first endorsed it (however reluctantly), Martí reminded readers that a government that had always supported slavery could not be expected to promote the principles of freedom.[30]

According to Martí, disorderliness, arrogance, and fear had caused previous revolutionary struggles for independence to fail.[31] That such problems were generally born of racial and class differences was obvious. But they were also born of ideological distrust between civilian and military leaders of the Revolution.[32]

Backed by a poor, largely black army with little to lose and everything to gain, the power of the military to decide the fate of civilians—not just planters, but businessmen and professionals—was both frightening and formidable to financially successful white members of Martí's audience. Recognizing this, Martí reminded readers that whatever happened, the black population of Cuba and the attendant legacies of slavery would not just disappear. To drive home this point, Martí cited the words of Rafael Serra, who was, in turn, celebrating a highly influential essay on the pragmatics of black appeasement published in Cuba by the famed independence veteran and orator Manuel Sanguily. "Peace," wrote Martí, quoting Serra, "is only in jeopardy where there is a system that produces an indignity [so great] that it excites a sense of righteousness in the most docile of peoples."[33]

Martí faced a challenging dilemma. The appeal of a renewed revolution depended on its leaders' ability to convince Cubans that armed struggle might achieve the justice that Spain, with its corruption, privileging of peninsulars, and monarchical government, had negated for so long. As a radical believer in the need and possibility of achieving a just society, Martí could not deny that Cubans of African descent had suffered the greatest injustices of all. But as a revolutionary activist, Martí knew that he could not appear to imply that the needs of one group dictated the needs of another. This was especially true when it came to dealing with the problem of racial equality and racism in Cuba. Clearly, the formula for remedying the injustices in question had to be as radical and profound as the injustices themselves in order for it to succeed. Yet, from Martí's perspective, pitting one group against another could only result in an inversion of roles. In the case of a society as divided as Cuba, a balance of power and of interests had to be struck. In founding and organizing the PRC, Martí believed he knew how to achieve this.

Transcending Race and Class: The Activism and Messianism of José Martí

In keeping with his analysis of "Our America," Martí considered that success of Cuba's revolution and the viability of any future Cuban republic depended on the delicate balancing of opposing social forces in both the discourse and the practice of a revolutionary state. Thus, Martí founded the PRC in New York as a model government for both the Revolution and the Republic. He intended the PRC to mediate the socially democratic visions of nation that Martí himself encountered among emigré cigarmakers and the highly exclusivist visions that predominated among the professional emigrés with whom he had more continuous contact. He organized the PRC to serve as an umbrella organization for hundreds of emigré clubs and secret revolutionary societies on the island.

Combining grassroots participation with centralized authority, Martí located the PRC's headquarters in New York and employed conservative middle-class professionals as its staff. Yet, he formulated the statutes for the party with a core group of leading labor activists and cigarmakers that included various men of color in Florida. The results were a set of resolutions and a revolutionary program that reiterated a commitment to mediating differences of class and color through "cordiality," "brotherhood," and "common action." Importantly, PRC resolutions promised that the new revolution would "not work directly for the current or future predominance of any class" but for all. A perfect example of the multilayered discourse Martí would adopt in bringing together nationalists of all stripes, the PRC program promised to rid Cuba of the authoritarian and bureaucratic colonial government. In its place, the PRC would found "a new and sincerely democratic society" that would nonetheless be "capable of conquering, through the orderliness of real labor and the equilibrium of social forces, the dangers of impetuous freedom in a society composed for slavery."[34] Martí hoped that his message of social unity through the restrained and controlled dispensing of social justice would appeal to the most radical as well as the most conservative nationalists. Between lines in which he exalted the security of peace between former slaves and former masters in a free Cuba, Martí wrote in 1893, "The world is an equilibrium, and we must put into balance the two sides of the scale while there is still time."[35]

Indeed, revolutionary activists in other emigré communities expressed a more radical platform than Martí's PRC. Although Cuban emigrés in Jamaica later joined the PRC's network of revolutionary clubs, the political program of their "Separatist or Radical Party," published in 1890, went much further than the PRC's statutes of 1892. Unlike the PRC, Jamaica's "Radicals" openly endorsed the "absolute freedoms" of thought, speech, and association as well as a standard of universal suffrage that extended to women. They also proposed the guarantees of racially integrated public education, prohibition of child labor, and state-sponsored programs to encourage the development of a class of independent black farmers as a means for subverting the structural inequalities of slavery.[36] Like Martí, they denounced U.S. imperial pretensions and perceived a threat to the viability of a new revolution in New York's pro-imperialist nationalist community whose newspapers, such as *El Progreso*, spearheaded the view that black integration to the nationalist cause jeopardized Cuba's future.[37]

For Martí, conservative voices were hard to dismiss as they were not physically distant but direct competitors for the constituency of the PRC. In 1889, Enrique

Trujillo, publisher of *El Porvenir*, the emigré newspaper with the longest-running and widest circulation in New York, openly appealed to white racism in order to justify why independence and not U.S. annexation provided a better means for controlling blacks in the Republic. In his view of the ideal future "nation," blacks would be assimilated by whites and eventually eliminated from the population as the state prevented their numbers from growing through prohibitions on black immigration.[38] As we shall see, Martí's right-hand man on the PRC staff, Tomás Estrada Palma, not only shared this view but also actively pursued it in both the 1895 War and the early years of the Republic. Thus, Darwinian interpretation of racial hierarchy that proposed the innate degeneracy of blacks and their probable extinction formed one of the bases for Trujillo and many other white emigré leaders to develop pro-imperialist nationalism. While emigré Radicals in Jamaica condemned these views, Martí took a different approach. He sought to engage and thereby neutralize the divisive power of the right wing.

Even as he founded and promoted La Liga, Martí struggled to contain racial fears among conservative white Cubans in New York City on whose approval the viability of the PRC rested. Frequently, Martí warned his black colleagues in La Liga not to make too much of their activities so as not to give too radical an impression of the PRC. As the PRC's membership grew to several hundred clubs in the U.S., Mexico, and places as far away as France, Martí's efforts to attract a broad base of support increased his sense of the need to control the image of the PRC as well as his own. For Martí, it was critical that his affiliation with black activists such as Serra and with their work on behalf of the social advancement of blacks not appear too radical. He avoided reviving the phantoms of the "uppity" black and the "arrogant" mulatto stereotypes that were so deeply inscribed in the Cuban psyche by the island's slave past. Thus, Martí warned Juan Bonilla in 1890, "Be careful with La Liga, which is like those small bodies that once illuminated by the sun, cast a shadow much greater than they are themselves."[39]

Although he never stopped reporting on La Liga's activities or exalting their importance to the overall cause of Free Cuba, Martí strategized with Serra about how to represent the implications that La Liga's work would have for the Revolution and thereby the Republic.[40] The issue seemed particularly problematic whenever Cuban emigrés gathered to commemorate the anniversary of the launching of Cuba's first war for independence in 1868. In 1888, for example, Martí merely invited Serra to the event, seeing the latter's presence there as symbolic enough. Apparently, for Serra to have been asked to speak might have alienated key emigrés in the movement.[41] By 1893, however, conditions had substantially changed. The PRC statutes had been approved by all affiliated clubs; veteran officers were expressing admiration for the work of Martí; and even *El Porvenir*

MYSTIC, MESSIAH, AND MEDIATOR

had begun publishing communications from the working-class clubs of Florida lauding Martí's work in "the unification of the great Cuban family."[42] Jubilant that he could not only invite Serra to attend the event but also ask him to preside over the formalities as an official speaker, Martí made sure to remark, "*Nothing too concrete*, so that it doesn't look too ostentatious and so that we don't reveal what our paths are. Ships depart more quickly when they are not announced."[43] The remark's significance lies not only in its pragmatism but in its subtle reference ("so that we don't reveal what our paths are") to private conversations and personal convictions that Martí and Serra shared. As this example illustrates, there was both a private Martí and a public Martí.

Privately, Martí often revealed his anxiety over the virulent campaign of racial fear Spain had once again launched to discredit independence in Cuba. Writing to Emilio Nuñez in the months prior to establishing La Liga with Serra, Martí admitted, "Already it is possible to see how here too [among patriots], negative passions such as these arise, and it is being said that blacks are little more than beasts."[44] In fact, the founding of La Liga may have represented a response to such critiques and an effort to contradict culturally static views of blacks. On a personal level, Martí was convinced that differences between whites and people of color most ascribed to race were more accurately due to differences of culture. Having come to this conclusion, Martí pushed himself to its ideological limits by privately meditating on the hypothetical proposition of an interracial marriage between his own daughter and a black man. Martí took his convictions to the point of endorsing this ultimate taboo but predictably asserted that "the black [*negro*]" in question had to live up to his would-be father-in-law's intellectual and personal expectations.[45] Martí never published these thoughts, and it is likely that he never intended to do so. Written in short, emotive phrases and peppered with doodled images (including one of New York's Statue of Liberty), the manuscript gives the impression that Martí was thinking through the personal implications of the public logic he espoused.

In short, Martí faced an audience that included activists like Serra who favored independence as a vehicle to racial equality and public figures like Trujillo who favored it as the path to greater racial control of blacks by whites. Given Martí's conviction that the PRC should embrace all Cubans who favored independence, no matter their reasons for doing so, it is not surprising that Martí's public discourse and private correspondence took such complicated forms.

Hoping to mediate the most extreme of racial fears by moderating the principal targets of them, Martí wrote several essays on key black and mulatto figures of the revolutionary movement. In order to undercut enduring rumors that the well-educated and prestigious mulatto general Antonio Maceo would one day aspire to a role in the future state beyond that of a military man, Martí depicted Maceo as a farmer who had spent years contentedly tilling the soil with his own hands.[46] Similarly, Martí lauded the much darker Rafael Serra as an exception to his race and his class and an example of the kind of ideal worker that access to education and a "higher" culture could bring.[47] In this way, Martí silenced the question of racial equality in order to promote rights of equal access instead.[48]

Although some activists, such as those in Jamaica or members of La Liga, may have been more radical in their endorsement of specific policies that ensured greater equality for blacks in the long run, certain aspects of Martí's discursive inclusion of blacks and blackness to Cuban identity remained unrivaled. For example, Diego Vicente Tejera, a close friend of Martí during the late 1880s and arguably the most famous socialist organizer of Florida emigrés in the 1890s, did not go as far as Martí in his efforts to include blacks and negate the credibility of a Cuban "race war." Whereas Martí emphasized the rootedness of apparent racial differences in culture and argued for the equal capacity of blacks, Tejera addressed the problem in ways that some blacks, like Serra, might have found offensive. Thus, Tejera spoke openly about "the positive state of intellectual inferiority in which the colored race finds itself" and only hesitantly suggested that "this condition of inferiority . . . may be passing, because it does not depend precisely on an innate mental deficiency, but to the absolute lack of education in a race that until now has been enslaved."[49] If Martí argued that the willingness of blacks to sacrifice themselves in war for Cuba's independence proved their worth, Tejera argued that the "race of color . . . has to work twice as hard now to prove with ease their respectability."[50] Moreover, while Martí skirted the idea that blacks needed to "whiten" themselves in order to achieve equality with whites, Tejera celebrated the propensity of the "colored individual [to] imitate the white in his manners and social tastes, demonstrating in this way a noble desire to elevate himself and providing proof of his admirable skills of adaptation." Indeed, Tejera went so far as to reference blackface theatre and the popularity of *danzón*, an emerging style of Cuban music characterized by overt African-derived rhythms, in order to show that whites might gain something as well from cultural exchange with blacks. This was the case even though, as he put it, the sector of colored society that such whites imitated was "the least worthy of imitation."[51]

By comparison, the subtlety of Martí's discourse, even its polite and respectful tone, implied that he spoke not only *about* blacks and their fitness as citizens but also *to* them. Martí's sensitivity showed that black Cubans were as much a part of his audience and a part of Cuba as those whose wealth, class, education, and

MYSTIC, MESSIAH, AND MEDIATOR

sophistication made them automatically acceptable members of a future Cuban society or, for that matter, any society.

Publicly, then, Martí walked the tightrope between the expectations of conflicting nationalist groups. Consciously, Martí hoped not to scare off social conservatives with a personal interest in preserving the privileges they already enjoyed. Class extremes, he suggested, could be mediated with delicacy, not tyranny: "*Even just a crumb* of the advantages accumulated in the exploitation of slavery will make relations among the Cubans more firm and generous in the Republic."[52] Importantly, pro-imperialist nationalists like Estrada Palma and some revolutionary nationalists among the military officers in the field would continue to read the silences and subtleties on race and class through which Martí reached out to critics before 1895 as evidence of the need for gradualism. For them, Martí supported a nation based on extremely limited or very slow social change that would develop naturally with time, not as the product of state directives or demands from below.

On the other hand, popular nationalists chose to inhabit Martí's silences and discretion, transforming them into evidence of Martí's advocacy of total liberation from injustice and inequality. "Martí, within and outside the process of the war, was a radical revolutionary," Rafael Serra wrote in 1896.[53] That proponents of multiple nationalisms interpreted Martí in multiple ways became apparent not so much in his life as immediately after his death. Still, multiple memories of Martí originated in the multiple visions of nation that Martí legitimated and the multiple images of himself as a leader and representative of those visions that he created.

During his years as an independence activist, Martí never lost sight of the past even as he glossed over its complexities in order to achieve the immediate and long-term goal of inspiring Cubans to believe in what past wars had rendered impossible: independence and nationhood. Drawing contrasts between Cuba's colonial situation and the "redemption" that the Revolution offered, Martí also policed remembrances of the past and worried about the implications that conflicted memories would hold in the Revolution and the Republic. In a letter in which he refuted one writer's specific memory of what he had said and why, Martí noted, "I say this because evocations of the past are, as much in the military sense as in the political, precisely one of the greatest dangers of living politics in Cuba."[54] On issues of particular sensitivity whose discussion only led Cubans to realize how divided their future projects for the nation were, Martí attempted to create a countermemory that not only minimized divisions but rendered them meaningless. Consequently, Martí attacked the notion that slavery had been based on color over class and, in another moment, ridiculed the idea that class exploitation derived from irreconcilable interests. He even went as far as to insist that given the proper attitude, Cubans would realize that "class" never really existed at all. Class, like race, Martí argued, was a mutable, social construction that could be mitigated for the benefit of all in an orderly and socially peaceful Republic.[55]

The messianic qualities of Martí's message of social unity made it especially infectious and morally persuasive. However, these ideas were not contrived but integral to Martí's sense of himself and perception of politics. The idea that his work on behalf of Cuba imitated that of Jesus Christ and that all great men who had served as liberators of their countries—Simón Bolívar, San Martín, and Miguel de Hidalgo—were messiahs obsessed Martí.[56] Accordingly, Martí characterized anniversaries of the dates associated with previous independence struggles as "sacred" and denounced anyone who defamed or conspired against the future struggle of Cuba as a Judas who "nails Christ to the cross of the thief."[57] When Spanish authorities arrested Martí for disloyalty as a teenager and his father secured his release into exile, Martí first expressed his identification with the destiny of a god-man who, like Jesus, had to ritually humble himself for the liberation of others: "Martyrdom for the fatherland is God himself. . . . I feel that God within me, I have that God within me; for this God within me, you [the Spaniards] should feel pity, more than horror or disdain."[58] Later, Martí was not beyond comparing himself to the ever-faithful Jesus and his often-doubting followers to Jesus' mercurial apostles. "What does it matter that Peter denies if Jesus triumphs? Peter denied and Jesus triumphed," Martí remarked in his report on a recent trip to the Florida communities in the PRC organ *Patria*.[59]

Martí also saw his personal sacrifices in messianic terms. After his wife left him out of disgust for his obsession with Cuban independence, she publicly humiliated him by seeking the help of his political rival Enrique Trujillo and secured the Spanish consulate's consent to legal guardianship of their only son.[60] Martí wrote to a close friend, "Not even to you—who means so much to me—can I tell of my continuous sacrifices, of my home lost to the affairs of the fatherland. . . . I have already said more than I should have. I am without strength, still very bad. My cross, when shall it finally arrive?"[61] Even Martí's own mother, Doña Leonor Pérez, chastised him in messianic terms: "You'll remember that I've been telling you since you were a little boy that everyone who puts himself in the role of redeemer is bound to be crucified and your worst enemies are those of your own race."[62]

Martí's identification with Jesus Christ prompted him to draw secular, political lessons from his story. Perhaps it was for this reason that he recommended

Renan's *Life of Jesus* to La Liga. Never wanting to appear as if he solicited support-ers for the Revolution, Martí acted as if a higher consciousness had led them to demand Martí's presence among them. When visiting emigrés in Florida, Martí often depicted himself as a self-sacrificing servant of the people rather than the self-appointed leader that he was.[63] Martí was also renowned during his lifetime for embracing opponents and "turning the other cheek" in significant ways. As his personal correspondence with men like Trujillo reveals, Martí did court his critics, often relentlessly, and they in the end often succumbed in order not to ap-pear ungracious before Martí's boundless generosity.[64] Even Enrique Collazo, a veteran general with whom he had sustained a virulent public debate in 1892 over the failures of past independence struggles, grudgingly came to admire Martí despite his disregard for Martí's heroic personal style. Indeed, Collazo provides one of the few critical characterizations of Martí that survived his death:

> Martí was small of stature, thin; he had the movement incarnated within him; . . . refined in temperament, an intelligent and tenacious fighter who had traveled widely, he knew the world and its men; being excessively iras-cible and absolutist, he managed always to dominate his character, trans-forming himself into a friendly, affectionate, attentive man, disposed always to suffer for others, the supporter of the weak, teacher of the ignorant, pro-tector and generous father of those who suffered; aristocratic in his likes, habits and customs, he took his democracy to its limits; he dominated his character to such an extent that his feelings and actions often stood in con-tradiction to each other; apostle of the redemption of the fatherland, he achieved his objective.[65]

Collazo's cynical image of Martí as a ruthless strategist contrasts sharply with other contemporaries' image of him as a selfless idealist. Possibly, both images coexisted because both were true.

But for all his words and gestures, Martí realized that powerful images were not enough. Discourse alone did not spark either action or belief. Actions on his part and that of the PRC were required to retain the faith of those most in need of change, Cuba's popular nationalists, and those who most feared change, the pro-imperialist nationalists. Two critical examples stand out in this regard: the first involves Martí's integration of emigrés who had once favored annexation of Cuba to the United States, and the second, Martí's intercession on behalf of Florida cigarmakers who launched a violent strike a year before the war.

As discussed above, Martí came to believe that inclusion and co-optation rather than dismissal and disdain were the best responses to the potential criti-cisms that conservatives could launch of a renewed war. If such critiques and rumors of a race war emerged from New York's emigré groups, their effects would be harder to combat given the United States' inevitable opposition to the war and potential to thwart its progress, either on behalf of its own interests or those of Spain. Thus, as early as 1889, Martí recognized an important difference in the motives behind North American annexationism and emigré annexationism. Feeling that emigré annexationists were really misguided nationalists, Martí expressed sympathy for them, a group that "loves their fatherland with as much fervor as anyone and serves it according to their understanding of it."[66] While he did not share the "logic" of their beliefs, Martí worked hard to integrate this group into the PRC fold, eventually making such former annexation proponents as Fidel Pierra and Estrada Palma strategic players within it. As we shall see, inclusion in the PRC gave them a space to express their vision for Cuba in the form of pro-imperialist nationalism, not annexationism.

Even more critically, when working-class emigrés demanded that Martí prove where the PRC's sympathies lay, Martí and the PRC responded. This turning point came in December 1893 when cigarmakers in Key West struck only to watch their emigré employers conspire with local North American officials to contract Spanish strikebreakers from Havana. When their union asked that the PRC send legal help, Martí dispatched Horatio Rubens, chief legal counsel for the PRC throughout the 1895 War. Amazingly, Rubens used U.S. immigration law to crush the defense. For the first time in their labor struggle and history of repeated requests for mediation of their labor disputes by former revolutionary chiefs, cigarmakers could declare a resounding victory.[67] The victory was as much theirs as it was Martí's, the PRC's, and the Revolution's. Recognizing this, Martí publicized these events widely, writing in both English and Spanish. According to Martí, the hypocrisy of the United States regarding democracy and civil rights had been fully revealed. No longer could any Cuban deny the duplicity of U.S. business interests or the way in which the U.S. government could—if unchecked—compromise its principles in pursuit of profit. "We have, Cubans, no country but the one we must fight for," he declared.[68] That country was Cuba, and for many popular nationalist emigrés, it was also a nation that they deeply identified with the figure of José Martí.

Conclusion

Although many of his speeches invite the opposite conclusion, Martí recognized that people did not put aside their class interests or racial identities in conceiving visions of nation. Both ideals and interests informed them. For Martí, mediating opposed identities and interests for the sake of social unity meant reframing the concept of community in broadly appealing terms. Martí did not so much choose terms to make the fractures, hierarchies, and differences that divided Cubans disappear so much as he created a discourse that drove these divisions into hiding. Martí sensed that the emigrés he was trying to organize had to experience this concept of community in both word and deed. In the end, Martí did not propose a vague set of principles for revolution.[69] His strategy and his discourse were precise in their selective engagement of images, values, and ideas that would and did appeal to all. Harmonizing their contradictions into a single discourse of unity, Martí brought together various emergent nationalisms behind the cause of independence and structured them into an institutional base that exemplified the coexistence and toleration of ideological polarities. In the short term, the unification of so many Cubans abroad and their official connection to militants in the field through the PRC was Martí's greatest achievement. In the long run, however, it was also the Achilles' heel of the Cuban revolutionary movement.

From the time of Martí's death in May 1895, members of the PRC and officers of the military who admired Martí struggled to keep the spirit of unity alive through invocations of his image and idealized memories of him as a self-sacrificing messiah, mediator, and mystic. Carrying out the Revolution of 1895 required that Cubans of all ideological persuasions and backgrounds confront the legacies of the past that colonial society and their former position in that society embodied. For some, remembering the past through the myth of Martí, the quintessential icon of social unity, became a discursive mandate for radical social change. For others, it became the ritual substitute and even the antidote to change itself. Once the fighting began, the Revolution would no longer be a crucible that fused together ideas, interests, and identities that belied conflicting visions of nation. Rather, the practice and process of revolution itself came to act as a prism.

TWO

· ·

Revolutionizing Cuba Libre, Civilizing
the *Manigua*, 1895–1898

ON THE AFTERNOON OF May 19, 1895, a column of Spanish soldiers under the command of José Ximénez de Sandoval approached the Cuban rebel camp near Dos Rios, Oriente. Earlier that day, General-in-Chief Máximo Gómez had ordered José Martí to remain in the rear flank of his troops.[1] Stubborn as always, Martí defied Gómez's orders. Venturing forth with only Colonel Angel de la Guardia at his side (a name ironically meaning "Guardian Angel"), he quickly paid the ultimate price. In his first encounter with the enemy, Major General and President of the Republic-in-Arms José Martí fell from his horse, mortally wounded under a hail of enemy gunfire. Exultant Spanish forces recovered the body and carried it on horseback to the town of Remanganaguas, where they buried it in a common grave, depriving Martí of even a simple coffin. Wishing to exploit their victory to the fullest, Spanish authorities in Havana commanded Ximénez de Sandoval to exhume the body and bring it to Santiago de Cuba where he should preside over a proper Christian burial.[2]

Months later, Gómez recalled these events with remorse, pain, and guilt. To him, Martí had died "so prematurely and so without glory." That February, Gómez had traveled to Santo Domingo with Martí and Enrique Collazo, a veteran of the Ten Years' War and, until recently, Martí's foremost critic. The cooperation of the three leaders was symbolic of the state of social unity they had called on patriots to achieve. Convinced that the cause of the Revolution would be better served with Martí at the helm of the PRC in New York, Gómez had persuaded Martí to abandon his plan to join rebels in the field. But just six days prior to Gómez's embarkation for the island and Martí's scheduled departure for New York, a copy of the PRC organ *Patria* arrived at Gómez's home. Weeks ahead of schedule, *Patria* announced that Martí's party had already made landfall in Cuba. It was a fatal error for which Gómez blamed the overzealous Tomás Estrada Palma, a man he had distrusted since the Ten Years' War.[3] The move seemed calculated to serve Estrada Palma's ambitions. Once the copy of *Patria* was in Martí's hands, its effect was immediate. "'After this, General,'" Martí had declared dejectedly, "'I cannot possibly show up in New York.'"[4]

For the revolutionary forces on the island and emigré communities abroad, the loss of Martí scarcely a month after his arrival at the front came as a devastating blow. Their fears attest to the tenuous nature of the social unity behind revolution that Martí's discourse and actions had helped to construct. The Spanish press only added to such fears with unsubstantiated rumors of the death of other rebel chiefs.[5] Commenting on current rumors in Santiago, one patriot remarked: "The General wounded, Martí dead, Paquito Borrero dead and the majority of the leaders dead; What do you make of that? The only thing left to say is that the Revolution is over."[6] Some emigrés worried about the possibility that the civilian-military alliance Martí had forged would collapse: "My wife has been weeping, I can scarcely sleep, thinking night and day of such a terrible possibility."[7] Rebel officers like General José María Aguirre concurred: "The most grave, sad and painful news that we have received so far has been that of the death of Martí. . . . Who has done what he has done?" Aguirre concluded that Martí's death was one of the first tests that the Revolution would face. However, if the rebels were truly committed to its progress, they would not falter. Revolutions produced "the liberators, the Bolívars," he wrote. It could not be the other way around.[8]

Indeed, the process of carrying out revolution differed fundamentally from that of preparing for one. No one can say with certainty that Martí's survival would have made the adjustment any easier. In the field, Cuban rebels faced not only Spain but, more important, the differences among each other that Martí's PRC and official revolutionary discourse had worked hard to hide. The harmonizing of identities, expectations, and cause had to be continually renewed and reinforced on a daily basis. Unity could not be taken for granted. This chapter analyzes the internal dynamics of the 1895 War in order to reveal how difficult this challenge truly was. Through the very practice of revolution itself, Cubans asserted, mediated, and negotiated the political and social differences in the nations that they imagined and for which they fought. They did so on two fronts: a diplomatic front overseen by the PRC in New York and its supporting civilian network of emigré clubs abroad, and a military front in Cuba overseen by army officers and the Government of the Republic-in-Arms, a legislative body elected in liberated zones that served as a mediator of policy between the PRC in New York and the rebel army on the island.

After fighting commenced, the ideological elements making up the Revolution crystallized in stark contrast to each other. Independence from Spain remained, at times, the only common ground that Cuban guerrillas, emigré workers, and PRC leaders shared. Still, even as the discursive seams binding different nationalist visions quickly frayed, mutuality of circumstance and of action worked to maintain a unity of purpose. In the following pages, we will explore how revolutionaries and their supporters expressed the three central nationalisms of Cuban independence through acts of defiance, confrontation, debate, and negotiation with one another in the midst of war.

Male and female *mambises* (rebel soldiers), emigré workers, *pacíficos* (rural noncombatants), female spies, and others espoused *popular nationalism*. This was a diffuse but radical set of principles for self-determination that included a commitment to racial (and, in some cases, gender) equality, socioeconomic access, and political justice through a grassroots-controlled democracy. Together with discursive expressions of popular nationalism, this chapter examines how popular nationalists acted on their vision of nation in the midst of the *manigua*, especially through the strategies and nature of the warfare involved. As in all previous independence wars, *manigua* referred to the zones liberated by the revolutionary army or their camp sites. Originally, however, *manigua* referred to the hideouts of runaway slaves in the forested highlands of Cuba. As we shall see, transformations in the meaning of the word conveyed the efforts of popular-class revolutionaries to define the goal of freedom on their own terms within guerrilla-controlled areas. This occurred despite the internal efforts of some officers of the Liberating Army to patrol these liberated/liberating zones, regiment them, and generally ensure that the *manigua* would be as hierarchical and structured as they wanted the Republic to be.

Socially conscious and politically reformist leaders of the Liberating Army promoted *revolutionary nationalism*. Among the most prestigious officers of the Cuban military were some of the more radical revolutionary nationalists. These leaders, such as Antonio Maceo and Máximo Gómez, envisioned a society that would break cleanly with the Spanish colonial past and redistribute resources to those previously constrained by the legacies of slavery and monocultural capitalism. Importantly, these officers hoped to build a paternalist Cuban state that would reward socioeconomic opportunities to those whose personal sacrifices during the war and commitment to change in times of peace would make them especially worthy citizens. However, revolutionary nationalism did not so much emphasize the development of democratic participatory channels or institutions, as popular nationalism did. Rather, it championed the role of patrician-caudillos who could lead, evaluate, and carry out policies for the good of their popular-class constituents. In this sense, revolutionary nationalists championed a top-down concept of how the future Cuban state would relate to its people and rooted this concept in the hierarchical model of discipline and cultural codes of honor that characterized the Liberating Army.

For Tomás Estrada Palma, the PRC support staff, and white professionals of the Cuban exile community, the Revolution was meant to bring about political change and thereby the means by which to move Cuba down the road to greater social progress. Having built new lives for themselves as lawyers, teachers, small business owners, physicians, and journalists in New York, Key West, and Tampa, these Cubans expressed a unique and contradictory brand of *pro-imperialist nationalism*. Stressing continued reliance on the plantation model for Cuba's sugar-centered economy, these nationalists believed in improving rather than modifying or demolishing the order of society basic to the Spanish colonial regime. For them, foreign investment, individual initiative, and adherence to the standards of civilization they admired in U.S. society could solve Cuba's problems.

All in all, the Revolution did not simply clear the way for an accommodation of multiple visions of nation into a mutually agreeable project that later fell apart, after or because of the U.S. military intervention of 1898. The Revolution that had been forged behind multiple, often contradictory tenets in the 1880s and 1890s was eventually funded, fought, and lived in the same manner. On two fronts, at home and abroad, strategies of warfare, finance, recruitment, and retention of soldiers and supporters straddled, obscured, and often challenged the boundaries between elite and subaltern understandings of protest, rebellion, and social order. At first, the need to perceive each other's actions as fulfilling a collective end made the lived process of armed struggle a flexible one. In this process, excuses could be made and justifications rendered to explain why certain actions or policy decisions were taken, even when nationalists of all visions disagreed about their implications or disliked their long-term results. However, if the integration of multiple visions of nation in the 1895 War made it ideologically accommodating at the outset, the outcome of internal struggles among revolutionaries revealed that by 1898, it was nothing of the kind. As explored below, the experience and perception of guerrilla warfare during the course of the war catalyzed the process of separation that distinguished nationalist elements from one another.

Negotiating Nations in the Manigua, Interpreting the Revolution

In the 1895 War, the process of collective action, argumentation, and negotiation over the use and meaning of guerrilla tactics formed the nexus of alliance and conflict through which popular and revolutionary nationalists battled with each other for ideological dominance within the ranks of the Liberating Army. As historians have long recognized, the confluence of guerrilla actions with the strategies of popular-class resistance on which Cuban peasants and slaves historically relied for their own survival contributed greatly to the successful recruitment and retention of the majority of fighters. Tactics such as raiding plantations, stealing livestock, and extorting ransoms, tribute, or "protection" money against future raids formed the principal guerrilla strategies of all three of Cuba's independence wars. Often reliant on the looting of stores and the sacking of plantations, the Liberating Army could be seen to mimic the actions of rebellious slaves, organized rural mobs, or common bandits. For Spanish loyalists, the concept of "bandit" became interchangeable with that of a Cuban guerrilla as the ordering of life and economy in the countryside took on arbitrary and chaotic patterns.[9]

For the Liberating Army's military officers who planned such strategies and controlled their execution through direct chains of command, the revolutionary process was orderly, just as the future nation they imagined would be. Dictating the pace and scope of social justice and distribution of material rewards from above kept it that way. On the other hand, those long subjected to the abuses of colonial authorities or rural elites took a different view. Many preferred to see the social and political content of the world-turned-upside-down scenes that characterized rebel invasions of towns and plantations as models for future political action by a popular nationalist state.[10] Glimpsing the Revolution for the first time on the occasion of such raids inevitably invited former slaves and the rural poor to equate the nation the Revolution would found on the reversing of extreme class disparities. Thus, the experience of guerrilla warfare confirmed simultaneously the legitimacy of two different concepts of revolution and visions of nation, both that of popular nationalist soldiers and of revolutionary nationalist officers.

In this context, the participation of former bandits acquired special significance. To possible recruits considering whether or not to join the Revolution, the inclusion of people the Spanish considered criminals in the ranks of the Liberating Army represented the ultimate test of its leaders' commitment to a radical reconfiguration of power in society. Oftentimes, bandit bands were wholly recast as military units, their former leaders transformed into officers under the title of *comandante* (commander). Like the cases of former slaves who became generals in the course of the war, the Revolution's identification with the struggle of rustic, rural common folk made it more appealing and empowered the poor to conceive of the nation in terms intimately related to their own experience and definitions of freedom. Making this connection, between the personal and the collective, the emotional and the political, formed the basis for the emergence and expression of popular nationalism in the midst of war.

Bandits-turned-soldiers did not just include small-time thieves but exceptionally infamous recruits whose reputations for rebellion were not necessarily limited to the social or economic realm. For example, the Spanish had condemned Manuel García, known as "El Rey de los Campos de Cuba" (King of the Cuban Countryside), to political exile during the 1880s for keeping the spirit of revolution alive between wars through his bandit activities. Exiled to Florida, García worked as a cigarmaker and became deeply enmeshed in the highly charged labor politics of Key West and Tampa. When he returned to Cuba in 1888, he did so as a secret agent of a revolutionary club in Key West and promptly resumed his attacks on property and the rich. This time, however, García donated the funds he collected from ransom payments and other "crimes" to the cause of independence, contributing an estimated $75,000 to PRC coffers. In turn, he hoped the Republic might provide what the colonial government would not: amnesty and the opportunity to make a fresh start.[11] As traditional peasant songs, or *décimas*, dating from the 1895 War attest, his and other bandits' examples helped shape the popular nationalist vision of nation in terms of reversing the social order and revising the cultural credentials through which social acceptability could be judged.[12] Personal gain did not necessarily sully the purity of one's contributions to the goal.

For their own reasons, revolutionary nationalist officers often encouraged their subordinates to think in such terms by linking loyalty to the Revolution with the possibility of material gain. Officers regularly engaged in displays of material redistribution and personal patronage. In addition to tolerating plunder in order to draw recruits from plantation workers, officers also endorsed the use of violence against the people and property that protected and symbolized the old colonial order, even if they did not directly threaten the rebels. Through such means, the Revolution symbolically inverted the legacies of slavery and class privilege. In the short term, revolutionary nationalist leaders saw such steps as necessary to the demolition of Spanish rule. In a letter to Salvador Cisneros Betancourt, president of the Republic-in-Arms after the death of Martí, Serafín Sánchez described Gómez's and Maceo's invasion of western Cuba in bloody terms. Citing their troops' coordinated assault on Spanish forces in the cane fields of the sugar plantation, or *ingenio*, "La Teresa," Sánchez praised the ease with which the gentlemanly style of cavalry officers combined with the unbridled fury of machete-wielding foot soldiers.[13] A few days later, Sánchez admitted to having "macheted to death some civilians [*macheteando unos civiles*]" along with a Spanish soldier from Lajas while holding up a train.[14] In evaluating these events, Sánchez expressed only measured remorse for the "beautiful ruin and desolation" unleashed on the province of Matanzas. There, "towns, sugar estates, railway stations, stores, bridges, dikes and whatever had been built by the Cuban settler [*hombre colono cubano*] burned in only ten days," he wrote. In addition to taking some 500 rifles from Spanish soldiers and the homes of the *pacíficos*, rebels also expropriated 4,000 to 5,000 horses.[15] Ironically, even as Sánchez celebrated plunder for the sake of Revolution, he condemned the Spanish for plundering (*trampeando*) Cuba.

However elite officers may have justified them, the tactics themselves symbolically legitimated acts of class warfare and confirmed that the ultimate authority of the Revolution lay in building an entirely new society on the rubble of the old. These tactics also invited ideological exchange between the popular nationalism of soldiers and the brand of revolutionary nationalism that patrician officers like Sánchez and his immediate superiors, Generals Maceo and Gómez, espoused. Sometimes revolutionary nationalist officers went as far as to sanction the redistribution of wealth outside of the context of plantation raids by encouraging conscious acts of expropriation from the *pacíficos* they encountered, not all of whom were poor. In doing so, these officers effectively ruptured the boundary between the "gentleman's war" they saw themselves to be fighting and the war of social protest that soldiers of the laboring classes were fighting. The war diary of medical doctor Eugenio Sánchez de Agramonte, who passed his free moments in the *manigua* reading Victor Hugo's *Les Miserables*, illustrates this.[16]

We passed through the main street of the Town of Tapaste (2,000 souls). Ugly and sorry place. Its inhabitants are quite insipid and uncultured [*incultos*], only the gentleman priest . . . is worthy of special attention. The wife of Dr. Crowley went as far as to kneel before me because [the rebel soldiers] had taken her horse named Guajamón. And she actually called herself a Patriot! The Pharmacist . . . complained to me that a soldier had asked him for his overalls . . . he says that he suffers from an allergy to plants and brush [*Nemoptisis*]. . . . And the soldier who gives his blood so full of health to redeem the Fatherland of all . . . ? Oh, human egoism! What degraded beings. What fruits can such beings produce [for liberty]?[17]

At times, Sánchez de Agramonte admitted that the Liberating Army relied on armed intimidation to recruit *pacíficos* for such undesirable tasks as carrying the wounded on a march. Yet, he apparently sanctioned this practice with the same conviction he held toward poor soldiers' expropriation of personal items.[18]

In taking the side of rebel soldiers against individuals who might otherwise have been his class allies, Sánchez de Agramonte contributed to the perception that the Revolution was about turning the world upside down by living out, at least occasionally, that ideal. However, officers who sanctioned plunder and acts of redistribution did not necessarily advocate a radical, redistributive vision of the future Cuban nation. Like Sánchez de Agramonte, the revolutionary nationalist lens through which officers perceived guerrilla tactics refracted their implications in terms that emphasized the gratitude of troops, not their long-term expectations. This idea was critical to their vision of how social change in the new nation would work: as a top-down, patron-client process dependent on their authority. Yet, whenever possible, these officers sought to control the frequency and direction of guerrilla tactics so as to manage better any alternative interpretations of the war and its results that subordinates might perceive. The following examples illustrate critical moments in which the guiding principles of revolutionary nationalism conflicted with those of popular nationalism.

In order to prevent the objectives of military campaigns and their "carnivalesque" aspects from getting out of hand, rebel leaders relied on strict standards for enforcing codes of honor and discipline among the troops. Not surprisingly, perhaps, bandit-recruits were frequent targets of military reprimands and persecution. More than one bandit-officer suffered the consequences of exhibiting excessive zeal in the carrying out of raids. In his diary of the war, Sánchez de Agramonte succinctly reported on July 6, 1895: "C. Joaquin Leiva, former bandit, has been tried and executed by firing squad. He sullied the prestige of the Revolution, making deals and harassing families."[19] On another occasion, he reported, "4 men, soldiers of our ranks, were executed after having been convicted of robbing the homes of *pacíficos*."[20] According to Ricardo Batrell Oviedo, the only black veteran to publish an account of the war, other former bandits-turned-officers were much more likely to suffer this fate if they were black. Military officials also fully exploited such cases. For instance, after the execution of Commander Severino Ricardo for conspiracy to conceal goods belonging to the Revolution, white officers put his body on display and ordered soldiers to parade before it. Through such means, claimed Batrell Oviedo, white officers made sure that black subordinates knew in whom the power resided to judge the difference between criminal acts of greed and selfless acts of heroism.[21]

The summary executions of such soldiers-turned-bandits or bandits-turned-soldiers reveal how fine the line between stealing for personal gain and stealing for the fatherland could be. If officers themselves initiated acts of theft, plunder, and the like, the legitimacy of such acts might go unquestioned, especially if the officer was a white aristocrat like Sánchez de Agramonte and not a black former bandit like Severino Ricardo. However, as the penal code of the Republic-in-Arms shows, revolutionary nationalist officers tolerated and recognized the contrary class interests and libertarian values of popular nationalist soldiers. These factors were a threat only if they spiraled out of control. Accordingly, the penal code strove to guarantee order by preserving gentlemanly standards of masculine honor and civility as the Revolution's underlying ideals.

According to the penal code, theft was defined as such only when committed "with the intention of benefiting monetarily [*con ánimo de lucrar*]" and when such acts were carried out "with violence or intimidation of the persons [robbed] or by the use of force on the objects [stolen]." Other types of theft that did not directly employ violence on owners of the property seized, or did not display the earmarks of undue remuneration to the thief, fell outside the criminal category of *robo* and were therefore not punishable. On the other hand, thieves whose acts had led to the deaths or mutilation of the persons robbed (or those who came to victims' aid) were punishable by execution. Acts of thievery most resembling banditry were sanctioned just as harshly, even if no deaths or mutilation occurred. These included cases in which the victim of a robbery was detained for more than twenty-four hours (arguably, a situation too close to the kidnap-and-ransom tactics of bandits to accommodate within the Revolution) or when any robbery was committed "*en cuadrilla.*" The latter occurred "whenever three or more armed thugs cooperate" for such ends.[22]

Interestingly, the code's toughest measures related to the court-martialing of soldiers for sex crimes, labeled "Crimes against Honesty." Regarding the social construction of morality, there was little room for negotiation of boundaries. For example, the code meted out punishments ranging from summary execution for rape and *rapto* to arrest and confinement for those committing bigamy. Rape was defined by the code quite progressively as the violation of a woman by using "force, violence, or appropriate intimidation"; under conditions in which she was deprived of her mental faculties because she was "unconscious or without her senses, for whatever reason"; or if she was twelve years old or less, regardless of the circumstances. *Rapto*, a culturally specific term implying the kidnapping and eventual sexual exploitation of a woman as a concubine, was punishable by death if committed against the will of the woman, irrespective of her age. In cases in which the woman claimed to have joined the man voluntarily, he was still subject to arrest and confinement if she was between twelve and twenty years old. So all-encompassing was the definition that simply attempting to seduce a girl between these ages merited the same sentence, especially if the claim were made by the girl or by any male or female guardian of the girl. Moreover, men convicted of such crimes were subject to public humiliation, as their sentences would be "publicized by all the means available to the Tribunal."[23] While such a punishment was supposed to humble a soldier, it was to be carried out with caution, ostensibly to counter the possibility that any negative publicity might only add to his *hombría* (macho image). Revolutionary officials who drew up the code apparently worried that gendered acts of violence might be committed across class and race lines, thereby defying traditional lines of white patriarchy. Unlike sanctioned acts of theft, this was not a phenomenon they were prepared to endorse.

Military and civilian leaders viewed infractions such as these as expressions of dishonorable manhood. That black masculinity was long associated with myths of uncontrollable sexual promiscuity and that the vast majority of soldiers comprising the Liberating Army were perceived as black played a central role in their assessments. Indeed, while the race-free discourse and records of the rebels make it difficult to assess what percentage of soldiers self-identified as black, perceptions of the army's overwhelming "blackness" may have mattered more, in the long run, than actual numbers. After the war, black veterans certainly promoted the idea of a black majority in the army, as we shall see. And during the war, the Spanish fanned white racial fears by claiming that the Revolution's goal was not a "Free Cuba" but another all-black republic like Haiti. Given these realities, revolutionary leaders may have felt especially compelled to define and selectively to enforce what they considered proper codes of conduct among the troops, since dominant ideologies of modernity equated morality and civilization with whiteness and linked criminal savagery with blacks. In the end, the revolutionary leadership reproduced rather than challenged the dominant stereotypes of the time by meting out punishment and identifying culprits of moral crimes according to traditional racialized standards.

For instance, cases of black officers leading "immoral" lives in the *manigua* were tolerated but were also well-publicized as bad examples, while similar actions taken by white soldiers went largely unnoticed.[24] On the other hand, some officers whose lack of education, darker complexion, and poorer origins conspired to render them more vulnerable to attacks on moral grounds did face court-martial. One such case was that of the former slave General Quintín Banderas, who faced court-martial for keeping a mistress, despite the fact that his accusers (chief among them, Máximo Gómez) readily admitted that this was a generalized practice. Nonetheless, they prosecuted Banderas for doing so openly, in contempt of the rules of civilization and insurgent masculinity set up by his white, social, and (so they considered) moral superiors. Although Banderas was never charged with violating any section of the penal code, he was still stripped of his rank.[25] Judged unfit to lead the kind of nation that his revolutionary nationalist accusers imagined, Banderas embodied a countervision of nation in which they wanted no part.

Expeditionaries of the vessel *Honor* led by the immensely popular and renowned black generals Flor Crombet and Antonio Maceo. They arrived at the front in April 1895. (Courtesy of the Archivo Nacional de Cuba)

As these and other cases show, many white officers viewed and treated black soldiers as social inferiors, servants, and generally unworthy partners in the Revolution and nation that would result. In the process, such white officers legitimated the aristocratic notions of "natural" entitlement and racial legitimacy that underlay more conservative forms of nationalism. Nevertheless, the Revolution created situations in which acts of bravery and national commitment might overrule issues of race or status. It did so in battle and in the *manigua* by allowing the development and engagement of multiple notions of identity and visions of nation within the same field of action and discourse of social unity.[26] Popular nationalists may have interpreted such moments in the same light as officer-sanctioned raids on plantations. The willingness of some leaders to demand adherence to a raceless discourse of inclusion along the lines as that articulated by Martí undoubtedly encouraged this view. For example, Martí's childhood friend Fermín Valdés Domínguez, who served as personal secretary to Máximo Gómez in the 1895 War, took precisely this stance, going as far as to criticize fellow officers who did not require the use of raceless language and ideals among their troops.[27]

Expeditionary force on its way to the rebel front in Cuba on board the *Dauntless*, August 22, 1896. The U.S. Coast Guard worked hard to prevent vessels carrying recruits and supplies like this one from reaching the revolutionaries in Cuba. (Courtesy of the Archivo Nacional de Cuba)

But regardless of their leaders' positions, notions of freedom were intimately connected with notions of honor that soldiers defined for themselves. The Revolution remapped the *manigua*. Once a term meaning the forested hideout of a maroon community, the *manigua* became in the 1895 War a liberated and liberating zone that allowed soldiers—together with the women, children, and elderly who formed the noncombatant support forces—to redefine tasks considered demeaning in other contexts. In the *manigua*, skills once useful to blacks as slaves, such as reconnaissance work, the skills of traditional healers, or storytelling, gained a new affirmation and respectability.[28]

The presence and role of women played a critical part in the elaboration of this experience. Despite the military's term *impedimenta* (impediment) for describing the participation of women and children, their participation did not obstruct the military's actions. Because the rebel army was a nonprofessional guerrilla army, the *impedimenta* made their activities possible in the first place. In providing basic services of food preparation, health care, and emotional comfort for male members of the revolutionary forces, women contributed to the redefinition of the *manigua* as a liberated zone. Here, traditional female roles acquired new meaning and thereby added to the redefinition of popular visions of the nation as a communal democracy. Women did far more than simply facilitate the actions of men. Indeed, Lynn Stoner reports that no fewer than twenty-five women achieved officer rank during the War of 1895, including three colonels and more than twenty captains.[29] In this and other ways, women took full advantage of the spaces opened up by the *manigua* to construct their own understandings of nation.

Magdalena Peñarredonda y Doley represents a dramatic example of this. A native of the western province of Pinar del Río that had remained deaf to calls for revolution during the first two independence wars, Peñarredonda had nonetheless supported independence since the 1850s. When she was in her teens, her father—himself a captain in the Spanish army—had incarcerated her and her sisters in their own home for cutting their hair in solidarity with patriot women in Camagüey. The women were protesting the execution of the independence conspirator and slave-owner-turned-abolitionist Joaquín de Agüero.[30] Like Martí who was called "El Delegado" (The Delegate) by emigré workers in his lifetime, Peñarredonda became known as "La Delegada" and "General" for her longtime service, first as an agent of the New York revolutionary junta in the 1870s, then in the island-based PRC underground from 1893 forward. The political remained personal for Peñarredonda, so much so that the cause of Cuba Libre led her to separate from her husband, an Asturian-born businessman, with the start of the 1895 War.[31] Nonetheless, for the first two years of the war, she exploited her personal relations with family members and Spaniards, including high-ranking enemy officers, to become a secret communications operative for the troops of Antonio Maceo in the area between Havana and Vuelta Abajo, Pinar del Río.[32] When she was eventually captured and imprisoned for espionage by the Spanish, La Delegada organized the female prisoners with whom she was housed in Havana's Casa de las Recogidas, a home for prostitutes, female vagrants, and other social deviants. Together, they staged protests against their inhumane conditions.[33]

First as a spy and later as a prisoner, her support of the Revolution was unswerving. Sounding a bit like Máximo Gómez, whose letters to Tomás Estrada Palma endorsed total war, she remarked in her letter to Estrada Palma shortly after Spanish loyalists proposed autonomy for Cuba in 1896: "What a bunch of pretenders! And there are still some Cubans so vile that they think [only] of agreements and pacts with them. Before we should suffer such humiliation and shame may all [on the island] be reduced to ashes."[34] Writing in April 1896, Peñarredonda celebrated the honor of destitute female peasants ("Those poor *guajiras* are surely heroines"), rounded up as if they were "beasts of burden" into Governor Valeriano Weyler's concentration camps.[35] She also railed against the lavish spending of Havana's patriot aristocrats, accusing them of hypocrisy and duplicity: "With what in Havana is spent on frivolities, *I would dare use to maintain all the towns of Vuelta Abajo*. And may they not say that they don't have, for at all hours, they can be seen in parties, spending money."[36] On her role as counselor and instigator of revolt among the captives of Havana's female prison, Peñarredonda proudly remarked on her maternal dominion over them, saying, "They only stop protesting and complaining when they know I have a headache. Daily they consult with me and confide in me their sad histories."[37]

For Peñarredonda, offering comfort, inspiration, and sympathetic leadership to poor women reflected the ideal social relations between a future state and society that the 1895 Revolution was all about. A revolutionary nationalist, she valued her benevolent role in the top-down process of fomenting social change, much as key military figures like Máximo Gómez did. However, it is not commonly believed that La Delegada ever saw battle. Thus, while her activities as a spy may have been equally dangerous, others who did see battle but lacked the necessary social origins and breeding that Peñarredonda enjoyed may have been rewarded in ways disproportionate to the extent of their service. For example, the poor black woman María Hidalgo Santana from Matanzas spontaneously risked her life at the head of the infantry to carry the Cuban flag after its bearer fell to Spanish bullets. Although shot seven times as a result, Hidalgo Santana survived to see eight more battles and to achieve the rank of captain.[38] How many more women made similar sacrifices that went unrecognized by the Liberating Army?

It is well known that *mambisas* served as messengers and carried official letters or reports through enemy territory. Legend has it that many hid scrolled messages in the deep heart of the mariposa, the fragrant lilylike flower that grows wild in the mountains of central and eastern Cuba. They then wore the flowers in their hair or behind their ears. Although written documentation of this legend is lacking, many elderly Cubans claim that it was for this reason that the mariposa became the national flower during the Republic.

Men such as Rafael Rodríguez Santos received the rank of captain for the similar service of carrying secret correspondence from the PRC and military communiqués from the field to agents in the urban underground of Santa Clara province. However, after Weyler instituted policies of "reconcentrating" rural populations in cities and increased patrols in the countryside in 1896, Rodríguez Santos's wife, Teresa Rosado Santos, began to carry out these duties. Yet, they were not similarly rewarded. Rather, as Rosado Santos's youngest daughter, Luisa, explained a century later, military officials saw women like her mother as supplementing men's roles or as serving as men's substitutes. The women did not necessarily see it that way. Rosado Santos, for example, felt that her services to the

Revolution should have been recognized and rewarded. Her husband had always refused a government pension on moral grounds, saying that he did not fight for the Revolution in order to get paid for it later. After Rodríguez Santos's death, Rosado Santos sought certification of her husband's activities during the war from Antonio Argüelles y Ferrer, the PRC's delegate in Cienfuegos, and claimed his pension. "After all," her daughter remarked, "she deserved it—perhaps more than he did."[39]

Although all too brief, the discursive legacy of literate women patriots speaks to the depth of revolutionary consciousness that *mambisas* felt. A novena, or Catholic prayer, sent to Estrada Palma in November of 1897 by a woman named Teresa de Jesús conveys how closely the concept of nation could cut to the core of one's identity and beliefs. Titled "Novena to the Most Holy Virgin of Charity of Cobre, intercessor and protector of Cubans," the prayer is, in its raw simplicity, a powerful statement:

> I commend my sons to you
> Whom today the Fatherland takes from me
> Because it needs them
> To make its freedom . . .
>
> You who are also a mother,
> The voice of a mother you hear
> Your pain was also great at the passion of Jesus,
> In every revolution there are martyrs of an idea
> Like he who died in Judea
> On an contemptuous cross;
> For the sacred memory of the martyrs of Cuba
> My voice rises to heaven
> In fervent prayer;
> In peace their souls find repose
> On the breast of glory,
> While your name history
> Preserves with honor.[40]

This prayer invited female believers to identify their personal suffering in Cuba's revolution with that of the semidivine mother of Jesus Christ. Drawing overt parallels between Cuba's martyrs and the martyrdom of Jesus, whom Rome's imperial authorities had accused of being a revolutionary, Teresa de Jesús legitimated Cuba's national struggle for freedom with a universal struggle for spiritual redemption. At the same time, her prayer linked personal interest to political interest, individual experience to collective experience, and local memory to national consciousness. For women who may have recited this prayer and others like it, the struggle and the suffering that defined the Revolution ensured the birth of the nation, just as their own struggle and suffering as mothers had given birth to its founders.

These women's actions and their explanations of those actions implied a yearning for a different kind of liberation. They located this liberation in a communal entity that was possibly more ambiguous than that of black soldiers only because the chances for achieving it seemed less certain to them. If life in the *manigua* was the contemporary version of the nation envisioned by ex-slaves, then the *mambisas'* moral universe of suffering for the promise of future justice can be seen in a related light. Both represented dimensions of the popular nationalist nation. Essentially, then, the *manigua* can be understood as "time-out" spaces where the customary ordering of the world according to blackness and whiteness, poverty and wealth, and honorable and dishonorable notions of gender could be questioned and even restructured. However, these were highly patrolled "time-out" spaces where the hierarchies and inequalities that formed the basis of colonial society struggled to reassert themselves. The following pages explore how the significance of these "time-out" spaces within the Revolution and their meaning for the future Republic diminished as the pro-imperialist nationalist leaders in the PRC and the priorities of revolutionary nationalist officers changed.

PRC *Leaders Civilize the Revolution from the United States*

A few days after Martí's death, General José María Aguirre speculated on the fragility of the dualistic framework of the Revolution that Martí had established from New York: "He who is here does not command the one who is over there nor the one who is over there command the one who is here. This one fights and that one helps. That one sends men, arms, munitions and this one employs them. . . . [But] over there, there is peace, over here, war."[41] Indeed, the radically different contexts from which the civilian and military wings of the Revolution experienced the war and formulated its objectives would prove critical to its direction in the years to come.

After Martí's death, PRC leaders in New York quickly consolidated their power as the authoritative voice of the Revolution before the world. Acting independently of many emigré clubs and increasingly of army officers in Cuba, PRC leaders actively suppressed the more radical, socially transformative nationalism espoused by top rebel officers, the mass of popular-class soldiers, and their social counterparts in the United States. They did so by centralizing control over the image of the Revolution and articulating a much more politically conservative project for the Cuban nation within the United States.

Almost immediately, evidence of how differently PRC leaders perceived the war and the nation for which Cubans were fighting emerged in the contrasting interpretations that emigré leaders and emigré workers gave of the memory of Martí. The views of popular nationalists in New York and Florida coincided with those of *mambises* writing from rebel camps in Oriente and of exiled Cubans in Santo Domingo. Both praised Martí as a "redeemer" who had found his "Calvary."[42] The "love of these people has made José Martí into an idol," reported one emigré to *La Nación*, the Buenos Aires newspaper for which Martí had long worked. Within a month of his death, Cuban cigarmakers in Key West triumphantly prophesied a second coming of "the Apostle" and disseminated the millenarianist conviction that Martí was still alive, despite official claims to the contrary, a view that survived long after the end of the war.[43] But if faith in Martí implied faith in the war, PRC leaders were not as comfortable with either claim. In a curious public speech honoring Martí in November 1895, pro-imperialist nationalist lawyer Lincoln de Zayas observed that the difference between those revolutionaries who adored Martí as a "demigod" and those who recognized him simply as a man came down to matters of class and relative refinement. Martí, like Jesus, Zayas said, had never doubted his cause. Zayas, on the other hand, was one of the doubters.[44] Contrasting memories of Martí were becoming a function of conflicting nationalisms.

Driven by men who did not share Martí's passion for keeping the United States out of the war, the PRC responded to Martí's death by focusing its strategies on exactly the opposite goal: that of bringing the United States into the war. Blinded by ambition and an unshakable faith in their own convictions, these emigrés perceived no contradiction between the goal of Cuban political sovereignty and the means they devised for ensuring that goal. By fanning the flames of U.S. expansionism and endorsing the values of individual expansionists, PRC leaders and their emigré supporters encouraged the public and U.S. officials to identify with the cause of Cuban rebels by seeing these rebels as cultural and political extensions of themselves. PRC leaders detected no conflict between the idea of nationhood and the idea of intimacy with a foreign power because they themselves had for so long lived within the borders of that power.

Arguably, PRC leaders invoked the tenets of a unique emigré nationalism whose constant referencing of U.S. interests and social values made it "pro-imperialist" long before U.S. imperialism asserted itself on Cuba's war-ravaged shores. Born of their own cultural assimilation to U.S. social and political norms, these emigrés saw the United States' recent history of liberating the South from the perdition of slavery and the West from the "backwardness" of Indians as inspirational. Thus, the nationalism these Cubans expressed was, from the beginning, dependent on the United States for its ideological legitimacy. Achieving modernity through gradual social change and rapid, foreign-financed technological improvement were two of this nationalism's primary goals. PRC leaders rooted both of these goals in an idealized interpretation of U.S. society and the image of a gratefully compliant future Cuban public. Many New York emigrés of socially conservative convictions shared their convictions. For example, one New York emigré merchant wrote to Estrada Palma, "As we say in this country, you are the 'right man in the right place' for your perfect knowledge not only of men and the things of our beloved Cuba, but also of the United States, with whose life we must be eternally tied if we want to be a nation."[45]

Like this merchant, Estrada Palma's confidence in the benevolence of U.S. intentions and influence was matched by his confidence in the ability of Cubans like himself to lead Cuba toward the brighter, enlightened future of modernity and social progress he imagined as his nation. In December 1895, one of Estrada Palma's first official acts as Martí's successor in the PRC was to make his case for U.S. recognition of Cuban belligerency rights to the U.S. Department of State. In appealing for the support of U.S. officials, Estrada Palma interpreted his countrymen's reality through the lens of a life experience he had gained largely as a citizen of the United States. His letter to U.S. Secretary of State Richard Olney is punctuated with parallels between the cultural values, political beliefs, and even the history of Cuban revolutionaries and the people of the United States.

On one hand, Estrada Palma insisted that the 1895 Revolution was not, as the "Spaniards charge, . . . a movement of negroes" and clarified that there were only three generals of color, all of them "mulattos."[46] He also cast the actions of Cuba's war chiefs in line with those of U.S. officials in the recent U.S. Civil War. Cuban guerrillas' attacks on private property, he argued, resembled those of the Union Army's fiery "march to the sea" that broke Southerners' political will by smashing the symbols of economic power.[47] On the other hand, Estrada Palma also provided U.S. State Department officials with a transcript of a letter he had written to rebel commanders, asking them to exercise restraint when dealing with the property of U.S. citizens.[48] Estrada Palma's appeal to U.S. officials and the public could not be "pro-imperialist" without being "nationalist." It had to be both because Estrada Palma understood what he was doing as both. In an 1896 address to the U.S. people that dismissed Spain's recent gestures toward the granting of greater autonomy to Cuba, Estrada Palma presented "proofs" of the "capacity of the Cuban white and colored to rule themselves." Insisting that

Cubans had nothing in common with the Spanish because of Cubans' "knowledge of modern institutions" and "democratic sentiments," he also contended that "the colored people of Cuba have reached a higher stage of culture than that of the United States." In short, he claimed, "We are Americans; we breathe the pure air of free institutions, and we contemplate with envy the government of the people, by the people and for the people."[49]

Most historians who have analyzed the figure and actions of Estrada Palma have tended to see him as an indisputable annexationist or puppet of U.S. interests from the beginning.[50] Still, before radical social mobilizations led to the collapse of his government in the Republic many years later, Estrada Palma had written only one openly annexationist text, at the time of his incarceration in a colonial prison for his activism during the Ten Years' War.[51] Moreover, the actions and discourse of PRC leaders provide for an alternative interpretation. Love and the desire to secure the best possible future for Cuba made pro-imperialist nationalists like Estrada Palma viable partners in the Revolution, not just in Martí's eyes but—more important—in their own.

Stressing foreign investment and reliance on a more industrial, corporate plantation model for Cuba's sugar-centered economy, these Cubans believed the Revolution needed to be founded on the tenets of turn-of-the-century Latin American Liberalism. Championed in the 1890s by political elites in countries as diverse as Brazil, Colombia, Guatemala, and Mexico, this ideology emphasized education, the building of modern infrastructure, state encouragement of the agro-export trade through large-scale farming, an accelerated program of racial "improvement" (usually through white immigration), and sufficient control of the lower classes so as to ensure a steady supply of labor. According to the tenets of positivism to which most late nineteenth-century Liberals subscribed, benefits would first accrue to those responsible for progress in the first place (elites and the state) and eventually trickle their way down to the masses.[52] Still, pro-imperialist nationalist leaders of the PRC did not find inspiration in Latin American Liberalism alone. They found the most critical components of their vision for Cuba in the mythical ideal of a mostly white, culturally homogeneous, and politically conservative "America" that, to their eyes, already existed in the United States.

Having lived for as many as twenty years in a country that imagined itself the pinnacle of "modernity" and "civilization," PRC leaders projected their pro-imperialist nationalist vision of the nation onto the Revolution through their policies and their rationalizations of those policies. Tomás Estrada Palma, Gonzalo de Quesada, Benjamín Guerra, and other top PRC heads who had become U.S. citizens during their exile did not expect to make Cuba a part of the United

States. Rather, they expected to recast Cuba as a smaller version of the United States. This "Americanized" Cuba would nonetheless remain eminently Cuban —or at least as "Cuban" as they were. It did not matter to these emigrés that many revolutionaries—including prominent military officers such as Antonio Maceo or Máximo Gómez—did not share their enthusiasm for U.S. models of culture and conduct. Steeped in the urban milieu of bourgeois New York society, their own sense of *cubanidad* was an amalgam of nostalgia, ambition, Liberal ideology, and unshakeable faith in the United States. For them, the nation extended forth from a pro-imperialist nationalist identity.

Ironically, PRC leaders interpreted the organization's function and elaborated the pro-imperialist nationalist image of nation within a discourse of civilization and modernity meant to appeal more to the U.S. public than to the armed revolutionaries in Cuba themselves. During the course of the 1895 War, PRC leaders increasingly dismissed the demands of black and working-class emigrés. They also denied the necessity for guerrilla tactics in order to bring about a successful conclusion to the war in the field. This process began with the PRC leadership's reorganization of power in the absence of Martí.

Martí, like Estrada Palma, had held most of the reins of control over the PRC network during the last months of his life as undisputed president and "plenipotentiary delegate" of the diplomatic legation. However, unlike Estrada Palma, Martí had demonstrated a history and a style of taking seriously the views and interests of traditionally marginal elements like workers and blacks. After Martí's death, Estrada Palma could not be bothered with such elements, let alone actively engaged in the articulation of their views. Surely, Martí may have been less than democratic in his willingness to oversee the control and direction of the PRC. However, Martí's personal trips to hotbeds of discontent in order to serve as peacemaker had made him a trustworthy patron in the eyes of Florida and New York's working-class emigrés. By contrast, under Estrada Palma, the PRC became increasingly isolated from these communities and oriented toward emigrés with ties to island planters or U.S.-based businesses that had openly sponsored projects for U.S. annexation in the past. Estrada Palma's amenability to elite interests, while comparable to Martí's, was not balanced by sensitivity to popular-class needs or opinions. Moreover, Martí's PRC had seen U.S. support for the cause of Cuban independence as dangerous, while Estrada Palma's PRC saw it as vital. Such differences proved critical in more ways than one.

After the PRC formally recognized Martí's death in July 1895, the Revolution as the PRC perceived and presented it took a decidedly conservative turn. Former foes of Martí, like Enrique Trujillo, who had considered the Revolution too radical under Martí's direction and the influence of Florida's "militants," subsequently declared their solidarity with the new PRC. Formally known under Martí's editorial watch for its discussions of race, class, and Cuban identity, *Patria* quickly dispensed with social themes altogether under the new editorial direction of Enrique José Varona — except, of course, whenever the opportunity to minimize black participation in the Revolution presented itself.[53] As if inspired by the new, post-Martí journalistic climate, once-ardent Autonomist Raimundo Cabrera began publishing his magazine, *Cuba y América*, in New York. From its pages, Cabrera and others glossed the history of working-class mobilization for the Revolution in Florida as the work of Spanish bosses and owners of various cigar factories in Key West and Tampa. Silencing the centrality of workers in fomenting financial and moral support for the Revolution, *Cuba y América* depicted their employers and exploiters as the genuine heroes of independence rather than as the reluctant pragmatists that they really were.[54]

In response to these developments, radical black emigrés like Rafael Serra founded a newspaper fully focused on the racial and socially oriented aspects of the independence project that Martí had sponsored and that the Revolution endorsed. Edited by Serra, *La Doctrina de Martí* recruited and received the public support of such white middle-class and working-class patriots of Tampa, Ibor City, and Key West as Eligio and Nestor Carbonell, Antonio Palacios, Rosendo Rivero, and Emiliana Brava.[55] Appropriating Martí as a symbol of his revolutionary nationalism, Serra openly criticized the emerging social conservatism of those who would confuse "war" with "revolution" by carrying out the former without furthering the latter: "There are those who believe that to revolutionize is to *remedy* a system, or to add or take something away, . . . when this is nothing more than to *evolutionize*. Revolution pulls the tree out by its roots, and plants new seeds. Evolution leaves the tree with the possibility of recovering because it only chops away at its trunk or its branches. The tree of colonialism in Cuba must be attacked at its roots. We must revolutionize."[56] Significantly, however, Serra did not so much refer in his critiques to the attitudes of the PRC under Estrada Palma's leadership — Serra regarded Estrada Palma as a personal friend and confidante until at least 1902[57] — as much as he referred to the small but extremely powerful group of wealthy exiles who threatened to turn the PRC ever more firmly toward their interests alone.

However appealing the tendency to view Estrada Palma as a sellout to conservatives at best and an annexationist at worst, such a view obscures otherwise important points of ideological contrast along the spectrum of pro-imperialist nationalism. These differences help explain why Martí chose his staff the way he did: compared to others, Estrada Palma and his colleagues were mild and compassionate moderates whose central role in the Ten Years' War and later membership in early PRC-affiliated clubs Martí had always appreciated. On the other hand, more conservative emigrés, led by Enrique Trujillo, Hector de Saavedra, and Enrique José Varona, belonged to the Sociedad de Estudios de la Jurídica y Economía (Society of Legal Studies and Economy [SEJE]). This was an "exile" version of Havana's influential Sociedad Económica de Amigos del País (Economic Society of Friends of the Country), founded by slave-owning sugar planters at the end of the eighteenth century in order to encourage the social and economic progress of the island. The disappearance of Martí's populism and the rise of even more "centrist" elements in the PRC undoubtedly brought about a thawing of relations and patriotic promises from Trujillo and the like. Nonetheless, the SEJE still worried that PRC leaders remained vulnerable to the wild excesses of radicalism that the SEJE associated with popular nationalists. In the winter of 1896–97, such feelings exploded onto the public arena when de Saavedra took it upon himself to denounce the PRC's leadership before a meeting of the SEJE in New York. Although no details of de Saavedra's charges were ever published, so shocking were his allegations (and the Society's apparent endorsement of them) that the PRC Advisory Council in New York was forced to call for a formal vote of confidence on behalf of Estrada Palma.

According to Eduardo Yero, a member of the PRC's Advisory Council, the editor of *Patria*, Enrique José Varona, only reluctantly agreed to publish the vote, one in which all emigré revolutionary clubs in the United States and elsewhere participated. Amazingly, Yero found himself forced to write a defense of the PRC in *La Doctrina de Martí*, *Patria*'s socially radical and highly critical rival. Despite its role as the PRC's official party organ, Yero charged, *Patria* had become an unofficial *vocero* (voicebox) for the SEJE.[58] A few weeks later, the SEJE came under such heavy criticism for betraying the Cuban cause that it was forced to dissolve. Manuel Sanguily, a member of the SEJE who had attacked Yero, eventually came around to making peace with him for the same reason.[59] In the end, it seemed that Martí's legacy of insisting on social unity in the face of war, no matter how sharp the differences, bore fruit. The image of social unity before the public eye came first, no matter how great the ideological conflict that it belied.

Exemplifying this, Hector de Saavedra saved his complaints for private correspondence. Part of de Saavedra's ire derived from the sense that Estrada Palma had been giving him and other more prestigious emigrés the cold shoulder while courting the advice of men who were his social inferiors. For months, de Saavedra had been trying unsuccessfully to convince Estrada Palma that he should use PRC funds to subsidize Domingo Figuerola Caneda's emigré newspaper in Paris, *La República Cubana*, a policy that the PRC extended to Florida's emigré newspapers that catered to a working-class readership.[60] According to Yero, de Saavedra was also pressing Estrada Palma for a job as the PRC's vice secretary, a desire that also went unfulfilled.[61] Thus, de Saavedra resented the fact that despite Martí's death, current PRC leaders seemed reluctant to do away with the connections he had established to popular nationalists:

> There is a tremendous internal struggle here. The Society of Legal Studies had to disband out of patriotism, for not providing fodder to the chatterings of a certain "democratic black" element here that calls us "the intellectuals." . . . [The PRC now has] an Advisory Council, dogged by two blacks, Serra and Figuero, and various cigarmakers with Yero in the lead that dominate [Estrada] Palma through terror and make or pretend to establish the doctrine that they, those of the rabble, are the only ones with the right to direct things in Cuba. With imagine what future end![62]

de Saavedra clearly did not want to mention or even "imagine" such an end: prominent black and working-class leadership in the future state and majority popular-class rule. In light of such racist and elitist attitudes, Estrada Palma's pedigree as a middle-class reformer emerges in sharper relief. One can only guess what direction the PRC might have taken if Estrada Palma had bowed to de Saavedra's wishes and appointed him to a leadership position.

Possibly as a way of appeasing the demands of such critics, Estrada Palma increasingly defined his tenure at the PRC helm in authoritarian terms. However, his strategies may have backfired with pro-imperialist nationalists like Saavedra, who were more conservative than himself, and with popular nationalists alike. Part of the reason the PRC never managed to sway New York's congressional or senatorial delegates in favor of either granting belligerency rights or recognition of independence may have to do with the influence of the SEJE. Many members held property and commercial interests in Cuba or, as lawyers, represented U.S. citizens who did. As a result, they pressed first the Cleveland and then the McKinley administration for restraint. Only in the context of a full-scale U.S. military intervention were Northeastern corporate interests and their representatives in Congress prepared to consider seriously any alternative to Spanish rule.[63]

However, if those in the SEJE camp viewed Estrada Palma as too radical, working-class emigrés and their supporters in New York and Florida saw him as not radical enough. Florida's emigré activists were perturbed by the reorganization of PRC statutes coming on the heels of the Government of the Republic-in-Arms' confirmation of Estrada Palma as president. The new statutes allowed Estrada

Palma to hold both the presidency of the PRC and the office of supreme delegate for the clubs simultaneously. In March 1896, the Florida clubs appealed to the man known for being Martí's closest friend, Gonzalo de Quesada, as a possible alternative candidate. After turning down the position of PRC secretary, de Quesada dared not openly accept the nomination of the clubs to run against Estrada Palma. However, he did admit that Estrada Palma was well aware of the support de Quesada had among grassroots supporters for the position of delegate. He also insinuated that if Estrada Palma announced his own candidacy, it would be to squelch the advance of any potential rival.[64]

Only one month later, events confirmed de Quesada's predictions. The Government of the Republic-in-Arms and PRC leadership rewrote the statutes of the PRC so that whomever the Government of the Republic-in-Arms appointed as president of the diplomatic legation would *automatically* become the supreme delegate of the network of revolutionary clubs. No vote by the clubs on the matter was required. The move effectively centralized power and eliminated Estrada Palma's accountability to the very working-class and grassroots organizations that had been responsible for formulating the PRC's program with Martí in the first place.[65]

In general, Florida emigrés were disconcerted by this and other PRC attempts to curry favor with New York conservatives at the expense of broader participation and consultation. In the summer of 1896, Nestor Carbonell, president of Club "Ygnacio Agramonte" that had originally invited Martí to speak in Tampa five years earlier, complained to Estrada Palma. The leaders of West Tampa, especially Fernando Figueredo, he said, had purposely misinformed other more politically progressive clubs of the visit of a PRC representative. Significantly, Figueredo had been one of a minority of local revolutionaries who had disdained Martí as far too radical.[66] As a result, Tampa's clubs—numbering over sixty—did not turn out to greet the official visitor, nor did they participate in the activities surrounding his stay.[67] But critics of the new revolutionary leadership's style of pro-imperialist nationalist "democracy" were not confined to the leadership of Florida's revolutionary clubs.

Cuban cigarmakers residing in the United States were, as a whole, highly politicized. Spain had deported many of them for labor activity. For harboring socialists among them who were also self-proclaimed nationalists, the cigarmakers of Florida were considered especially radical.[68] Martí had clearly attempted to neutralize radical tendencies among Florida's cigarmakers by rejecting the idea of class struggle and had gained the approval of their employers in the process.[69] However, Martí's PRC had also actively supported cigarmakers in their pivotal strike of 1893–94. By contrast, Estrada Palma took a minimalist approach. Either

Revolutionary club in Tampa, Florida. The diversity of ages, race,
and gender represented among the members is striking.
(Courtesy of the Archivo Nacional de Cuba)

he ignored workers' interests altogether or engaged them only on a superficial
level by subsidizing newspapers such as Ramón Rivero's *Cuba* in order to curb
the influence of socialist or anarchist rivals.

Still, popular nationalists in Florida resented and resisted such changes, often
through invocations of their memories of Martí. From the summer of 1897 to
the early months of 1898, Diego Vicente Tejera, socialist intellectual and close
friend of Martí, delivered numerous lectures in Key West's San Carlos Theatre,
the place where Martí had delivered his most famous appeals to workers. Lecture
topics included "Blacks and Whites," "The Cuban Woman," future political parties in the Republic, the potential for a socialist Cuba, education in democratic
societies, and the image of Martí himself as an ideal citizen who recognized the
rights of all.[70]

Ironically, the war reduced the supply of Cuban leaf tobacco, and economic
conditions in Florida worsened. Industry management used various antilabor
techniques as a way of cutting its losses. More committed than ever to building a
new society in Cuba that minimized employers' power over them, cigarmakers,
who had loyally contributed one day's earnings per week to PRC coffers since the
start of the war, began to bristle with anger toward the PRC. As early as the fall
of 1895, cigarmakers vociferously protested Estrada Palma's efforts to appease
the right through favoritism and symbolic acts that confirmed ideas of class

privilege. For instance, at one point the PRC covertly financed the room and board of a group of recruits from the upper crust of emigré society for Enrique Collazo's expedition from Florida. Meanwhile, poorer recruits, stationed in Ibor City, had to depend on the meager support their comrades at the cigarmakers union could supply. Using the official letterhead of their guild, Unión Tabaquera, the cigarmakers of Ibor City affirmed their commitment to the Revolution but insisted that Estrada Palma, "without distinction of rank or color . . . treat the same all members of the expeditionary forces of Ibor City and West Tampa, of Ocala and Jacksonville, because we do not understand [the ways] of *aristocratic people,* but of patriotic ones."[71] Further, the cigarmakers demurred to PRC paternalism in sending eloquent emissaries to rally the support of workers instead of sending negotiators who could seriously address their needs.[72] Workers found the practice insulting: "We do not desire that they (the representatives up there [in New York]) give us a chain of pretty and well-chosen words, but rather that they speak to us sincerely and clearly: for the question is, to be or not to be, and as the Americans themselves would say, less talking and more business."[73]

Over time, several factors convinced the New York leadership that popular-class elements in its structure and movement were largely superfluous. Economic hard times coupled with long strikes in Tampa's cigar-making factories had meant not only fewer contributions to the PRC from Florida's workers but also a corresponding wane in Estrada Palma's interest in this sector. The PRC increasingly turned its attention to challenging the objections of the Cleveland administration to the war. Given this priority, PRC leaders perceived the specific demands and class consciousness of workers as problematic, especially between the fall of 1896 and the spring of 1897 when Estrada Palma was fighting off his critics from the right. In this regard, the PRC's investment in subsidies to emigré newspapers with a working-class readership exemplified PRC leaders' utilitarian response. Ramón Rivero, a former factory reader and editor of *Cuba,* assured Estrada Palma that even if workers linked their anticapital activities to their patriotism, he did not. Rather, he saw himself as a neutralizing agent who publicly supported them while privately putting *patria* first.[74] *Cuba,* he wrote, represented precisely the PRC's policy of moderation because it "lash[ed] away at the hardliners and gradually kill[ed] off the spirit of anarchism, planted in our artisans by its advocates, the Spanish."[75] In other words, Rivero admitted that his and the PRC leaders' vision of *patria* was dramatically different than that of workers. He also confessed that pro-imperialist nationalists' engagement of popular nationalist emigrés' concerns extended only to the symbolic and the rhetorical.

In the wake of the Florida strikes and the SEJE's disbandment, Estrada Palma moved to institutionalize pro-imperialist nationalist tenets in the structures of

PARTIDO REVOLUCIONARIO CUBANO
CLUB
"GENERAL JORDAN"
MARTÍ CITY, OCALA, FLA.

DIRECTIVA:—1. Juan García Ramírez, Secretario.—2. Juan Pereira Ramírez, Presidente.—3. José García Ramírez, Tesorero.—4. Manuel García Ramírez, Vocal.—5. Juan Noroña Díaz, Vocal.—6. Celestino García Ramírez, Vocal.—7. Lorenzo Valdés Díaz, Vocal.—8. José Valdés Hernández, Vocal.—9. Juan José Buttari Gaunaurd, Vocal.—10. Fortín Castro, Vocal.—11. Ramón García Ramírez, Vocal.—12. Juan Barreto Díaz, Vocal.

Leadership of Club "General Jordan" in Ocala, Florida, known to Cuban emigrés as Martí City. The name was apparently misspelled by the printers. In the Jim Crow era of Florida, the racial diversity of the club's governing council spoke to the very different kind of republic many emigrés hoped to found.
(Courtesy of the Archivo Nacional de Cuba)

the PRC and to further ingratiate himself with conservatives. He decreed the restriction of male suffrage for the next PRC elections to only those Cuban emigrés (sixteen and older) who had contributed a rifle or 500 bullets to the army in the last two months. So obviously class-biased was the decree that even Ramón Rivero expressed shock. Writing to Eduardo Yero from Tampa, Rivero saw that the decree "gives the vote to whomever has the means to buy it and leaves out in the cold the humble people [in Florida] who are currently unemployed but were the old contributors." Writing on the same day to Rivero, Yero minced no words in his assessment: "From the first to the last letter, [the decree] has been dictated by the Spanish spirit which is poisoning us and which kills." Such a system was tantamount to legitimating the post-Zanjón, Spanish version of elections in which poll taxes were charged:

> The decree is a political crime, a legal one and in all senses, and in its articulation it is the mystification of Liberalism and of democracy about which so much is said in its preamble. . . . The Revolution has not been made so that anyone can transform himself into Romero Robledo with his consort of lackeys to be seated in its Congressional Chambers. I rebel against such underhanded stunts pulled by pygmy bureaucrats who can't see past their noses. . . . As for me, I will say that these and other things that are happening in Cuba fill me with foreboding and they give me the impulse to fall upon those who think themselves little idols, in order to reduce them to what they are in reality, only clay.[76]

The nature of the pro-imperialist form of nationalism these men espoused was inextricably wedded to the ideals and standards of "modern civilization," a condition that they had already attained but to which most Cubans—or so they thought—could only aspire.

Attaining such a standard would require of the Revolution and the emerging nation patience, unswerving confidence in PRC leaders, and respect for a social order modeled on that of the United States. For PRC leaders, inculcating the values and customs of modern civilization into the Cuban nation began with the war effort itself. They attempted to achieve this in two ways. First, they carried out a publicity campaign in the United States meant to highlight their own perspective on Cuba's past and future. Second, they tried desperately to enforce "civilized" standards of conducting warfare in calling for the protection of property and good personal treatment of wealthy loyalists by the Revolution's military cadres.

As many historians have shown, the "yellow" press and specific newspaper moguls played a critical role in popularizing support for the Cuban war among the U.S. public and expansionist Washington officials. Such efforts were central to building momentum for U.S. intervention in 1898. However, PRC leaders also organized a concerted strategy to manipulate public attitudes for the benefit of their own pro-imperialist nationalist vision for Cuba. The PRC employed media specialists who toured the greater Northeast and cities as far west as Chicago.[77] Key among these was Fidel Pierra, a Cuban-born businessman who had spent his teenage years learning English in the U.S. and faced extradition upon returning to Cuba for his activities as a Freemason and publisher of liberal newspapers. After escaping Spanish persecution and arriving in New York City in 1872, Pierra had become a prominent member of Brooklyn's working- and middle-class emigré communities, largely through the patronage he offered various mutual aid and "free-thinking" societies.[78] As a PRC agent under Estrada Palma's direction, Pierra's travels promoted the Cuban cause in New York, Rhode Island, Pennsylvania, Ohio, and Virginia in the first two years of the war alone.

Typically, Pierra would arrive in the host city by train, where he would be met by a delegation of prominent local citizens and politicians who escorted him to his hotel and frequently offered to pay his expenses. Pierra always turned down such offers in order to keep the 1895 Revolution from bearing any resemblance to the joint Cuban and U.S. filibustering ventures to annex Cuba of the 1840s and 1850s. During his stay, Pierra would attend both large public gatherings and small, intimate meetings with the politically and socially powerful. Yet, the sheer range and number of citizens who flocked to his speeches (often amid fierce weather) reflected the extent to which U.S. citizens of various classes felt an affinity for the Cuban cause. Pierra worked hard to associate this cause with his audience's own national myths of social progress and inclusive democracy. In Cleveland, Ohio, over 3,000 people turned out to hear Pierra's address extolling the sacrifices and suffering of Cuba's virtuous aristocratic men at the hands of greedy and cruel Spaniards; 10,000 ribbons advertising the event had been sold in advance. The Cuban American League of Cleveland, formed immediately thereafter, promised to generate more propaganda materials, all proceeds to go to PRC headquarters in New York. Pierra also made sure to meet with reporters of all the local newspapers and gratefully to turn down offers by local men who promised to raise armed volunteer militias and put them at the disposal of the Liberating Army.[79]

Pierra's success in generating solidarity for Cuba among Northern veterans of the U.S. Civil War and, possibly, former abolitionists only underscores the nature of PRC efforts to appeal to U.S. Americans' perceptions of themselves as models of social and political progress.[80] For example, in November 1895, the Philadelphia Brigade Association, a veterans organization, mobilized a coalition of Protestant and Catholic ministers who joined them in signing a petition to

Congress that demanded immediate recognition of the Cuban Republic. The next day, Governor Claude Matthews of Indiana, together with Estrada Palma, presided over a rally on behalf of Cuban independence.[81] While Pierra undoubtedly hoped to appeal to as broad and diverse a U.S. public as possible, he never neglected to pay special attention to those who could make not only a political difference in Washington but an economic one in Cuba once independence was achieved. Thus, despite the fact that the working class made up the vast majority of over 1,000 supporters who turned out to hear him in Providence, Pierra's reports to the PRC emphasized the views of "the better society," including the mayor and representatives of the local men's athletic club.[82]

Like Pierra's speeches, PRC propaganda materials, such as English-language books like *Free Cuba* by Rafael Merchán and *The History of the War* by Gonzalo de Quesada, emphasized three themes that leaders believed would most appeal to U.S. sensibilities: the colonial administration's corruption and frequent embezzlement of island revenues; the near absence of a public school system for the Cuban majority; and Spain's persecution of rich revolutionaries who unselfishly sacrificed their nobility and wealth for "freedom."[83] As such, Pierra echoed other PRC leaders in their appeals to the White House by insisting that blacks comprised no more than one-third of the army's enlisted ranks (instead of the two-thirds that they probably did) and celebrating the presence of titled aristocrats in their officer corps and provisional government.

In making the case for U.S. recognition of Cuba's belligerency rights to Washington's high society, the PRC enlisted agents even more polished than Pierra. Through the culture-class idiom of refined taste and a keen fashion sense that typified the image of some agents, the PRC hoped to demonstrate their validity as future leaders of a Cuban nation cast in their own pro-imperialist nationalist design. For example, in a memoir of his longtime association with emigré leaders Martí and Estrada Palma, PRC counsel Horatio Rubens recalled the impact of Ricardo Díaz Albertini's appointment to the PRC's Washington office: "Albertini was valuable; he had a social flair. . . . He was a fixture in fashionable circles in Europe and America, among people who shuddered delicately at 'those disturbed conditions.' . . . Many people, nevertheless, marveled that so polished a man of the world would consort with 'revolutionists.' Albertini's clothes were from England, though; his shoes from Italy; his ties from France and made to a special specification of form. He danced beautifully; he dined with a manner. He knew knives and forks."[84]

By way of contrast, Rubens noted that Albertini's good taste served to eclipse that of his less worldly though equally pompous PRC colleague in Washington, Gonzalo de Quesada, who he noted "wore removable cuffs." As Pierra stated in a

speech in Washington, the object of such efforts was to contest Spanish represen-
tations of the revolutionary forces as consisting of "only some ignorant Negroes,
a few white people of the lowest class of society, some bandits and a few foreign
adventurers."[85] Through men such as Albertini, the embodiment of European
etiquette, and Pierra, of U.S. sensibilities, the PRC showed the Cuban cause for
what it "really" was: a struggle to promote a Euro-American–styled civilization
led by white, elite Cubans in an otherwise barbarically ruled and savage land.

Accordingly, Pierra and other PRC publicity "commissioners" sent a glamor-
ous and appealing message to economically privileged sectors of U.S. society,
making the Cuban war seem like the latest philanthropic cause of choice. Thus,
between May 25 and 30, 1896, Pierra held a lavish "Cuban-American Fair" for the
war in Madison Square Garden, advertised under the motto "Cuba appreciates
sympathy—she must have assistance."[86] The fair collected $19,000 for the war
effort but cost a whopping $14,000 in expenses.[87] Indeed, the holding of celebra-
tory dances, balls, and other such events by affiliated emigré clubs projected a
sophisticated, cosmopolitan image of Cuba's society and cultural prospects that
were in keeping with the Liberal philosophies of PRC leaders. Often, the self-
sacrificing white hero of Cuban independence took center stage in the form of
José Martí. Pale, meticulously (if starkly) dressed, and thin enough that his ro-
bust intellect contrasted with the appearance of physical frailty, Martí had during his life fulfilled the standard of Victorian-age masculinity so glorified in the
romantic literature of the time.[88] Forgetting that Martí's desire to embody this
image probably cost him his life, pro-imperialist nationalist emigrés identified
with Martí's frailness and through him portrayed themselves as the "minds"
behind the Revolution. Thus, PRC club "José Martí" of Manhattan organized an
evening of music and English-language theatre for a U.S. audience, promising
that one of the scenes of the dramatic production would include a bust of Martí
on the stage.[89] Through appropriations such as this, pro-imperialist nationalists
proved that their community represented the Revolution's cultural and cerebral
soul. Like popular nationalists who remembered a suffering, messianic Martí,
they originated an image of Martí that meshed with the values peculiar to their
vision of nation.

Educated, middle-class, and wealthy emigré women played a critical role in
the construction of an image of Cuba Libre founded on pro-imperialist nationalist principles. By 1898, out of approximately 200 PRC clubs, no less than 49 were
made up of women. By 1898, the PRC counted between 1,000 and 1,500 women
members.[90]

Using the sacrifice of their own personal wealth as an analogous symbol to the
property and wealth sacrificed by white, economically privileged soldiers, rich

PRC-affiliated revolutionary club of Philadelphia called "Hermanas de Martí" (Sisters of Martí), April 19, 1893. Note that, two years before his death in 1895, these women chose to appropriate the figure of Martí as an expression of their nationalism. (Courtesy of the Archivo Nacional de Cuba)

ladies in West Tampa were moved to send a collection of diamond and other precious gem-encrusted jewelry to New York as a donation to PRC coffers.[91] Similarly, the statutes of the all-female "Disciples of Martí" club recalled the heroic principle of sexual self-denial typified in the ideal Victorian male by requiring all its female members to be unmarried. Further, they prohibited members from dancing at the very parties the club arranged to raise funds for independence until it was achieved.[92] Celebrating the star-quality of its central hero, the letterhead of the club featured a sketch of the face of José Martí heralded by the club's name and a halo of tiny, boldly printed hearts.[93]

Moreover, magazines like Raimundo Cabrera's *Cuba y América* frequently carried descriptions of such activities and photographs of women's clubs on their "society pages," a column redefined to include only social engagements strictly connected to the cause of Cuba Libre.[94] Elite women supporters of the Revolution in exile also contributed to the PRC's civilizing mission through the nature of their fund-raising activities and the items they chose to send to the *manigua*. Thus, Carmen Mantilla, now widely considered to have been Martí's common-law wife, reported in April 1895 that her own club, "Hijas de Cuba," would be holding a bazaar and a party under the patronage of New York emigré socialite Emilio Agramonte. As usual, the benefits of the events would go to PRC coffers. In one month alone, Mantilla reported that Hijas de Cuba had collected $1,000.[95]

Of course, the frivolity associated with such events may have been a rightful byproduct of the optimism generated in the early phase of the war, especially among emigré women who were not palpably aware of the hardships suffered by revolutionaries in the field. Nonetheless, emigré women found their analogue among female supporters of the Revolution in Cuba. The secret PRC-affiliated club "La Cubanita" of Cienfuegos offers a case in point. Composed of an entirely female membership, La Cubanita sent packages to rebel units in the *manigua* from 1897 to 1898. While other clubs in Tampa and underground traffickers in Havana channeled hundreds of bundles of clothes and shoes for general distribution to the most needy of rebel troops,[96] La Cubanita, directed by Ritica Suárez del Villar y Suárez del Villar, specialized in shipping high-quality goods and personal luxury items to economically privileged officers. Thus, a typical entry in her secret log of "war supplies" from November 1897 featured four pounds of chocolate, a dozen cans of milk, a box of sweets, and a jigger of "Beef Esteak Sauce."[97] Alberto Abreu, of the fabulously wealthy (and Parisian-based) Abreu family, received multiple woolen shirts and cashmere pantaloons along with cigarettes, cans of Spanish sausages, and the occasional woman's dress (*vestidos de señora*) for outfitting a needy lover. One Colonel Bravo received many a linen handkerchief, undershirt, and warm scarf.

In this way, La Cubanita upheld the code of elite masculine respectability by providing women and children of officers with the proper accoutrements of honor, status, and culture even when their men—because of their duties to the war—could not. Thus, Suárez del Villar ensured that Colonel Esquerra's wife was always fashionably attired, sending her many gowns, measures of cloth, and even dress patterns. She did the same for Carlos Trujillo, supplying him with children's clothes, toys, women's dresses, sweetened condensed milk, cinnamon, chocolate (both solid and powdered), and, at one point, a gallon of sherry. Trujillo apparently forwarded these items from the field to his family.[98] Only once in La Cubanita's sixty-seven-page, double-sided register does Suárez del Villar specify a shipment as destined for the rank-and-file soldiers: in the summer of 1898 (after U.S. troops had landed), she sent fifty bundles of clothes, shoes, and hats "to the forces" of General José de Jesús Monteagudo.[99] The club's log of shipments is overwhelmingly dominated by entries of luxury goods meant to ensure the personal comfort of individual upper-class men whose aristocratic tastes ran far afield of the practical or mundane. These efforts on the part of elite women revolutionaries, regardless of the senders' good intentions, could not

CLUB " JOSE MARTI " FUNDADA EN COSTA
RICA, POR MARIA CABRALES ESPOSA DEL
GREL, MACEO, A LA XXXXXXXXXXXXXXXXXXX
APARECE AL CENTRO

PRC-affiliated revolutionary club "José Martí," founded in Costa Rica by the
exiled wife of General Antonio Maceo, María Cabrales, at the start of the 1895 War.
(Courtesy of the Archivo Nacional de Cuba)

help but uphold the standards of civility and traditional class structure that the
PRC's New York office and fellow pro-imperialist nationalists on the island saw
as paramount to their cause.

But the PRC did not restrict its activities in promoting a "civilized Revolution" to the sponsorship of progressive women, informational events, or gala
parties held to raise funds. Consistently, it relied on the engagement of sympathetic agents among the U.S. press and, on occasion, on methods of direct manipulation in the leaking or reporting of war news. The process of "packaging"
the Cuban Revolution of 1895 for U.S. consumption was not a one-sided affair,

dominated by the burgeoning U.S. media industry, but was quite dialectical. It involved the conscious efforts of PRC leaders to shape and represent the Revolution of 1895 in terms meaningful both to them as pro-imperialist nationalists and to the very sectors whose economic interests and political connections they sought to exploit.

In fact, PRC courting and reliance on U.S. reporters to tell the Revolution's story from their side was well known and commonly accepted, even by secret revolutionary agents operating in Havana.[100] For example, the PRC patronized the trip of New York war correspondent Franc R. E. Woodward to meet Antonio Maceo's troops in Cuba by providing him with letters of introduction for Martí, Gómez, and Maceo along with the commissioned rank of captain in the Liberating Army.[101] Sylvester Scoval, of New York's *World*, accompanied an expedition of Cuban emigrés departing from Key West with arms for the Revolution in the spring of 1896.[102] So trusting was the relationship between PRC leaders and the press that U.S. reporters were called upon to scout out Spanish spies among fellow media correspondents on the war front and to warn the leadership of their identities.[103]

Far less known was the fact that Fidel Pierra secretly penned dozens of articles on Cuba's society, history, economic condition, war, and political future as a republic for such influential newspapers as New York's *Sun* and *Journal*, *New Republic*, *Peterson's Magazine*, *Shipping and Commercial List*, and the *Boston Herald*. As Pierra admitted, most of the articles were not signed by him "because it was preferable that they be presented as if they were the product of U.S. pens so as to inspire greater confidence" among readers. So successful was Pierra at this political and discursive masquerade that he bragged about a front-page piece he wrote on Spanish governor Valeriano Weyler's anti-insurgent policies for the *Journal* to the PRC's second-in-command, Joaquín del Castillo. According to Pierra, the article had been read as testimony of U.S. public opinion before the U.S. Senate at the request of Senator John Sherman in early 1896.[104]

These developments underscore the ideological orientation of PRC leaders toward the practices, beliefs, and institutions of the "modern" sectors of U.S. society. More important, they also reveal the lengths to which the PRC would go to ensure U.S. diplomatic recognition, mediation, or even military intervention on Cuba's behalf in as short a time as possible. The need for such a solution grew into a veritable obsession between the summer of 1895 and late 1897 as Estrada Palma, de Quesada, and other PRC agents scrambled to garner congressional, and then presidential, support of Cuba's right to belligerency and/or independence. The results—continuing hostility from the White House and faltering enthusiasm in Congress—fell far short of PRC expectations. The need to turn the tide diplomatically and end the war categorically was crucial to PRC leaders for two reasons. First, they were committed to maintaining the structures of a plantation society under the Republic. Second, liberal principles dictated that they attract foreign investment to the country in order to assure future growth. The longer the fighting dragged on, the further Cuba's economy and few symbols of modernity (like the railroad and telegraph system) were reduced to rubble by their own rebel forces and Spanish troops alike. Not surprisingly, then, PRC efforts brought them into conflict with the Revolution's military cadres.

Financing Freedom, Confronting Costs:
PRC *Leaders and the Cuban Military*

Conflicts over the meaning of "revolution" and its implications for the prospect of nation-building among civilian and military leaders were perhaps best illustrated in the divergent approach and attitude of each toward the strategies of warfare employed by the Liberating Army. In order to face the larger and better-equipped Spanish army, Cuban rebels relied on weapons—including machetes—often imported secretly from the United States to the war front. To buy arms, print the PRC's official newspaper, *Patria*, subsidize the newspapers of other clubs, and provide stipends for PRC agents, revolutionaries in Cuba relied on the expropriation of supplies from island plantations. In particular, they demanded direct cash payments from planters, whom they threatened with the destruction of their crops and sugar mills. In exchange for the Liberating Army's protection, such cash payments were called a revolutionary "tax." Like plantation and town raids by rebel forces, this taxation strategy became a mainstay of their activities. Of course, many planters felt besieged on all sides and only reluctantly agreed to fill the Liberators' war chests. Few planters wholeheartedly supported the patriot cause. Emilio Terry, owner of the world's most valuable sugar mill and subsequently touted as a patriot, was typical. Terry grudgingly paid off the PRC, only to maintain a squadron of Cuban soldiers in the service of Spain (known as *guerilleros*) to fend off rebel attacks.[105] Máximo Gómez described a typical encounter with a planter in this way:

"Do not order the destruction of the sugar mill, because that is savage" the landowner began to shout, and I answered him: "Sure, then why don't you get those little Spanish soldiers out of your house [*Pues sáqueme Ud. los soldaditos españoles de su casa*] and pay for your reasonable share to the revolution, or go with your sugar mill back to Spain. What is in Cuba belongs to the Cubans." And the landowner then began to deal with the revolution, and she, being honorable, shall know how to respect and fulfill her contracts.[106]

Alternating subtle and direct means of coercion, revolutionaries in the field found the policy extremely effective. Judging from the financial reports of the PRC during the first two years of the war, the Revolution could not have survived without the collection of planter tribute. Together with similar "taxes" levied on mining companies, amounts totaled nearly half a million dollars.[107]

However, Máximo Gómez, as supreme commander of the Liberating Army, and Antonio Maceo, as second-in-command, understood the purpose of such tactics to extend beyond that of merely financing the war. Such revolutionary revenues, garnered by taxing the rich to benefit the poor, foreshadowed a redistributive role for the state. Under a Republic, or so the Manifesto of Montecristi had pledged, soldiers of the Liberating Army would be compensated with land and resources.[108] Thus, revolutionary taxation served to instruct planters and rebel soldiers alike on how differently society would be structured after independence. Like redistributing plunder to soldiers, this was a process that revolutionary nationalists should directly control. For Gómez, the money collected in tribute meant nothing if the social character of the Revolution was weakened or its goal of demolishing the foundations of colonial society was compromised.[109]

Gómez cheered on the tactics of Antonio Maceo, whose successful invasion of western Cuba he attributed to Maceo's adamant refusals to accept any bribes from wealthy Creoles, a group he cast as "the powerful ones, partial to the [Spanish] tyrant." In response to such offers, Maceo had ordered his troops to burn every property in sight, "destroying and purifying the origins of such greed." These origins were historical and deeply rooted in the rationale of class-color distinction that formed the logic of exploitation to which colonial elites had appealed in order to subject less powerful Cubans for generations. "Everything is collapsing, and the little that is left standing, Spain herself is occupied with destroying. All the better," concluded Gómez.[110] For his part, Maceo declared himself little interested in entering into a compromise with either colonial aristocrats or the United States for any reason.[111] If the United States was genuinely concerned with ending the war for Cuba's sake, he challenged, then let it make possible the shipment of enough arms and munitions to equip properly the Cuban rebels.[112] Otherwise, his implied, no wing of the Revolution should trust the U.S. government or actively court U.S. interests.

Through the lens of pro-imperialist nationalism, Estrada Palma and Salvador Cisneros Betancourt, the first president of the Government of the Republic-in-Arms during the 1895 War, were naturally limited in their enthusiasm for such measures. Although they appreciated Gómez's newfound respect for and inclusion of civilian leaders like themselves in his plans, they also recognized that neither attitude granted them any authority over the extent of guerrilla attacks.[113] Hoping to impose his criteria nonetheless, Estrada Palma frequently met with and responded to the concerns of U.S. investors, even writing letters to the Government of the Republic-in-Arms on behalf of specific investors to request guarantees for the protection of their properties and their right to make improvements on them. He did this because of their influence in Washington; but he also did this because he wanted them to feel comfortable with the idea of continuing their investments in a pro-imperialist nationalist Republic.[114]

In a letter to one investor explaining the need for such measures, Estrada Palma rationalized them as less barbaric and more humane than blockading a town or fortifying its central plaza, normally the seat of colonial government. Further, he described the future free Cuba as "the home of Cubans and Spaniards, who, as members of the same family, will live in peace and harmony, as members of the same nation. . . . Spaniards should continue living in Cuba, because they, as a [social] element of hard work and order, should serve . . . to give impetus [and] the right direction to the young Republic."[115] At one point in the summer of 1896, Estrada Palma proposed having all payments of taxes go directly to the PRC through the planters' accountants already in New York. He even proposed organizing a planters' association to defend their interests and make the tax collection more efficient.[116]

Such activities and proposals infuriated the revolutionary nationalist members of the Cuban military. Understandably, combatants felt their efforts to destabilize plantation society and punish colonial elites for their tacit support of Spain were being undermined by the very people the Revolution had charged with defending their actions abroad. In September 1896, Gómez responded to Estrada Palma's proposals in no uncertain terms. Emigrés' willingness to negotiate with agents of the planting elite abroad and to restrict the strategic targets of the Liberating Army had taken away the rebels' greatest weapon—fear. Moreover, a PRC proposal to allow planters to harvest sugar in exchange for money donations was preposterous. "In Cuba," Gómez insisted, "it is not possible for anyone to work. Work is a crime against the revolution. Not understanding this from the beginning is the reason that we have seen extended the hours of our triumph. . . . They ought to pay and pay heavily [*pagar gordo*], only and for nothing more, than that we should respect their properties, and to him who does not pay, well he is already lost [to the cause] and he has no reason to make any rational claim, let alone a just one. What is his should be destroyed."[117] The military leadership turned the PRC leadership's tax proposals down on all counts.[118]

Often, Estrada Palma adopted an accommodating stance with officers like Gómez, even recognizing the positive message of strength that the Revolution sent the world in levying taxes on Cuba's elite. Yet, he was also not afraid to go through extraofficial channels in order to implement the PRC's own plan for ending the war. For example, he instructed "Mario" (a conspirator in the Havana underground) not to ship any dynamite or other explosives sent by emigré clubs in Key West to revolutionaries in the field. Mario proceeded to contact Rosario Sigarroa, a principle organizer of arms shipments in Tampa, and directed her to turn down the offer of dynamite. Mario explained Estrada Palma's logic (which he apparently shared): "In this way, . . . our people will not grow accustomed to anarchist methods [in preparation] for the day that we will be alone."[119]

But try as they might, Estrada Palma and the rest of the Revolution's leaders —military and civilian—would not be able to turn back the clock.[120] In fact, by the second year of the war, Estrada Palma and his cohorts were convinced that the war had reached a stalemate. As a solution, the PRC began plotting ways outside of military victory to end the war and still gain independence from Spain. It is not clear whether the military leadership at any level (including Máximo Gómez) was ever informed of these plans. However, Estrada Palma and the PRC acted with the full knowledge and consent of civilian leaders like President Cisneros Betancourt of the Government of the Republic-in-Arms on the island every step of the way.

Beginning in the spring of 1897, PRC leaders concocted various covert schemes meant to win U.S. and/or Spanish recognition of Cuban independence. Acting as plenipotentiary delegate of the Revolution, Estrada Palma, Vice-Delegate Joaquín del Castillo, José Zayas, and Benjamín Guerra signed a contract on behalf of the PRC and the Republic in May. The contract involved John R. Dos Passos, a man described in Estrada Palma's official report to the Government of the Republic-in-Arms as a "rich lawyer from New York." In exchange for the sum of $1 million in bonds of the Cuban Republic, Dos Passos was given six months to orchestrate "the recognition of the Cubans as an independent nation by the United States or Spain." He was also to arrange "the evacuation of the Island of Cuba by the Spanish forces."[121] However, Dos Passos was apparently able to secure only a private meeting between Estrada Palma and President McKinley's brother.[122]

Therefore, by June 1897, Estrada Palma was already negotiating another deal, this time with a syndicate of Wall Street brokers led by Samuel M. Janney. Anxious to preserve Cuba's propertied wealth, he wrote to Janney in June, "It must be understood that my Government will not be willing to pay such a sum after the time limited, as every day that passes increases the ruin of the island & lessens the value of Spain's sovereignty."[123] According to the original terms of the contract and amortization scheme signed by both parties on October 1, 1897, the Republic of Cuba agreed to pay Janney and his cronies the sum of $150 million in 4 percent gold bonds issued by the future state. Payment would begin January 1, 1903, and end in 1953. In return, Janney would convince the Spanish Crown within three months from the date of the contract to sell the island of Cuba to the Cuban revolutionaries.[124] Custom receipts under trust to the U.S. Department of the Treasury would guarantee the money. Moreover, U.S. treasury officials would serve as independent inspectors, ensuring payment and preventing internal graft — a former mainstay of the Spanish colonial government.[125] Although the Janney group had not let him in on their precise plans, Estrada Palma assumed that they planned to woo Spain with $100 million while keeping $50 million for themselves.[126]

In his report to the Government of the Republic-in-Arms, Estrada Palma explained his reasons for seeking out such alternatives. Chief among these, he declared, was his contention that Spain could never defeat the Cubans through force of arms. However, he also doubted that the Cubans could defeat the Spanish quickly enough to save the material foundations of production that the kind of nation he wanted to build would need to grow.[127] Citing reduced sugar production, declining voluntary contributions, and what he predicted as the eventual demoralization of the Liberating Army, Estrada Palma foresaw no better option for halting the bloodshed and the "final destruction of the territorial wealth of the island."[128]

Sadly, Estrada Palma vested greater faith in those who rejected the tenet of absolute Cuban sovereignty than in the honor of compatriots who were willing to give their lives for it. Following the contradictory logic of pro-imperialist nationalism, Estrada Palma added that U.S. inspection of the Cuban customs house "does not infringe in the most minor way on the sovereignty of the Republic of Cuba." Rather, U.S. inspections would make Cubans more honest.[129] Because the Government of the Republic-in-Arms ultimately approved his actions, one can only assume that there were many powerful members who agreed with him. Such officials — emigré and otherwise — rejected the principle of societal transformation that informed the nationalisms of many rebel officers, popular-class soldiers, and working-class emigrés in the United States.

Conclusion

The process of war and the implementation of revolution in practice frequently involved many levels of contradictions — contradictions of official discourse versus lived reality, of popular-class versus patrician standards of honor, of guerrilla tactics versus regimented assaults, and of libertarian versus "civilized" lifestyles based on etiquette and hierarchy. Ultimately, these contradictions would provide the basis for complicity with changes in PRC policies. Popular nationalist soldiers perceived in their leaders' endorsement of the methods of guerrilla warfare a commitment to destroying the regime of plantations and inequality as a foundation for postwar society. As wartime conditions became more critical and devastation of property increased, the potential for a radical restructuring of society along the lines imagined by popular nationalists also increased. Acting in accord with the tenets of their respective visions of nation, revolutionary and pro-imperialist nationalist leaders rushed to prevent this from happening, both in the PRC and the Liberating Army.

By 1898, pro-imperialist nationalist leaders of the PRC largely succeeded in centralizing structural control over the image of the war and the diplomatic representation of its ends in their hands. This process eventually brought about the marginalization of all other nationalisms whose interests and goals conflicted with those of the PRC leadership. Largely conditioned by the urgent circumstances of the war, the absence of Martí, and the deaths of radical revolutionary nationalist officers, pro-imperialist nationalists emerged as the most coherent, dominant force within the Revolution. Meanwhile, conditions in Cuba worsened as rebels held the countryside and the Spanish held the towns. As deaths in Spain's concentration camps increased, support among the U.S. public for an end to Cuba's humanitarian crisis rose to a fever pitch. Ever amenable to U.S. public opinion and impatient to stop the destruction of Cuba's structural wealth, PRC officials leaned eagerly into the political winds that augured U.S. military intervention.

In the end, it would be the McKinley administration's decision to intervene militarily, the U.S. Congress's support of intervention without guarantees of future independence, and the PRC's miscalculation of what such an intervention meant that interrupted the natural course of the war.[130] Once the United States declared war against Spain in April 1898, the possibilities for nationalists to shape Cuba's political destiny independently of outside accountability had radically changed. U.S. intervention finished the task that PRC leaders had begun by sealing off the paths that might have led popular nationalists to become equal partners in the military and civilian project of constructing a national state. However, as the next chapter suggests, the internal political limitations that characterized the early Republic had as much to do with struggles launched among Cubans during the 1895 War as it did with the policies of the first U.S. military occupation (1898–1902). Popular nationalists, like revolutionary nationalists, survived the 1895 War to wage battle over the right to see their respective vision of nation implemented. Through conflicting memories of the Revolution, nationalists articulated differences in the kind of nation they expected to achieve. They also interpreted the means for reviving a spirit of social unity differently, through conflicting images of José Martí.

THREE

....

Cuba Libre in Crisis

The Origins of U.S. Imperial
Hegemony, 1898–1902

BY JULY 1898, the U.S. and Cuban militaries had achieved victory over Spain. Yet, Cuba's thirty-year struggle for independence had come to an ambiguous and confusing end. Cuban rebels had no other choice than to make the most out of a situation they could neither predict nor control. For emigré activists and supporters, the coming months would bring more anxiety than joy. Everywhere, former sources of U.S. support for Cuban independence seemed to have reversed course. Not only did the United States exclude Cuban rebels from claiming their own victory over the Spanish, but U.S. diplomats barred representatives of the Cuban forces from peace talks in Paris, thereby allowing Spain to cede sovereignty over the island to the United States. Meanwhile, U.S. press accounts of the war advanced the view that because Cubans had supposedly mattered little in the struggle against Spain, they now mattered even less in the political process that would determine its results.[1]

Within weeks of the Spanish surrender, three different institutions had emerged to represent the Revolution, each claiming the greater right to defend and achieve the goal of independence from the United States. The U.S. occupation of the island suddenly made U.S. officials the principal power brokers and mediators of differences among leaders of the civilian and armed wings of the Revolution. The army, under Máximo Gómez, refused to lay down its arms without guarantees of independence from the United States. The PRC in New York continued to assert its right to command negotiations in Washington. At the same time, the legislative and executive branches of what had been the Government of the Republic-in-Arms during the war reorganized themselves into the Representative Assembly of Santa Cruz, Camagüey, with the claim of constituting a provisional government. As during the war, nationalists of all stripes could be found on every side of the three-way divide. However, the new context of political uncertainty exacerbated preexisting tensions. Backed by military force, U.S. officials held the power to recognize or dismiss the authority of revolutionary leaders and any influence they might exercise in determining Cuba's fate. Amidst this climate of insecurity, envy, disdain, and fear, distrust fractured the revolutionary leadership even more than issues of ideology.

Unwilling to surrender control of their own or Cuba's destiny to each other, most revolutionary leaders proved equally unwilling to admit that the U.S. government would not recognize any authority but its own. After months of seeking recognition of their respective organizations' authority from the U.S. government, the Liberating Army, the Representative Assembly, and even the PRC voluntarily dissolved. One by one, each group's collaboration with U.S. officials helped the United States assert its right to exercise ultimate control. Their complicity and, in some cases, cooperation eventually annulled each body's right to exist and, in the case of the Representative Assembly, undermined its members' legitimacy as representatives of the Revolution in the eyes of the Cuban people.

Caught between nearly 40,000 destitute popular nationalists and a foreign army that made up its own rules for political engagement, Cuban leaders clung to one of the few principles that their respective nationalist visions shared: three years of guerrilla warfare had made them wary of popular empowerment and proponents of top-down structures of command. Although Cuban leaders never came to agree on the terms of the process, their active or tacit support for the U.S. policy of paying off desperately poor but still armed insurgents dismantled the Liberating Army. Indeed, rebel leaders' support for this policy effectively eliminated the last obstacle to U.S. control.[2] Thus, by March 1898 when the disarmament process began, the crisis of authority at the top of the Revolution's former ranks threw the prospects of nationhood and the elements that comprised all three Cuban nationalisms into disarray. Nonetheless, while nationalists' strategies for achieving their respective visions of nation may have changed, the ideals that guided them did not necessarily go away.

This chapter tells the story of how the three forms of Cuban nationalism that emerged in the process of preparing and living the Revolution of 1895 responded to the discourse and practice of U.S. imperialism from 1898 to 1902. Essentially, it contends that nationalists' engagement of U.S. imperialism made the establishment of U.S. hegemony possible. Those responsible for making that hegemony possible reached beyond the political elite to include workers, teachers, and even some popular-class veterans themselves. Popular nationalists' efforts to see aspects of their vision of nation fulfilled, if only through the actions of a new imperial state, inadvertently legitimated a long-term role for the U.S. government in Cuba's internal affairs. At the same time, the revolutionary leaders' complicity with a U.S.-directed political process recast them in the role of emerging political elites whose desire to establish a dominant place for themselves obscured the fact that the basis for their power resided with U.S. officials and not the Cuban masses. Threatened by popular nationalists' successful engagement of U.S. imperialist policies and their subsequent marginalization, revolutionary and pro-imperialist nationalist leaders struggled to reconstitute their own authority by constructing the myth that social unity had been achieved during the 1895 War. They also articulated that myth collectively, for the first time, through the image of José Martí.

Because U.S. imperialism emerged at precisely the same time as Cuban nationalisms did in the 1890s, the policies, attitudes, and discourse of U.S. officials charged with carrying it out reflected a similar degree of contradiction. Surely, most U.S. officials interpreted the occupation as a colonial conquest in which policies of "tutelage" such as public schooling, public works, and political pluralism served the utilitarian ends of foreign exploitation. Still, others took such policies seriously, even to the point of subverting the objectives of Washington administrators. Although U.S. officials acted as agents of neocolonialism regardless of their beliefs or actions, many popular nationalists, especially women, veterans, and teachers, exploited the opportunities for liberation that U.S. "tutelage" opened up. This, in turn, meant that the institutional and discursive spaces that U.S. imperialists constructed to confine Cubans actually allowed some Cubans to experience them in unintended ways. Instead of seeing U.S. imperialist structures as controlling, some Cubans came to see them as democratic and even internally liberating.

Constructing U.S. Imperial Hegemony from Below

Undoubtedly, the disaster in which average Cubans found themselves when U.S. troops first landed on Cuba's eastern shore necessarily colored their analysis of U.S. relief efforts and intentions. The combined impact of colonial and rebel policies had laid the island waste. Under the command of Captain General Valeriano Weyler, Spanish troops had ordered the evacuation of the Cuban countryside and the concentration of *pacíficos* in cities and towns. Before being marched at gunpoint to the concentration camps where nearly a quarter million of them perished, Cubans had witnessed the burning of their homes and the sacking of their possessions.[3] Prohibited from bringing foodstuffs along with them, peasants' livestock was summarily killed so as to prevent them from falling into the hands of rebels. Of the 3 million head of cattle available in 1895, only 10 percent had survived. Of 350 sugar mills in operation, only 40 remained.[4] However, while U.S. relief efforts, especially those of the Red Cross, alleviated the worst suffering among *pacíficos*, the end of the war seemed to increase it for many *mambises*. Before the island-wide disarmament policy went into effect in 1899, sheer hunger had reduced some veteran soldiers to stealing money, clothing, and food, a process that quickly earned them the title of "bandits." General Leonard Wood, then governor of the province of Oriente, authorized the execution of such "brigands" without trial or hearing. Decisions made by U.S. officials to deny veterans the right to commemorate the death of war heroes like Antonio Maceo and to exclude them from ceremonies marking the end of Spanish rule only added to tensions. In both Santiago and Havana, December and January were marked by rioting and anti-U.S. demonstrations.[5]

Given this context, how could former supporters and participants in the 1895 War engage or resist the agents and policies of imperialism? As we shall see, many Cubans furthered goals derived from their visions of nation by whatever means U.S. imperial agents put at their disposal. As *décimas* from the period attest, memories of the recent past and Spain's policies of terror served as points of comparison with the style and nature of U.S. rule.[6] For many popular nationalists who found themselves dependent on U.S. aid or employment for survival after 1898, engagement of U.S. imperialism and rationalization of their participation in its projects and discourses was unavoidable. The fact that some of the most active participants and opponents of U.S. policies in Cuba were women is also significant. Marginalized by a PRC and a military that had seen them as auxiliaries at best and "impediments" at worst, female popular nationalists proved themselves eager to assert a much more autonomous, self-defined role in the processes of social improvement that U.S. forces set in motion.

Captain Magdalena Peñarredonda, the prominent link in the Revolution's urban-rural espionage network, provides a case in point. Even before the occupation, Peñarredonda inadvertently contributed to the legitimation of a U.S. role on the island when Weyler's repression of *pacíficos* radicalized her views.[7] Eventually, Peñarredonda came to believe that the Spanish meant to exterminate the lower orders of the Cuban population,[8] a conclusion with which some foreign observers agreed.[9] Desperate to remedy the condition of *reconcentrados* as best she could, Peñarredonda had urged U.S. involvement through William J. Calhoun, an Illinois judge and agent of the McKinley White House as early as 1896. "[W]e shall all die before we surrender to Spain," she insisted, implying (intentionally or unintentionally) that without U.S. aid, there was no end in sight to human and material costs.[10] Calhoun's subsequent report to McKinley was greatly influenced by Peñarredonda's statements. First, like Peñarredonda, the report clearly confirmed that the Liberating Army would fight to the death and, in the long run, would probably win. Second, it presented the revolutionaries as the enemies of annexation and the Spaniards and wealthy, loyalist Cubans as its staunchest supporters. In short, Calhoun's report gave McKinley all the assurance he needed to proceed as he did. Whatever her intentions, Peñarredonda clearly shaped U.S. policy-makers' positions on Cuba. Ultimately, the same U.S. policy-makers who marginalized Cuban revolutionaries and courted Spanish loyalists for positions in the U.S. administrations were the same ones who relied on testimony like hers to justify the intervention on humanitarian grounds.

How shaky these grounds actually were became increasingly obvious to Peñarredonda and others from the start of the intervention. In the first few months after Spain's surrender, Clara Barton's Red Cross found that the U.S. military was prohibiting its ships loaded with food for starving *reconcentrados* from landing in Cuba.[11] Similarly, the initial provisioning of tens of thousands of daily rations to the people of Santiago by the U.S. Army came at the price of Commanding General Leonard Wood's authoritarianism and courting of Spanish officials. Fresh from fighting Indians in the U.S. West and invigorated by his own personal capture of the Apache "bandit" Geronimo, Wood even hired a press agent to publicize his dictatorial methods in Oriente at home, some of which became the stuff of legends.[12] Displays of bravura in Oriente coupled with Wood's strict courting of the Spanish colonial order soon paid off.[13] White House officials eventually rewarded Wood for his antics when they asked him to replace the island's original military governor, John R. Brooke, who was deemed "soft" by comparison.

In response—and to the delight of General Wood—all the Cubans in Brooke's cabinet resigned. Subsequently, Wood completely reorganized all levels of Cuba's civil government, choosing candidates for posts "who are in sympathy with U.S. American ideals." Although Wood recruited some Cubans along with loyalists and former Spanish officials, many of Wood's emigré appointments were the archconservative former members of the SEJE who had criticized Tomás Estrada Palma's supposed sympathy for blacks and workers during the war.[14] Moreover, Governor Wood took important steps to consolidate the support of key colonial institutions, especially the Catholic Church.[15] Together with the Cuban "propertied classes," Wood considered Spaniards the genuine "people of Cuba" since, in his estimation, they were the only islanders of pure race. He also applauded their open annexationism.[16]

Not surprisingly, Peñarredonda joined labor activists returning from Florida and intellectuals who had supported the Revolution in denouncing Wood.[17]

Other female patriots like Peñarredonda found Wood's courting of clergy particularly disturbing, since the Spanish priests and bishops who had supported the reconcentration and justified the massive loss of Cuban life still dominated the ranks of the Church.[18] Recognizing this, the Vatican appointed a new archbishop for the seat in Havana. However, when it became clear that the Vatican had not chosen a Cuban but an Italian for the post, Peñarredonda organized a largely female "Popular Committee" to accuse Wood of orchestrating the act. Most insulting to the protestors was the fact that U.S. officials had slated the new bishop's arrival in Havana for February 24, 1900, the fifth anniversary of José Martí's Grito de Baire, the 1895 Revolution's call to arms. The Popular Committee defamed Donato Sbaretti as a puppet of U.S. imperialism and called for his resignation. For Peñarredonda and her fellow activists, Sbaretti's appointment and arrival offended the memory of martyred soldiers and civilians. It also subverted the cultural sovereignty of Cuba by dismissing memories of Martí and the War of 1895 as if they no longer mattered. In order to counter the belief that Cuba's nationalist past had all but expired, Peñarredonda recruited living symbols of that past in order to remind other Cubans as well as U.S. rulers that the struggle for independence continued. The demonstrations counted not only on the participation of war widows but also on the presence of Máximo Gómez and former president of the Republic-in-Arms, Salvador Cisneros Betancourt.[19]

However, the participation of prominent revolutionary leaders in the women's campaign was exceptional, not typical. Most revolutionary leaders did not understand what the fuss was all about.[20] Although they did not achieve the appointment of a native bishop, the protestors' demonstration at the port of Havana forced many Cubans to rethink the implications of imperialist actions and call for Sbaretti's resignation.[21] Thus, at a time when no civilian or military body of the Revolution asserted its authority, let alone unity, women activists achieved what revolutionary leaders could not. They re-ignited the flame of hope: the symbolic act of remembering their expectations for the nation helped popular nationalists conceive the possibility that some of those expectations still lay within reach.

Even when female patriots approached the U.S. occupation from a different angle, their actions often served a related purpose. Many middle- and popular-class women played a critical role in deciphering the cultural code of U.S. imperialism, often translating its key tenets of civilization, enlightenment, and progress through their activities in ways indigenous to their experience and local setting. Some continued the work of "civilizing the *manigua*" in the home and on the street much as they had done during the 1895 War by founding feminine social clubs modeled on the PRC's revolutionary clubs. Through example, word, and

94

deed, such clubs sought to generate a base of popular pressure for the absolute independence of the island.[22] Having contributed moral principles and gendered ideals of motherhood and compassion to the project of making Cuba free, they now vowed to build a nation in which the same values applied.

Ironically, similar convictions may explain why so many women flocked to the U.S. imperialist project of public education. Thousands of women, most of them with little previous work experience in the public sector, responded to the call of Alexis Everett Frye, the superintendent of public schools during the occupation, to "uplift" the masses of Cuban children. One woman who channeled popular nationalist perceptions of the wartime experience into a teaching career under Frye's tenure was Ritica Suárez del Villar y Suárez del Villar, founder of Club "La Cubanita," an all-female underground revolutionary club. Temporarily at least, working in Frye's public schools seemed to return some of the autonomy to act out of a self-defined interpretation of the nation that formal participation in the male-dominated structures of the Revolution had compromised. In many ways, Suárez del Villar's activities as a teacher echoed earlier stances she had taken on behalf of her own nationalist ideals long before the 1895 War.

The daughter of a planter from the town of Trinidad, Suárez del Villar had acquired a public reputation for rebellion at the tender age of seventeen. Invited to attend a ball at Trinidad's aristocratic Liceo society in 1879, Suárez del Villar had dressed in the colors of the Cuban flag and pinned a red carnation to her breast as a protest to the Liceo's general hispanophilia. When she refused to dance with a Spanish cavalry officer, the man denounced her as a *mambisa* and publicly humiliated her by shearing off her long hair with a pair of scissors.[23] Later, a scandalous affair with her first cousin (her parents were already first cousins) further jeopardized her family's social standing and forced them to move to Cienfuegos in order to separate the lovers.[24] In the late 1890s, however, revelations about her activities during the 1895 War rehabilitated her reputation as a self-appointed revolutionary who contested the constraints of traditional society. As founder and president of La Cubanita, Suárez del Villar achieved local celebrity in 1899 when Máximo Gómez visited her in Cienfuegos.[25] Indeed, she herself became known as "La Cubanita" in honor of her club and more than twenty years of work for the Cuban cause. During the U.S. occupation, Suárez del Villar would continue to fight for women's empowerment and her own social credibility, but she often did so by exploiting the existing patriarchal culture's ideals of feminine weakness. Known as much for her commitment to independence as for her hypochondria, Suárez del Villar's activities as a teacher promoted a vision of nation fashioned in her own terms.[26]

In the spring of 1900, Suárez del Villar passed the island-wide teaching exams with flying colors. "Illness," however, and the need for constant care from her personal physician, Luis Perna, deterred her from accepting Cienfuegos's nomination to attend the Harvard Summer School for Cuban Teachers that Superintendent Frye had organized that year. When Suárez del Villar subsequently requested appointment as the director of a public school, her request was initially denied. Indignant, Suárez del Villar took her cause to the editorial board of *Mariposa*, a newly founded women's newspaper in Trinidad. Although the editors confirmed that she deserved an appointment, they also cautioned against her bravado: "Human passions are fatal but her Christian and patriotic soul should respond like Jesus did: Forgive them, Lord, for they know not what they do."[27] Suárez del Villar apparently did not agree and continued to press for a job through personal channels. Finally, the insistence of Perna, a member of the all-Cuban school board, yielded her appointment. In September 1900, Suárez del Villar became principal and teacher of Public School No. 16 on the corner of Cristina and San Carlos in downtown Cienfuegos, a job she relished. At the time, Enrique José Varona, the pro-imperialist nationalist editor of the PRC's *Patria* and Governor Wood's minister of education, declared the need to "replace soldiers with teachers" in order the carry out the final phase of the 1895 War and civilize the Republic.[28] Suárez del Villar responded to the call in her own way.

In December 1900, Suárez del Villar formally requested that the local school board authorize her to declare December 7—the anniversary of the death of Antonio Maceo and Panchito Gómez (Maceo's assistant and the son of General Máximo Gómez)—a day of mourning for her school. She also wanted to dedicate a Catholic mass to their memory. Both requests were summarily denied. Suárez del Villar decided not to press for a mass (perhaps out of deference to the U.S. military government's separation of church and state) but went ahead with plans to commemorate the heroes' deaths. In response, the school board warned her that she stood in violation of their regulatory code.[29]

By May of the following year, Suárez del Villar had dismissed the warning. As the sixth anniversary of Martí's death drew near, she chose not to consult the school board at all but to lead her students in a day-long act of commemoration. She took her students on an excursion to the plantation of the wealthy Abreu family, an insurgent base during the war. There the girls received small patriotic mementos from their teacher and gathered flowers that they weaved into a wreath upon returning to the school. Suárez del Villar later told the girls stories of the great deeds and valor of Martí and had them place their wreath before his portrait.[30] Many of the girls were moved to tears by her stories of sacrifice and heroism. The school board, on the other hand, was not moved. Before long, Suárez del Villar found that her job was in jeopardy.

Apparently, her chief adversary on the school board was Colonel Luis Yero Miniet, an important local figure in the Liberating Army. Attempting to suppress any controversy that disciplining her might cause, the school board attempted to shut Suárez del Villar's school down. At first, it reassigned all her students to other schools, but Suárez del Villar continued to hold classes and students continued to attend. Then, as soon as the academic year ended, the board redrew the school districts so that Suárez del Villar's school was left without pupils. Frantic to reestablish her position and confirm her good intentions, she solicited the support of Máximo Gómez. But having just negotiated the $3 million payment to his troops with the McKinley administration that earned him the censure of the most important civilian leaders of the Revolution, Gómez feared that his "recommendation might well be tossed into the trash bin of useless papers." When Spanish terror reigned, he noted, "it was different, but now [Weyler is] gone and already nobody remembers any of it. I will do what I can for you, by other means. That is better. Your loving brother, M. Gómez."[31]

In the end, Suárez del Villar defiantly reopened the school in September 1901, but upon receiving a plain note signed by the president of the school board asking her to return her keys, she surrendered them, closed the school, and never taught again. She did not fully recover from the public humiliation her dismissal represented. Throughout her life, she lamented the ingratitude her compatriots showed her. In the last testimony published before her death at the age of ninety-nine, Suárez del Villar commented, "[Afterward,] I forgot about the School . . . , but I continued to commemorate on each anniversary my dead loved ones, without the necessity of the Constitution, now vigilant [of these matters], obligating me to do so."[32]

Quite possibly, Suárez del Villar had understood why honoring a black war hero like Maceo in Cienfuegos—founded as a consciously Francophile "white" settlement in 1817 and long known for its racial intolerance—would have caused waves at the time. In fact, she might even have asked permission to hold the event for Maceo and Panchito Gómez with this in mind. However, La Cubanita clearly never considered that honoring the death of Martí would stir so much controversy, let alone cost her her job. As a *mambisa*, Suárez del Villar was unprepared to imagine that veteran officers and civilians would one day consider her memories of the war threatening. Yet, from the moment that she sought a teaching position, her candidacy had been opposed. Ignoring the advice of sympathetic editors at *Mariposa*, Suárez del Villar had nonetheless pursued her goal, as if her talents and experience entitled her to the role. In so doing, she acted on the popular nationalist principle that women's value to the war had lain in their unique ability to uphold the standards of civilization and morality. For Suárez del Villar, the same logic still applied in times of peace. Thus, these men not only discounted the sacrifices she had made for the Revolution but also accused her of violating the very "social rules" of her status as "a lady" that society imposed and that she had once defied and redefined as an underground activist during the war.[33]

In short, Suárez del Villar's experience testifies to how sensitive and potentially dangerous independent, uncensored interpretations of revolutionary figures and the Revolution itself could seem to Cuba's emerging political elites. During the war, inclusion of marginal groups into the hierarchy of power proved conditional on their acceptance of a new brand of patriarchal authority. However, once Suárez del Villar moved to begin inculcating her own unorthodox values as a *mambisa* into the next generation of *cienfuegueras*, she had gone too far. In the end, Suárez del Villar's conversion into a woman who believed girls would and should exercise greater control over their destiny (and therefore greater influence over society) overwhelmed her acceptability. Like some officers and soldiers of color had done during the war, Suárez del Villar had violated the chain of command that revolutionary nationalist leaders had envisioned as integral to the building of their nation.

Moreover, Suárez del Villar did not necessarily play by the rules set down for her by U.S. authorities, either. The school registration form she submitted to the board members on December 14, 1900, reveals a notable reluctance on her part to follow the curriculum guidelines set forth in Frye's *Manual para maestros*. Of the fifty-three pupils attending School No. 16, Suárez del Villar identified thirty-six as white and thirteen as "colored" or *hembras de color*, reporting that all of them received the same level of instruction. Classes included orthography, reading, writing, arithmetic, geography, grammar, drawing, vocal music, and Cuban history. However, under the heading of "U.S. American history," she listed zero, indicating that she did not teach that subject to her students.[34] Frye insisted that this subject be taught alongside Cuban history as a means for undermining the values of belligerency, a policy that school board members deemed especially important in the case of female youths.[35] From this perspective, Suárez del Villar's commemorations represented the straw that broke the camel's back. Both the source and content of her popular nationalist memories made those with different ones nervous.

However exceptional, Suárez del Villar's story provides a number of clues as to the motives of the thousands of young Cubans, especially women, who joined Frye's "pacifist army" of teachers. The public *magisterio* drew recruits from a broad social spectrum that included *mambisas* like Rita Flores de Campos Marquetti, the mulatto wife of a revolutionary general, and Erundina Fernandez de Borges, formerly affiliated with the famed girls preparatory owned by María Luisa Dolz, Cuba's only female doctor of philosophy.[36] Still, most women and men who became teachers were overwhelmingly young in age, and the vast majority of them had never been teachers before. Along with other factors, the youth of these teachers played an important role in facilitating the discursive and ideological dialectic that Frye's system of public education established between popular nationalism and the hegemonic process of U.S. imperialism.

Driven by paternalist officials who themselves represented the socially reform-ist impulse of imperialist and progressive political movements current in the United States, Frye's system of public education strove to fulfill the promise of uplifting the Cuban masses and of "rescuing" the Cubans from themselves. Frye brought to life the humanitarian discourse of U.S. intervention by enlisting the aid of the United States' most prominent, liberally minded pedagogues such as Wilson L. Gill, organizer of the first "scholastic city" in New York, and Marie Keil, the promoter and founder of the first U.S. kindergartens.[37] A native of the tiny island community of North Haven, Maine, Frye had been a public school teacher himself for eight years, first in a primary school in Quincy, Massachu-setts, and later at the Normal School in Cook County, Illinois. Between earning degrees in legal studies and in the emerging field of education from Harvard, Frye had served as superintendent of the San Bernardino school district in Cali-fornia for thirteen years. He also gave more than a thousand influential lectures on educational methods and issued various geography texts that achieved a cir-culation of over 2 million copies among U.S. schoolchildren.[38] Perhaps more than any other imperial official, Frye believed that the U.S. mission was to bring about a "democratization" of Cuban society through "U.S. Americanization." Thus, in his attitude, actions, and person, he embodied the greatest contradic-tion of U.S. imperialism, namely, the notion that as Cubans became increasingly "American" culturally and Cuba became increasingly "American" politically, Cubans would become more civilized and Cuba, by default, more indepen-dent, rather than dependent. Cuban teachers readily exploited and engaged this contradiction.

The system that Frye implemented demonstrates not only how U.S. imperial-ism could be paternalistic but also, more important, why that paternalism was frequently interpreted as liberating and democratic instead of confining and colonial. Copied from the state of Ohio's liberal model, public schools in Cuba were governed by boards of education elected by the parents of school-age chil-dren (regardless of their state of literacy) and controlled locally. In addition, for the first time, Cuban teachers were considered civil servants of the state. The contrast with Spanish policy was striking. Under Spain, teachers' salaries were so low that colonial law required the parents of all children who were not indigent to subsidize salaries with amounts specified by the municipal government. Delays in the payment of the state portion of teachers' salaries often lasted a year or more. So chronic did this situation become that it gave rise to the popular nineteenth-century expression "He is hungrier than a schoolteacher."[39] During U.S. intervention, however, teachers received set monthly salaries of fifty to seventy-five pesos, depending on the cost of living in the area in which they taught. In exchange for attending normal schools during the summer, teachers also received paid vacations. Despite some school directors' calls for increases, these salary rates provided financial security and a comfortable standard of living at a time when severe unemployment was the order of the day.[40] Moreover, U.S. policy provided all teachers, regardless of their gender, equal pay for equal work.[41]

Ramiro Guerra, one of the most prominent historians of the Cuban Republic, began his career during the U.S. intervention as a rural teacher in his native Pinar del Río, then Cuba's most illiterate province.[42] Guerra recalled how this policy of gender equity positively affected the position of young women in their homes. Besides offering an alternative to domestic dependency, teaching elevated these women's power and prestige, since they were often the sole source of monetary income for their families. According to Guerra, the requirement that teachers attend normal schools and learn to live in cities independent of their families also enhanced their self-esteem. The knowledge and sophistication they acquired subsequently fostered greater social regard for them in the local communities where they taught and lived. Moreover, noted Guerra, the new imperialist emphasis on education made support for teachers fashionable, rather than suspect, among local elites. Encouraged by the modernization and future-oriented discourse of U.S. imperialism, many lawyers, doctors, and scientists began to consider the social implications of their work in relation to pedagogy for the first time.[43]

Indeed, Frye not only set a high standard for the treatment of public employees that teachers would continue to demand in the Republic, but he also encouraged high expectations among Cubans for the social mobility that a public education might provide. That the educational system in Cuba cried out for reform in 1898 is undeniable. At the time of the intervention, Cuba possessed only 312 schools with a total enrollment of 34,597 students. By 1902, Frye's efforts had increased the number of schools to 3,628 with a total of 172,273 girls and boys registered. Of these, 62,864 were either black or mulatto, with slightly more girls than boys enrolled.[44] By contrast, in 1899, only 198 black or mulatto Cubans nationally had received some level of higher education, compared to 8,629 whites. Thus, by making education broadly available to those whose parents had long dreamed of such opportunities, U.S. officials like Frye garnered the praise of many popular nationalists for whom this seemed an impressive, even revolutionary, achievement.[45]

Although not enough schools were built to meet the needs of Cuba's school-age population, those children who could attend school expressed their enthusiasm for learning by attending 79 percent of the time nationally. When compared to the dismal levels of enrollment achieved under the Estrada Palma administration (1902–6) and second U.S. intervention (1906–9), Frye's commitment to maximizing resources in order to ensure high rates of attendance was exceptional.[46] Oddly enough, it seemed that the rapidity of what could be achieved under U.S. rule overshadowed a paradoxical reality: that popular nationalists were pursuing the course for a more socially just nation through terms set by a new colonizer.

Indeed, Frye's version of "Americanization" drew thousands of new teachers. By 1901, the government had achieved a total certification of 5,566 teachers out of 6,603 applicants.[47] Espousing the democratic principle of individual merit over experience, Frye opened the profession to any and all who were able to pass a certification test. Although the new system angered many older teachers who sensed an implicit critique of their training under the Spanish, the exams did not put off many applicants.[48] Apart from the six normal schools he established in each provincial capital, Frye also opened a normal school for kindergarten teachers in Havana. In order to ensure equal access to the schools, admission quotas were set in proportion to the population of each province. Candidates received a scholarship of $240 a year to attend the school.[49]

In fact, the modernity of ideas and bureaucratic efficiency that Frye's administration attempted to instill in the minds of teachers and students alike worked to foster the support of many Cubans whose revolutionary experience, youth, or ideological persuasion predisposed them to socially progressive or innovative approaches. For example, the director of *Revista de Instrucción Pública* responded to a teacher's inquiry concerning the use of corporal punishment by rejecting such measures as detrimental to the development and emotional health of both the child and the teacher. Anyone who resorted to brutality in order to gain respect was not a teacher, he wrote.[50] That public schools in Cuba, unlike the United States, were not racially segregated also seems to have helped project the idea that the public school system was a model of racial democracy and social liberalism. The experience also changed the attitude of some teachers like Francisca Rojas de Astudillo who openly lamented the fact that schools had not been open to black children years earlier.[51]

In keeping with the arguments of Martí, Rafael Serra, and others that perceived racial differences derived from unequal access rather than from biology, Frye's teaching manual emphasized culturally chauvinistic ideas to explain the various "races" of the world to students. Teachers were to depict the presumed inferiority of certain races as determined by their climatic and cultural environment rather than as the simple product of an inferior nature.[52] On the other hand, when it came to certain cultural taboos on gender, Frye backed away from rather than stirred up a fight. Although Frye mandated a coeducational public school system as a goal, he did not enforce the measure. So long as both girls and boys could be guaranteed access to equal education, local school boards could decide if schools would be coeducational or not.[53]

Such flexibility in the administration of public schools exemplified the softer side of imperialist politics and discourse with respect to the best, most persuasive methods for "Americanizing" Cubans. This was the indisputable goal of U.S. imperialist policy in establishing Cuba's public educational system. The military government spent thousands of dollars equipping Cuban students with free translated textbooks that included such titles as *Libros primero y segundo de lectura* by Sarah Louise Arnold and *Historia de los Estados Unidos* by Justo P. Parrilla.[54] Certainly, individual companies such as Champion, Pascual & Weiss made a fortune from contracts arranged with the military government. One of this company's own advertisements boasted of having sold 400,000 reams of paper, 240,000 books of penmanship, and 17,500 orator stands for use in Cuban public schools.[55] Apparently, Frye himself added to his own personal fortune by translating his world geography text into Spanish and requiring its use in Cuba.[56] However, at least one Cuban newspaper reported that Frye had "not taken one cent of his salary or even of his royalties for the publication of his books, distributing it all through acts of charity." In all, the newspaper reported that Frye had doled out $3,355 and had not received remuneration from the interventionist government for travel expenses or the cost of food.[57] In truth, Frye had originally refused a salary. However, General Wood insisted on one, apparently as a way to assuage suspicions about the profits from Frye's geography text. Frye agreed, though he ordered it reduced to $2,500 per year.[58]

Inevitably perhaps, Frye's willingness to offer Cubans a central role in his administration sometimes placed Cuban nationalist interests in the service of U.S. imperial gain. For example, Frye's appointment of an all-Cuban panel for the selection of school textbooks provoked an ironic debate in the pedagogical press. According to the Cuban-owned *La Escuela Moderna*, panelists' refusal to use history books that had been printed in Cuba under Spanish rule automatically granted Samuel Small, book publisher and owner of the rival magazine *La Escuela Cubana*, a monopoly over the Cuban textbook market. Small fired back that any lessons Cuban children might learn from American books were preferable to those the Spanish had wanted them to learn.[59]

Responses to this predicament varied. Some Cuban schoolteachers like Ramiro Guerra and Ritica Suárez del Villar chose not to use a textbook at all and relied on their own memories of Spanish rule and Cuba's revolutionary struggle to instruct their students on the history of Cuba. Still others drew political lessons from the problem. For instance, *El Vigilante*, a small newspaper published in Guanajay, Pinar del Río, deemed Small's attitude as illustrative of the difference between the negative form of U.S. imperialism that corporate capitalists represented and the positive form that Frye stood for. Under the headline "¡Qué Grande!" (How Big!), editors insisted that "the Yankee people are not Small, they're Frye."[60]

On the other hand, Frye's system often worked in reverse. That is, Cuban teachers found creative ways to put U.S. imperialism to the service of popular nationalist goals. For example, on October 10, 1899, the teachers in the town of Güines collectively called the suspension of classes in order to commemorate the anniversary of the start of the Ten Years' War, known as "El Grito de Yara," in 1868. In doing so, they defied the orders of the town's U.S.-appointed mayor, a general of the Liberating Army, who would not endorse a holiday not approved by the U.S. government.[61] Similarly, the teachers' almanac of 1901 began with a poem that parodied the contradictions of U.S. imperialist discourse through the jargon of mathematics. While the almanac did not include any holidays not sanctioned by the imperialist state, it culturally defied the underpinnings of that state by designing the academic calender as a *santoral*, or calendar of saints' days.[62] In taking these small but symbolic actions, Cuban teachers voiced their rejection of those aspects of U.S. imperialism that conflicted most sharply with their own notions of popular nationalism. At the same time, they also consciously engaged those elements that furthered the cause of nation as they understood it.

Frye's organization of an expedition of Cuban teachers to Harvard University for training in the summer of 1900 best illustrates the way in which the popular nationalism of Cuban teachers became entangled with U.S. imperialism, appearing to satisfy both agendas at once. The brainchild of Frye, the expensive trip was funded by the private donations of Boston-area citizens. At a total cost of $70,000, donations benefited 1,256 Cuban teachers. Of this number, more than half, or 655, were women, but only a tiny fraction were black or mulatto. Originally, Frye had invited 1,455 teachers, although some, like Suárez del Villar, declined for personal reasons. Also attending were one Filipino teacher and ten Puerto Ricans.[63] As Frye explained in his letter to Harvard president Charles Eliot, "We want the teachers to breathe the atmosphere of the greatest school in

America. . . . We want these teachers to have the culture that comes from travel. We want them to carry this culture back into their Cuban homes and the Cuban schools. We want these teachers to know our country, to know our people. We want the ties between the two countries drawn closer, so that all feeling of antagonism may melt away, in order that our country may do a higher and better work for Cuba."[64] By exposing Cuban teachers to the pedagogical rigor and resources of the United States' oldest academic institution, Frye, Eliot, and others hoped to impress them with the evidence that the modernity and democratic culture of U.S. society were worthy of emulation.

Brought on board steamers of the U.S. Navy, Cuban participants in Harvard's summer program seemed keenly aware of the irony that their presence in Cambridge represented.[65] Many teachers evidently interpreted their presence there as a testament of their commitment to Cuba's national sovereignty and took the opportunity to state as much. Some expressed these feelings in a book of autographs preserved at Harvard. "We Cubans feel a deep sense of gratitude to U.S. Americans, and it will be all the greater the day that our Cuba is independent," wrote José de C. Palomino of Matanzas. "The independence of Cuba will be one of the glories of the fatherland of Washington: the most lively expression of the great virtues of this generous people," remarked Miguel Barceló y Pérez of Santiago. Enrique Rodríguez Batista insisted, "[As] a teacher of the school of Punta Brava [the town in Pinar del Río that crowned Maceo's western invasion], I desire to see as soon as possible the flag of the solitary star fly above Morro Castle in Havana."[66]

Others were less laconic in their appraisals, giving voice to their hatred of the Spanish and underscoring the positive cultural impact that U.S. imperialism as they experienced it was having on them, and through them, other Cubans. While a few voiced an uncomplicated admiration for the United States that bordered on advocacy of annexationism rather than any brand of nationalism, such views were decidedly in the minority.[67] More common were expressions of gratitude to Harvard University and Frye, as distinct from the U.S. government, for having provided teachers with this unique inside view of U.S. society. These teachers clarified that their purpose as Cubans was not to copy U.S. society exactly or to become a part of it but to create their own unique, independent democracy in Cuba. Thus, a man who wrote under the simple title of "a teacher from Oriente" remarked, "I am a worshiper [*Soy idolatro*] of the United States only for the fact of having *thrown out* of Cuba the power of the Spaniards. If one day it should occur to the U.S. Americans not to leave one Spaniard in Cuba, that day, I shall only shout, 'Long Live Cuba Libre!' I believe the United States should, rather than educate, *dehispanicize* Cubans, only in this way shall we be independent."

Under the heading "Where will all of you go to dance?," a reference to the carnival season, this cartoon satirized and ridiculed the upwardly mobile sectors of Cuba's working class and professional middle class during the U.S. military occupation. Contrasting with the elegantly dressed wealthy woman on the left (who will dance at the home of the marquis) are the pathetic figure of a public school teacher, a well-dressed mulatto couple, and a cross-dressed woman heading to the bohemian Teatro Tacón of Havana. (From *El Fígaro*, March 4, 1900, 97)

Teacher Pedro Aragonés, future mayor of the city of Cienfuegos under the Liberal dictator Gerardo Machado, offered similar comments.[68]

Aside from these individual pronouncements, the Harvard experience not only provided teachers with occasions to express their forms of nationalism actively and collectively but also demanded that they define it in terms of the U.S. imperial presence. Some popular nationalist teachers opted to interpret their engagement of U.S. imperialism in the most idealistic way. For example, when General Wood visited the teachers at Harvard, his prognosis that the example of Cuban teachers augured an imminent transition to independence elicited a furor of cheers from the audience.[69] One Cuban teacher who served as a translator remembered the overwhelming inclination of Cuban teachers to "cubanize" commemorations of U.S. history by reading it through the prism of their own recent past. For example, when Cuban teachers took a field trip to the site of the Washington elm, one teacher remembered that their own heroes had shown the same valor as the U.S. anticolonial rebels, long before "the Americans came to help us."[70]

Often, Cuban teachers raised their voices in saluting Cuban independence side by side with many U.S. citizens. Such events gave Cuban teachers the opportunity to carry out something of a "countercolonization" of U.S. public spaces that defied the rules set in their homeland by U.S. military forces for the expression of nationalist sentiments. Thus, precisely when U.S. law prohibited the flying of a Cuban flag over public buildings in Cuba, teachers greeted the sight of Frye raising their flag over the center of Harvard Yard with sheer "delirium." Throwing Frye onto their shoulders, they paraded him around as their hero.[71] Another remarked that the sight of that flag made the teachers feel as if they had become their country's "Liberators," marching across Anglo-Saxon lands as if they were crossing a field of battle in Cuba with the Revolution's flag at the head. Similarly, when the U.S. flag was flown over Boston Commons in celebration of the Fourth of July, Frye equipped his teachers with over 3,000 small Cuban flags for distribution to Boston's public school children, who put away the U.S. flag and waved the Cuban flag instead.[72]

Some teachers felt overwhelmed by the need to make sense of the contradictions that such a personal engagement with U.S. imperialism highlighted. According to the Boston area press, Cuban teachers wrote an average of 400 to 500 letters home a day.[73] One letter, sent by teacher José Filas Torres, captured the awe many must have felt as well as the bittersweet longing to found a nation of their own:

Here everything is admirable, everything is made by machines, by electricity. . . . 700 trains leave [the city] daily and 80 to 100 thousand passengers travel aboard. . . . The Public Library has over one million three hundred thousand volumes and its building, which covers more than two acres, cost two and a half million dollars. . . . The free woman here lives on her own; there are beautiful ones, pretty ones and they are wholly complaisant with us; everywhere we go they happily show their affection for us with little flags and waves. . . . Bicycles and ugly old men run through the streets and parks like bands of flamingos do in our valleys of Vuelta Abajo. . . . My friend, I am not an annexationist. I cannot be an annexationist; but I am enchanted: who could give something like this to the Fatherland! Enthusiasm and determination we do not lack.[74]

In this way, Filas Torres brought to life the intense popular nationalist convictions that Frye's version of imperialism paradoxically evoked in Cuban teachers.

After years of war and a lifetime of frustration with the rigidity of Spanish colonial rule, the education system established by U.S. imperialists inspired Cuban teachers to believe that the realization of a prosperous, modern, and intellectually progressive future for Cuba were genuinely possible. At a personal level, Frye reinforced their aspirations symbolically, both in word and in deed. Even before arriving at Harvard, word of Frye's uniquely sympathetic imperialism spread on the island. Under the headline "Mr. Frye: Boxer," Trinidad's *El Telégrafo* reported that when the captain of the USS *Sedgewick* insulted over 400 female Cuban teachers on board by making them wait to be admitted to their cabins without explanation, Frye defied the captain's orders and admitted them himself. Apparently incensed that Frye should side with his racial and social inferiors, the captain threatened to toss Frye overboard. To the delight of the teachers, Frye responded by knocking him out cold.[75] In addition, when Frye returned to Cuba with the teachers, he clarified his reasons for planning the trip in no uncertain terms. While attending a formal reception organized by the mayor in Sagua la Grande, Frye declared that his personal goal had been to "destroy [Americans'] erroneous beliefs" regarding the cultural and intellectual fitness of Cubans for self-government. He felt that the trip to Harvard had transformed U.S. perceptions of Cubans and that this was his "greatest glory."[76]

Clearly, Frye's populist form of imperialism earned him the love and respect of thousands of Cuba's popular nationalist teachers. But it also got him fired. Indeed, General Wood eventually fired Frye for subverting U.S. imperialist goals. As Wood explained in a letter to Secretary of State Elihu Root, "[Frye] is a dangerous man in the island and his influence on the teachers and the children was in the direction of the most intense radicalism as to the future relations between Cuba and the United States."[77] However, after being forced to resign his post, Frye stole the scene from Wood once again by announcing his upcoming marriage to a Cuban teacher from Cárdenas whom he had met at Harvard.[78] As part of the announcement, Frye distributed 100,000 copies of "La Bayamesa," Cuba's (as yet) unofficial national anthem, to the students of the public schools and their parents. In explaining his gift, Frye expressed hope that his own future biracial children would proudly sing the anthem of their Cuban forefathers. Encouraging readers to be prideful of their "Latin" heritage, Frye revealed the depth of his own scorn for the attitudes of U.S. officials by predicting that one day, Cubans would turn the tables on the United States and dominate the world, just as their Roman ancestors had done.[79]

Frye's public school system demonstrated how U.S. imperialism could be both generous and self-serving. As with perhaps all hegemonic processes, Cuban teachers' participation in it proved ideologically liberating as well as structurally confining. By engaging its contradictions and exploiting them for nationalist ends, many of these teachers emerged from the marginal positions to which gender, class, and race threatened to keep them confined, becoming as they did so central players in the development of Cuba's political possibilities.

The case of Cuba's organized workers during the intervention illustrates a similar process. On the whole, the response of the interventionist government to worker activism was quite repressive. And yet, the few successes workers achieved allowed many to interpret the U.S. presence as favorable to their interests, especially in the wake of severe Spanish repression of all forms of labor activism. Just as former female patriots of the Revolution saw the expansion of opportunities for a role in a new struggle for nation after 1898, so the relative acceptability of labor rights to some interventionists created new discursive and organizational spaces for black activism. Such experiences held important implications for future popular-class agitation that addressed inequalities of race and class in the Republic. They also reinforced popular nationalists' belief that the discussion and mitigation of such inequalities stood at the center of the nation that the 1895 War was all about.

U.S. Imperial Hegemony at the Intersection of Race and Class

In January 1899, only months after the cessation of hostilities with Spain, Cuban stevedores, or dockworkers, in Cárdenas, Santa Clara province, staged their first strike of the intervention. Known as the Currency Strike (la Huelga de la

Moneda), stevedores originally took the action because they wanted payment in the higher valued U.S. dollars, in which most goods were sold during the U.S. occupation, rather than in Spanish gold. The strike ended peacefully with workers receiving a 100 percent increase in their daily wages as a result.[80] Days later, stevedores in Havana followed Santa Clara's lead and held a strike demanding not only wage increases but also overtime pay as well as double pay on holidays and night shifts. Since most if not all stevedores were black (dock work had long been a "black" profession), the incident is especially significant. The response of recently appointed local authorities was swift. Remarkably, however, a famed Cuban war veteran, rather than U.S. officials, repressed the workers by force.

General Mario Menocal, newly designated chief of Havana's police, not only swung his officers into action with clubs but actually recruited workers from among Cuban troops formerly under his command for the task of breaking the strike. Not surprisingly, the effect was electric. Popular nationalists in Florida organized a mass meeting to protest the incident. On February 24, the anniversary of the Grito de Baire, emigré workers addressed a letter to Máximo Gómez. They could scarcely contain their shock. At issue was the willingness of a former rebel commander, under the influence of imperialist officials, "[to order] his soldiers [to descend] from their high pedestal to the less than exalted role of strikebreakers."[81] So criticized were Menocal's actions around the city that at least one veteran published a manifesto in his own defense when the worker daily *El Reconcentrado* accused him of aiding the police. Saying that no patriotic Cuban could collaborate with the "police of the ferocious domination, that is of the Terror," José Cruzado y Bado signed the manifesto "I await either death or absolute independence."[82]

The force of public outcry soon combined with pragmatism to convince current governor general John Brooke that Mario Menocal should back down. Although Menocal would employ his tactics more successfully against the same workers a few weeks later, all these strikes eventually ended in the strikers' favor with revisions of the wage scale and other benefits some months later.[83] In the case of this incident, stevedores and emigré workers alike might easily have interpreted Menocal's actions as seeking to promote the interests of U.S. imperialism. Yet, as workers in the port system, their employer was the imperial state itself. Here, Menocal's attitude proved much less democratic and much more authoritarian than that of U.S. imperialists themselves. That a former revolutionary general would repress workers while a U.S. military governor protected them could not but have a confusing effect.

Furthermore, the fact that black stevedores dominated Havana's docks and that blacks played a prominent role in the leadership of the Cárdenas strike should not be overlooked. Indeed, acts of U.S. "benevolence" toward black and mixed race workers would repeat themselves in the general strike organized by Havana's bricklayers in September 1899. Described in great detail by Philip Foner elsewhere, this strike's relevance arises from the prominent leadership of two figures, both dark mulattoes: Enrique Messonier, president of the General League of Workers formed only days before, and Evaristo Estenoz, leader of Havana's bricklayers guild.[84]

Messonier had been a labor activist from Santiago whom the Spanish exiled to Key West for his revolutionary sympathies during the war. Before returning to Cuba, Messonier signed the letter that Florida emigrés sent to Máximo Gómez in order to protest Menocal's brutal behavior earlier that year.[85] Yet, while he protested its repression, Messonier chose not to support the strike and condemned the violence it was causing for "lead[ing] the country to the abyss." Like other nationalists, Messonier had adjusted his principles in relation to Cuba's new imperial context. Although other historians have interpreted the position of Messonier as a self-interested betrayal of labor, it seems probable that he feared that the escalation of the strike would provide a pretext for imperialists to prolong their stay in Cuba, perhaps indefinitely.[86]

On the other hand, Estenoz—from his jail cell in Havana—cooperated with authorities by offering to call off striking bricklayers in exchange for his freedom. Still, Estenoz did not surrender in defeat once freed. Although the strike entailed the use of repressive measures by police and the jailing of hundreds of male and female strikers, it ultimately ended with important gains for workers. In return for calling off the strike, Estenoz and other leaders managed to negotiate guarantees of an eight-hour day for the bricklayers from their employers. General Brooke then recommended that this policy be extended to the public establishments of all municipalities in order to prevent further strikes of public employees—a recommendation that was apparently carried out. As a result, Havana's bricklayers effectively became the first workers in Cuba to achieve the eight-hour day.[87]

The fact that these labor successes were achieved under the governorship of General Brooke rather than that of his militantly authoritarian successor to the same post, General Wood, is not coincidental. One can only wonder how such incidents may have contributed to President McKinley's decision to hasten Brooke's departure. Still, the importance of these examples lies in how workers translated their working-class consciousness into popular nationalist terms and how the power of that discourse forced U.S. imperialist officials to respond.

At the same time, examples of U.S. flexibility on issues of working-class politics and race were few and far between. That black Cubans experienced an intensification in the public tolerance and official sanction of racism in this period has been well documented.[88] So well known were General Wood's racism and that of U.S. officials generally that individual white Cubans sought the protection of the interventionist government when black Cubans sued them for discriminating against them in public establishments.[89] On the other hand, it is significant that black Cubans confided sufficiently in the U.S. military's stated commitment to enforcing the law that they bothered to bring such cases to trial in the first place. Further, there is evidence that whites, ostensibly opponents of Cuban independence, attempted to manipulate the racism of U.S. officials in their favor by spreading false rumors and submitting equally false reports of a black conspiracy to General Wood from the spring of 1900 to that of 1901. Hoping to incite a U.S.-sponsored repression of Cuban blacks and cast suspicion on individual revolutionaries such as Quintín Banderas, Carlos Roloff, and Juan Gualberto Gómez, one man wrote several reports to U.S. military authorities. These reports detailed how blacks—with the aid of some whites—planned to establish an all-black republic. Among his recommendations to Wood was the suggestion that he mobilize forces immediately in order to prevent disaster and that he "wipe clean" the newly organized Rural Guard of "a certain element" predisposed to committing acts of violence.[90]

In reality, such rumors and reports proved to be wild exaggerations, born of racist intentions. However, General Wood took them seriously, dispatching Rural Guard units under veteran general José de Jesús Monteagudo, the future mastermind of the military repression of black Cubans led by Evaristo Estenoz in 1912, to find evidence of any such conspiracy. Monteagudo found none, save a few minor robberies and roving bandits.[91] Yet, one can only imagine how such rumors and U.S.-sponsored intelligence missions to decipher their relevance negatively affected the psyche and perspective of Cuban blacks.

In voicing their protest to imperialist policies, many black veterans of the war understood the racial dimensions of the U.S. military occupation from the vantage point of popular nationalism. For example, in June 1900, black general Jesús Rabí and veteran officer Saturnino Lara wrote Antonio Maceo's white assistant José Miró a letter in which they expressed pain over the humiliation the Liberating Army had suffered because of the United States. For Rabí, the potential for conflict ran high. "We would be extremely proud," he pointedly stated, "to have you by our side the day that we should need you, [given our belief] that the arrival of that day is inevitable."[92] The fact that Miró was a white man who had served more closely than any other officer with the martyred and internationally known General Antonio Maceo must have figured prominently in Rabí and Lara's invitation.

Nevertheless, it is important to note that many blacks took a cooperative and engaging approach to U.S. imperialist officials. General Wood's decrees limiting the expression of African religious culture through the playing of African drums provides a case in point. Despite the fact that such decrees specifically attacked the legitimacy of African-derived culture, some blacks refused to believe that they implied outright repression. Thus, the Mutual Aid Society of African Lucumís of Our Mother of Cobre and Saint Lazarus requested a permit in order to play drums at their Sunday meetings—one which municipal mayor and veteran general Alejandro Rodríguez promptly denied.[93] Some blacks, born in Africa and brought as slaves to Cuba long after Spain banned the slave trade, asked the U.S. government to intervene on their behalf against the actions of white Cubans. Gathered under the leadership of Reverend William George Emmanuel, these Africans began a campaign in the winter of 1901 to gain U.S. sponsorship of a project to return them to Africa.[94] Later, the same group complained to Wood of another grievance. The Cuban Constitutional Assembly, Emmanuel charged, had decided to include them as citizens of Cuba—effectively nullifying their African heritage by decree—without consulting them or giving them a choice on the matter. By contrast, the proposed constitution provided Spaniards resident in Cuba the right to decide which citizenship they would hold. Not surprisingly, Emmanuel gained the full support of Cuba's most conservative pro-Spanish newspaper, *Diario de la Marina*, which published a full-page exposé on the nobleness of the African colony's enterprise.[95] Enough of these ex-slaves wanted to leave Cuba that at one point, Emmanuel signed a petition on behalf of 18,000 addressed to the government of the Congo Free State. The petition requested that they be allowed to settle in King Leopold's Congo as Belgian colonists.[96]

These examples demonstrate the diversity of reactions to U.S. imperialism that black Cubans—and Africans—represented. When it came to judging their experience through the lens of popular nationalism or, quite simply, consciousness of race, blacks in Cuba negotiated the greatest degree of freedom. Under the first U.S. military intervention, some Cubans found the way to negotiate for greater rights as workers and, in sharp contrast to their recent experience under the Spanish, managed to advance their cause. Like Cuban teachers, striking workers made the most out of a context of foreign intervention and fragmenting nationalist alliances among the Revolution's leadership. Some Cubans, such as white racists like Wood's informant or African nationalists like Emmanuel, acted on the belief that the U.S. presence benefited their interests. Others, like black workers, veteran labor activists like Estenoz, and Frye's teachers, exploited and inverted the paternalist benevolence of U.S. educational policies, interpreting their cooperation through the lens of popular nationalism. Like Magdalena Peñarredonda or Ritica Suárez del Villar, they strove to implement the particular understanding of the nation that they had derived from the war through acts of personal liberation and collective experiments in democratization. In the process, the contradictions of U.S. imperialism and, more important, the contradictory ways in which Cubans interpreted U.S. imperialism made the construction of imperialist hegemony possible from below—at least in the fractious and uncertain period from 1898 to 1902.

Thus, despite the fact that it had been the Revolution's civilian and military commanders to whom U.S. officials had first turned in order to consolidate their hold over Cuba, these groups became increasingly less central to the process of building U.S. hegemony. Seeing how quickly the structures of power were returned to the hands of foreigners undoubtedly changed the perspectives of these nationalists on the viability of their own visions of nation as well as the place of popular nationalists within them. Thus, it is perhaps not surprising that once U.S. forces initiated the process of withdrawing from the island by mandating islandwide elections for a constitutional convention, Cuban leaders attempted to re-mark the boundaries of their authority over the future of Cuba through the figure of José Martí.

Constituting a Unified Cuba: Memory and the Unifying Myth of José Martí

In November 1900, thirty-one delegates convened in Havana for the purpose of drafting a Cuban constitution. Although neither Washington nor Governor Wood gave any guarantees that the promulgation of a Cuban constitution would lead to independence, the entire process, including islandwide elections for the delegates, took place at the behest of U.S. officials. General Wood called the convention in the hope that it would produce a basis of laws for the establishment of the Republic favorable to U.S. interests. Wood and officials in Washington also hoped to stem the rising tide of frustration among Cubans and alleviate discomfort among the U.S. public in a presidential election year with the continuing ambiguity of U.S. policy. Despite Wood's efforts to "pack the convention" with pro-U.S. delegates by proposing limits on suffrage and engineering a publicity campaign to intimidate voters, the vast majority of the delegates, with few exceptions, came from the civilian, military, and emigré ranks of the Revolution. Like the municipal elections held earlier, voters seemed immune to the criteria that U.S. imperialists attempted to impose on them.[97]

Once elected, however, the susceptibility of delegates to U.S. influence proved an entirely different matter. During the four months in which the convention held sessions, concerns over how U.S. officials would respond to proposals and final votes remained constant.[98] Although delegates began their work by changing the name of the theatre in which sessions were held to "El Teatro Martí," debates quickly revealed how little ideological unity their visions of nation shared.[99] A key debate on the right of universal male suffrage, for instance, revealed the fundamental differences separating pro-imperialist nationalists like Gonzalo de Quesada from revolutionary nationalists like civilian leaders Manuel Sanguily, Salvador Cisneros Betancourt, and Juan Gualberto Gómez and their military counterparts such as General José Miguel Gómez. In the end, de Quesada and Domingo Méndez Capote, former vice president of the Republic-in-Arms, voted with the only delegate who had been a Spanish loyalist, Eliseo Giberga, against universal suffrage rights. All three felt that it would stall the modern progress of the nation.[100] During debate on the matter, the position of revolutionary nationalists was equally unequivocal. Sanguily railed at the idea that any Cuban "aristocrat" or member of the "middle class" was any more qualified than the *clases populares* or the *pueblo obrero* to vote. The spilling of blood had instilled the right of universal suffrage into the collective consciousness of Cubans, he insisted, and it could not be refused.[101]

In dealing with other issues, however, revolutionary nationalists' views seemed to splinter depending on what they thought the implications of constitutional mandates might be for the long-term prospects of independence — prospects that many recognized as laying in U.S. hands. For instance, Sanguily and José Miguel Gómez worried that universal access to primary education might not be deemed a constitutional matter but one better left to local governments to decide. Conditions for suspending constitutional guarantees and the rights of individual citizens to associate and organize were similarly problematic.[102] Whenever the issue of U.S. pressure arose, only Cisneros Betancourt argued that the U.S. position on any internal convention debate did not matter since ratification of the Constitution meant that a Cuban nation formally existed in the minds of Cubans, whether the U.S. recognized it or not. As far as he was concerned, he was "still in revolution."[103]

Although they had exchanged weapons for words, it did seem that some delegates to the convention felt they were still very much at war — this time against an enemy whose ambiguous ends and contradictory actions proved much harder to defeat. Perhaps it is not surprising, then, that when truly divisive issues such as definitions of equality and rights under the law did arise, delegates to the convention retreated into the language of social unity that had served to quell debate and disguise divisions before and during the war. In the end, no antidiscrimination clauses or references to race appeared in either the final document of the 1901 Constitution or the debates leading up to it. Article 11 simply declared Cubans "equal before the law."[104]

In early August 1901, the idea that the language of social unity could serve as both a discourse and a practice of postwar politics was put to the test. That month, a scandalous argument erupted among convention delegates. Apparently, Eliseo Giberga, the rabid hispanophile and former Autonomist who opposed independence, had attacked José Martí in a public forum. Even more horrifying, Giberga had derided Martí in the context of rejecting a proposal that all delegates voluntarily donate one peso a month to a pension fund for Martí's elderly, blind and indigent mother.[105]

The incident sent shockwaves through the pro-independence community of Havana. Immediately, former and emerging political elites struggled to take control of the situation and benefit from the fallout. Thus, *El Mundo* and *La Discusión*, Havana dailies with normally divergent political sensibilities, rushed to prove their revolutionary credentials. First, these newspapers raised donations to purchase the house in which Martí had been born for his mother, Doña Leonor Pérez. Second, they helped veteran leaders organize a banquet at the Teatro Nacional that would render homage to Martí and generate proceeds for Doña Leonor's pension fund.[106] But most significant of all were the justifications that both pro-imperialist nationalist and revolutionary nationalist leaders gave for their collective reaction.

In responding to the incident, military and civilian leaders had essentially adhered to a strict code of silence. Veteran leaders unanimously condemned Giberga's criticisms of the Revolution and its leaders outright while limiting public debate on the precise nature of those criticisms. The strategy appeared aimed at halting interrogations of the past that might illuminate the public's analysis of the revolutionary leadership's behavior and authority in the present. Fully cloaked in the myth that revolutionaries had achieved and maintained complete social unity during the war, the image of José Martí emerged for the first time at the center of political leaders' frenzied activity in their own defense.

In the days and weeks following Giberga's outburst, constitutional delegates engineered the omission of any written account of what Giberga had said from the *Diario de las sesiones de la Convención Constituyente*, an otherwise complete transcription of the convention's proposals, debates, voting record, and final deliberations. Stripping of the record took place under the watch of Méndez Capote, pro-imperialist nationalist president of the convention, and Cisneros Betancourt, initiator of the pension proposal for Martí's mother. At the same time, leading veterans outside the convention mobilized quickly to denounce Giberga and to confirm their solidarity with Cisneros Betancourt.[107] Calling themselves the Supreme Veterans' Council, twenty-two generals, lieutenants, and colonels of the Liberating Army joined civilian intellectuals to issue a manifesto. Signatories included Cisneros Betancourt, president of the Supreme Veterans' Council, as well as its officers, Juan Gualberto Gómez, General José Miguel Gómez, and even Martí's former critic General Enrique Collazo. Its terms were revealing. Ignoring the depth of discord that characterized constitutional debates over such basic issues as the popular vote and the separation of church and state, the manifesto denied any current ideological divisions among them and insisted that such divisions had played little or no role in the past, either:

> [This council] understands that it is not necessary to explain or even justify its protest, disclosing [in this way] the great merits of the immortal Apostle of Cuban independence. The whole of America, the entire civilized world, recognizes in Martí one of the greatest figures of humanity, and history when it speaks, glorifies his work as one of the highest, most exalted ever achieved by our contemporaries. . . . If in Martí, [Giberga] has intended to offend *the noble idea that he embodied*, a truly censurable act has been committed, because *the same idea* is held by those who were the auxiliaries, comrades and co-believers [*correligionarios*] of José Martí, now living representatives, disposed to defend it.[108]

Despite the words of praise the manifesto heaped on Martí, it actually said very little about him. Rather, its writers asserted Giberga's greatest crime did not lie in his attack on Martí the man but rather in the implications that his attack held for Martí as a symbol. Claiming to be "living representatives" of the "noble idea" of ideological unity, veteran leaders confirmed their authenticity as Martí's partners in blazing Cuba's heroic past and assailed any limits to their own authority in the present.

Ironically, amidst the blustering and fanfare of ex-revolutionaries-turned-politicians, Doña Leonor gained little in the way of amelioration of the economic hardships she suffered in her old age, a condition that Martí's unmarried sisters (now Doña Leonor's caretakers) were powerless to do much about. In the end, the Giberga scandal inspired returning Cuban emigrés from Florida, many of whom were cigarmakers, to complete the payments on her home (also Martí's birthplace), and she eventually began to receive a monthly pension. However, her pension apparently only amounted to twenty-four dollars annually.[109]

So why did veteran leaders make such a fuss? The answer is simple. Since Giberga was the only member of the convention to have opposed Cuban independence, his attacks on Martí represented an indictment of its future viability in the context of U.S. intervention as well as of the myth of total unity behind

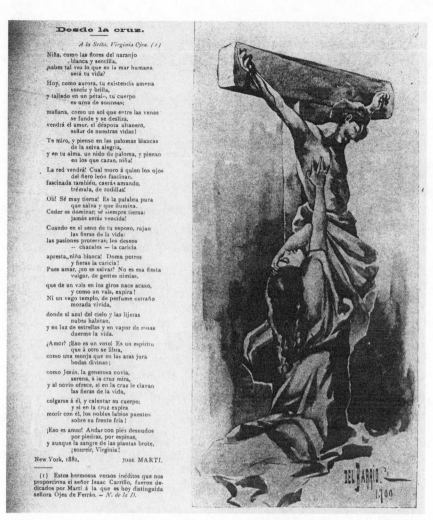

An example of the early imagery of Martí as Cuba's messiah. This image, accompanied by Martí's love poem to a young woman, features the icon of Cuba Libre, cast in the role of Mary Magdalene, weeping at his feet. (From *El Fígaro*, March 11, 1900, 111)

the cause of Cuba's sovereignty that was coming to underlie it. Standing at the fork in the shifting road to nationhood that U.S. intervention had created, the Revolution's former leaders denied their complicity and culpability in the growth of U.S. hegemony by claiming intimate affiliation with the ultimate symbol of nonconformity, José Martí. In this way, they accomplished two goals. First, they diminished current conflicts among themselves and dismissed public concerns for their future implications. Second, they mandated that the Cuban public close ranks around their leadership in the same way that they had once supposedly closed ranks behind Martí. Thus, one year before the Republic was inaugurated, manipulating history and the public's memory was already becoming standard practice for avoiding the reality of ideological conflict over the nature and direction of the nation in Cuban politics.

Conclusion

The uncertainty and triangulation of political power among revolutionary elites, the popular classes, and U.S. officials that had characterized the U.S. military did not go away with the withdrawal of U.S. forces on May 20, 1902. In fact, U.S. acceptance of the Cuban Constitution signed by convention delegates in February 1901 and the U.S. military withdrawal hinged on the convention's acceptance of the Platt Amendment. Formulated and ratified by the U.S. Congress, the Platt Amendment ensured the United States' right to intervene politically and militarily in Cuba's internal affairs whenever it deemed necessary. It also represented an insurance policy for those U.S. officials who would have preferred to continue direct domination of Cuba indefinitely. Some pro-imperialist nationalists like Estrada Palma and de Quesada apparently felt that it was the kind of compromise they had been looking for all along, an external "check" in the system that would assure that the policies of the Cuban Republic did not stray onto a socially radical path. Revolutionary nationalists were divided. Some, like Sanguily, voted to accept the amendment in order to end U.S. occupation, while others like Juan Gualberto Gómez and Cisneros Betancourt voted against it because they recognized that the Republic would be born only to live in the shadow of other, potential occupations.[110]

Both views were correct. The U.S. military occupation would probably not have ended without acceptance of the Platt Amendment. And as history has shown, the early Republic was born only to live in the amendment's shadow. Still, the origins of U.S. imperialist hegemony can be found as much in the actions of individual Cuban leaders as in popular nationalists' interpretations and engagement of the policies of imperialist agents. The fact that some Cubans found spaces within the confines of imperialist discourse and policy for expression of their ideal of nation and partial liberation would have profound consequences for the future of the Cuban Republic.

FOUR

························

From Revolution to Involution

*Conflicting Nationalisms at the
Crossroads of Race and Class*

ON MAY 20, 1902, U.S. military forces withdrew from Cuba, leaving the reins of government and nominal pledges to respect the island's national sovereignty in the hands of President Tomás Estrada Palma and his newly appointed cabinet. After nearly thirty years abroad, Estrada Palma waited until the last minute to return to Cuba, conducting his campaign for the presidency from New York and arriving in Havana only days before his inauguration. Months earlier, Governor Leonard Wood's administration had greatly facilitated Estrada Palma's chances of winning by carefully crafting a system for the registration of presidential candidates in order to drive his only real rival, the anti-Plattist revolutionary nationalist general Bartolomé Masó, from the running. Given the uncontested nature of the election, voter turnout was light.[1] Still, the election may well have ended the same way since Estrada Palma managed to reproduce in his campaign the very dynamic between himself and the public on which José Martí had relied to galvanize support for the War of 1895. That is, Estrada Palma's campaigners avoided making specific promises on issues of policy for the new republic, depending instead on his affiliation with the PRC and the invocation of Martí's tried and true discourse of social unity to gain supporters. Certainly, both Estrada Palma and Masó claimed to be the legitimate heirs of Martí.[2] However, Estrada Palma's absence from the actual scene of the election and the open nature of his appeal invited Cubans to interpret his plans for the nation on the best possible terms—their own.

In contrast, Masó illuminated with precision his ideological perspective and plans for the nation. In one of many public manifestos, Masó roundly condemned the U.S. intervention for having "threatened [Cubans'] existence as a civilized people" with its policies of generating disorder and corruption. Instead of taking advantage of the chance to reconstruct the country's wealth through state protection of its native industries, the United States had left Cuba at a greater disadvantage than when it arrived. In the future, free trade and the rebuilding of the plantation system were necessary, Masó argued, but were not to be dictated in U.S. terms. Importantly, Masó characterized the "class of color" as "the most essential factor" in Cuban society and promised blacks a central role in Cuba's political development and "public life." He also reached out to a progressive group of Spanish loyalists, the liberally democratic Autonomists, because he felt that they shared the same social ends for Cuba.[3] Finally, and perhaps most important, the Masó campaign espoused a total commitment to the repeal of the Platt Amendment and condemned any moderation on this goal as tantamount to annexationism.[4] With all these points, Salvador Cisneros Betancourt, Masó's running mate, agreed.[5]

Estrada Palma chose a different tack. Downplaying the relevance of the Platt Amendment and claiming he would replicate the social unity that Cubans had supposedly achieved during the war, Estrada Palma gained credibility among a surprising array of nationalists, all of whom could find in him what they could not in Masó: that is, the symbolic legitimation of their own nationalist concerns. In many ways, the Revolution's leaders, like Cuban voters, were faced with deciding where the greater threat to Cuba's sovereignty lay. Revolutionary nationalists like Máximo Gómez, Manuel Sanguily, and Emilio Nuñez decided that the Platt Amendment was an immediate threat but believed that a moderate government under Estrada Palma would reduce social tensions, inspire the popular classes to trust the state, and thereby eliminate the potential for another U.S. occupation.[6] Others found the greater threat in appeasement of Spanish loyalists. Thus, José Miró, Antonio Maceo's right-hand officer during the war, backed Estrada Palma because he thought that Masó was nothing but a spineless "peacock" whose reconciliation with Spanish Autonomists risked provoking Cuba's peasants and impoverished veterans into open revolt.[7] Quite different concerns led some radical labor and race activists to see Estrada Palma as the only appropriate choice. In a speech before Santiago's all-black Club "Maceo," Enrique Messonier depicted Estrada Palma as the only candidate capable of reversing the recent U.S. takeover of small holders' lands in Oriente and overturning this latest version of development based on "slavery." Urging listeners to vote for Estrada Palma because he came the closest to emulating Martí, Messonier blamed U.S. officials for instilling distrust and a form of rabid, antiblack racism among Cubans that they would otherwise not have felt. Estrada Palma, he said, would end all that.[8] Other returning emigrés campaigned for Estrada Palma in like terms, describing him as one of the "apostles of the Cuban Christ" (Martí) and a "new pine," despite the fact that both Masó and Estrada Palma's roots in the Ten Years' War had made them "old pines" by Martí's standards.[9]

Ironically, the bases on which nationalist leaders of every stripe justified their support for Estrada Palma proved mistaken on all counts. It was precisely Estrada Palma's lack of moderation, espousal of hispanophilia, advocacy of the rights of U.S. capital over native labor, and antiblack and antidemocratic policies that brought Cuban nationalists into violent confrontation and the brink of U.S. intervention, not the other way around. These rationalizations for supporting Estrada Palma's candidacy illustrate two key issues. First, they show that Cubans held fast to the memory of social unity forged during the war as the means for conserving and defending Cuban sovereignty. However, they infused it and its iconic representative, José Martí, with different meanings. Second, they demonstrate that while popular nationalists like Messonier worried about revamping the social order in terms of race and class, revolutionary nationalists like Máximo Gómez, Sanguily, and Miró focused on keeping social tensions at bay and the popular classes under control in order to prevent a second U.S. intervention.

This chapter explains how these two different approaches to understanding the role of the republican state informed political action once the goals of Estrada Palma's pro-imperialist nationalist administration became clear. Events taking place in the first years of the Republic illustrate how conflicts that had existed among nationalists long before suddenly began to flare into open conflagration. Ultimately, the Estrada Palma administration's pro-imperialist nationalist policies became the primary target of both revolutionary nationalists' and popular nationalists' rebukes. Yet, the struggle and critiques they launched against Estrada Palma's administration only brought popular nationalists and revolutionary nationalists closer together on a strategic level, not an ideological one. In that sense, the lessons that each sector drew from the past and the series of confrontations that punctuated the Estrada Palma administration in the present moved them farther apart.

Estrada Palma's administration made little or no effort to negotiate or incorporate the expectations of other nationalists. Guided by the principles of their own pro-imperialist nationalism and secure in the belief that the United States now stood behind them, Estrada Palma and his cabinet did not feel they had to do so. Rather than break with the colonial laws, social mores, or authoritarian policies of the colonial past, Cuba's first national government adopted official positions and enacted measures that built on its colonial legacies. These measures repressed civil liberties, marginalized popular-class interests, and consolidated the plantation system as the basis for a foreign-dominated capitalist economy. Fearful of losing what political control they had acquired as newly elected members of Congress, most revolutionary nationalists, whether they had opposed Estrada Palma's candidacy or not, became increasingly wary of the rising anger, frustration, and radicalism expressed by two key sectors of popular nationalists: black veterans and organized workers.

Between 1902 and 1906, Cuba's political elites moved away from revolution, defined here as the inversion of the colonial order, as a mandate for guiding and justifying their actions in the Republic. As a result of key encounters with popular nationalist forces, especially black veteran activists and striking workers, they turned increasingly toward political *involution*, the selective retrieval and incorporation of the colonial order, as the basis for political power. Analyzing battles among nationalists over issues of race and class, the following chapter shows that both revolutionary and pro-imperialist nationalists shared a common commitment to keeping their popular nationalist constituents in line and containing the pace of change through a predictable and orderly pattern of policy-making by the state. At the same time, popular nationalists sought to expand the reach of the *manigua* outside the war in a context of peace. In marches, strikes, manifestos, and an independent press, they began to defy the hostile, suspicious attitude of former revolutionary leaders by assigning a redistributive role to the state, much as soldiers had demanded from officers during the war. Moreover, they used references to such practices during the war to justify their agenda in the present. Through discourse and political action, popular nationalists strove to "decolonize" Cuban leaders of what they perceived were Hispanic- and U.S.-derived forms of thought and belief that denied them the political autonomy and right to impose their needs on the state. Indeed, the first two years of Estrada Palma's administration represent the first spin of a political cycle that would come to define interactions between national leaders in command of the state and popular nationalist activists outside it for much of the early Republic.

Using the Past to Shape the Present: Contested Claims to the Legacy of José Martí

Many Cubans inaugurated the Republic by demonstrating their willingness to engage the social and class needs of others as beneficial to the whole, much as they had done during the war. During this period, competing claims to the legacy of Martí revealed at the level of symbol and discourse what events gradually bore out. To build a future "with all and for all" as Martí had promised, Cubans had to draw lessons from the past. The fact that they drew different lessons set the stage for the political battles soon to come.

When Estrada Palma returned to Cuba shortly before his inauguration in the spring of 1902, he did so as a man who had spent nearly thirty years in exile in Europe, the United States, and Central America. No longer forced by circumstances into the less than auspicious role of schoolteacher and manager of a summer boarding house in upstate New York, Estrada Palma was anxious to gain the social acceptance and political legitimacy that had been denied him for most of his life.[10] Although he had married the daughter of a former president of Costa Rica, Estrada Palma possessed few personally charismatic traits and even fewer accoutrements of aristocratic breeding.[11] Indeed, he was not even Catholic but a convert to Quakerism, a religion alien to Cuba and associated with U.S. Anglo-Saxon culture.[12] Supporters of Estrada Palma glossed over such contradictions through a similarly contradictory image of Martí. On May 19, the anniversary of Martí's death and a day before Estrada Palma's inauguration as first president of the Republic, *La Discusión*, the conservative Havana daily owned by former SEJE member Hector de Saavedra, hailed Martí as "God's messenger on earth," who, like Estrada Palma, had learned the value of liberty from U.S. Americans: "From the coasts of the United States we were sent the inspiration of the Revolution. . . . God elected the 19th of May to harvest the life of the Apostle. America of the North chose the 20th of May to proclaim our Republic. . . . Gratitude to the land of honor and liberty: the United States!"[13]

As president of the PRC, Estrada Palma had been keenly aware of the suspicions he aroused in elite-class Cubans, largely because of his close association with Martí. Yet, he was also aware of the need to cultivate the image of intimacy with Martí in order to keep the loyalty of popular nationalists and appear interested in their concerns. Through symbolic action, Estrada Palma believed he could achieve the support of both groups. Thus, when he took charge of the first Cuban government, he acted much as he had when he had been president of the PRC. To gain the support of the popular classes, he made periodic gestures of paternal understanding backed by little if any action on their behalf. To gain the support of conservative and wealthy elites, on the other hand, he combined gestures of respect for their interests with actions meant to amalgamate their authority with his own. Estrada Palma had chosen Luis Estevez y Romero, a highly aristocratic lawyer who was also the husband of wealthy planter Marta Abreu, to be his vice president.[14] Estrada Palma's choice made him socially and politically more attractive to the very group that had benefited the most from the U.S. intervention and hoped to continue doing so from the new Cuban state: Spaniards, ex-

loyalists, and the emerging professional elite that serviced the needs of U.S. capital.[15] By comparison, Estrada Palma did little more for those who had benefited
the least from the intervention than to appropriate the symbols dearest to their
hearts. For many, the dearest was Martí.

La Lucha, Havana's most liberal and formerly Autonomist newspaper, testified to the extent of Martí's appeal, publishing a variety of articles on him that
tapped into an image of Martí that equated him not with the United States, as *La
Discusión* had, but with local conditions and revolutionaries in Cuba.[16] By acting
in ways overtly mimetic of Martí's social habits and political style, Estrada Palma
hoped to exploit this image of Martí as well, projecting himself as a representative of the people who had been spiritually anointed by Martí. For example, after
maintaining New York's black emigrés at a distance for years, Estrada Palma
invited three of them, including Rafael Serra, to accompany him aboard the ship
that returned him to Cuba. The oddity of the sight did not escape the attention
of Havana's press.[17] Upon arriving in Oriente, Estrada Palma met with delegations of teachers, visited the widow of General Calixto García, and agreed to eat
the scrawny white chickens that an impoverished revolutionary matron offered
him.[18]

Once in Havana, Estrada Palma continued to act the part of Martí, reviving
memories of him as a relentless pursuer of his worst critics. Graciously, the new
president organized meetings with political opponents, both within and outside
ex-revolutionary ranks. However, if Martí had hoped to bring his critics to the
table of compromise, Estrada Palma only wanted to bring his critics around to
his way of thinking. Meetings with former foes of the Revolution went better
than those with former colleagues. For example, the Casino Español, a social
club supported financially by the Spanish Crown and famously denounced by
Martí, visited Estrada Palma and was warmly received.[19] Principal among the ex-
revolutionaries who agreed to meet with Estrada Palma and left feeling deceived
was Salvador Cisneros Betancourt, Masó's former running mate. Apparently,
Estrada Palma's invitation had misled Cisneros Betancourt into believing that
they might actually discuss the issues of Cuba's sovereignty and the need for
social reforms. In describing their encounter to the press, Cisneros Betancourt
reported that Estrada Palma had characterized him as "radical," adding, "'You
are under a delusion Marquis, and I must [correct your impression] at once: I am
a conservative.'" To this, Cisneros Betancourt replied that he was a conservative
too—insofar as "conserving" the Revolution's goal of "absolute independence"
was concerned.[20]

By eating dinner with war widows, appearing with black activists, and holding
well-publicized meetings with former comrades-turned-political-rivals, Estrada

Palma ritualized the principles of social unity and mutual accord that were so important to the war as the symbolic foundations of his government. However, Estrada Palma appeared to forget, rather than to forgive, the differences of interest and perspective that inspired the formulation of these principles in the first place. He also ignored what social unity had meant in the practice of war: that is, negotiation and compromise for mutual gain.

One of the few surviving labor newspapers of the period, *El Proletario: Seminario Obrero Político*, represented in its editorial staff, financial contributors, and audience a significant cross-section of Cuban society whose nationalisms, both revolutionary and popular, forged a rich, historically inspired alliance. The paper's board of directors included noted members of the middle class who were doctors and lawyers as well as emigré leaders such as Dr. Juan O'Farrill, current mayor of Havana, and Dr. Fermín Valdés Domínguez, personal assistant to Máximo Gómez during the war and Martí's childhood friend. Other members of the board were skilled tradesmen such as José Domínguez, a master bricklayer; José Paredes Gómez, a painter; and Leonor Armenteros, a midwife. One of the principal editors of the paper was Carlos Baliño, founder of the first Socialist Party in Cuba and a labor activist of great renown among emigrés in Florida.[21] Although it frequently featured articles on socialist thought, the newspaper decried the idea of establishing a socialist utopia as unrealistic and problematic. In sharp contrast to anarchist newspapers such as *¡Tierra!*, most of which remained under Spanish direction, *El Proletario* encouraged native workers to forge ties with mainstream political parties so that workers' demands could be directly integrated into a pluralistic, democratic state.[22]

Moreover, the newspaper rooted its prescriptions for the state in the original party program of the PRC, of which Articles 4 and 6 flanked its title: Article 4 declared that the PRC did not intend to perpetuate in the Republic in any new form "the authoritarian spirit and bureaucratic composition of the colony" but rather to establish a new society on the "legitimate abilities of each man" and through the "order of real work and the equilibrium of social forces." Article 6 pledged to put the national treasury at the service of the most deserving of its citizens and in this way found "one fatherland, cordial and wise." According to *El Proletario*, all Cuban workers interpreted these promises as the rightful legacy of José Martí, of which they declared themselves its principal heirs and protectors:

We are in the midst of the period [of] constituting the Cuban Nationality. For that Nationality . . . the Cuban proletariat has struggled at all times. . . . Martí, . . . from the beginning, looked for the better and the greater guarantee of the success of his labor of redemption in the *humble ones.* . . .

[If] he were alive, they would not dare, as they so dare today, with inaudible effrontery . . . to proclaim—oh pitiful ones!—that the American Intervention, [had more to do with securing Cuban independence] than the efforts and sacrifices of her sons! . . . No, the Cuban proletariat cannot turn its back on its work. . . . [In the words of Martí,] "It is my work, I should not abandon it."[23]

The problem with the Republic, *El Proletario* charged, was that its leaders were no longer acting like the paternalistic caudillos that the *mambises* and revolutionary supporters had known during the war. Rather than redistribute rewards to soldiers on the basis of need and service to the founding of the country, leaders were acting like *caciques* who rewarded loyalty and obedience with personal handouts. *Caciquismo*, editors explained, was an archaic form of rule that selectively apportioned rights of political participation through social status and not merits or need. Today's state was *caciquista* precisely because Cubans had felt as if they were still being governed by Spanish "*virreyes* [viceroys]."[24] The president did not have half an hour to meet with a delegation of workers who had repeatedly solicited his attention, claimed *El Proletario*'s editors. However, "he has had more than enough time to regale archbishops and foreign millionaires with banquets." Furthermore, whenever workers have had occasion to protest their conditions, "we have been lectured on the Treaty of Paris, we have been shown that in the North there is a formidable sword raised over Cuba, a sword that cannot wait to fall and annihilate us." To this situation, *El Proletario* proposed, there could be only two solutions. One was to fight the domination of Cuba by foreign capital by seeking ties to the international labor movement. The other was to reject Estrada Palma and press alternative caudillos, the revolutionaries-turned-politicians who were now engaged in founding political parties of opposition to the state, for the sake of change. Under Estrada Palma's watch, Cuba was being ruled by self-absorbed Creole surrogates of foreign interests. Consequently, Estrada Palma's attempts to create social unity by courting the Revolution's former foes did not imitate Martí; they betrayed him.[25]

The signs of inclusion on which Estrada Palma relied to win the backing of black and lower-class Cubans ultimately proved to be nothing more than the gestures of a shallow and self-absorbed politician. Yet, the signs themselves and the ways in which Cubans interpreted them demonstrate two related ideas. First, Estrada Palma's efforts to cloak himself in the memory of Martí reveal how quickly that memory was being transformed into a myth of unity through which foundational struggles over the shape and definition of Cuban national identity were forged. Reconstructed, perhaps in equal parts, from the recollections of nationalists who knew him and expectations of those who did not, this myth circulated among popular nationalists who relied on his image to express their deeply rooted and conflicting beliefs about the nation and the state. Second, the Republic's first battles over who could legitimately claim the legacy of Martí were, symbolically, the Republic's first battles over which vision of nation was more authentically true to conflicting nationalists' memories of the Revolution and their respective image of Martí. For many popular nationalists, marginalized sectors were the most authentic representatives of the nation they had conceived during the war and, consequently, the most deserving constituents of the state.

Importantly, *El Proletario*'s editors offered the Revolution's emerging political elites the opportunity for engagement and negotiation. That is, they sought to remind revolutionaries-turned-politicians that, from their perspective, the state's purpose was to institutionalize the values of the Revolution's liberated zones. There, the economic rules and social conventions of the colony had been subverted by the need to maintain the fluidity and integrity of the community as a whole. In the coming months, black veterans and workers transformed the vision of the nation they had developed in the revolutionary struggle and cultivated during the U.S. intervention through the exchange and interpretation of memories of the war into a political plan of action. The result was direct confrontation among nationalists over the role and nature of the state.

Race, Nation, and a Hispanophile State: The Veterans' Movement of 1902

During the first year of the Republic, the state employed a discourse of social unity that silenced issues of race with blatantly discriminatory hiring policies for positions in the public sector such as the army, Rural Guard, and police. Because applications for government jobs required high educational qualifications and social references (both standards to which only a tiny number of black Cubans could have aspired), government posts were disproportionately allocated to Spaniards and former opponents of the Revolution. Many black Cubans who worked in government offices did so as messengers and office boys. Some areas of government, such as the diplomatic corps, were entirely limited to whites. Over twice as many Spaniards worked for the Estrada Palma government as blacks.[26] Moreover, even when black Cubans were hired, their reception by public employees of the same division was not necessarily tolerant. Nor, it seemed, did the state require it to be.[27]

Reasons for this had to do with the nature of the nationalism guiding the new republican state. After four years of U.S. military rule, the "pro-imperialist" components of the nationalism Estrada Palma and his allies espoused no longer derived exclusively from the emigré values of U.S. culture and society that they had developed and articulated in exile. Rather, they increasingly reflected a pro-Spanish sensibility that promised to improve upon colonial legacies by adapting them to a U.S.-inspired modernizing mold.

Upon taking office, Estrada Palma moved immediately to install the old civilian leadership of conservative emigrés who had organized the war effort in the United States as the core of his cabinet. He also reserved key cabinet positions, including the Minister of the Department of Governance, Finance, and Justice, for the primary leaders of the pro-Spanish Autonomist Party—all former enemies of Cuban independence and proponents of a Hispanic identity for Cuba.[28] In courting Spanish loyalists, Estrada Palma confirmed a pattern of appointments and a style of government instituted by the U.S. military over the previous four years. Estrada Palma, however, was not merely imitating U.S. strategies of co-opting Spanish loyalists. Long before the U.S. intervened in Cuba in 1898, Estrada Palma had already calculated the benefits of including Spaniards in state priorities. In official reports to the Republic-in-Arms and private letters, Estrada Palma had often cited Spanish immigrants as the sole conduits of the values of hard work and personal initiative amidst a sea of (apparently) lazy Cubans.[29] After 1902, Estrada Palma's inclusion of Spaniards came at the cost of excluding Cubans of African descent.

Oriente's representative to Congress, Antonio Póveda de Ferrer, made precisely this point when he wrote Estrada Palma to demand that he confine his appointments to Cubans who had favored independence. Moreover, Póveda de Ferrer insisted that the government standardize the language with which all citizens were addressed by authorities of the state in line with the 1895 Revolution's policy of eliminating all forms of racial labeling in documentation and public discourse of the Liberating Army. The Republic's unexpected return to Spanish colonial styles for addressing citizens by their racial identities, Póveda de Ferrer wrote,

> deeply disgusts and humiliates the social classes who deserve and have a perfect right to demand that they be treated with all due respect. We are living under the command of a democratic Constitution that does not establish privileges of any kind among the diverse members of the Cuban family. Mr. President, in order to suppress this aged and undignified practice, a bottomless source of definite bitterness for mulattos and blacks, there are reasons of internal politics, of moral order and of patriotic convenience

that doubtlessly, should be evident to a just and good soul as yours, Mr. President.[30]

The recovery of racial labeling as a state and, therefore, a societal norm signified the ideological and discursive involution that Estrada Palma's pro-imperialist nationalist state promoted in its attempts to recast revolutionary Cuba along culturally Hispanic and racially ordered lines. It also paralleled similar policies of the U.S. military's interventionist government under Governor Wood. In 1900, a delegation of Cubans had presented Governor Wood with a similar petition, asking him to decree the prohibition of racial epithets in public discourse and documents. Like Póveda de Ferrer, petitioners proposed that the term "citizen" should be employed instead, because Cuba's "colored race has already proved its value and capability." Convinced that Cuban blacks would rebel and establish another "Hayti" if encouraged to forget their "racial condition" and believe in their social worth and equality, Wood had ignored the petition.[31]

Unlike Wood's petitioners, Póveda de Ferrer had not included in his letter to Estrada Palma the explanation that Cubans of African descent were entitled to legal equality with whites because of their service on behalf of independence. Since he was addressing a fellow revolutionary, he probably believed he did not have to. And yet, events in 1902 quickly proved the weakness of this logic. Given Estrada Palma's history of appeasing racist pro-imperialist nationalist emigrés during the 1895 War in return for their support, his rejection of the need to enforce the discourse of raceless and classless social unity in the Republic is not surprising. As he did during his tenure as president of the PRC, Estrada Palma seemed to take black activists' toleration of his concessions to conservative elites for granted.

In both the 1900 and 1902 cases, black veterans protested the orientation of public policy away from wartime revolutionary norms—norms they interpreted as actively subverting the legitimacy of the Spanish colonial past. For them, the fact that both the U.S. military and Cuba's first independent state endorsed a hierarchical structuring of Cuban society along traditional racial lines was nothing short of alarming. From its inception in the spring of 1902, increasing parallels in the policies of the U.S. and Estrada Palma administrations began to cast the latter's historic motivations in a new light. His actions as well as inaction on a number of racial issues led many popular nationalist black veterans to conclude that Estrada Palma was not building the socially just nation for which they had fought but was rebuilding the Spanish colony that they had toppled.

Consequently, as soon as the U.S. military withdrew its forces, black veterans demanded state action to correct the social disadvantages that Cuba's colonial past conferred on blacks. Pro-imperialist nationalists justified state inaction using the reverse logic: that is, they insisted that a colonial past no longer existed since blacks had freed themselves of it by securing Cuba's freedom. "In Free Cuba," the president declared, "we are now all of the same color." This meant that candidates for civil service would be evaluated on their "merits," just as Martí had promised. But merits, as Estrada Palma defined them, meant that Cubans were employed "according to their capacity." Fulfilling the duties of civil service in a civilized government required educational training and the "higher" cultural values of white, elite society that, in his view and, by default, the view of his subordinates, most black Cubans lacked.[32]

To black veterans, on the other hand, "merits" implied proof of prior service to the nation as a prerequisite to the employment security that the state offered in contrast to the wider economy.[33] Estrada Palma's failure to honor such service and to require social and educational standards beyond the reach of most veterans implied a betrayal of the latter's interpretation of the nation. From his perspective, however, Estrada Palma was simply putting into practice pro-imperialist nationalists' own conflicting view. Indeed, many veterans felt doubly discriminated against: first, for their African heritage and the educational differential that it necessarily implied; and second, for being forced to compete for jobs with former enemies of the Revolution in a government that owed its existence to patriots like themselves. By the summer of 1902, black veterans expressed their already mounting frustration with what they perceived as the state's ideological betrayal of the nation in a campaign that drew attention to the irony of their plight.

In June 1902, a group of black veterans requested an audience with the president and his new cabinet to lay out their grievances and explain the relationship between race and nation as they saw it. For this task, nine black mutual aid societies led by the prominent popular nationalist veteran General Generoso Campos Marquetti organized a commission that eventually met with Estrada Palma for two hours. Campos Marquetti criticized the hiring process for government jobs, singling out Havana's police force as especially symbolic. Significantly, though, Campos Marquetti did not embrace the validity of political patronage as an end in itself that other revolutionary nationalist leaders offered as a counter to Estrada Palma's laissez-faire rule. The only Cubans of color who held government jobs did so at the behest of Juan Gualberto Gómez (one of two mulatto congressmen), he recognized.[34] Reliance on the generosity of an individual caudillo did not resolve the fundamental problem at hand: how to enforce the idea of racial equality as a hallmark of the Republic and an unconditional principle of the state. This view—that the building of a nation required participation from below in order to ensure a rupture with the old colonial order—distinguished popular nationalist veteran leaders like Evaristo Estenoz and Campos Marquetti from their revolutionary nationalist counterparts.

Campos Marquetti later explained to reporters how he and Estrada Palma had come to loggerheads in the course of the meeting over what a nation founded on equality and democracy meant for state policy regarding race. Campos Marquetti asserted that the state needed actively to champion the interests of black veterans, without whom the Revolution would not have been possible. In contrast, Estrada Palma countered that to make such a claim on racial grounds was to betray the raceless basis on which the Revolution had been founded. As Campos Marquetti explained, "We went to the president to ask that he put the Eleventh Article of the Constitution [guaranteeing the equality of all Cubans] into practice and he tells us that our requests are inconvenient; we ask that the Republic might be established on a foundation of democracy and he responds that we are racists. We ask for access to public employment and the Chief of Police denounces as liars those who have not committed such a crime."[35] In response, Campos Marquetti concluded, "The truth is, Mr. President, this is not what we expected from the Revolution and things cannot continue like this."[36]

Three days later, a second commission of black Cubans, this time comprised entirely of veterans, met with the president. Significantly, the commission's primary representative was Colonel Evaristo Estenoz, the black labor leader responsible for negotiating an end to Havana's 1899 General Strike and winning management's consent to an eight-hour day for his union. Like Campos Marquetti, Estenoz articulated the frustration of veterans of color with the attitudes of pro-imperialist nationalist state officials who cloaked their favoritism of whites in the mantle of Martí. Commission delegates reiterated Campos Marquetti's view that a system of political patronage that admitted blacks to its ranks on the basis of convenience and tokenism was not democratic and most certainly not a goal for which they had fought. Such a system only used blacks while it ensured their continual denial of equal opportunity under the law.[37] The fact that Estrada Palma interpreted this policy of tokenism as ideologically true to the Revolution's own tenets and practices especially angered these veterans. They wanted Estrada Palma to admit publicly the fitness of black Cubans for state jobs, whether or not they met the cultural standards that former colonial elites expected. As racially conscious activists who had joined the Revolution to promote the interests of blacks and see them integrated into the republican system of power, popular nationalists like Estenoz could not reinterpret the Revolution that they themselves had experienced in Estrada Palma's hispanophile and hispanocentric terms. Essentially, Estrada Palma's recalcitrance on racially discriminatory issues asked them to do precisely this—forsake their interpretation and their own memories of the Revolution for his.

Importantly, many revolutionary nationalist leaders were equally critical of Estrada Palma's continuation of policies established under U.S. rule and his preferential treatment of Spaniards. Like black veteran activists, these leaders condemned Estrada Palma and his pro-imperialist nationalist cabinet in the name of Martí. However, as Bartolomé Masó had done earlier, they saw the greater threat in the reaction that Estrada Palma's policies might provoke in the masses and the response the United States would take as a result. In 1902, Liberals such as Juan Gualberto Gómez denounced the complicity of Estrada Palma for "deviating" from Martí's plan to establish a republic that was "eminently Latin, born without any obligation to our Saxon neighbors and . . . principally [founded] in solidarity with Spanish America." However, Gómez saw all Cubans who put sectoral interests above the U.S. threat to sovereignty as culpable of betrayal. If they did not "return to practicing the doctrines and observing the methods of the Apostle," he warned, "his project shall never be fulfilled" and upon the "apathetic, cowards and villains" would fall the "eternal damnation of history."[38] Similarly, in a speech commemorating the Grito de Baire of February 24, 1902, at the Teatro Martí, the future Liberal leader Mario García Kohly expressed similar sentiments, warning that Cubans who put self-interest before social unity would sell their souls to the devil. The United States, the "Mephistopheles of Cuban patriotism and honor" who cowered before a portrait of José Martí, was the devil figure in Goethe's drama *Faust*.[39] As their actions later bore out, these leaders' antipathy for Estrada Palma's pro-imperialist nationalist values did not translate into sympathy for those most affected by them, poor black veterans and working-class popular nationalists.

In many ways, pro-imperialist nationalists' attitude toward the demands and viewpoint of black veterans found its ultimate expression in the case of General Quintín Banderas. A veteran of all three wars for independence, Banderas had been stripped of his rank of general near the end of the War of 1895 for acts of sexual license, despite comparable behavior on the part of white officers who were not similarly tried. Poor, landless, unemployed, and semiliterate, Banderas turned to friends in Congress for a job but was offered only the humble position of gatekeeper at the House of Representatives. Subsequently, Banderas appealed to Estrada Palma for a monthly pension that would allow him to retire with honor. In response, the president sent over a personal donation of five dollars with his assistant. Banderas made no secret of the disgust and horror with which he greeted this act. In a curt letter to Estrada Palma, he wrote, "In reply to the pittance [*limosna*] that you pretended to give me, sending over with your assistant a five dollar bill on the day I personally solicited a destiny from you, in accordance with my aptitudes, in the Republic over which you preside and to which I have contributed in establishing with the sacrifice of my whole life, [an act] which I shall never regret; I enclose a card which confirms the profession by which I provide bread for my family, given to me by a foreign commercial establishment." The business card read "Quintín Banderas. Division General of the L[iberating] A[rmy]. Chief of the Propaganda Department of the House of Crusellas Bros., & Co. Makers of Soap."[40] Rejected by the new national government, Banderas had found work in a Spanish-owned business as a public relations agent. The irony could not have been lost on anyone, including Estrada Palma. Clearly convinced that his merits qualified him for a job and treatment as an equal, Banderas insisted, "Rather than being children, we are men and with dignity."[41]

Banderas's attitude speaks to the desperate frustration that black veteran activists felt. How was it possible for a fellow revolutionary to deny them the dignity that they deserved and at the same time honor the Revolution's former enemies? The answer lay in the very different kind of nation that Estrada Palma and his supporters had imagined and now attempted to enforce. Conflict quickly spilled into confrontation. A few weeks after the black veterans' commission met with the president, the newly organized Association of Veterans of Color summoned black Cubans of various political and social persuasions to a historic meeting at Havana's Teatro Albisu in order to discuss possible strategies of response to the state's inaction on racial and veterans' issues.[42] Representative Juan Gualberto Gómez served as moderator, but conspicuously absent was Martín Morúa Delgado, the only nonwhite member of the Senate, a staunch supporter (at the time) of Estrada Palma and a former factory reader among emigré tobacco workers in Florida. Having opposed the veterans' movement altogether, Morúa Delgado declared the meeting counter to the goals of the Revolution and refused to attend.[43] While much spirited debate dominated the session, Gómez's concluding speech summarized the tone and course of action that he and most other revolutionary nationalist leaders of the liberal opposition—both white and black—would adopt.

His message was ironic, for it combined items stipulated in the PRC's Manifesto of Montecristi with the strategy Martí had used to refute Spanish claims about black rebels meant to discredit the Revolution. These claims characterized the independence struggle as nothing more than a glorified race war, meant to establish another Haitian-style "black republic."[44] Rather than admit that continuing feelings of racial prejudice against blacks were a problem that neither the Revolution nor emerging political elites had resolved, Gómez blamed U.S.

influence for any displays of racial hatred against blacks.[45] Gómez did not see the Revolution's policy of silencing race and the continued subsuming of racial identities under the rubric of *cubanidad* in the Republic as problematic. Consistent with his espousal of racelessness as a tenet of revolutionary nationalism during the war, Gómez scorned the view that ignoring race as a factor in apparent social inequalities and discrimination could only ensure its perpetuation. "If one day," he warned, "—may it never come—the black race here needs to battle with the white, whether provoked or unprovoked, you will have to look for another man to advise you and guide you. Because I represent the politics of racial fraternity, and if this were to fail, the feeling of honor, the respect which I owe my past . . . would oblige me to disappear from the political scene, with the failure of my opinions."[46]

By contrast, popular nationalists of less prestige and no position in government office like Campos Marquetti and Estenoz recognized that silencing race could reinforce rather than eliminate race prejudice. Cuba's context had radically changed since the Revolution. No longer did wartime conditions require leaders to respond to the needs of constituents and no longer would mutual dependence prompt people to hide their differences for the sake of unity. For popular nationalists, calls for social unity now meant calls for active negotiation, not obedience to leaders' commands or the receiving of handouts along the way. Black veterans now demanded the systematic, not pragmatic, redistribution of wealth and power as a policy for remaking the old order. And they did so with the knowledge that they had made the state possible in the first place.

However, as Juan Gualberto Gómez's attitude showed, they faced a bitter reality. When deployed by the Revolution's former leaders, the very features that had once made the raceless discourse of social unity and the image of Martí that championed it liberating to blacks during the war now worked to confine them. Both pro-imperialist and revolutionary nationalists were stuck in the past. The premise for inclusion that ensured black participation in the independence struggle as ostensibly equal citizens now served to justify continuing state discrimination against blacks. When transferred from guerrilla war to republican reality, the ideal of racial fraternity that Martí and other leaders had once championed as a way of including blacks and discussing their historic condition as the foundation of social unity behind the Revolution now took on a different role. The ideal of racial fraternity as the key to social unity in the Republic was nothing more than a discursive substitute for policy changes that would have addressed the historical legacies of slavery and altered the social order in order to ensure black inclusion in the new system of power.

The question of why Gómez and Morúa Delgado did not see this can be partially answered by considering their views on the relationship between race and nation. As revolutionary nationalists with long personal histories of working for the expansion of opportunities for blacks under Spanish rule, Gómez and Morúa Delgado were committed to pursuing the social transformation and unification of their society in terms of race.[47] Seeing Cuba's sovereignty under constant external threat from the United States, Gómez felt that any public airing of political divisions over issues as historically heated as race could end Cuba's chances for independence—just as they had ended them before, in Cuba's first two independence wars. Moreover, by acting on their own and eschewing his advice in their meetings with the president, veteran activists circumvented his authority as an authentic founder and defender of the nation. They also, therefore, betrayed the principles of revolutionary nationalist nation that he derived from the war and to which he continued to be true.

Like Gómez, Morúa Delgado long believed in education and the cultural integration of Cubans of African descent to the racially white, literate, and European-derived culture of the elite.[48] Gómez (like Martí) was a cultural chauvinist who believed that all black Cubans' "inferiority" derived from their limited access to higher, European cultures. For Gómez, the Spanish colonial practice of distinguishing blacks and mulattoes was an artificial barrier that promoted white supremacy and prevented the advancement of the "people of color" as a whole. Morúa Delgado, however, continued to espouse the belief that blacks were a separate race from mulattoes. Perhaps because he was a darker mulatto than the French-educated Gómez, Morúa Delgado's social origins as the son of a Spaniard and a black slave forced him to work much harder to earn acceptance in white society. Thus, he proved reluctant to share power or lower the standards of acceptability set by white society that he had himself met in order to advance the interests of uneducated blacks whose cultural "crudeness" he found embarrassing.[49]

Yet, despite Gómez's and Morúa Delgado's radically distinct perspectives on race, they both came down on the same side when it came to judging the validity of black veterans' appeals. The irony of their unexpected alliance shows the depth to which both committed to a particular definition of what social unity meant and how to achieve it. Social unity for them required blacks to silence the origins of their injustices in racial discrimination, past and present. Both rejected the use of overt racial discourse in the Republic and consequently rejected the right of popular nationalist black veterans to define the nation for themselves and on their own terms.

In the end, Estrada Palma adopted an opportunistic attitude toward the appalling economic circumstances of the majority of black veterans. Abandoning

Havana at the height of black veterans' street demonstrations in the late summer of 1902, Estrada Palma traveled to his former home in Oriente to demonstrate his goodwill and ongoing relationships with other "loyal" blacks. During the visit, Estrada Palma rewarded select black officers who had *not* publicly criticized his administration or lent any support to the black veterans' movement with government jobs.[50] These were men who did not contradict Estrada Palma's vision of a nation led and shaped by white men like himself. Only when angry veterans threatened a revolt did Estrada Palma's administration finally permit the payment of war claims. Once again, the greatest beneficiaries were black loyalists who later repaid his favoritism by endorsing Estrada Palma's conservative "Moderate" Party, founded in 1904.[51] Unfortunately, the indemnities were too little too late for the thousands of veterans who had resorted to selling their claims to speculators and now faced excessive debts.[52] Moreover, veterans in some areas were so poor that they could not even afford to travel to submit their claims to municipal governments.[53] Thus, in ways not unlike his revolutionary nationalist opponents, Estrada Palma showed how much he prized submission to authority as the principal criteria for granting rewards.

In the early months of the Republic, the treatment of black veteran activists crystallized the political intransigence for which the pro-imperialist nationalist state would become best known. For their own reasons, revolutionary nationalists responded to the veterans with either passivity or outright hostility. Popular nationalists found themselves alone in their struggle for practical, structural change.

A short time later, Estrada Palma reinforced the implications of his confrontation with veterans by demonstrating in symbolic ways his commitment to the task of re-Hispanicizing and modernizing the identity of Cubans through the state. On November 10, 1902, nearly 10,000 Cubans—most of them rural peasants—planned a march through the streets of Havana to protest Estrada Palma's decision to continue the ban on cockfights and related forms of gambling that the U.S. military had imposed.[54] The next day, Juan O'Farrill, Havana's mayor and former Florida emigré and member of *El Proletario*'s board of directors, bowed to pressures from the national government. He prohibited all shoe-shiners who did not own chairs from exercising their trade. O'Farrill justified the decree with the contention that shoe-shiners (many of whom were minors) were failing to improve themselves and society by attending school. "On the contrary," the decree observed, "they cause damage to the culture of the country."[55] To this series of blatantly anti-working-class measures, Estrada Palma's administration added a number of antiblack actions.

On the same day, the only black member of the Secret Police guarding the

Presidential Palace received a letter from Estrada Palma's office. In light of a reception to be held there the following night, the letter stipulated that "the watchman for the night be a white person." The black detective, whose superiors had judged his job performance as impeccable until then, was understandably outraged.[56] Moreover, it was this same presidential reception that mulatto senator Martín Morúa Delgado declined to attend since Estrada Palma had neglected to invite his dark-skinned wife and daughters.[57] Significantly, black revolutionary nationalist leaders responded differently to these incidents than they had to veterans' demands for critical changes to state policies. In fact, their outraged reaction proved the start of a pattern: whenever pro-imperialist nationalists' actions undermined or contradicted the authority of revolutionary nationalists, the latter violated the criteria they set up for popular nationalists to follow in the name of social unity. In this case, Juan Gualberto Gómez invoked an overtly racial discourse in his interpretation of social unity and Martí—an act he had just attacked popular nationalist blacks for doing. Apparently, his greater power and authority gave him, and not those he viewed as clients, the right to do so. From the pages of *La República Cubana*, Gómez issued his response: "Is this in accordance with the doctrines of Martí, with the creed of the Revolutionary Party, with the democratic ideas for the triumph for which white and black heroes fought side by side? . . . We appeal to all sincere and dispassionate people. Is this right? . . . Is it right that in the Cuban *patria* which we all made together, colored men may only enter the Palace of the President as servants?"[58]

However, shared outrage over the extremes of Estrada Palma's hispanophilia seems to have overshadowed the irony of Gómez's response. In a final insult to revolutionary and popular nationalists alike, the presidential reception had culminated in the honorary bestowal of Asturian nationality on Estrada Palma by a group of his invited guests. Flabbergasted, editors for the liberal daily *La Lucha* sarcastically hailed him: "Long live the grandiose bash of Don Tomás! And long live as well the honorary Asturian!"[59] Indeed, the act represented an obvious affront to the suffering and honor of those who had fought in Cuba's thirty-year struggle against Spain. It also highlighted the contrast between the pro-imperialist nationalist view of the elements constituting "Cuban" identity and those of other nationalists. But Estrada Palma's acceptance of Asturian citizenship also carried a weighty message of implicit racism against people of African descent. Historically, Asturias was the only province of Spain never entirely conquered and governed by the darker-skinned Moors who invaded and ruled Iberia for 700 years prior to 1492. For this reason, the prince or princess of Asturias traditionally retained a preferential right of accession to the national crown of Spain.[60] Estrada Palma and his guests apparently found such implications flattering. Despite his

Creole pedigree and the fact that he had spent most of his adult life in the United States rather than Cuba, Spanish residents had symbolically admitted him to their historically noble and racially "pure" ranks.

By late November 1902, both pro-imperialist nationalist and revolutionary nationalist elites confronted a movement of social protest unlike any they had seen since before the war. Led by black and white cigarmakers, many of whom had formed the core of working-class supporters of the PRC and the Revolution from exile in Florida, a general strike paralyzed Havana and shook the foundations of Cuba's political economy. Importantly, the strikers' demands did not center on wages but rather on the practical implications of a Republic founded on the increasingly contested ideal of racial fraternity as the foundation of social unity as the Revolution's political leaders actively defined it. The course of the strike and the ire it aroused dramatized the preoccupation of Cuba's popular classes with the fate of the nation they still hoped to achieve as well as the anxiety with which former revolutionary leaders perceived that nation. As had occurred during the black veterans' movement, neither pro-imperialist nor revolutionary nationalist leaders sanctioned popular nationalists' demands for structural change. Although the latter expressed sympathy for their cause, they bristled at the strikers' brash displays of autonomy. Estrada Palma's administration rejected both the nature and content of strikers' demands.

Worker Defiance and Political Recalcitrance in the General Strike of 1902

On the same night that Estrada Palma accepted honorary membership in the crème de la crème of Spanish society, the Central Committee of Enrique Messonier's General League of Workers held an organizational meeting to prepare to strike.[61] Led by cigarmakers from factories owned by the Havana Commercial Company, a U.S. trust, these men and women readied themselves for a protracted struggle. Their main grievance was not pay. Rather, strikers hoped to define national interests in working-class terms and gain the right to organize for the protection of those interests. Specifically, strikers sought to elect factory commissions whose authority would be recognized by management. Because they were paid by the piece and had a greater knowledge of the quality of materials with which they worked than their employers, cigarmakers also wanted to be included in the pricing process for cigars currently set by management. Most important, cigarmakers wanted the Havana Commercial Company to guarantee that Cuban children would be admitted to the factories' apprenticeship programs in the cigar trade at all levels, without distinction of race or ethnicity.

In what was emerging as a general pattern, first under the U.S. military and then under Estrada Palma's administration, Spaniards enjoyed preferential treatment over Cubans in the U.S.-dominated cigar industry. U.S. factory owners believed the Spanish to be of purer race and therefore capable of superior, more efficient work. Whereas in other sectors of the economy, white Cubans seemed unwilling to side with black Cubans over the preferential hiring of Spaniards, Cuban workers in the cigar industry operated quite differently. According to census figures for this period, nearly half of all native cigarmakers identified themselves as Cubans of color.[62] Indeed, distinctions among cigarmakers were not based so much on race (as defined by the combination of biology, phenotype, culture, education, and wealth, as tended to be the case when Cubans at large made distinctions among themselves) as on nationality. Thus, what one U.S. labor analyst called "an element of race antagonism" between Spanish and Cuban cigarmakers, both black and white, may more accurately have been understood as an ideological and historical divide. Key players in Cuba's independence struggle and members of Martí's popular base for the PRC, Cuban cigarmakers saw themselves as guardians of its ideals. In the Republic, they institutionalized their difference from Spaniards, former enemies of independence, by forming their own multiracial unions within the same industry and even the same factories.[63] Using the idiom of nation and the right of access to its resources, strikers cajoled, intimidated, and challenged workers of other sectors of the economy to join their strike or become "traitors."[64]

Popular nationalist interpretations of Martí's ideals of racial fraternity and social unity among Cubans lay at the heart of strikers' demands. At first, sympathy for the strike transcended class, national, and nationalist boundaries. Many of Havana's doctors and pharmacists offered their services to strikers free of charge, and the Cubans who remained in Florida's emigré communities sent $1,100 in supplemental strike funds.[65] Strikers requested and gained the support of revolutionary nationalists close to Martí such as Fermín Valdés Domínguez. Eventually, a wave of sympathy strikes paralyzed the regional economy, encompassing such diverse sectors as the Department of Public Works, sixty tobacco factories in three cities, breadbakers, and the city's typographers, along with college students at the National University of Havana. The notoriously all-black Bahía dockworkers also lent their support. Their strike under U.S. occupation in December 1899 had been brutally repressed by pro-imperialist nationalist ex-revolutionaries serving as a police force. Havana's bricklayers union, led by black veteran activist Evaristo Estenoz, also supported the strike. For his part, Estrada Palma initially countered news of the strike by attending a gala dinner for Cuban consuls at the Casino Español. When asked for his opinion on current events,

Estrada Palma declared himself "optimistic," adding that "the situation could not be more satisfactory."[66]

Three days later, violence between strikers and police erupted on the streets of the capital. When one worker resisted arrest, police armed with billy clubs began attacking the crowd along the wide, central boulevard of Galiano. Chief of Police Rafael Cárdenas fled the scene in order to gain Mayor O'Farrill's approval for the use of force against the strikers. Returning from the mayor's office with what he understood to be carte blanche approval for repressive measures if the strikers did not disperse, Cárdenas apparently tried tactics of persuasion first, inviting one striker to use his coach as a platform from which to appeal for calm from the crowd. The latter, however, responded by showering the coach with insults and a hail of rocks.[67] In response, Cárdenas ordered his force of mounted police to attack the crowd and disperse them at all cost. The resulting battle between strikers and police lasted three hours.[68]

However, Cárdenas had miscalculated the political momentum building in favor of, rather than against, the strikers. Initially at least, some revolutionary nationalists took the opportunity to express their hostility toward the hispano-phile policies of the Estrada Palma government by siding with the strikers. With tensions on the street rising, the coalition holding the political majority in the House of Representatives, a group called the National Convention, or Nacionales (later, the core of the Liberal Party), adopted a resolution favoring the strikers' demand for open apprenticeships.[69] O'Farrill positioned himself as an objective mediator by meeting with factory owners at the same time that police clashed with demonstrators. But Cárdenas's brutality caught the mayor off-guard. After learning of police excesses, O'Farrill telephoned station headquarters to order the release of five workers unjustifiably detained. He also ordered that his office be contacted in case of further workers' arrests "for acts of violence, insults, disobedience or analogous offenses."[70] Finally, he issued Cárdenas's suspension. In his place, O'Farrill appointed a new chief of police, José Ugarte. Cárdenas, in turn, presented his complaints to the receptive ear of President Estrada Palma.[71]

In the meantime, O'Farrill continued to pursue the path of mediation, in line with his commitments to the revolutionary nationalism he had come to espouse among emigrés in Florida.[72] Then, a mutual desire for independence and nation-hood, however differently defined, had united them against Spanish factory-owners. O'Farrill was convinced that he could make something similar happen now. Addressing the Cuban Congress in a written appeal, O'Farrill explained the justness of the workers' demands regarding open apprenticeships for Cuban children. Those who controlled the tobacco industry, he argued, had acquired their monopoly through colonial privilege. Today, they sought to maintain that privilege by keeping Cubans out of their own national industry. "Do the men and children who were born across the sea, in foreign and far distant countries, have more right to enjoy the benefits of this country, to develop its wealth, to take part in all the manifestations of its social and political life, than those . . . whose fathers conquered the liberty of this country with their heroic sacrifice?" he asked. "Of course not. History and nature are opposed to it; equity and science forbid it."[73] O'Farrill's arguments subsequently inspired Senator Morúa Delgado to propose a bill that would have required the preferential hiring of Cubans in all sectors of the economy irrespective of race.[74]

But as usual, Congress was exceptionally slow to act. Just outside its halls, in the center of Havana, tensions rose by the minute. For having personally "insulted" police officers charged with maintaining public order, twenty-four strikers were arrested on November 20. In turn, Mayor O'Farrill decreed the release of sixteen strikers arrested on similar grounds the previous day.[75] The next day, at the National University, college students joined strikers in jeering and pelting nonstriking laborers of the Department of Public Works with rocks. At the same time, all municipal police captains declared their loyalty to Cárdenas and pledged to continue his policies. The latest adherents to the strike included guilds of bakers and carpenters. The city's public waste employees considered joining the movement as well.[76] Indeed, even the anarchist labor press, long dominated by Spanish workers, took advantage of cigarmakers' radicalism to call for an all-out war against capital. Under the headline "War without Quarter! To Blood and Fire!," *El Reconcentrado* incited workers, "For honor! For dignity! . . . The struggle between capital and labor is at hand."[77]

Aimed at paralyzing the city economically and socially, these tactics and threats put pressure on political authorities to force recognition of strikers' demands and a settlement with management. The pressure was both practical and ideological. Mayor O'Farrill's sympathy for strikers and their right to demonstrate provides clear evidence of its efficacy. However, in the process of the strike, participants gained confidence in the democratic process that characterized the nightly meetings at Teatro Cuba and the public decision-making in which strikers and labor leaders jointly engaged. The success of this small, local, and grassroots democracy only encouraged a loss of faith in the tentative, bureaucratic nature of that constituted under the state. If unanimity of voice and action could be achieved among workers of such diverse trades and interests, why did they need anyone to fight their battles for them? If politicians wanted to help them, they could force management to deal directly with the strike's Central Committee on terms of equality and cordiality. As support for this attitude grew among strikers, they became increasingly critical of the paternal benevolence that revolutionary nationalist leaders wanted to bestow on them. Not surprisingly, perhaps, the strikers' autonomy and sense of entitlement regarding their right to impose their interests on the state earned them the same rebuke from revolutionary nationalist circles that the actions of black veterans had.

By November 22, O'Farrill announced that the Central Committee no longer wished to consider his proposals for mediation. Apparently, strikers wanted plant owners to meet directly with the committee and thereby recognize it as a duly constituted authority of labor. This they refused to do, a refusal facilitated by the insistence of Mayor O'Farrill that he and not the workers' representatives oversee the process of exchange. Later, O'Farrill would claim that it was the "tumultuous" character of the strikers' behavior that forced him to resign as mediator.[78]

O'Farrill's withdrawal from the negotiations marked a turning point in the radicalization of the strike as well as the possibilities for state intervention at any level in support of workers' rights. From November 23 to the morning of November 26, Havana came to a complete standstill, with authorities and strikers battling openly in the streets. Once the typographers guild joined the strike, all major newspapers ceased publication, and Havana's literate public was deprived of media coverage.[79] Lack of access to information only made matters worse. Both the municipal and presidential branches of the state joined forces in repressing the strike. Perhaps in partial deference to Estrada Palma for agreeing not to interfere in the dismissal of Chief of Police Cárdenas, Mayor O'Farrill agreed to ban all open-air, public assemblies. City police were issued 30,000 bullets. Estrada Palma ordered his only national armed forces, the Rural Guard, on stand-by for potential duty on the streets of Havana. Only through the intervention of Salvador Cisneros Betancourt, acting as president of the National Council of Veterans, was Estrada Palma's Minister of Governance, Diego Tamayo, persuaded to delay the deployment of the Rural Guard. But his patience proved short-lived. On November 24, the Rural Guard launched a full-blown assault on crowds, ostensibly to protect the Presidential Palace from attack. In the end, at least 114 workers were wounded, 80 were imprisoned, and 5 were dead.[80] Efforts to halt the city's trolleys and prevent members of the bourgeoisie from getting to their jobs and running their errands had shifted police tactics into high gear. Mounted police charged crowds at Cuatro Caminos and Monte, both points in the center of the city, where dozens of workers were injured.[81]

Convinced that he could not guarantee order short of using all-out violence on strikers, Chief of Police Ugarte threatened to resign. In reply, both O'Farrill and Minister Tamayo decided that the need to establish public order superseded citizens' newly acquired constitutional rights to free assembly and expression. On November 24, they gave Ugarte full authorization to use whatever means necessary to end the "tumult" overtaking the city. Police spent the rest of the day repressing strikers for verbally insulting them and for allegedly provoking or committing acts of vigilante violence.[82]

A short time later, Mayor O'Farrill's sudden reversal of position backfired when a large crowd of angry strikers appeared at Estrada Palma's doorstep. That afternoon, the strikers wound their way down Obispo Street toward the Plaza de Armas, site of the Presidential Palace and the center of state power in Cuba. Stopping at O'Farrill's office, the strikers were carrying the body of a black worker who had been beaten by police. Bloody and half-conscious, the black worker was near death. Infuriated, strikers demanded the suspension of the officer responsible. Although O'Farrill would not meet with them, he ordered that the wounded striker be cared for at the closest Casa de Socorros, an emergency aid facility operated by the Catholic Church. But the strikers refused to go away. Frantic, O'Farrill turned to Minister Tamayo, who had been consulting with him and Ugarte earlier that day. Fearing that the Presidential Palace might be the strikers' next destination and panicked that the mob might assault the president, O'Farrill and Tamayo ordered an immediate dispersal of the unarmed strikers by force. The police accomplished this feat in minutes, "*alcanzando palos hasta los mirones* [even to the point of beating bystanders]." Ironically, General José Miguel Gómez, the revolutionary nationalist who later founded the Liberal Party and claimed to represent the interests of peasants, workers, and black veterans in his 1905 presidential bid against Estrada Palma, delighted in the spectacle. From a municipal office nearby, he watched and later congratulated the police for their fine and effective performance on behalf of an orderly and civilized nation.[83]

Amazingly, both O'Farrill and Tamayo would subsequently be accused of not having done enough. In the aftermath of the bloodshed of November 24, fellow cabinet members' attacks and Estrada Palma's disapproval forced Tamayo to resign.[84] For his efforts to rein in police and release imprisoned workers based on the unconstitutionality of charges against them, O'Farrill, along with individual workers and editors of anarchist newspapers, was tried by a special court organized in Havana to deal with the fallout of the strike. Incredibly, authorities originally charged O'Farrill with sedition against the state. However, he was eventually convicted of the contradictory crimes of abuse of power and dereliction of duty. Despite its blatant violation of the 1901 Constitution, the state's official justification for creating the special court was that the strikers had called into question both the viability and the stability of the Republic. Not only had they jeopardized Cuban independence in the as-yet untested context of the Platt Amendment, prosecutors argued, but more important, the barbarous and anarchic course of the strike had endangered the sanctity of civilization itself.[85]

It is significant that revolutionary nationalists who closed ranks against the strikers did so publicly for reasons similar to O'Farrill's logic for changing course. Captain Magdalena Peñarredonda was the first to initiate efforts by the national headquarters of the veterans association to mediate the dispute on behalf of workers. It was because of her eleventh-hour private appeal to O'Farrill on the night of November 24 that members of the strike's Central Committee were not arrested and those who had already been were released.[86] Also, thanks to Peñarredonda, a racially and socially diverse coalition of prominent veterans met with the strikers. These included General Máximo Gómez, Salvador Cisneros Betancourt, and Juan Gualberto Gómez. In sharp contrast to O'Farrill, who had met with the Central Committee only in the sanctity of his own office, the veterans' commission joined the strikers at Teatro Cuba for a mass meeting and public debate.

Initially, the workers received the veterans with suspicion and hostility. As popular nationalists, the workers had seen their own vision of direct democracy in action on a nightly basis at the Teatro Cuba. Daily, they had brought that vision to the streets in order to raise the consciousness of others and make them witness the kind of society that Cuba might prove capable of becoming—a revolutionary one. For these reasons, the strikers had little patience for the speeches of wartime caudillos who presumed themselves qualified to mediate a labor dispute. Still, events in the last few days may have convinced many workers that the mediation of caudillos might be the only option open to them. Strikers appeared willing to hear what they had to say.

One veteran whose remarks did nothing to endear him to this audience of popular nationalists was Máximo Gómez. Brandishing the usual warning that autonomous actions by popular-class sectors undermined the future of the fatherland by angering the United States, the general was particularly blunt: "Public order should be inalterable. I am against all procedures which compromise public order." Ignoring any parallels that might have been drawn to the black veterans' movement, Juan Gualberto Gómez focused his comments on the need for Cubans to put aside their class interests as the criteria for creating social unity. However, Gómez did offer to mediate the strike with employers. Nonetheless, strikers declined the offer, probably because Gómez, like O'Farrill, insisted on forcing them into the role of clients. Dismissing workers' accusations that he would not take their interests seriously, he asserted that their leaders' authority should be the workers' first recourse to action: "The Veterans have a right to believe that the Republic risks grave danger. If outside dangers were to threaten her, they would rise up in arms; but [the dangers] are internal, blood of our blood, and we come here to interpose ourselves in order to settle the danger of the fatherland. We fear neither the authorities nor the workers. We are not bourgeois nor are we representatives of the Government. We are simple mediators. And if it is said that the fatherland is secondary, then we have no role here."[87] The statement was emblematic of the dramatic shift from revolution to involution that former leaders of the 1895 War had taken. As pro-imperialist nationalists had done, revolutionary nationalists like Máximo Gómez and Juan Gualberto Gómez had come to decide that the greatest risk to sovereignty was not the United States but popular nationalist provocateurs whose radicalism they needed to control.

Still, lessons drawn from the veterans' movement seemed to convince strikers of the need for pragmatism. Eventually, they agreed to submit to Juan Gualberto Gómez's authority and let him negotiate with employers. However, despite around-the-clock efforts, the owners of the factories agreed to none of the workers' demands. By November 29, the Central Committee and the General League of Workers that had initiated the strike declared it a catastrophic failure. Workers returned to their jobs, demoralized and dependent on their supporters in Congress to seek political restitution.[88]

Significantly, though, while popular nationalists had to give up their struggle for constitutional protection and an end to preferential treatment of Spaniards in cigar factories, revolutionary nationalists mobilized to defend their own authority vis-à-vis both Estrada Palma's administration and their popular nationalist rivals for power. In his address before fifty-six members of the House, Representative Juan R. Xiqués Arango of Camagüey denounced the government's brutal deployment of public force against its own people as an affront to the democratic process and a mockery of shared governance. Moreover, he and other radical Nationals demanded accountability. The executive branch could not simply override the authority of Congress or the Constitution at will.[89]

The next day, General Enrique Loynaz de Castillo introduced legislation calling for Estrada Palma's administration and Havana's municipal offices to make public all communication, decrees, and evidence relating to the incarceration, brutalization, and persecution of "the multitude of citizens" during the recent strike in outright defiance of constitutional law.[90] However, the Nationals' proposal was never voted on by the House of Representatives: within minutes of its presentation, almost all the Republican representatives—supporters of Estrada Palma—left the House chambers. In the absence of a quorum, the Republicans' action not only silenced debate but also successfully ensured the dismissal of the legislation. This incident initiated a long chain of similar situations in which pro-imperialist nationalists would undermine the foundations of democracy through the manipulation of institutions for years to come. It also effectively ended hopes for a solution to the General Strike and workers' concerns more broadly through the new kind of "command structure" that revolutionary nationalists were so keen to employ: political process.

The General Strike of 1902 marked a pivotal moment in the history of the early Republic. On one hand, it left the state under Estrada Palma stripped of its legitimacy before a great number, if not the majority, of Cuba's popular classes. By the end of the first year of the Republic, the ideological differences separating revolutionary nationalists and popular nationalists emerged in sharp relief. However, Estrada Palma's administration demonstrated that as far as pro-imperialist nationalists were concerned, making policy was a zero-sum game. They would impose their plans on others, including opposition leaders, without negotiation or consultation. This reality pushed other nationalists into the position of realizing that they had more to gain by coming together strategically, if not ideologically, for the sake of dislodging administration officials from power. By 1904, when pro-imperialist nationalists organized into the Moderate Party, the stakes seemed higher than ever. In the name of modernity, Estrada Palma's administration proposed a radical solution to the problem of internal threats and continuing social unrest from black and working-class sectors: the re-racialization of Cuban society through state-subsidized white immigration.

Saving Cuba: White Immigration as the Ultimate Solution to Race-Class Defiance

After 1902, the Estrada Palma administration increasingly turned a deaf ear to complaints from below. In the early months of 1903, revolutionary nationalist politicians formally created a system of authority in which they invited popular nationalists to participate and through which they hoped to exercise greater control. Thus, in 1903 the Liberal Party came into being. Shortly thereafter, Estrada Palma's supporters formed the Moderate Party. In addition to using the techniques of political terror to silence Liberal opposition (discussed in the succeeding chapter), Moderates funneled their energies toward the major legislative task of passing a bill for the selective immigration of European, "naturally" hard-working agricultural laborers.

By the spring of 1906, the administration achieved wide congressional support for this project among Moderates. It was a policy whose purported benefits for the culture and economy of future generations Estrada Palma had extolled for years. Reported in the media as a successful experiment for agricultural and industrial expansion that had already been tested in Argentina and Chile, the project resonated with the majority of Cubans in the upper echelons of society. Of course, many of these Cubans had been loyal to Spain during the war and, like the Spanish, may well have disdained Cuba's revolutionaries as black "uncivilized savages." As newspaper articles, rumors, and the criminalization of African-derived popular expression in this period attest, conservative elites and the Cuban state culturally mystified the lower classes, seeing them as contaminated by violent instincts or perverse tendencies born of a mixed, nonwhite racial heritage.[91] Between 1903 and 1906, pro-imperialist nationalists adopted a social-scientific rationale that underscored their promotion of white immigration. By inoculating society with new blood and new cultures that augured a prosperous, united future, the project promised to neutralize continuing conflicts over a past shaped by slavery and revolutionary struggle.

Underlying this rationale was the idea that until independence, Cuba had gone about solving its need for cheap agricultural labor in ways detrimental to the cultural evolution and economic modernization of the country. As Dr. Juan Santos Fernández, president of the Academy of Science, argued in 1906, Estrada Palma's espousal of Spanish immigration represented the best untried solution to Cuba's social and cultural stagnation, especially as seen in the light of the rapid evolution of other countries such as Germany and the United States. As in ancient Greece, the attention of these countries to the physical characteristics of their populations had produced the kind of "vigorous people" responsible for their unsurpassed standard of progress, or so Santos Fernández theorized.[92]

Because Cuba had relied on "immigration" from Africa, Yucatán, and Asia to solve its short-term labor problems in the nineteenth century, Santos Fernández contended, it had jeopardized the long-term prospects and proliferation of its people. The supposedly inferior characteristics of these races only reinforced in their descendants the "impulsive forces that produce the political crime of rebellion." The presumed effects of a tropical climate on human passions had already naturalized this condition in Cubans. Ignoring the effects of war and slavery on Cubans' reproductive rates, Santos Fernández argued that the island's low density of population was evidence of the infertility and inviability of its racially mixed people. In Latin America and the Caribbean, he claimed, racial mixing had caused the nobler features of "purer" races to mutate and reappear "as they do in animals; from there comes the regressive savage type, the cruel, thieving, hypocritical atavist."[93] Citing the famous dictum of the early nineteenth-century Argentine statesman Alberdi, "To govern is to populate," Santos confirmed the belief current among European scientists that Spanish workers were the racial group most adaptable to the unique challenges of hard labor in the tropics. To build the Panama Canal, even the United States had turned to Spain, he said. Now, so must Cuba.[94]

Incredibly, while black leaders such as Morúa Delgado, black newspapers such as *El Nuevo Criollo*, and the labor press denounced the immigration project, all strategically avoided the racial and racist dimensions of the proposal. Ostensibly, they wanted to avoid reviving old debates over the place of race in public discourse and thereby guarantee the cooperation of popular nationalist activists with revolutionary nationalist Liberals who opposed the plan and held positions in Congress. Moderate proponents of European immigration, however, took the opposite tack, openly couching their arguments on explicitly racial grounds. Before the black veterans' movement and General Strike of 1902, many of the same proponents had touted their project in strictly cultural terms, referring to it as an antidote to the decline of Hispanic customs and norms in the Republic.[95] However, by 1906, proponents now felt little need to disguise overtly biological racial arguments in a national discourse of social unity that reified culture.

By the time the project for state-sponsored immigration made it to the floor of Congress in February 1906, the administration, Moderate politicians, and the vast majority of former Spanish loyalists, now allied with the Moderates, had constructed a vast political machine. It favored guns and terror as a means of consolidating a monopoly on local as well as national political power.[96] As a result, the bill titled "Project for an Immigration Law and National Growth" can be understood as an ideological manifesto representing the extremes to which those of the pro-imperialist nationalist sector, led by Estrada Palma, would go in fulfilling their own ideal vision of the nation. Article 10 of the bill stipulated which immigrants the state favored and whose passage it agreed to sponsor. "Individuals of the Caucasian race may consider themselves sheltered under this law," the bill read, as long as such individuals demonstrate their "good conduct and laboriousness in the country or countries of prior residence." Article 17 further explained which groups were "excluded from the privileges which this law concedes." Key among these were the "individuals and families of the race of color, be they black, Malaysians, Mongoloid, of the Oceanic races as well as the copper-toned and all mestizoes, and the gypsies also known as *zíngaros.*"[97]

Asserting that the "state of agitation and chronic turbulence" of Latin American nations since their independence had driven European immigrants north to the United States, the bill's proponents explained the logic behind their own project for national development in this way:

> This constant migratory current [to the United States] has powerfully contributed to the making of the American Union, in little less than a century, into one of the richest, most civilized, progressive and powerful peoples of the earthly globe; meanwhile, the nations of Latin origin remained sta-

tionary, backward, poor, and some, because of their innumerable revolts, arrived even at the brink of barbarity. Among these peoples, fortunately, various heard the striking of the hour in time [to establish] order, work and peace—Mexico, Chile, the Republic of Argentina and Brazil, opened their doors to European immigration, which has begun to leave its benevolent influence on the progress of those peoples of our race. . . . *There are no opinions contrary to the idea of fomenting a white population; all agree on the necessity of attracting as quickly as possible the greatest number of European families who may be settled in our countryside, to contribute with their number, their example, their activity and their energy to develop production, helping us to consolidate the bases on which to set our contemporary institutions.*[98]

As supporters of the law clearly articulated, their aim was not to make Cuba an appendage of the United States but a leader among Latin American peoples, as equally strong, economically productive, and "racially" vibrant as North American society as well as American "leaders" in the south, especially Argentina and Brazil.

Representing a historical understanding of the Cuban nation that contradicted at all levels both revolutionary nationalists' interpretation of the nation and the popular nationalist views of black veterans and workers, this document ignored and thereby defied the foundational promise of a Republic built on racial fraternity and social unity. Apparently, for pro-imperialist nationalists, it was no longer necessary to rationalize or even engage these ideals. These ideals, like those who continued to espouse them, regardless of interpretive differences of meaning, had become equally expendable. Re-racializing Cuban society was the only alternative to the demise of the modern, culturally Hispanic, and biologically white nation that they imagined.

Significantly, the bill that President Estrada Palma eventually signed into law on July 11, 1906, did not make mention of racial exclusions—a circumstance owed mainly to the efforts of black congressmen. With Juan Gualberto Gómez fraudulently defeated in the elections of 1905, Martín Morúa Delgado and Rafael Serra, a one-time supporter of Estrada Palma, worked ceaselessly to impede passage of the law with these provisions in the Senate. Nonetheless, while sponsors of the bill silenced an explicit definition of which groups the law excluded, they did clarify which groups it included. Of the $1 million made available for the payment of immigrants' passage to Cuba, $800,000 was earmarked for immigrants from Europe and the Canary Islands. Apparently aimed at increasing the preponderance of "Aryan" features in Cuba's population, the law apportioned all remaining funds for the exclusive recruitment of laborers from Sweden, Norway, Denmark, and northern Italy.[99] Denied their critical contributions to Cuba's past, blacks had no future in the Cuban nation as pro-imperialist nationalists imagined it. Thus, a new Cuban nation would emerge, embodied by new Cubans: white, docile, and energetic servants of their masters' republican state.

Conclusion

The immigration project as conceived and understood by pro-imperialist nationalists was the ultimate expression of their own specific vision of nation. Racially exclusionary and predicated on the ideological purity of "objective" science, immigration was meant to be the solution to Cuba's colonial legacy of racial divisions, labor inequality, and vast socioeconomic disparities. Most revolutionary nationalists and popular nationalists could not support it, although for strategic reasons, they chose to silence the racial dimensions of their objections to the project. Instead, they drew the common conclusion that regardless of how they may have remembered the practice of social unity and defined current methods for achieving it in the Republic, Estrada Palma's immigration law not only isolated it but did away with the concept altogether. Circumstances had clearly changed since 1902, and the stakes were higher than ever before. While Estrada Palma had been willing to listen to demands couched in racial terms during the veterans' movement of the first months of the Republic in 1902, the General Strike of that fall had hardened his government's position. While both political elites believed that popular nationalists had to be controlled, Liberals still wanted to do so through a political, democratic process. Estrada Palma's pro-imperialist nationalists, however, focused on how best to eliminate them as a participatory force from the political scene.

In taking such a course, pro-imperialist nationalists dismissed the opportunities for implementing the socially transformative goals of the Revolution and the construction of state hegemony that the first years of the Republic might have otherwise required. But, as the Estrada Palma administration would discover, the cost of dismissing these opportunities would be measured in the inability of the state to maintain itself without recourse to violence.

As this chapter indicates, the Constitutional Revolution of 1906 that followed this process resulted from many individual rebellions against the legitimacy of the state that began as early as 1902. Importantly, both popular nationalist activists and revolutionary nationalist leaders staked out their claims of authenticity as heirs of José Martí during this same period. In this sense, they differed fundamentally in their approach to the Republic than Estrada Palma. For him and many other pro-imperialist nationalists, the Revolution was no longer, if it had ever been, a model for the Republic. It had simply been and should remain a means to an end. Yet, for every failure of the Estrada Palma administration to live up to or even recognize the Revolution as a model for governance, there had been revolutionary and popular nationalists who contested the legitimacy of the state's policies through the myth of social unity they saw reflected in Martí. In this sense, the Constitutional Revolution of 1906 represented a collective, mass effort to redeem the myth of Martí by reenacting the process that had brought them together eleven years earlier.

FIVE

· ·

Political Violence, Liberal Revolution, and
the Martyrdom of Martí, 1904–1906

BETWEEN 1904 AND 1906, Liberal leaders achieved for the first time since the 1895 War a massive, cross-class, cross-racial alliance among popular and revolutionary nationalist sectors. To do so, they revived the flexible, discursive style and paternalistic political practice that had proved so effective during the 1895 War. As the 1906 Constitutional Revolution illustrates, revolutionary nationalist leaders of the Liberal Party consistently refused to trust their popular nationalist followers, from the political "rank and file" to midlevel reformists. These reformists formed a marginal political elite comprised of black leaders such as Quintín Banderas and other veterans-turned-labor-and-race-activists such as Evaristo Estenoz whose commitment to social change was more radical than that of revolutionary nationalist Liberals. These Liberals counted on the allegiance of this marginal elite to secure a broad, popular-class constituency for the emerging apparatus of the Liberals' armed revolt against Tomás Estrada Palma's regime. Once the victory of the 1906 Revolution was at hand, though, Liberal leaders came to fear the revolutionary potential of the popular classes and the marginal elites who had mobilized them. The result, in many ways reminiscent of events in 1898, was a second U.S. intervention and another fragmentation of alliances that had been forged along the road to armed revolt.

Largely unexplored by historians of Cuba, the two-year period of political repression on which this chapter focuses represented the first cycle of state violence, revolution, and foreign intervention that would repeat itself throughout the course of modern Cuban history in the twentieth century. Keeping this in mind, it is easy to see the propensity to violence as a solution and harbinger for change manifested in the First Republic. Here, violence began not only to take new forms but also to touch new groups of people. Previously, many of these people had seen themselves as immune to and disconnected from the violence perpetrated on "others" by virtue of their respective social positions in the former Spanish colonial system or their insulation from the realities of the 1895 War that exile in a foreign country had provided. Therefore, unlike the situation of Cuba in the nineteenth century, violent protest and warfare in the early twentieth century would not take as its overarching goal the ousting of a foreign power from Cuba—at least not until 1933. Rather, its goal was to silence, intimidate, and even eliminate other Cubans who would not submit to the state's ideological landscape of nation. Pro-imperialist nationalist officials of the Estrada Palma administration and their allies at the local and national level were the first to adopt such methods, setting a precedent that revolutionary nationalists would later emulate.

Such political infighting proved instrumental to the process of consolidating U.S. imperial hegemony in the Cuban Republic. Yet, even as worries about the United States receded before the struggle to control the state, commemorations of José Martí, Cuba's greatest former critic of the United States, intensified in importance and increased in number. From 1904 to 1906, Martí's name and image became deeply associated with each group of nationalists' respective ideological vision. In 1905 and 1906, pro-imperialist nationalist leaders presided over the public unveiling of two nearly identical national monuments to Martí, the first in Havana's Central Park and the second in Cienfuegos Central Park.[1] Both events took place in the presence of tens of thousands of Cubans at the behest of pro-imperialist nationalist officials who were personally responsible for the policies of state terror then affecting the country. Curiously, these officials shared the spotlight with opposition Liberals who, by 1905, had become not only their ardent political enemies but also targets of state repression. Thus, for the first time in the early Republic, a period of intense social division and political crisis became the staging ground for ritual commemorations of Martí as a symbol of social unity. Rather than moments of solidarity that conveyed a toleration of ideological difference for the sake of a singular vision of nation, commemorations of Martí became crucibles for testing the resilience of Cubans' commitment to conflicting images. Sharp and distinct interpretations of the meaning of social unity were precisely the elements that commemorative occasions such as these tended to highlight. Through word and deed, Cubans asserted the authenticity and authority of their respective nationalism by refusing to surrender control of, ownership of, or intimacy with Martí to any other side.

In this period, the significance of Martí acquired both a historical function and a contemporary political purpose: each group of nationalists now remembered Martí as the primary catalyst for the social unity that they insisted on

Thousands of Cubans attended the unveiling of the first national monument to José Martí in Havana's Central Park, February 24, 1905. President Tomás Estrada Palma and General Máximo Gómez presided over the event. This photograph originally appeared in the commemorative edition of *El Fígaro* (February 24, 1905). (Courtesy of the Archivo Nacional de Cuba)

having forged during the 1895 War. Through carefully crafted, related narratives that focused on the martyring of Martí, Cuban nationalists commemorated his death in ways that explicated its meaning for present political circumstances. For pro-imperialist nationalists, the meaning of Martí's death lay in the birth of the Republic and the mandate for rule they claimed in his name. They saw Martí's ecstatic faith in creating a consensus of cooperation as a foundation for rule as much naive as it was delusional. Thus, the exceptionality of Martí's idealism implied that it could not and should not be duplicated. Conformity with Cuba's present circumstances was the best way to commemorate Martí.

By contrast, revolutionary nationalist opponents focused on Martí's martyr-dom in order to legitimate their own right to reclaim power in the state. Re-membering the suffering of Martí and revering his messianic qualities meant identifying their own leadership with his legacy and their ability, in time, to complete Martí's mission. On the other hand, for popular nationalists, it was not Martí's death that mattered so much as his life. Focusing on Martí's life gave his martyrdom meaning. Fulfilling his life's work in the Republic meant having leaders who identified with the most marginalized of Cuba's masses, not leaders who demanded that the Cuban masses identify with them.

Through these narratives, Cubans created a collective origin myth of social unity rooted in the messianic martyrdom of Martí. Even as they all commemorated Martí and invoked his memory in related ways, each group blamed the other for having violated the sacred standard of unity incarnated in Martí and for jeopardizing the divinely sanctioned role in history that it proscribed to Cuba. Consequently, they also raised the stakes for determining how that standard might be fulfilled.

Intimidation and Betrayal:
The Making of a Republican Political Culture

Under Tomás Estrada Palma's presidency, pro-imperialist nationalist officials defined the nation in terms of the promotion and protection of "civilization," a catch-all concept implying the white racial standards, wealth, and level of education that pro-imperialist nationalists ascribed to themselves. So exclusionary had Estrada Palma's vision become that by 1905, he seemed to see only his circle of supporters as qualified members of his pro-imperialist nationalist nation: "In Cuba we have a Republic but no citizens."[2] Only by ridding Cuba of its politically rebellious and therefore socially undesirable elements could the Republic fulfill administration officials' and their supporters' expectations of nation.

In the end, the state's repression of potential constituents it perceived as "enemies" actually encouraged these "enemies" to define themselves in such terms. That is, Estrada Palma's mounting conviction that the greatest threat to state sovereignty came from internal enemies within Cuba turned out to be a self-fulfilling prophecy. Starting with the elections of 1904 and continuing through the consolidation of Estrada Palma's bid for reelection on the Moderate Party ticket in early 1905, violence became a primary means of political coercion for the government. Eventually, it also became a major means of social protest against the government.

For the first time since Spanish rule, state authoritarianism and violence manifested itself in the day-to-day, local rhythms of people's lives, especially between the winter of 1905 and the summer of 1906—a period when state repression was at its height. The sources of discontent that eventually led Cubans to take up arms against the state did not derive from any single act of repression, such as the breakup of a labor strike or public demonstration. Rather, they emerged from the rigidity of the context that Estrada Palma's government had set up in economic, political, cultural, and even discursive terms. Increasing numbers of Cubans could find nothing resembling their understanding of nationalism in Estrada Palma's pro-imperialist nationalist rule, as its policies emerged to serve only the interests of foreigners and officials like himself. This process began with the Republic's partial elections for Congress in 1904, to be held independently of foreign supervision for the first time.

Galvanized by their opposition to Estrada Palma and hoping to create a mass following, revolutionary nationalist veteran leaders and popular nationalist activists formed the National Liberal Party, with representatives and party organs in every province.[3] Key figures included men who had both contested and promoted the black veterans' movement, such as Juan Gualberto Gómez, Martín Morúa Delgado, and Generoso Campos Marquetti. Also prominent were Estrada Palma's former Minister of Governance, Diego Tamayo, and the newly reinstated mayor of Havana, Juan O'Farrill, both of whom had suffered indictment by the special court set up to try labor leaders of the 1902 General Strike along with local officials who had repressed them. O'Farrill and Tamayo, whose methods had not been repressive enough to suit the tastes of pro-imperialist nationalists, defected to the other side. Undoubtedly, the spectacle of seeing leaders and activists who had taken opposite sides during the social crises of the previous two years join forces to win the elections must have terrified supporters of Estrada Palma, largely members of the Republican Party. Even more threatening was the fact that many Liberals had once been members of the National Convention Party, a party whose platform was totally antithetical to the administration's free trade policies and laissez-faire approach to social issues.

In line with revolutionary nationalist goals of gradual social change, the National Convention Party championed high tariffs for the protection of nascent national industries, state regulation of labor including minimum wage and nondiscriminatory hiring guarantees, the "absolute equality" of citizens, and the breakup of *latifundia* (large-scale plantation agriculture) in favor of small-scale family farming.[4] Since leaders of the National Convention Party now formed the core of the Liberal Party, it was safe to assume that these ideals still held a great deal of sway among Liberals. Moreover, the Liberals managed to recruit rising stars from among the organized working class as well as from the young professional sector to its ranks. Examples included popular nationalist activist Evaristo Estenoz and public school official Arturo R. Díaz. As a leader of Havana's bricklayers guild, Estenoz represented a profession dominated by black Cubans.[5] He had also played a central role in the failed black veterans' campaign. Arturo Díaz, the brash editor of *La Escuela Moderna* and a personal friend of Alexis Everett Frye, had made a similar name for himself. During the General Strike of 1902, Díaz showed his solidarity as a popular nationalist with workers' rights by resigning the post of general superintendent of public schools under Estrada Palma as a protest of the state's repression of workers.[6] From the perspective of popular-class constituents, Estenoz's and Díaz's affiliation with the Liberal Party could not help but demonstrate its commitment to social change. Weeks before the February election of 1904, Estenoz and Díaz teamed up with several others to print a manifesto extolling the virtues of four Liberal candidates, including Juan Gualberto Gómez and Generoso Campos Marquetti. Cuba, the manifesto read, "cannot continue on the path chosen. [Our] agriculture requires the protection that the State is obligated to give it. . . . The working classes should not be always eternally exploited, nor shall commerce and industry live trapped in a confined circle."[7]

But just as midlevel agitators for the Liberal Party like Díaz and Estenoz consolidated its image as socially progressive, pro-imperialist nationalist Republicans shifted their position further to the right. In the spring of 1904, they called for the revision of the constitutional clause that provided full universal male suffrage. In response, *El Fígaro* demanded an accounting of prominent politicians' individual views. In arguing that this "capital mistake" of the Constitutional Convention should be rectified, one Republican actually justified his position on the basis of José Martí's warnings against rule by the *incultos* in Martí's essay "Nuestra América." Others claimed that the pure, honest, unwitting souls of Cuba's illiterate classes would forever put the wrong men in power. By contrast, Liberal leaders vociferously denounced any limitations on suffrage, characterizing the suggestion as a basic betrayal of the tenets of the Revolution and its many martyrs. Orestes Ferrara went as far as to demand extension of suffrage rights to women.[8]

The Republicans' efforts to restrict suffrage represented a last-ditch effort to prevent their own demise at the polls through fair elections. Eventually, fraud became a primary recourse. Mainly through the direct manipulation of "scrutiny boards" charged with registering voters and counting ballots, Republicans snatched "victories" in every province but Havana. Most of these victories belonged to roughly hewn, mainly professional and middle-class Liberal candidates with popular-class constituencies. In the overwhelmingly Liberal province of Santa Clara, Governor José Miguel Gómez secured a Republican landslide by ordering that Ramón Valdéz, a schoolteacher and member of the local scrutiny board, be severely clubbed by local law enforcement. In Cienfuegos, Republican senator José Frías organized a gang of thugs that became known as the "Partida de la Porra," whose purpose was to pursue and beat up Liberals. The same thugs later assaulted the Liberal Party clubhouse in the nearby town of Rodas, causing the death of at least one member. It was not the first time, nor the last, that a prominent Liberal was assassinated publicly.[9] Liberals, in turn, attacked José Miguel Gómez in the press, accusing him of treachery in the Ten Years' War and of collusion with Autonomists in the War of 1895. They did not, however, react violently.

Nationwide, the results of Republican machinations were obvious. In Oriente, where the Liberal ticket featured such stars as Juan Gualberto Gómez, Republican-affiliated candidates achieved easy victories. Although Oriente's Liberals eventually secured the annulment of election results in the provincial supreme court, Republicans in Havana refused to recognize any change. Similar events took place in both Pinar del Río and Camagüey.[10] Indeed, the only province in which the Liberals won handily was Havana, a result that Republicans attributed to fraud.[11] In all, of the thirty-one seats in the House of Representatives and forty-six senatorial seats open to election, the Republicans and affiliated conservative parties claimed twenty seats in the House and twenty-six in the Senate, giving pro-imperialist nationalist candidates a majority.[12] With both chambers of Congress as well as the presidency in pro-imperialist nationalist hands, Estrada Palma's administration then conspired with former Autonomists to create the Moderate Party and, through terror tactics rather than fraud, consolidate one-party rule.

No longer able to rely on the electoral process to ensure a role in the state, revolutionary nationalist leaders in the Liberal Party tapped the long-standing anger that popular nationalists felt toward the Estrada Palma administration and publicly reversed their earlier stances on workers' rights and the plight of black veterans. Such moves undoubtedly served to consolidate already existing alliances with popular nationalist leaders active among workers and black veterans. Thus, Liberals attacked Estrada Palma for having engineered a congressional majority in order to pass his white immigration project, a proposal they depicted as a continuation of earlier repressive measures targeting the movements of workers and black veterans that many revolutionary nationalists among them had once condemned.[13] The Liberal press also championed the cause of black veterans as never before. When a small group of black veterans rose in arms against in Oriente for reclamation of war pay, the Liberal press recognized the justice of their claims by condemning the Cuban Congress's recent appropriation of $25,000 to buy the daughter of U.S. president Theodore Roosevelt a diamond necklace for her wedding day.[14] The effect of the Liberals' critique proved powerful enough to force Estrada Palma into doing what he had always refused: granting veterans their war pay. Veterans eventually received over $57 million in cash and bonds.[15]

Nonetheless, Estrada Palma managed to maintain a surplus of nearly $20 million in the state treasury, a fact of which he was consummately proud and to which he made constant reference. While Estrada Palma interpreted this surplus as the greatest evidence of his government's break from a colonial past of debt and internal corruption, Liberal critics tended to see it as proof that the state was hoarding public wealth despite the obvious suffering of the masses.[16] Liberal attacks on Estrada Palma's miserly government easily found a receptive audience among many popular nationalist veterans. For them, the redistributive role played by leaders in the midst of the guerrilla war of 1895 continued to serve as a potential model to be emulated. Revolutionary nationalist politicians who condemned Estrada Palma for his state's "avarice" appeared to endorse this model.

Aside from using fraud and corruption to reengineer the political process away from democratic principles, pro-imperialist nationalists also relied on the same means to ensure economic circumstances favorable to their vision of a modern nation based on foreign investment, a plantation economy, and a stagnant social order. For example, one resident planter testified that a U.S. land company interested in buying his mill had sought and gained the clandestine protection of the state's armed forces to compel a sale. Paramilitary elements of the Rural Guard, operating on behalf of the Bahía Honda Land Company, used intimidation and violence to prevent the planter from attracting the labor force he needed to restore his mill. Moreover, he reported, the Bahía Honda Land Company had also dedicated itself to buying and selling the land of small farmers who, "lacking instruction as well as money," could not produce property titles, since most of them had been destroyed in the independence wars.[17] Indeed, knowledge of the pro-imperialist nationalist state's role in facilitating a U.S. takeover of land was so widespread that one U.S. citizen from Des Moines, Iowa, took it upon himself to warn Estrada Palma of the damage his policies could cause the Republic in the long run. The promise of the Revolution, he reminded the president, had been a Cuba dominated by a class of native, small farmers.[18] Liberal critics of the administration's policy of encouraging foreign ownership went as far as to dub it an extension of "Manifest Destiny."[19]

One of the sectors of society deeply affected by the political and cultural dimensions of Estrada Palma's economic policies was public instruction. In the opinion of the large number of teachers who would later participate in the Constitutional Revolution of 1906,[20] the greatest victims of the parsimonious state were Cuba's children. As a former teacher himself, Estrada Palma initially made much of his government's commitment to education, promising in his first message to Congress in 1902 to build enough classrooms to educate all Cuban children.[21] A few months later, the president of Havana's advisory board for education proposed a budget of one million pesos for the construction of schools to meet the needs of capital alone. But to this, the administration balked, charging

TABLE 1. Teachers Employed at the Start of the Academic Year, 1900–1907

	Whites			Of Color			
Year	Men	Women	Total	Men	Women	Total	Grand Total
1900	—	—	—	—	—	—	3,613
1901	1,389	2,026	3,415	41	77	118	3,533
1902	1,353	1,826	3,179	38	83	121	3,300
1903	1,477	2,025	3,502	47	112	159	3,661
1904	1,402	1,925	3,324	41	118	159	3,486
1905	—	—	—	—	—	—	—
1906	1,171	2,167	3,338	51	157	208	3,546
1907	1,194	2,383	3,577	59	203	262	3,839

Sources: La Instrucción Primaria: Revista Quincenal Publicada por la Secretaría de Instrucción Pública, December 25, 1902, 465; December 10, 1904, 279; January 10, 1905, 341; April 10 and 25, 1907, 630; December 10 and 25, 1908, 426.

Note: September marked the start of the academic calendar; all numbers are for September of each year.

that the majority of Cubans would be "scandalized" by such a thought.[22] In fact, the Estrada Palma administration spent less money on supplies, building repair, and teachers' salaries in public schools than had been the case under the mandate of Alexis Everett Frye during the first U.S. military intervention.[23]

However, statistics on the number of teachers employed in September, the start of each school year, from 1900 to 1907 show that the supply of teachers from the time of the first to the second U.S. intervention was relatively stable. (See Table 1.) Even as the number of white teachers fluctuated, teachers of color, both male and female, made continual if minor advances, increasing their total from only 118 nationwide in 1901 to more than twice that number by 1907. Moreover, women of both racial categories increased their representation in the academic workforce, with the number of female teachers of color more than doubling between 1900 and 1907. Reasons for this rise remain unclear. However, it seems that Frye's efforts to open up the school system as a legitimate space for women to work independently and honorably continued to bear fruit. Despite the budgetary limits and other practical constraints the profession faced in these years, women joined the profession in ever greater numbers, possibly augmenting their politicization as a group and further diffusing popular nationalist sentiments among the popular- and middle-class children they taught.

However, during the same period that women's participation increased in the profession, the total number of children matriculated in public schools declined radically, dropping by over 20,000 children between 1904 and 1906 alone. Since colonial times, enrolling children in school had meant that their families could no longer count on their potential labor to supplement household income. Not surprisingly, in a worsening economic situation of scarce jobs and reduced access to subsistence lands, sending children to school easily became a luxury that fewer and fewer Cuban families chose to afford. Black families suffered the most. Cuban government statistics show that the matriculation of black children declined disproportionately to both their representation in the school-age population (five to nineteen years) and to the total number of children actually registered in school.[24]

Declines in the number of children able to attend school and the willingness of the administration to look the other way on such matters profoundly disturbed many popular nationalist teachers. Before Superintendent Arturo Díaz and Secretary of Education Eduardo Yero resigned their posts in the last month of 1902, *La Instrucción Primaria*, a publication of the Department of Public Instruction, became a venue for the airing of grievances. According to an article reprinted from the newspaper *Un Maestro Rural*, the root of all problems was the national government's overt politicization of local *juntas escolares* (school boards). These *juntas* increasingly dedicated themselves to the firing and hiring of teachers on the basis of personal whim or the desire to distribute political patronage. Another rural teacher testified to a particularly alarming case. According to the teacher's letter to Yero, the local board of education conspired to get rid of a particular female teacher whose political views members found distasteful. Still, because of her obvious qualifications for the job and high degree of personal prestige, the board decided to pass a regulation requiring that all the female teachers whom they hired be unmarried. Only a few days later, however, board members realized that the woman they had meant to appoint in the teacher's place no longer qualified because she was married. Amazingly, they solved the problem by amending the regulation they had just passed to allow for the hiring of married female teachers on the condition that they be reproductively "sterile." Understandably, the writer minced no words in expressing her outrage.[25] Female popular nationalists, arguably the greatest beneficiaries of Frye's populist version of imperialism, had become despised pariahs under a pro-imperialist nationalist administration.

With time, the situation of corruption and patronage in the public school system only worsened. In general, Cubans began to perceive the Department of Public Instruction as a giant political machine, created for the purpose of dispensing favors or even state salaries for jobs that existed only on paper, not improving society. Cubans called such "jobs" *botellas*, literally "bottles."[26] At a time when breast-feeding was the only means for nourishing an infant for the majority of Cuban women, the term implied that politically connected "babies" survived shortages of regular breast milk (a metaphor for hardship or unemployment) by gaining access to "bottled milk."[27] By 1904, the situation had gotten so bad that word of it reached the ears of Alexis Everett Frye. In January of that year, Frye wrote a detailed, open letter to Juan R. Xiqués Arango, a radical Liberal then in charge of the Commission on Public Instruction in the House of Representatives. In 1902, Xiqués Arango had condemned the state's repression of strikers and other congressmen's complicity with it as a violation of the Cuban Constitution.[28] Frye urged Cuban congressmen to press for legislation that would make teachers' contracts binding and their dismissals less open to local *juntas'* flights of political fancy.[29] Xiqués Arango might well have done so, but only a short time later he lost his seat in Congress due to the political machinations of the Republican Party.

Clearly, the political, economic, and social evidence for how far pro-imperialist nationalists would go to secure the implementation of their vision of nation was undeniable. Equally powerful was the discursive, culturally based evidence that, in the eyes of other nationalists, defied the very basis of Cuban sovereignty by looking to foreigners, rather than to local Cubans, for its authenticity. Many Cubans not directly affected by the state's economic policies resented the growing signs of U.S. influence on daily culture as well as the persistence of Spanish colonial mores in island life. For actively encouraging this by the nature of its economic policies, they blamed the Cuban state, not imperialism itself.

For example, Ezequiel García, a popular nationalist veteran and longtime critic of Estrada Palma who had supported Bartolomé Masó for president, pointed to the proliferation of the symbols of foreign power as the source of the problem. These were not evidence of Cuba's modernity, as Estrada Palma's government contended, but of its stagnation. While the Cuban Senate building and government plaza were still decorated with symbols of the Spanish monarchy such as lions, shops like "*The* Marquesita" and "*The* National Bank of Cuba" were staffed entirely by U.S. citizens. For García, Cuba was trapped in an imperial limbo from which the state made no effort to free it. Even Cuba's national postage (presumably not redesigned since the departure of the U.S. military) carried the face of Thomas Jefferson rather than that of José Martí or Antonio Maceo, he noted. He finished the article with the rhetorical question, "But what do such details matter? Do they impede a rise in the price of sugar or that one should eat and live?"[30] For García and a growing number of Cubans, the state's economic priorities translated into a cultural and social crisis that was ideological in origin.[31] Of course, for pro-imperialist nationalists, such signs indicated that Estrada Palma's policies were working, not failing: Cuba was becoming a diminutive, Hispanicized version of the United States.

In defining their opposition to the state, revolutionary and popular nationalists' reference to the revolutionary past became unavoidable as well as instructive. Even if Cubans had not agreed then on what kind of nation they wanted to build, they at least had agreed on the mutual right to argue over the contours and direction of the state. During the 1895 War, these "arguments" had taken place among revolutionaries (in Cuba and in exile) within a discursive field that equated proper behavior, social tolerance, and communal accountability with the collective cause of building a better Cuba. However, the state's growing reliance on violence and its assumptions about the expendability of opponents demonstrated the extent to which Moderates had abandoned the discourse of mutual engagement and toleration. Ironically, but perhaps inevitably, interrogations of the past meant to justify their actions led pro-imperialist nationalists, like their ideological opponents, to articulate the origin of their vision of nation as a historically united one through narratives on the martyrdom of José Martí.

Entombing Martí, Resurrecting the Republic: Struggles over the Meaning of Martyrdom

In the summer of 1904, administration officials saw signs of growing political divisions in society as the Liberals mobilized their campaign for the coming presidential elections less than a year away. Recognizing that the old Republican Party's credibility had been tarnished by February's electoral scandals, they worried about the threat that a Liberal presidency would pose to their social and economic plans for the nation. In May of that year, they expressed their pessimism toward the capacity of greater Cuban society to determine its future by insisting that Cubans were not yet "worthy" of "the twentieth of May," the birth of the Republic. From their perspective, Martí's "tomb" was the "cradle of the Republic" from which most had not yet emerged. Cubans needed to recognize that Cuba was currently experiencing its own "way of the cross" just as Martí had in the past, an allusion to Jesus Christ's grueling walk to the place of his crucifixion and simultaneous humiliation before jeering crowds. As such, they had to make themselves "worthy" of the freedom that Martí's martyrdom provided by being similarly humble, or so counseled the conservative newspaper *La Discusión*. Cubans would accomplish this by offering selfless support for "all who represent the advancement of our culture, the growth of our people, and the prestige of our government."[32] Cuba was a "modern Israel" that had rid itself of its ancient oppressor, Spain.[33] More than a Bolívar for Cuba, Martí was a Christ who had already redeemed Cuba with his death.[34]

The idea that Martí's role had ended with his death and that Martí's greatest quality had been his humility conveniently conformed to pro-imperialist nationalists' expectations regarding the role of other Cubans in "Free Cuba." For some pro-imperialist nationalist officials who commemorated Martí and the pro-Moderate press that supported them, the notion that Martí was not only supernaturally inspired but also divine often went hand-in-hand with the idea of his insanity. One writer went so far as to identify Martí with both the divinity of Jesus Christ and the delusional idealism of Cervantes' famous character Don Quixote. An ordinary Spanish peasant who believes he is a glorious knight of moral justice, Don Quixote projected his fantasies and desires onto the world around him. Martí's idealization of Cuba's future, insisted La Discusión, recalled the image of Don Quixote, who mistakenly confused a dust-covered and ugly peasant woman named Aldonsa with a gorgeous and dazzling lady whom he called Dulcinea. In Martí's case, Aldonsa/Dulcinea turned out to be none other than Cuba itself: "A magnanimous knight who took 'It doesn't matter' as the slogan of your shield, you didn't hear [the reality around you], your ascetic profile, pale and sad, you left to the world a fantastical dowry. In your mind of a poet, Patria was an unhappy, destitute maiden who implored your generous help and became your faithful lover until your death when you tossed sweet life at her feet like a white and immature rose."[35]

Two years later, La Discusión editorialized even more directly on the role of Martí: "Without Martí, without his dream, without his insanity [sin su locura], without his fixed idea, . . . Cuba would not be free: independence was decreed [by his death]; Martí was the apostle, the human means. And he was also, because he had to be so, the martyr. He had to fall, he had to die, before the ideal could be realized, so that he could serve as the definitive vestment for sacrifice, his historic shroud the secular struggle with no other end than that of duty and the accomplishment of the mission."[36] In other words, Martí's historic role and legacy could be reduced to his necessary and timely death. By "the coincidence of destiny," in the words of La Discusión's editors, the day of his death "joined with his triumph, the triumph of his ideal" in the Republic as the current government was constructing it.[37]

On the tenth anniversary of Martí's death in 1905, House president Santiago García Cañizares, a highly conservative Republican from Las Villas who had been elected through fraud, echoed these thoughts at the legally prescribed "solemn session" of both houses of Congress. Saying that the majority of the Cuban people "still had not realized that the revolution had ended" with the inauguration of the Republic, García Cañizares explained that this was why they did not know how to enjoy the "freedom in which we live today." One could only pray that Cuba's leaders would follow Martí's example of "preach[ing] with saintly ire against apostasies and betrayals" and "force [our political life] to begin the slow and cautious march" toward nationhood despite the impatience and ignorance of others who threatened it.[38]

These "others" included both popular nationalists and revolutionary nationalist Liberals. The Cuban Workers Party insisted that workers were already worthy of freedom and that they had been not only the "first to aid" Martí in his efforts to attain it but always "the first to strike out" for the task. They reminded *La Discusión*'s readers of this by paying to print their own statement in its pages, dedicated to Doña Leonor Pérez, Martí's aged mother, a day after editors issued the paper's official commemoration.[39]

However, popular nationalists did not generally confine commemorations of Martí to the anniversary of his death as political elites did. Perhaps popular nationalists chose not to focus on that day precisely because they did not wish to lend credibility to the politicians' official interpretations. Or perhaps they simply did not find the source for inspiration in Martí's death so much as in his life. For many popular nationalists who invoked Martí's name as a symbol of the promise of social unity, the Republic did not represent its fulfillment under the present regime, but its opposite. Fulfilling Martí's life's work lay ahead: "Cuba . . . might still become, one distant day, the vision of the Maestro Martí: a new *pueblo*, with new peoples; of sincere democracy, that may serve as an example to the whole world, . . . [with] a government of the people, by the people and for the people."[40] In addition, while *La Discusión* depicted Martí's messianism in terms so exceptional that they bordered on inane or even insane, *El Proletario* saw Martí's proximity to Jesus Christ as a source of empowerment. If Cuba was the modern Israel, workers were Jesus' ardent disciples, struggling against the hypocrisy of political elites just as Jesus himself had struggled against the Pharisees, leaders of the Jewish community who collaborated with imperial Rome in Jesus' day.[41]

For similar reasons, Cuba's popular nationalists appear to have responded with great enthusiasm to a completely fictionalized dime novel on the life of Martí. Published anonymously for the first time in 1901 and printed in multiple editions through 1905, *Martí: A Historical Novel by a Patriot* was the work of Franco Rander, a little-known writer.[42] Quite consciously, Rander seems to have manipulated facts drawn from a thirty-year period of Martí's historical life to create a sensational, romantic narrative that would appeal to a broad urban readership. Whether or not readers recognized the artificiality of the story is irrelevant to interpreting the possible sources of its popularity. So little did "facts" matter to the publisher, the author, or the readers that no one ever bothered to change such obvious errors in the text as the date of Martí's death, given as May 21 instead of May 19, a mistake every reader would have been able to detect.[43]

Inspired by Martí's own account of his imprisonment in a colonial jail as an adolescent, the novel casts Martí in the role of an eighteen-year-old rebel bent on breaking a poor, elderly, and abused black man out of Havana's political prison. In the subsequent course of events, Martí goes into hiding in the home of his friend's ex-girlfriend, Carolina, now an upper-class prostitute whose principal clients include the governor general of the island, among others. Eventually, Martí and Carolina fall into the role of star-crossed lovers, although Carolina's abiding sense of honor and Martí's immaculate state of sinlessness (the author describes Martí as "never having sinned") keep them from consummating their passions.[44] The story's allusion to the legend of Jesus' stoic but loving tenderness toward Mary Magdalene is clear. Once Martí is arrested, Carolina attempts to rescue him by sleeping with any Spanish official who might secure his release. Rife with clichés and sappy, ridiculous plot twists, the novel is blunt in its depictions of Carolina's raw sexuality and its conscious inversion of the ideas of gender and racial honor prominent in the colony and early Republic. Often, the author seems to want to remind readers of just how much the making of Cuba's revolution for independence called traditional mores and the social order into question. While the novel depicts the poor and destitute in heroic terms, wealthy loyalists are shown to be vulgar, destructive savages. Praised by the omniscient narrator as Cuba's true patriots, side characters critical to the survival of Martí and propagation of the Revolution include small businessmen, former slaves, and men of color who are Martí's closest allies and confidantes. Moreover, Carolina, a prostitute who sleeps with Spaniards, is not a character whom readers are meant to scorn or pity. On the contrary, as her ex-boyfriend and Martí's coconspirator says to her admiringly in one scene, "I can see that the Cuban cause, in order to triumph, needs more women like you."[45]

Carolina uses her knowledge of Spanish plans to aid Cuba's self-appointed revolutionaries, and when Spain forces Martí into exile, she manages to so affect him that his last thoughts rest on her as he leaves the port of Havana for exile in New York. In turn, Carolina takes to the field with Oriente's *mambises*, eventually dying in battle in the same manner as Martí, "also shot through by a bullet. She died exclaiming: Long Live Free Cuba!"[46] Effectively, Martí's own death appears as an incidental afterthought. The story continues well beyond Martí's death scene with an explanation of how thousands of "young and enthusiastic *guajiros* [peasants]" quickly joined the ranks of the Liberating Army.[47] Importantly, the novel concludes that the "work of the great Martí" for which monuments should be erected in his name was not the Republic but rather the struggle of the Revolution itself—one that in the novel's epilogue has just begun.[48] Arguably, the novel's popularity derived from the alternative set of cultural values and ideological principles that guided popular nationalists' interpretation of the past, the martyrdom of Martí, and the meaning of social unity as the foundation of a racially inclusive, socially radical nation both in the war and the Republic.

In many ways, Liberals' commemorative appropriations of a martyred Martí as the incarnation of social unity were far less articulate and far more vague than popular nationalist versions, fictional or otherwise. Unwilling to champion the life and words of Martí for fear of inciting the frustrated popular nationalists into premature action, Liberal leaders also refused to concede the triumph of the 1895 Revolution to pro-imperialist nationalists whose betrayal of electoral democracy put any evidence of such a triumph on hold. In fact, by 1905, Liberal leaders seemed willing to sacrifice their image as a clean party whose inclusion of popular nationalist activists like Evaristo Estenoz had resurrected the promise of revolutionary social change through electoral democracy in the public's eyes. When the organization of the Moderate Party dashed the presidential aspirations of Santa Clara's Republican governor, José Miguel Gómez, Liberals not only accepted him into their fold but also decided to nominate him for president on the Liberal Party ticket.[49] Yet, Gómez's reputation was less than democratic. A historically reluctant convert to universal suffrage,[50] Gómez had most recently helped the Partida de la Porra terrorize Liberals in various towns of Santa Clara so as to ensure that Moderate candidates favored by the pro-imperialist nationalist administration would win. Liberals in his own hometown of Sancti Spíritus declared that the former general of the 1895 War, who had been "a Plattist and conservative yesterday, cannot today, by honorable convictions, be a liberal anti-Plattist today." Gómez, they charged, sponsored "assassination as a campaign tactic." They also condemned Estrada Palma in similarly revolutionary nationalist terms, arguing that he was "yesterday an elitist revolutionary [and] cannot today be—as he pretends to show by banding together with the old colonial Autonomists—a sincere follower of the creed of Martí condensed in this phrase: Cuba *with all and for all*."[51]

Nevertheless, Liberal advisers worked hard to improve Gómez's image after the nomination, hoping to equate him with the ideal of social unity incarnated in Martí. Gómez personally courted popular-class voters, especially blacks, and portrayed himself as a man of "the masses" who had nothing in common with the stiff-lipped and stoic Estrada Palma. Gómez went as far as to produce a phonograph of a propaganda speech he had given in which he used the "terms and sayings of the Cuban *guajiro*."[52] Moreover, a pamphlet later justifying the use of arms against Estrada Palma's corrupt state and excusing Liberals' complicity with its interventionist outcome implied no less than four times that the spirit of Martí had been resurrected in the figure of José Miguel Gómez.[53] Rather than appropriate texts or memories of Martí, Liberal campaign managers preferred to gloss the metamorphosis of Martí into Gómez by invoking the image of the good caudillo who had rewarded his popular nationalist soldiers and rural folk during the war. The central idea behind Liberals' claims was that Martí's "true" successors were none other than the Liberals themselves.

Like pro-imperialist nationalists who supported Estrada Palma and justified their right to rule by commemorating the death of Martí, Liberals entombed memories of Martí in a martyr's casket. In so doing, they hoped to contain discussion of the means by which the ideal of "social unity" could not only be defined through specific policies but also implemented as a priority of the state. Liberal leaders needed popular nationalist support to win the elections or, if necessary, force Estrada Palma to step down, but they stopped far short of genuinely allowing voters to set the agenda. At the height of their battles with Estrada Palma's authoritarian rule in 1906, at least one Liberal writer, Roque E. Garrigó, did remind followers of Martí's passionate critiques of U.S. imperialism. However, the reference was only meant to warn readers that they needed to vote for Liberals or face the collapse of sovereignty forever. Continued pro-imperialist nationalist rule could only lead to the U.S. annexation of Cuba, he predicted, because its extremism would soon lead to social explosion.[54]

Time would show that Garrigó was far from wrong. Between the organization of the Moderates in late 1904 and November elections in 1905, Estrada Palma's administration engineered the first waves of political terror in the republican era. Convinced that the loss of the presidency to the Liberals would mean sure disaster for the pro-imperialist nationalist nation they imagined, Moderates urged Estrada Palma to reorganize his cabinet along strict party lines. The resulting "Gabinete de Combate," or Combat Cabinet, as it became known to Moderates and Liberals alike, was dominated by two figures, Rafael Montalvo, secretary of public works, and Fernando Freyre de Andrade, secretary of governance, both formidable pro-imperialist nationalists among New York emigrés during the 1895 War. In the coming months, these men proved that they would stop at nothing to ensure Moderate control of local political systems and the national electoral process.

State Terror and the Remaking of a Revolutionary
and Popular Nationalist Alliance

Starting in the summer of 1904 and ending with the August Revolution of 1906, pro-imperialist nationalist officials at all levels of government, local and national, began to turn regularly to physical violence and psychological intimidation in order to ensure the continued triumph of their vision of nation. During this period, state agents refused to conform their exercise of power to any set of predictable rules, even the constitutional code of law that had brought the Republic and therefore the state itself into being. Consequently, Cubans of all social classes began to perceive the state's actions as legal and moral violations that left the state devoid of any legitimacy or moral authority before its citizenry. Such violations constituted a frontal assault on the memory of the struggle for independence and the expectations for political and social change intrinsic to it. Cuba's pro-imperialist nationalists had come to adopt an extreme view: the only way social unity could be achieved and their vision of nation consolidated was through the total surrender to their authority of the opposing side.

Despite the secrecy in which Moderates operated and the general climate of fear that facilitated their impunity, evidence about events is not in short supply. Once the U.S. military intervened in 1906, it carried out a meticulous investigation of Liberal charges against the Moderates at the local level. Since the Roosevelt administration favored the Moderates over the Liberals, whose revolutionary pedigree and populist instincts they did not trust, Moderate agents often accompanied U.S. field investigators in their work. Nonetheless, the U.S. military deemed Moderates' use of terror in over twenty municipalities indisputable. The following discussion centers on these cases. Orchestrated through the Gabinete de Combate in the Presidential Palace, Moderates in the provinces began to force the resignation of Liberals elected to municipal office by using agents in local law enforcement as instruments of harassment and intimidation. Typically, Moderates accomplished this by provoking armed confrontations between Moderates and Liberals in local towns, employing force and sanctioning the mass arrest of Liberal officials. They also intimidated Liberal officials and their allies into resigning their posts through Machiavellian means of rumor and innuendo that indicted the gender or sexual honor of Liberals' family members. Deprived of social prestige and business contacts since clients often shied away from men with sons and daughters of questionable sexual repute, the Liberals in question then surrendered their posts without further comment.

For example, as soon as the Moderate Party founded its headquarters for the town of Cruces in April 1905, Moderates "began to harass the Liberal element of the town, . . . trying to displease all of them, gossiping and lying to the extent that it affected the private lives of many of the best-known people in town." As elections approached for the local scrutiny boards that would oversee presidential elections in November, the Moderates asked the mayor of Cruces for permission to hold a parade on behalf of Estrada Palma's candidacy. The mayor then called on the police force, mainly Liberals, to follow the marchers along the parade route in order to discourage the Moderates from provoking or attacking Liberal bystanders. Local Liberal leaders asked the party faithful to remain indoors "so as not to give the Government any pretext to commit violent acts such as were committed [under similar circumstances] in Palmira and other places." However, since the formation of the Gabinete de Combate in early 1905, the Moderates had begun to rely on the Rural Guard as the political militia of the executive branch. When the parade started at sunset with the largely Liberal town police in tow, a local thug fired on police, signaling the Rural Guard to attack the police with their machetes. The following day, a Moderate judge arrived with orders to arrest all Liberal officials, including the mayor, the chief of police, and three policemen, and over thirty town residents. The officials and eight citizens were held in the Cienfuegos jail for more than a month before being released on bail. The condition for the release of town officials was that they agree to resign from office.[55]

In other cases, like those of San Luis and Guane, Pinar del Río, Moderate police arrested Liberal officials on trumped-up charges of falsifying government documents in order to force their resignations. Through such means, whole municipalities once dominated by Liberals were suddenly transformed into Moderate strongholds.[56] But municipal governments were not the sole targets of Moderate strategies; they also included school boards, police departments, and public employees. By September 1905, in the town of Lajas, three different police chiefs had been appointed in less than two months. The reason for this was that all three had been sent to jail when they tried to enforce the law or protect officials' lives to the detriment of Moderate electoral tactics. In other cases, police officers were simply arrested, jailed, and released only after elections for scrutiny boards that month ended. Because of their short- and long-term influence over future generations and voting parents, schools were special targets for "*Moderación* [Moderation]." Teachers and school superintendents, especially in the provinces of Oriente and Santa Clara, were summarily fired in the weeks before elections of scrutiny boards "for refusing to prostitute their consciences." Moderates even went as far as to abolish schools located in wards entirely composed of registered Liberals. In the municipal government of Havana, normally a fortress of Liberalism, Moderates succeeded in dismissing 130 public employees.[57]

Unaccustomed to scenes of such violence since the Spanish repression of independence rebels, small-town residents were especially horrified to discover that the targets of Moderate repression were not lower-class "bandits" or troublemakers hiding in the bush but wealthy, upstanding citizens living and working in their towns. Unable to dismiss those attacked as socially insignificant, observers were equally unable to rationalize their repression by the Rural Guard or Moderate members of the police force as apolitical. Moderate senator José Frías, a key organizer of the Cienfuegos project for erecting a monument to Martí in the city's Central Park, relied on his band of thugs, the Partida de la Porra, to make examples out of socially prominent Liberals. For example, the Partida de la Porra invaded Liberal representative Agustín Cruz's home in the fishing village of Santa Isabel de las Lajas and sent his family fleeing in their bedclothes onto the streets after a night of abuse under a hail of bullets.[58] In places such as Rodas, a small town near Cienfuegos, the climate of fear that the Partida de la Porra generated proved so paralyzing that Moderates found the resignation of Liberal town officials unnecessary. Moderates extorted votes and cash from the local population at will.[59]

The fact that Moderates referred to such strategies of coercion as a process of "moderating" local politics reveals the degree to which they believed the expectations of Cubans were getting out of hand. For Estrada Palma and his Gabinete de Combate, state-sponsored violence was understood as consistent with the need to contain radical elements of the recent 1895 Revolution, of which they had once formed a part. As pro-imperialist nationalists, they had espoused this policy of revolutionary "containment" all along but had not needed to carry it out until the recent mobilization of Liberals made real social change through legislative mandate a political possibility. But the overt political nature of Moderate attacks radicalized and unified citizens who might otherwise have been tempted to turn a blind eye to state-sponsored repression. For members of the popular classes, especially urban workers, the situation was particularly difficult. Moderates hoped to create the illusion of lower-class support by coercing them into joining the Moderate Party. The effect, however, was to galvanize opposition and increase the possibilities for cross-class alliances against the Moderates. As Salvador Cisneros Betancourt observed at the time, "The seeds of terror have been planted." More Cuban blood had been made to run in the streets of some provincial towns over the last few months, he remarked, than their residents had witnessed at any time during the wars for independence.[60] By making victims out of the "high and mighty" at a local level, Moderates humbled wealthy Liberals that poor people knew personally, recasting them in the role of fellow citizens. Consequently, state authoritarianism may well have rekindled ties of loyalty between willing revolutionary nationalist patrons and would-be popular nationalist political clients by giving them greater reason to sympathize with each other than they might otherwise have felt.

One of the best examples of this phenomenon occurred in Caibarién, on the northern coast of Santa Clara province. Because of the complicity of the national government, no elections for municipal offices had ever been held in Caibarién, and the same mayor who had ruled the town under Spain simply continued in office after the inauguration of the Republic. By 1905, this mayor had held his post for a remarkable twenty-nine years. Upon joining the Moderate Party, the mayor, "obeying the motto of the [central] Government," proceeded to arm thirty-two residents of the area as a secret police force. From then on, the secret police began to subject "the persons of worth of the Liberal Party" to round-the-clock surveillance and an unending stream of anonymous threats. Liberals in the Customs House and telegraph offices resigned, as did the municipal doctor.

However, according to Liberal leaders in the area, the brunt of Moderate harassment fell on the "sovereign *pueblo*, the *pueblo* that works for its living." That is, Moderates targeted the sponge hunters, fishermen, woodcutters, charcoal makers, stevedores, sailors, and day laborers who made up not only the majority of the town's population but also the bulk of supporters for the Liberal presidential bid. In late 1904, the newly "moderated" Customs House began to impose taxes on fishermen that were so high that they could not afford to fish. Fishermen who refused to pay the tax and fished anyway then became subject to fines. Liberal stevedores, "all of whom were black [*todos negros*]," were unable to obtain immunization papers from the port doctor, without which they could not report for work. Subject to ridiculously exorbitant new taxes, Félix Castro, the rich Liberal owner of a private railroad, found himself forced to close his railroad, laying off some eighty men in the process. Not surprisingly, Castro, together with thirty followers (possibly his own workers), was one of the first men to take to the countryside in armed rebellion against the state in 1906. At first, Caibarién's Liberal leaders reacted to the intolerable conditions by passing a resolution that dissolved their party. But after holding a public meeting attended by over 700 Cubans, they decided to take a hard line against Moderate intimidation. Moderates responded by switching tactics: "The Government offered each fisherman of sponges [and] fish, woodcutters or stevedores that if they would be *moderated* [*que si se moderaban*] they could fish for sponges much smaller than the law required, that they could fish anywhere they wanted, . . . the woodcutters could cut wood on any key owned by the Government and that stevedores would obtain their immunization papers." Not surprisingly, many of the more than 1,200 workers in such industries found the Moderates' offer hard to refuse. Still, when election day for scrutiny boards arrived, the Liberal vote was "drowned by the force of the bayonets." With their salaries and travel expenses paid by Estrada Palma's government, the Rural Guard, municipal police, 32 secret police, and 100 privately armed militiamen joined in the repression.[61]

Apparently, the efforts of Rafael Montalvo, secretary of public works, in Havana had served as a model for Moderates in Caibarién. After Montalvo's installation in the Gabinete de Combate, changes of personnel involved not only those in technical and clerical positions but also workers carrying out manual labor. "Hundreds of men were left without employment, and their places largely filled by Spaniards, improvised Cuban citizens," Liberal leaders complained. Through such means, the Moderates had hoped to provide themselves with a ready pool of willing demonstrators for campaign rallies as well as foot soldiers they could organize into "guerrillas" for the subsequent commandeering of polling stations. Significantly, Liberal leaders understood these strategies as highly racialized. By targeting blacks, the Moderates hoped to gain for their side the very sector of society from which all previous revolutions had drawn the bulk of their numbers. Using this logic, Liberals charged, the brother of Domingo Méndez Capote and the director of the new Department of Public Sanitation centralized control over scavengers and street-sweeps in Havana with state patronage. In return for their loyalty to the Moderate Party, Fernando Méndez Capote recruited "pardoned jail-birds and well-known *ñáñigos* of this city" as sanitation workers.[62]

That the Moderates did attempt to exploit black Cubans' growing disillusionment with the Republic through this and other means is clear. A September 1905 manifesto issued by a lower-level black Moderate in Pinar del Río invoked the historical memory of blacks' century-long struggle for freedom in order to legitimate the policies of the present regime. Implying that black Cubans had always been used as cannon fodder in the past, the manifesto warned that the same men who had called on blacks to sacrifice their lives for independence with false promises would soon turn to similar tactics. Once officers of the Revolution, they were now all Liberals.[63]

Nonetheless, few black Cubans cared to invest in the pro-imperialist nationalist–styled message of social unity that the Moderates were selling. The experience of Jorge Varela, a black veteran who accepted a job in Fernando Méndez Capote's sanitation department, represents a case in point. Varela, once a colonel in the Liberating Army, received a death threat in May 1906, apparently from his former black subordinates, after he accepted a job as a garbage collector from Méndez Capote. These veterans accused Varela of undermining their efforts to organize a new, armed movement against the government on behalf of democracy and of violating the nation for which they had all once fought and for which they had to continue fighting. "Colonel," the writers demanded, "don't you know that the President doesn't like blacks even enough to let them shine his shoes ... [?] Don't you see that they have given you nothing more than [the job] of captain of garbage, and that you are only one of the lackeys of the Government ... [made] to stick yourself in the pants of the [Méndez] Capote [brothers?]"[64]

Regardless of the outright hostility that many Liberals had shown toward autonomous black protests in the past, many black Cubans deepened their affiliation to the Liberal Party as a result of alienation from the national government's brutality. Even more so than during the 1895 War, blacks were disproportionately represented in the Constitutional Army organized to fight the administration in the summer of 1906, a matter discussed below.

The role of the national government in the "moderation" process that gripped the country from 1904 to 1906 was undeniable. In general, Secretary of Governance Freyre de Andrade took responsibility for interfering in local governments on behalf of the administration. This entailed allocating rewards to regional strongmen who worked for Moderate control in their areas as well as authorizing municipal mayors to ignore any instructions that emanated from a non-Moderate provincial source. In return for securing Moderate control of the municipal government in Sagua la Grande, for instance, Freyre de Andrade arranged for the public employment of all the male members of Brigadier José Luis Robau's entire family at extraordinarily high rates of pay.[65] But Estrada Palma himself also issued presidential decrees overturning political decisions and changes in leadership made at the level of municipal governments that might otherwise have hurt Moderate interests.[66] With Estrada Palma's full consent, Freyre de Andrade ordered the dismissal of thirty-two municipal mayors of the Liberal Party on charges of fraud or dereliction of duty, including (once again) Juan O'Farrill of Havana.[67] Importantly, Estrada Palma legitimated his actions on the basis of Spanish legal codes, not the Cuban Constitution. Under Spanish law, any evidence of dereliction of duty permitted the chief executive to remove and replace municipal officials at will. Nonetheless, the reasons he cited for removal of officials often rang quite hollow.[68] The fact that the officials Estrada Palma replaced had been elected to office rather than appointed did not matter. Moreover, the more obvious point that Spanish law should no longer apply in an independent republic, no matter the nature of its political system, also made absolutely no difference.

Still, Estrada Palma and Freyre de Andrade took the need to justify their actions seriously. As perhaps with all instances of state terror, deniability was central to the government's success. Freyre de Andrade's staff was careful to leave a paper trail that justified the ordering of policy reversals at the local level by the national government or sanctioned the removal of Liberals from municipal office. However fraudulent, victory at the elections remained a priority. Convinced that Moderates were fighting an uphill battle for modernity against backward and ignorant masses, Estrada Palma and his cabinet engineered a landslide victory for the Moderate Party in the November elections of 1905 that surpassed all expectations — including those of fellow Moderates.[69] When U.S. officials later questioned Freyre de Andrade about the use of the Rural Guard and the police to ensure a smashing victory for the Moderates, he replied that "he had simply opposed force with force." When asked about the extra 150,000 ballots that had been cast over the number of eligible registered voters on the island, Freyre de Andrade said that such a thing "was possibly true, but that it was impossible to hold an election in Cuba without fraud."[70]

In truth, much of the violent repression exhibited at the polls during the elections was unwarranted since Moderate domination of electoral boards had ensured that the names of Liberal candidates would not appear on voting ballots. Moreover, the leadership of the Liberal Party eventually called for Liberals to boycott the elections entirely, which most of them did.[71] Thus, the state's use of violence implied multiple agendas, only one of which was to ensure the Moderates' election. Other objectives had to do with the need of the state to assert its monopoly on the use of violence and to undermine the utility of contested, multiparty elections altogether. By attempting to establish a monopoly over violence and political power, pro-imperialist nationalists used force as a means of expanding the state's political presence, centralizing its authority, and coercing the integration of scattered populations into a unified system of control. Desperate to accelerate the process by which it might achieve modernity and thereby acceptance in the U.S.-dominated club of "civilized" and modern nations, Moderates acted in ways that, on the surface at least, seemed essential to establishing state stability and power. In other words, they propelled their project for a nation-state over the threshold of modernity before securing the structural and social rudiments so vital to the organization and existence of any modern nation-state.[72] Through excessive shows of force, the state sought to neutralize local revolutionary nationalists' competing claims to legitimacy and short-circuit any popular nationalist support for those claims. The Moderates seem to have decided that one-party rule through force strengthened the state and established the future of the pro-imperialist nationalist nation they imagined on firm ground.

Critical to the Moderates' plan for accelerating the state's ascent to modernity and their nation's rise to civilization was the discursive marginalization of political opponents as potential rebels and of the popular classes as untrustworthy "non-citizens." So convinced of the purity of their objectives were members of

Estrada Palma's cabinet by May 1906 that Freyre de Andrade summarized Cuba's situation—only months before the fall of the Republic—in this way: "Our Republic has just passed through a critical period, emerging from it with its credit fortified in the exterior and moral peace affirmed in the interior."[73] As the key architect of Estrada Palma's "reelection" strategy, Freyre de Andrade signaled his faith in the consolidation of Moderate power over society by deciding to turn his post of secretary of governance over to General J. Rius Rivera and to assume the role of president of the House of Representatives. Having secured Estrada Palma's return and the helms of both the House and Senate, Moderates assured themselves that the legislative construction of an ideal pro-imperialist nationalist nation was in sight.

Within days of the 1905 elections, it could have surprised almost no one that the first groups of revolutionaries took to the field, draping their flag of Cuba Libre in black. Unlike the independence wars of the past, Cubans everywhere had already chosen sides by the time the first shots of protest rang out. The word "*pacífico*" could not and did not apply to any significant proportion of the population as it had during the 1895 War, because the conditions that Estrada Palma and the Moderates had created did not allow for neutrality. Declaring one's political affiliation and making it a matter of public record was a necessary first step in the "moderation" process. However, the opposition did not organize itself under one distinct banner until the eve of the August Revolution of 1906 when the Liberal Party declared itself the civilian wing of armed rebels in the field. By then, rebels were organized into a broadly based Constitutional Army, complete with a funding and propaganda base in New York.[74] According to its Liberal leadership, the Revolution of 1895 had been reborn. How Cubans of different nationalist currents viewed this role in relation to the "nations" they defended changed forever the character of their nationalisms as well as the development of U.S. imperialism itself.

Reviving the Revolution: Liberals, Moderates, and the Battle to Contain Popular Nationalists

By the fall of 1905, the growing hostility of the Cuban public toward Moderate rule was palpable. Salvador Cisneros Betancourt testified to this when he observed that at the start of the Republic, the president had traveled freely all over the island without need of even a few bodyguards. By September 1905, however, so vulnerable had the president become that the "police and the Rural Guard are not sufficient for his safety; rather, it is expressly necessary that in the Palace . . . should be housed . . . a company of the Artillery Corps."[75] Still, the obvious reluctance of Liberal leaders to ally with popular nationalists in armed revolution clearly strengthened the Moderates' position. Whether out of concern over the renewed interest of the U.S. Senate in annexationist projects or out of fear that popular nationalist radicals would get out of hand, top Liberal leaders seemed indisposed to resort to organized force against the state.[76] After the fraudulent elections for scrutiny boards on September 23, 1905, José Miguel Gómez resigned as chief of the Liberal Party and booked passage to the United States in fear for his life.[77] Once in New York, he publicly denounced the situation in Cuba and called for U.S. diplomatic intervention to guarantee the holding of new elections.[78] He did not return to Cuba until January 1906, at which point he settled into a well-compensated job as manager for the Silveira Sugar Company's estate Quince y Medio.[79]

But if top Liberal chiefs were unwilling to risk everything the Republic had gained economically and politically since 1902 in pursuit of a more revolutionary and democratic nation, many midlevel and rank-and-file popular nationalist Liberals did not feel the same way. For them, no risk was too great. From their perspective, neither they nor the Republic had gained very much since 1902. Therefore, neither they nor the Republic had much to lose. As a Liberal Party manifesto conceded that September, "The same tricks were resorted to during the colonial days when it was desired to throw into prison or deport antigovernmental elements."[80] *La Lucha* echoed these sentiments, saying that yesterday, under the Spanish, a republican constitution was good only for the cleaning of rifles; today, the Constitution was good only for being ignored.[81] If Liberals who refused to take up arms expressed such indignation, those who did take them up expressed utter outrage. In late November 1905, only days before the elections of December 1, organized groups of rebels rose in arms under the leadership of Evaristo Estenoz in the area between San Antonio de los Baños and Alquízar, Havana province.

Because the rebels captured a minimal amount of equipment from local farms and engaged in only brief skirmishes with the Rural Guard before being arrested,[82] apparently only one historian has made mention of their appearance, let alone investigated their motives.[83] However, close inspection of the events immediately preceding the uprising as well as the evidence presented at the rebels' trial reveals a high degree of planning, coordination between urban and rural participants, and substantial financing. In fact, the greatest significance of this movement might actually lie in its failure. The fact that state security forces were able to abort this revolution suggests much more than just a high degree of vigilance exercised by the Moderate state; it suggests the possibility that foul play may have contributed to the Revolution's unraveling—foul play originating in the upper ranks of the Liberal Party itself.

On November 20, 1905, Havana's secret police filed a report with the special court judge who would preside over the rebels' trial only two weeks later. For some time, the secret police had been conducting a surveillance operation on the home of Evaristo Estenoz and the French fashion boutique operated by his wife. According to the investigating officers, Estenoz was nowhere to be found. Because Estenoz's mother-in-law accompanied his wife (a frequent occurrence whenever Estenoz traveled), the agent believed that Estenoz had gone to his home province of Oriente, presumably to collect funds for the armed revolt he was planning. Estenoz's mistress subsequently corroborated this theory. Additionally, the agent reported that an informant had overheard several prominent Liberals, including Máximo Gómez's former assistant, Orestes Ferrara, discussing the finer points of their conspiracy against the government in a Havana restaurant. Apparently, the rebels planned to rise in arms at various locations on both extremes of the island on the fifteenth of the month, although it is not clear whether this was meant to be November 15 or December 15, that is, before or after the elections. With the Rural Guard sufficiently distracted in the repression of these uprisings, rebels in Havana would then assassinate Tomás Estrada Palma. In the event of the president's death, the authority of the 1902 Constitution would call on the Liberal Alfredo Zayas, still president of the Senate until the Moderate "landslide victory" was ratified, to assume the chair of the presidency. At that point, Zayas would declare the recent election results invalid and force the calling of new elections, this time with both parties' tickets fully represented and fairly counted. The high degree of specificity this informant offered implies that he was not eavesdropping on a private conversation in a public place. Rather, he probably participated in the planning of the operation, then handed the names of his fellow conspirators over to police. According to the agent filing the report, all Liberals knew the informant well because he was a Liberal leader himself and "many of the Liberal Party fear him."[84]

Evidence against the conspirators included two large caches of arms confiscated from safehouses by the secret police almost a month before the uprising took place. Forcing their way into his home, agents surprised a twenty-two-year-old Havana mechanic who had stashed twenty-one boxes of gun powder (one of them weighing twenty-five pounds), eleven metal cases of finely pulverized gun powder (for the making of explosives), two boxes of grenades, 15,000–20,000 bullets for various types of guns, as well as many boxes and bags of bullets for use in .38-caliber revolvers and .44-caliber rifles.[85] Days earlier, secret police had raided another suspected safehouse where they found thirty-one packages of heavy paper (probably for making dynamite), forty-one brand-new rapid-fire rifles with their factory packing still intact, twenty-one *tercerolas* made for firing on horseback, a few pistols, and approximately 5,000 bullets. Most incriminating of all was a specially outfitted piano-shaped box that had been used for transporting the weaponry to and from the empty flat without arousing suspicion.[86] Finally, a few days following the roundup of the fifty-five rebels from the site of their encounter with Rural Guardsmen and camps in the field, two Spanish fishermen discovered a bomb hidden along a pier of the Playa del Chino.[87]

Evidently, rebels calculated that the combination of bomb blasts on the outskirts of the city and simultaneous uprisings in the countryside would draw the Rural Guard, the majority of whom were already stationed on the western and eastern halves of the island, away from the capital. This would open up the potential for a successful assault on the Presidential Palace. Since the total force of Rural Guardsmen was small (not more than 3,000 nationwide) and popular antipathy for the person of Estrada Palma high, the rebels probably believed that their plan was not as far-fetched as it was daring. However, someone clearly derailed their plans before they had a chance to get off the ground. Did more prominent Liberals (who later remained unnamed in the prosecutor's case) back out at the last minute, leaving the more dedicated to fight by themselves? Were Liberal Party chiefs attempting to sideline the more radical and independently minded members of their popular nationalist lower-level leadership? Could José Miguel Gómez, a former supporter of Estrada Palma and Liberal turncoat, have persuaded other Liberals to betray Estenoz?

Given the past leadership experience and youth of the rebels captured, one is tempted to believe that their plan to overthrow the state could have succeeded. As a former lieutenant in the Liberating Army, Estenoz's popularity as a labor leader only added to the prestige of the nine veterans topping the list of captured rebels, most of them officers of the Liberating Army, who had joined him in the uprising.[88] Although most of the veterans were natives of Havana province, two were from Santa Clara and Camagüey while Estenoz himself hailed from Oriente. The high incidence of identical patronyms among those arrested also indicates that kinship played a role in mobilizing participants in the area. Of the fifty-one rebels who stated their professions, the vast majority were working-class: twenty-eight were day laborers or manual workers (listed variously as *labrador*, *obrero*, or *jornalero*); seventeen worked in commerce or the service industry or exercised a trade such as shoe-cobbling or cigarmaking. The remaining six rebels included the ex–municipal mayor of Alquízar, one scribe, two property owners, a policeman, and a plantation sugar master. Only one man of the total held a criminal record, and only one sported a shady reputation as a gambler and speculator.[89] The rest appear to have been upstanding citizens whose alienation from the Republic was political, personal, or both. More than one veteran of officer rank among the rebels could claim no other occupation than that of day laborer by 1906. Presumably, despite their contributions to the Revolution, these veterans' economic conditions had not improved since before 1895. Quite possibly, they may have worsened. Fearful that popular nationalist rebel leaders might radicalize the Republic if they became heroic founders of a new revolutionary state, revolutionary nationalist Liberals may well have ensured their defeat. Significantly, many veterans unconnected with Estenoz's movement interpreted the rebels' ideological motives in this way, prompting concern among Moderate state officials and their supposed enemies in the Liberal Party leadership.[90]

A court found the rebels guilty of "the crimes of rebellion, conspiracy, sedition, disobedience, [and] public disturbance" in December 1905. Amazingly, though, the president took advantage of his right to grant the rebels amnesty six months later in honor of José Martí on the eleventh anniversary of his death.[91] Symbolically, his actions meshed well with the image of Martí that Moderates wanted to cultivate: it not only demonstrated Estrada Palma's authority over people's lives but also showed his willingness to forgive those who betrayed him, if only on the condition that they surrender humbly to his authority. But more than an act of political "forgiveness," the decree of amnesty might also have been calculated to widen the ideological rift among Liberal forces. By discrediting those who chose arms over words to express their opposition to the state, Estrada Palma may have hoped to increase their resentment of more powerful Liberals whom they already suspected of betraying them in the first place. If so, Estrada Palma's plot did not go as planned.

Although historians have depicted the "Constitutional Army" as a neatly organized revolutionary movement under the direct command of the Liberal Party, this view does not withstand close scrutiny. The independence with which various forces took to the field in August 1906 bears out the notion that popular nationalists were fighting for radical goals: many if not most revolutionaries outside of the Liberal Party's immediate leadership defined their goals in distinctly nonpartisan terms. That is, protesting the terror tactics and political corruption of the Moderates did not necessarily go hand-in-hand with either loyalty to Liberal leaders or adherence to their strictly limited goal: defense of the Constitution and true electoral democracy.

In mid-August 1906, sporadic reports of an armed rebel movement in Pinar del Río began to reach Havana. General Alejandro Rodríguez responded by stationing a large squadron of Rural Guardsmen before the Presidential Palace in the Plaza de Armas.[92] Meanwhile, in Vueltabajo, Pinar del Río, site of the 1895 revolutionary underground headed by Magdalena Peñarredonda, General Faustino "Pino" Guerra rose up in arms. Seconded by Colonel Ernesto Asbert's forces in Havana province, Guerra mustered rebel troops estimated to number around 2,000, possibly more. Alarmed at the discovery that the revolutionaries had siphoned recruits from the ranks of the Rural Guard, Havana's Secret Police ordered the immediate arrest of suspected conspirators and the searching of their homes in the capital. Named as the most prominent of the Revolution's organizers were the three sons of Generals Calixto García, José de Jesús Monteagudo, and Enrique Loynaz del Castillo and various leaders of the aborted revolution of 1905, including Evaristo Estenoz.

In addition, Juan Gualberto Gómez and a fellow black Liberal were apprehended in Santiago while on a political speaking tour. Because most men arrested were prominent Liberal leaders and all of them were veteran officers of the independence wars with popular-class constituencies, the police's decision to conduct seizures and searches in broad daylight shocked the Cuban public. Having turned up no evidence linking them to revolutionaries in the field, police released some suspects within seventy-two hours but kept the more important of them in jail. Rather than quell Liberal leaders' inclination to support the rebellion, police harassment seemed to prompt the most politically radical of them into action. After being arrested by one his former subordinates from the 1895 War, General Loynaz del Castillo carried out a daring escape from the vehicle transporting him to police headquarters. Days later, Loynaz del Castillo surfaced at Havana's city limits, the head of one of the fastest growing regiments in the Constitutional Army.[93]

Similarly, Evaristo Estenoz took the first opportunity to join a volunteer force that General Quintín Banderas had organized. Court-martialed for shirking the authority of white commanders during the 1895 War, Banderas had consistently articulated a libertarian interpretation of popular nationalism. Having suffered public humiliation and official disregard for the merits of his revolutionary contributions since then, Banderas emerged in 1906 as a symbol of black Cubans' discontent and general hostility toward the Estrada Palma regime. Although Banderas and Estenoz managed to escape Havana and integrate themselves to forces in the field, Secret Police confiscated the bulk of their resources from the home of another black rebel. These included twenty newly sharpened machetes, thirty-five explosives, and almost 400 bullets.[94]

Not surprisingly, the conservative press took full advantage of Banderas and Estenoz's high-profile, all-black regiment to discredit the Revolution as a socially radical, anarchic threat. Although Banderas's troops were almost immediately dispersed by a detachment of forces under the personal command of General Emilio Nuñez, the provincial governor of Havana, the August 26 edition of *El Fígaro* presented Banderas as the Revolution's principal instigator. Placed in the middle of a group of photographs of rebel leaders was a sharp-eyed, black-skinned image of Quintín Banderas that was four times larger than that of any other rebel. The contrast between his image and a similarly enlarged portrait of the handsome, white lieutenant of the Rural Guard recently killed in action served as a visual metaphor for the magazine's political views. While the Revolution represented racial disorder, cultural savagery, and political anarchy, the pro-imperialist nationalist state protected the social order, traditional standards of gender respectability, and modern civilization.[95]

Indeed, by the time *El Fígaro* ran the story, Quintín Banderas was already dead. Reduced to only fourteen men after the initial encounter with Nuñez's forces, Banderas's troops were assaulted after midnight by a force of forty Rural Guardsmen. Savagely attacked with machetes while they were sleeping, Banderas and two other men of color had little time to defend themselves. The Guardsmen also discharged bullets into the skull of Banderas to assure that he was dead. One of the other men's bodies was attacked with such force that the blade of the machete literally hacked him in two. Clearly, official accounts of the operation displayed all the earmarks of a professional assassination, not a military assault. It was meant to. Government authorities made no effort to conceal the bodies' mutilation, placing the cadavers on public display in Havana's morgue as early as noon of the following day. *La Lucha* described the multitude that turned out to see how state agents had treated these former heroes of the independence wars as "a human avalanche." Later, Banderas's widow (whom pathologists counseled not to see the body) showed up at the Presidential Palace to demand that authorities surrender her husband's remains. Estrada Palma refused, conceding only that Banderas should be given "a decent burial." Symbolic of the kind of threat that Banderas represented, the press reported that at the time of his death, Banderas carried only two Spanish dollars and three cents on his person.[96]

Days later, *La Lucha* published a letter found in Banderas's breastcoat in which he pleaded with the Liberal leadership to aid his forces and stated that his troops had been betrayed in the initial assault by Nuñez. When Liberal leader Baldomero Acosta promised to bring fresh recruits for his forces, Banderas waited for them at a designated spot. What Acosta brought instead was "300 *rurales*." Just as Banderas's men were watering their horses and relieving them of their saddles, they were attacked. For Banderas, this was no coincidence: "And that's why I find myself here alone, isolated from everyone."[97] His revolutionary nationalist allies in the Revolution were going to let him be killed, and Banderas died knowing it.

Certainly, the large number of black Cubans who joined the ranks of the Constitutional Army did much to fuel the paranoia of the state and encourage discomfort among their white Liberal allies. Because the state had no remaining credibility with the popular nationalists, the potential for the Revolution to exceed the goals of its leaders and explode into a fury of social upheaval was apparent to everyone. Moreover, the fact that the Revolution had begun in the western provinces as opposed to the east must have struck a chord with many. Since the nineteenth century, rebellion as a means of protest and change had been characteristic of Oriente, the cradle of all three independence wars, but Pinar del Río had become known as "*la bella durmiente*" (Sleeping Beauty) to most Cubans. Daily realities were defying the stereotype of a province that many considered to have been populated by sleepy, apathetic peasants. By August 23, the Revolution had spread eastward to Santa Clara province, a move that defied historical patterns and traditional expectations. There, Eduardo Guzmán and Orestes Ferrara amassed a force of 6,000–8,000 additional men.[98] By expropriating property from thousands of citizens as *mambises* had done in the independence wars, a large number of these forces were armed and mounted.[99]

But if the rebels had learned from their experience in the independence wars, Estrada Palma and his cronies had learned equally well. Recalling that the primary difficulty of the PRC lay in the acquisition and shipment of arms from the United States, the president immediately requested and received the right to purchase arms and horses from U.S. agents in New York.[100] To reinforce the small number of Rural Guardsmen on which its security relied, Estrada Palma's administration still had to resort to the hiring of 10,000 mercenaries (some of whom were common criminals) at exorbitant rates of pay. In the opinion of Alejandro Rodríguez, the commanding officer of state forces, the unruly militias "were worse than useless."[101]

Yet, according to official manifestos put forth by the revolutionary leadership, any fear that the destructive methods and radical underpinnings of the Revolution of 1895 could be repeated were wholly unfounded. As early as July 28, 1906, the Revolution's leadership issued a manifesto that declared the objectives of the movement to be threefold: first, to restore the power of the Cuban Constitution; second, to expel members of Congress elected through illicit or fraudulent means; and third, to ensure the holding of new elections. Additionally, the manifesto assured citizens that its purpose was not "revenge" or even the installation of an unelected official in the presidency. Electoral freedom, it intoned, was strictly the Revolution's highest goal.[102] On September 1, the revolutionary leadership reconfirmed its intentions, adding only that all political prisoners connected with the electoral repression of Liberals should be released: "We demand nothing and nothing shall we demand besides the restoration of legality."[103]

In the limited time the revolutionaries operated, they generally avoided giving property owners reason to fear them. Unlike the previous independence wars, for instance, the Constitutional Army refrained from attacking any U.S.-owned properties.[104] When questioned by reporters, rebel commanders like Pino Guerra generally skirted the inflammatory issue of tactics altogether. Moreover, they also tended to pledge allegiance only to the electoral process, not specific social ends. For instance, when a reporter from the *North American Review* asked Guerra whom he would support for president, Guerra replied, "If Tomas Estrada Palma should be elected by a fair vote, I would give him my whole support. But the present conditions are intolerable. If the American people had to endure such a Government as Palma's is today, they would not permit it to remain in power five days."[105]

This did not mean, however, that rank-and-file revolutionaries shared the same cautious perspective. Undoubtedly, the links between the unresolved expectations popular nationalists derived from memories of the 1895 War and the current situation were real. This was partly the case because countless former comrades-in-arms now stood in violent opposition to each other. More indisputably than ever before, all romantic illusions of the glorious "fraternal" past were daily being called into question.[106] If Moderates had insisted on invoking the collective memory of social unity during the height of political repression, they were not doing so now. Rather, in light of a violent revolution meant to topple them from power and destroy the pro-imperialist nationalist "nation" just as it was becoming a reality, the Moderates perceived their opponents as committing the ultimate betrayal of the past, a past whose struggles they interpreted in their own terms. For the popular nationalist rebels, on the other hand, a state that ignored their demands and subverted the electoral process, the only channel by which they could implement those demands, could not be allowed to continue. In relying on violence to enforce a standard of unity that eliminated the possibilities for dissent, Moderates attacked the foundation of the nation popular nationalists identified with Martí and created new martyrs to it. The brutal assassination of Quintín Banderas and the public desecration of his body provided only the most recent example of this. For the thousands of Cubans who filed past it, Banderas's lifeless corpse embodied Moderates' attempts to destroy the promise of the 1895 Revolution and their collective memory of past social unity. If Estrada Palma wanted to bury this memory, the revolutionaries wanted to exhume and resurrect it.

When revolutionary nationalists like Pino Guerra articulated an understanding of contemporary state injustices informed by the past, they tapped this collective memory of social unity as popular nationalists understood it. As Guerra stated at the start of the war, "I declare that I have not been able to consent since the 19th of August that I should be treated like a third-class Cuban in my own fatherland, in the same way that I could not consent to being treated like a second-class Spaniard in the colonial period. For this reason, since the date of the 19th I have felt as much a revolutionary as Maceo, Martí, Calixto García and Máximo Gómez were."[107] Hearing such words, popular nationalists could not help but feel that within their leaders' goals of political reform were their own goals of social change. But regardless of their confidence in Liberal leaders like Guerra, others might still feel that the revival of the Revolution gave them a second chance to construct their vision of nation.

One popular nationalist who expressed these feelings in 1906 was Father Agustín Miret in an open letter to La Lucha. Explaining his initial reasons for opposing the state, Father Miret said that the Moderates had gone to the extreme of pressuring Havana's Archbishop Sbaretti to relinquish his duties at the parish of San Juan y Martínez, Pinar del Río. Having been accused of subversive activities, Miret feared that today, Moderates might even try to kill him. After fleeing to the home of a friend in Guane, he reported that within four hours, 100 of "the faithful [feligreses]" had surrounded him in search of comfort and direction. Within a day, he wrote, the number had risen to 300:

> Today I have a thousand, disposed to lose their life before they consent to be trampled again. I am with my faithful not in the character of a guerrilla, but as a [self-appointed] military pastor, considering it a duty to be with them, rather than those in town, because they are in danger. And Jesus Christ counseled that the good shepherd should give up his life to help his spiritual brothers. My faithful are incorporated to the forces of the General Pino Guerra, which in the number of more than three thousand, have taken the towns of San Luis and San Juan and in a short time will take [the city of] Pinar del Río.[108]

Of special significance was the fact that Guerra's forces had taken these towns with absolutely no bloodshed and little resistance. So confident did local peasants feel of revolutionaries' intentions that they did not stop their work or abandon the fields, despite recent invasions of nearby towns.[109] Had the "war" continued in such a fashion, such Cubans might have expected the resulting state to be moral, forgiving, and tolerant in ways that they glimpsed among the Constitutional Army and celebrated through the messianic life and martyrdom of José Martí.

By early September, even Senator Adolfo Cabello, an independent who had nonetheless benefited from Moderate electoral fraud, was admitting publicly that the Moderate Party had no credibility. The primary objective now, he said, was to prevent a U.S. intervention. Estrada Palma, because of his history in past struggles and his long-standing motto of creating a society of "more teachers than warriors," would not support using force over negotiation, he predicted. The only solution was to find a way for him to step down with his "honor" intact.[110]

Despite the state's intransigence, there could be no doubt of its vulnerability: by early September, revolutionaries were poised at the gates of Havana, waiting only for the state's surrender to them as a nonviolent alternative to taking the capital by force. As a group of veteran generals led by Mario Menocal arrived by train from Oriente to mediate the conflict, at least one veteran officer expressed his doubts over the success of any such enterprise. By creating a climate of friendliness toward key architects of the state-sponsored terror in Estrada Palma's cabinet (namely Fernando Freyre de Andrade), Menocal was inviting disaster, he predicted. Why should the rebels pay any attention to mediators who were willing to ensure the impunity of the state?[111] On the face of things, any allowances that veteran mediators made to the state at this point must have seemed laughable. But, in fact, the Liberal revolutionary leadership did not oppose making concessions to the state. The problem was that Estrada Palma would not agree either to make or to receive them. That left only one option, or so it must have seemed to popular nationalist rebels: taking the Presidential Palace by force.

Yet, Menocal's efforts to diffuse support for this option encountered little if any resistance among Liberal leaders. By September 9, Menocal announced that they would be willing to lay down their arms if, in exchange for conceding that the president and vice president remain in office, all officials elected in the last elections resigned their posts and a new election law was drafted by both parties. In private conference with Estrada Palma that evening, Menocal and Dr. Eugenio Sánchez Agramonte obtained the pledge that he would accept the plan "in principle." However, Estrada Palma did not accept any changes at the municipal level of government, since he claimed any reversal would undermine his authority. He also warned that it would be impossible for him to press anyone "to resign an office obtained through election."[112]

Within days, however, Estrada Palma had completely reversed his position. As Menocal put it, "[He suddenly decided] that he did not propose to support that [agreement] nor any other, because he would make no agreement with those whom he considered rebels, criticizing Mr. Agramonte and myself for not having placed ourselves unconditionally at the disposal of the Government to put down the rebellion." Genuinely shocked, Menocal confirmed the change of circumstances with cabinet officials. Literally overnight, Estrada Palma had decided that his state could stand the test.[113]

What had happened was simple: having consulted with U.S. consul-general Frank Steinhart, Estrada Palma realized that he had another option beside those of surrender, negotiation, or fighting a war the state would inevitably lose. The option was to request with the greatest urgency that U.S. warships come to Cuba on the state's behalf. In his now infamous telegram to U.S. Secretary of State Robert Bacon dated September 8, 1906, Steinhart wrote that Secretary of State Freyre de Andrade had requested, in Estrada Palma's name, that Roosevelt send warships in order to quell the rebellion. Virtually quoting the Platt Amendment's conditions for intervention, he stated that "the Government is unable to protect life and property."[114]

Thus, Estrada Palma had worked to give the appearance of negotiation to veteran mediators while he waited to see what the United States would do. When he had accepted Menocal's plan in principle on September 9, he had still not received a reply. But by September 10, he had: Bacon wired back to Steinhart that two vessels were en route to Cuba. However, he warned of the great displeasure that the possibility of intervention caused President Roosevelt. Having just dispatched Elihu Root on a goodwill tour of Latin America, Roosevelt was doing everything possible to dispel fears that the United States planned to continue invading its neighbors and manipulating their governments. The recent acquisition of the Panama Canal Zone and the United States' all-out war against independence forces in the Philippines and continuing occupation of Puerto Rico were proving problematic enough. In Cuba, Roosevelt believed "actual, immediate intervention [was] out of the question."[115] But to Estrada Palma, Roosevelt's words were meaningless. The door to keeping the Cuban state and the Moderates' monopoly on power had been reopened. Estrada Palma was convinced that all he had to do was walk through it.

On September 20, U.S. envoys Secretary of War William Howard Taft and Secretary of State Bacon began negotiations with the government and rebel forces, mainly through Liberal Party president Alfredo Zayas, whose release from jail they managed to secure. From the first moment of their arrival, Taft was in constant communication with President Roosevelt. All three U.S. statesmen demonstrated a complete ignorance of the situation in Cuba. Knowledge of the extremes of political fraud and violence that the Moderates had committed over the previous two years came to their attention (apparently for the first time) only through the course of Taft's own investigations. For Roosevelt, it was simply a question of forcing the Moderates to accept a plan similar to that proposed by veterans.[116] However, Taft quickly discovered that the Moderates, most of all Estrada Palma, had only one solution in mind. Saying that any concessions on electoral matters "would be inconsistent with his dignity and honor," Estrada Palma issued Taft an ultimatum: "He and his cabinet say that the only course open to the United States is war with the insurgents and future control. . . . It is quite evident that Palma, and I fear, the Moderate party, are determined to force armed intervention by us."[117] Roosevelt's response to this was a combination of fury, exasperation, and panic. In an ironic twist of fate, he personally appealed to Estrada Palma's sense of patriotism.[118]

But the greater Taft's quiescence toward Liberal representatives became, the more Moderates' determination grew. They decided to play U.S. fears of real revolutionary change to their political advantage. As pro-imperialist nationalists, the Moderates feared revolutionary change as much as if not more than their U.S. imperial allies. Proponents of an idea of nation that had become increasingly antithetical to revolutionary change, they were prepared to salvage what they had already built of that "nation" at all costs, even if it meant giving up their right to direct its progress to a government staffed by foreigners.

As Estrada Palma expressed in an extraordinary joint session of the Cuban Congress on September 14, blame for the jeopardy in which Cuba's sovereignty and credibility found themselves rested firmly on the shoulders of revolutionaries and the rabble who supported them: "Who would have suspected, in the midst of the portentous prosperity of the country and the general well-being of our people, refuge of peace and progress; counting on millions of extra dollars in the Treasury, even after having paid the Liberating Army and set up a multitude of public works . . . who would have suspected . . . that there could be Cubans who might conspire among themselves to attempt by force of arms the subversion of a constitutional regime, substituting the Law of force and violence, order for anarchy, peace for war?"[119] Estrada Palma's parting words to the "nation" of Moderates assembled before him revealed more than just how out of touch with the needs of society they were; his words revealed how indifferent they all were to the alternative, aspiring "nations" for which thousands of Cuban revolutionaries had fought and had been willing to give their lives—just as much then as now.

In the face of Roosevelt's outright refusal to engage U.S. troops in combat and Taft's insistence on promoting political compromise, Estrada Palma decided to force a U.S. takeover of the island by threatening to abandon the government entirely. He made a mockery of Taft's recent accord with the Liberals to stop short of a U.S. intervention but guarantee the supervision of new elections. "They are abusing us and are taking the ground that it was our duty to sustain the Government at all hazards and put down the insurrection at all cost," Taft declared to Roosevelt.[120] Thus, in the end, Estrada Palma's strategy could not have hit its mark more directly. Taft had to admit that if all the Moderates resigned, the state would fall to the revolutionaries, the majority of whom he saw as "an undisciplined horde of men" with whom the majority of Cuba's "poorer classes and the uneducated" sympathized. Justifiably so, Taft feared that the refined revolutionary nationalist Liberals with whom he had been dealing were only "titular leaders" whose power to contain revolutionary change was limited by midlevel leaders and their followers' expectations.[121] Incredibly, some political observers believed that Liberals had ordered soldiers to refrain from a quick and easy capture of Havana in the hopes of achieving precisely the same end Estrada Palma now sought.[122]

By September 28, Taft reported that both sides were pleased with the idea of a U.S. intervention. The Moderates favored it because as Taft understood it, they preferred "annexation generally." The Liberals accepted U.S. military intervention "because they can earn their victory in the holding of elections" without fearing any repudiation of their results.[123] In short, the leadership of both parties had decided that any hope they had of seeing their images of nation fulfilled hinged on cooperation with the United States. On September 29, U.S. Secretary of War Taft declared himself provisional governor of Cuba.[124]

Conclusion

Only one month into the Revolution of 1906, Moderates' intransigence conspired with Liberal leaders' fears over the outcome of a popular nationalist movement meant to create the conditions for social change through war. The result was a transformation of U.S. imperial policy. No intervention would have been possible without the complicity of Liberal leaders who, at the last moment, panicked over the potential for social revolution that Cubans' mass demonstration of opposition to the state signified. U.S. officials had not intended to play the Platt Amendment card if it could be avoided. However, the transformation from mediation to intervention clearly served the United States' long-term goals.

Because all groups had understood social unity as the greatest challenge posed to organizers of the 1895 War for independence, the same groups—now acting in opposition to each other—understood their actions as the only way to recapture that unity. As their actions under Estrada Palma showed, pro-imperialist nationalists interpreted the fraternal struggle of the independence wars as a virtual surrender of the will and interests of popular nationalist followers to the will and interests of their leaders. Not surprisingly, then, they attempted to use this interpretation of Cuba's history as a model for guiding the political present: social unity signaled conformity to a pro-imperialist nationalist vision of nation and a pro-imperialist nationalist version of the state. However, in negating other Cubans' memories of social unity in the 1895 War, they inadvertently inspired them to act on such memories.

The state's use of violence to enforce a pro-imperialist nationalist standard of social unity prompted popular nationalists to ally with revolutionary nationalists in an armed movement meant to topple Estrada Palma's "false" Republic and create a new one. Ultimately, then, revolutionary nationalist leaders of the Liberal Party showed that they would rather have blamed Estrada Palma and the United States than admit their unwillingness to live up to the promise of social unity with popular nationalists that they had just mobilized. Thus, Liberal leaders were as responsible as Estrada Palma for inviting a second U.S. military intervention in 1906. Having opted for intervention over compromise, both political elites would transform José Martí's martyred body into a discursive corpse of betrayed memory and forgotten promises that they would continually try to bury in the coming years. Popular nationalists, on the other hand, would fight for the redemption and resurrection of Martí's same martyred body in this period.

Popular nationalists' memory of social unity in the Revolution and their inscription of it in the evolving myth of Martí as a martyred messiah and leader of the masses represented a combustible reserve of frustrated anger and passion. It was no wonder that revolutionary nationalist Liberals feared the implications of a coup against Estrada Palma: not only would the possibilities for achieving radical change have burst open, but Liberal leaders who instigated the coup would have faced tens of thousands of armed followers who expected them to act on their expectations and demands for social change that Estrada Palma had either ignored or betrayed. Nonetheless, despite the collapse of such a possibility with the second U.S. military occupation of Cuba in 1906, popular nationalist leaders like Evaristo Estenoz and other participants in the Revolution of 1906 did not give up the struggle to salvage and see implemented their own ideals of "nation." On the contrary, the manipulation of U.S. imperial interests as leverage in this struggle soon become a tactic on which popular nationalists would depend.

SIX

····················

Perceiving Populism in a
U.S. Imperial Context

*The Paradox of Popular Nationalist
Struggles, 1906–1909*

ON THE EVENING OF June 6, 1907, several U.S. soldiers joined a large crowd of Cubans for an open-air concert in Cienfuegos's Central Park. Nearly a year had passed since Liberal Party leaders launched a massive armed movement against the authoritarian state of Tomás Estrada Palma and the United States initiated a second military intervention in October 1906. With the help of 5,600 U.S. soldiers and 1,000 marines, Teddy Roosevelt's administration had successfully installed Charles Magoon, a federal judge, as provisional governor of Cuba. By the summer of 1907, the outward appearance of social peace reigned over the island while inward turmoil bubbled just beneath the surface. For leaders of the Liberal Party who had demanded free elections and Moderates who had repressed them less than a year before, the business of resolving disputes over the nature of any future Cuban state and the character of the nation it served remained unfinished. Additionally, widespread anxiety over the implications that a renewed U.S. occupation might hold gripped Cuba's popular nationalists. Listening to music in Cienfuegos that evening, concertgoers collectively expressed the frustration that percolated through Cuban society by showing a picaresque sense of humor in the face of political adversity. As one U.S. officer later reported, "On the Plaza last evening, the Cuban [municipal] band was playing on the ground, and there were a few [U.S.] soldiers listening to the concert. In the interval between pieces a member of the band took from his pocket a small United States flag, flirted it around to attract a Cuban audience, and with a significant glance at the soldiers blew his nose upon it. This thing was repeated a few times much to the satisfaction of his audience."[1] Irked by the raucous laughter emanating from the crowd, U.S. soldiers confronted the offending musician only to find his attitude equally irreverent. Neither he nor any fellow members of the band apologized for the insult.[2]

According to the commanding officer's report, the incident's significance lay in its transcendence: "[This action] clearly indicated the contempt in which the American soldier and everything American is held; matters of this character are continually coming to my notice. It is the firm belief of the mass of the people in the vicinity that we are afraid of them."[3] Pressed by the provisional governor's office, the mayor of Cienfuegos eventually agreed to fire the musician and promised to reestablish "cordial" feelings between the occupying soldiers and his fellow citizens.[4] However, the U.S. State Department's chief adviser in Cuba, Colonel Enoch Crowder, acknowledged just how highly strung anti-U.S. sentiments were in Cienfuegos and beyond. Keeping news of the incident quiet was the best way to keep islandwide sympathy for defiance of the U.S. presence at bay.[5] Crowder's advice spoke to the volatility of Cuban nationalists' situation. It also expressed the urgency with which U.S. officials now worked to maintain the mission of securing social peace in Cuba, at any cost.

Much had changed since the first U.S. intervention, not just in terms of the attitudes of Cuban nationalists but also in terms of the tactics of U.S. imperialists. Then, Cubans had proudly flown their flag in the company of its North American "sister," and the name of José Martí often accompanied that of George Washington in popular patriotic expressions and songs. By contrast, most Cubans during Magoon's administration did not participate in parades honoring North American independence and no longer chose actively to appropriate its symbols.[6] Disillusion and regret had replaced pragmatism and trust. Symbolic of this, the pro-imperialist nationalist editors of El Fígaro who had supported the Estrada Palma administration in August 1906 chose to grace the February 24, 1907, edition with an ambivalent image: "Cuba Libre," a toga-clad woman carrying an olive branch, wept desperately at the tomb of José Martí.[7] Equally symbolic, President Roosevelt broke with rules set during the first U.S. intervention of 1898–1902. He ordered that the Cuban flag remain at full mast on all government buildings in Cuba during the second U.S. intervention of 1906 to 1909. Nonetheless, all Cuban officials who occupied posts within the U.S. military administration still swore allegiance to the government of the United States as they had in 1898. They simply did so before both Cuba's flag and that of

EL FÍGARO

REVISTA UNIVERSAL ILUSTRADA

24 DE FEBRERO: CUBA.—MARTI.—1907.

The icon of Cuba Libre weeping at Martí's tomb on the anniversary of the Grito de Baire, or call to arms, for the 1895 War. The image reflects the mood of many Cubans after the collapse of the Constitutional Revolution of 1906 led to a second U.S. military occupation. (From *El Fígaro*, February 24, 1907, cover) the United States.[8] The historic symbol of independence no longer stood in overt contradiction to the objectives of the United States.

During his two years of rule, Magoon did more than simply satisfy Roosevelt's mission of securing social peace and enhancing the U.S. economic presence in Cuba. Guided by pragmatism, Magoon's actions in office brought about several unforeseen results. As this chapter shows, the Magoon administration's efforts to keep social peace in Cuba produced a number of important political and social gains for Cuba's working class and for key leaders of the defunct Constitutional Army with popular nationalist goals.

Convinced that they could no longer effect change from within the vertical channels of authority that revolutionary nationalist leaders offered them, discontented popular nationalists like Evaristo Estenoz broke away from the Liberal Party altogether. Estenoz, a large number of black veterans, and others formed an independent, marginal elite of civil rights activists who would foreground race issues in their campaign to influence the shape and policies of the state. Similarly, organized cigarmakers who had lost their battle against discriminatory hiring practices in 1902 changed their tactics for pressuring the state and employers. No longer convinced that native political elites offered more than lip service to their goals, cigarmakers focused their struggle on the imperial state's recognition of workers' right to strike. For both these groups, Magoon's mandate to create and maintain social peace in Cuba proved fortuitous.

Political elites did not dismiss the fact that the very groups whom Magoon chose to court were precisely those groups that pro-imperialist nationalist officials had repressed and revolutionary nationalists, many of whom were now Liberals, had perceived as a threat. Turning toward the United States as a means for keeping popular nationalists' agendas at bay, both revolutionary nationalists and pro-imperialist nationalists expected U.S. agents to act on their behalf. However, Magoon's failure to align himself with either the Moderate or Liberal Party and his policies of compromise toward socially radical forces proved that the United States could not be trusted to act on political elites' behalf. Consequently, between 1906 and 1909, political elites began to equate popular nationalist acts of social protest with traitorous solicitations that the United States usurp political elites' authority. In this regard, Magoon's administration marked a turning point in the history of the Republic. By 1909, nationalists of all currents and of all major political parties came to define their relationship to each other and the viability of their respective nationalist visions in terms of their relationship to the United States.

The U.S. Mandate of Social Peace and Cuban
Ideals of Social Unity under Magoon

For the Roosevelt administration, the need for a second U.S. military intervention in the late summer of 1906 could not have come at a worse possible time.
Having just completed the U.S. war of conquest in the Philippines, finalized covert operations to ensure Panama's independence from Colombia, and gained
rights "in perpetuity" over a U.S.-controlled canal zone in Panama, Roosevelt
now turned to improving the United States' declining image as a "democratic"
leader abroad. In this regard, his choice of Charles Magoon, a civilian judge and
the self-made son of a Minnesota farmer, personified the objectives of U.S. foreign policy in Cuba as the White House defined them. Possessed of a jocular
disposition, Magoon gave the impression of benevolent, political impartiality
coupled with a paternalist reluctance to use force. As one Cuban writer noted,
Magoon knew how to "walk around as Roosevelt wants the United States to do
in the world, without the 'big stick' that [Washington representatives] carry in
their hand."[9]

In line with the mandate of proving U.S. benevolence and political impartiality over weaker neighbors, Roosevelt directed Magoon to keep any conflicts that
might emerge over the course of the second U.S. intervention strictly among Cubans and not between Cubans and North Americans. While U.S. agents would
formally control military and governmental affairs in Cuba from October 1906
through January 1909, U.S. troops were to be kept in the "background to give
confidence, not do fighting" from the start. By making it appear that U.S. agents
in Cuba exercised a strictly advisory and administrative role on the island, Roosevelt hoped to create a situation in which fellow Cubans, not the United States,
remained the target of any local resentments that might arise. For this reason,
U.S. Army regiments stationed in Cuba took the title of the "U.S. Army of Cuban
Pacification."[10]

For Magoon, the revolutionary events of the summer of 1906 that brought
him to Cuba proved the need for the United States to act as supreme mediator
in Cuba's internal political life. He realized that continued hostilities among
political elites threatened to spill over into open, armed conflict that would inevitably ensnare the U.S. military. As late as March 1907, official intelligence
reports of unrest in provincial towns and the countryside continued to flood
onto Magoon's desk. This was especially true of Pinar del Río, focal point of
popular mobilization in the summer of 1906. There, various municipal mayors
had sworn in groups of 500 men on the pretext of protecting local tobacco farms
from roaming bandits. However, the guardsmen were "in reality . . . armed men

at the disposal of political parties."[11] Seeking to alleviate tensions and relax the lines of authority that Liberals and Moderates directed among constituents, Magoon hoped to balance the political forces in Cuba by keeping local political elites busy and by assuaging, whenever necessary, their more socially radical opponents. Implementing this policy, however, often brought U.S. imperialism into ideological conflict with the pro-imperialist and revolutionary nationalisms of Liberal and Moderate elites. Ironically, such conflicts also made it possible for greater maneuverability on the part of popular nationalists.

The youngest son of a frontier farmer, Magoon had spent only one year at the University of Nebraska at Lincoln before taking a job as a lawyer's apprentice and obtaining admission to the bar. Although socially deferential to political patrons like Roosevelt, Magoon's own life experience made him distinctly respectful of individual rights before social privilege as well as personally ambitious, qualities that served him well in embodying the new imperial character of successive Republican administrations abroad. Magoon began his career as President McKinley's chief legal adviser on the acquisition of territories abroad. Having served as governor of the Philippines and the recently acquired Panama Canal Zone before coming to Cuba, Magoon earned a reputation as a pacifier and appeared to relish this role even when it put him at odds with U.S. armed forces.[12] With this in mind, Governor Charles Magoon selected José Martí's only son, José Martí y Zayas Bazán, as his personal assistant only a few days after he arrived in Cuba in October 1906. Although Martí Jr. had sided with the pro-imperialist nationalist forces that backed the authoritarian tactics of Estrada Palma and Moderates, Magoon's symbolic inclusion of Martí's son and namesake indicated the surprising degree with which he took memories of the 1895 Revolution seriously.[13] In the interests of serving the United States' objective of social peace, the most important of these was, ironically, social unity. In his appointment of Martí's only son, Magoon illustrated U.S. imperialism's sudden and paradoxical appropriation of the unfulfilled legacy of the 1895 War: a willingness to negotiate interests for mutual gain.

In the first months of the provisional administration, Magoon orchestrated a number of political maneuvers meant to appease both political parties while consolidating as much power in the executive branch — that is, in his own hands — as possible. First, he made the disbanding of the massive Constitutional Army a primary order of business, compensating soldiers for surrendering their weapons and allowing them to keep expropriated war materials, such as horses, and paying their former owners for property losses out of the national treasury. Magoon also reached out to Liberals by investigating complaints of intimidation by former Moderates and, in a matter of weeks, restoring Liberal officeholders to power in twenty-two out of thirty-two municipalities that had filed complaints.[14] Hoping to regain their legitimacy and finding Magoon's relative generosity flagging, Moderates quickly recast themselves into the Conservative Party under the leadership of a new set of regional caudillos such as General Mario Menocal, the veteran who first attempted to defuse the revolutionary crisis that fall. Known for his willingness to repress black strikers during his tenure as chief of Havana's city police during the first U.S. occupation, Menocal had since shown his commitment to pro-imperialist nationalist values by working as the manager for the largest U.S.-owned sugar plantation in Oriente. With Moderates scrambling to resurrect themselves as born-again patriots, Liberals jumped eagerly into the role of political victims whose elected right to power the U.S. had come to restore.

In general, Liberal leaders like Alfredo Zayas and Juan Gualberto Gómez endorsed U.S. decisions on provincial complaints against the Moderates as fair and objective.[15] The way Magoon structured his government encouraged them to do so. First, he officially confirmed Liberals' complaints of fraud in congressional elections, thereby lending credibility to the Liberals' image as Cuba's only "true" democrats. Second, he left them little power or a platform from which to complain. After Secretary of War William Howard Taft annulled the "Moderated" election results of 1905 in the first days of the U.S. intervention, Magoon issued a decree providing that the Cuban Congress remain in permanent "recess" throughout the course of the U.S. intervention. This effectively transferred all legislative powers to the succeeding executive (Magoon) and sanctioned that he rule as previous U.S. military governors had done, that is, by decree. On the other hand, Magoon financially neutralized many national leaders' incentive to complain by permitting congressmen to draw their usual salaries until their terms expired and, in anticipation of the U.S. military's departure, by promising that new elections would be held.[16] Similarly, Magoon ensured the loyalty of Liberal military leaders like General Pino Guerra by putting him on the government payroll as the chief of the newly organized Cuban Armed Forces. Together with José Martí's son, Magoon promptly sent Guerra for training abroad.[17] He also kept Liberal and Conservative party chiefs such as Zayas, Juan Gualberto Gómez, and Domingo Méndez Capote busy with projects to draft new, fraud-proof electoral and municipal laws that would make the removal of elected officials from office more difficult.[18] Financially placated or otherwise occupied with legal matters whose implementation was hypothetical at best, the vast majority of the 1906 revolutionary leadership shrank into the bureaucratic background that Magoon's administration was only too happy to provide.

Only one major Liberal general and former congressman, Enrique Loynaz del Castillo, refused to cooperate with Magoon. Writing in perfect English, Loynaz del Castillo explained to Magoon that while "the Liberals have been disarmed ... the Moderates continue holding the Rural Guard, the judges and tribunals, and the whole administration [of Magoon's] Cabinet." Even the murderer of General Quintín Banderas and his accomplices in the Rural Guard were still in command of the same district in which Banderas was killed, Loynaz del Castillo pointed out. Such things contradicted the promises that Secretary of War Taft had made to Constitutional Army leaders while they were still in the field. "Believe me, Sir," Loynaz del Castillo concluded, "... I am sorry the Intervention came a week too soon."[19]

Blaming national leaders in the capital for having derailed a revolution, many revolutionary nationalist Liberals in the provinces felt the same way. Complaints that U.S. agents were allowing former Moderates to continue their abuse of Liberals emanated loudly from the provinces—apparently without much effect on Liberal leaders in the capital. For example, one manifesto published on November 23, 1906, in Pinar del Río charged that the Rural Guard was taking advantage of the U.S. mandate to disarm members of the Constitutional Army. In the process, these Guards—all former Moderates—harassed, beat, and even hanged innocent citizens without trial (at least one of whom was black) on weapons charges. The tone of the manifesto was irate: "Do we live among savages [cafres]? What is the point here? To force the people to make justice by their own hand? The Liberals put these facts ... at the consideration of Mr. Magoon, and ask for justice and nothing more than justice ... if public peace is to be a reality."[20]

These Liberals interpreted the evidence of U.S. "neutrality" as tantamount to U.S. complicity with the terror tactics of Moderates-turned-Conservatives. For example, in the fall of 1907, the mayor of Alquízar, Havana province, sent an urgent appeal to Alfredo Zayas by telegraph, asking that something be done to stop Rural Guardsman Rosendo Collazo from brutalizing the local population and newly restored Liberal government. In response, U.S. Army captain Powell Clayton Jr. traveled to the town to investigate the charges but did so in the company of none other than Collazo himself! Not surprisingly, when questioned by Clayton in the presence of Collazo, not one of the more than half a dozen prominent citizens who had filed complaints was willing to admit that any of their reports was founded. Even the mayor denied having sent Zayas the alarming telegram, saying that it must have been a mistake of the telegraph operator—a charge the operator adamantly refuted by retrieving the original message written in the mayor's hand.[21]

In this way, Magoon's "neutrality" policy did not neutralize Moderate sources of political violence and authoritarianism in the countryside, nor did it alleviate local resentment over the declining enthusiasm of Liberal leaders to defend the

PERCEIVING POPULISM

human and civil rights of citizens. However, cases like these ultimately served U.S. interests by undermining the leadership and legitimacy of Cuba's political elites. However persistent the complaints of their constituents, few Liberals in positions of power showed themselves willing to take a forceful stand before Magoon's government.

But if Magoon's efforts at appeasement and incorporation did not satisfy revolutionary nationalist Liberals in the provinces, the same actions thoroughly angered the recalcitrant pro-imperialist nationalist Conservatives. As Estrada Palma had done, Conservatives expected U.S. officials to endorse without question the dominance in local government that they had established over the preceding year through the "Moderate" political machine. By restoring most popularly elected Liberals to office, Magoon dashed these hopes. In the long run, however, Conservatives' greatest frustrations would come from Magoon's populist gestures toward the popular classes, gestures related to what they (and many Liberals) alleged was Magoon's abuse of the Cuban national treasury for the sake of satiating the selfish greed of the popular classes.

With regard to social policy, Conservatives counted on U.S. officials to live up to the racist and classist cultural values that they attributed to "Anglo-Saxon America" and proudly believed they shared. After all, Conservatives' vision of the nation depended largely on standards of modern culture and a march toward "civilization" that many had derived from living in the United States or from absorbing the multiple myths that the U.S. print media and politicians generated. As pro-imperialist nationalists, Conservatives believed Magoon would rely on these principles in shaping his policies for the social progress of Cuba. For Conservative Cubans, this meant putting goals such as greater racial equality and social equity aside until the lower orders of society had sufficiently "improved" themselves through education, the adoption of European-derived cultural traits, and hard physical labor. "We are in danger of becoming another Hayti [sic] if left to ourselves," a rich tobacco planter admitted to a U.S. journalist at the start of Magoon's tenure. "There are in this island many thousands of negroes not one step higher in civilization than those you find in the African jungles. These fellows will take the field with any leader to whom they are attached."[22] Thus, when Magoon promised to pacify the island and pave the way for greater degrees of progress in Cuba, Conservatives interpreted this as expanding upon the pro-imperialist nationalist process that Estrada Palma's administration had set in motion.

At first, Conservatives felt they had no reason to fear that Magoon would do other than they expected. In his first public address as governor, Magoon provided evidence of how much the Roosevelt-era brand of U.S. imperialism resonated with the principles of pro-imperialist nationalism. Speaking at the convocation exercises of the National University of Havana, Magoon attributed "Anglo-Saxon" superiority in the knowledge of self-government to accidents of history that had allocated to the United States the advantage of "two hundred years of education" in its arts. Further, Magoon confirmed the need for foreign capital to promote Cuba's economic development and applauded Estrada Palma, "that great man . . . [who] realized more than any of the Cuban people the necessity for bringing capital in here and convincing the world of the conservative character of your government." Ironically, Magoon warned of the danger of letting too much of the economy slip into foreign hands, a problem he blamed on the lack of industriousness thus far exhibited by Cuba's patriots: "[U]ntil you have a community of political influence and control which is affected by the conserving influences of property and property ownership, successful popular government is impossible." Magoon ended the speech with the cry, "*Viva la República de Cuba* [Long Live the Cuban Republic]." His words, spoken in the Aula Magna of the university and widely published in the Cuban press, must have been music to the ears of Conservatives.[23]

However, Conservatives began to suspect the commitment of Magoon to their ideals once it became clear how popular nationalist Cubans interpreted Magoon's early concessions to the Liberals. According to one Conservative, poor and working-class Liberals, whom he described as "almost all black," believed that the United States was on their side. It was no wonder, then, he charged, that so many Liberal blacks felt themselves empowered to commit atrocious crimes of social impropriety that undermined the stability of the social order and damaged the moral fabric of Cuban society. Since U.S. officials had arrived, he complained, blacks had begun congregating openly on street corners, showing off horses they had acquired in the 1906 Revolution (whose retention Magoon had sanctioned), insulting Spanish shopkeepers for not giving them credit in their stores, and generally "rebuk[ing] the white man, and making an insolent spectacle of themselves even with *Señoras*," that is, respectable, probably white, women. Some blacks even managed to commandeer free passage for themselves on trains, arguing that the authorities had granted this benefit to all "Liberal soldiers."[24] These acts of social defiance on the part of popular nationalist blacks angered Conservatives who interpreted racial standards of social deference as critical to the progress of Cuba's "civilization".

Even greater problems emerged with regard to Magoon's policy on immigration. While Magoon's administration did approve Estrada Palma's scheme for promoting white immigration, his efforts at implementation did not live up to its originators' calculations. For one thing, the number of immigrants from Spain and the Canary Islands dropped precipitously from a high of nearly 50,000 in 1905, before the second U.S. intervention, to less than 20,000 per year during Magoon's provisional administration. In addition, while over 35,000 of those immigrants arriving in Cuba appear to have stayed as island residents in 1905, less than 12,000 did so in 1906. By 1908, this number had been reduced to half: approximately 6,000 remained. As a representative of the Centro Asturiano critically observed, the vast majority of these workers were young males who had little intention of remaining in Cuba once they had made their money. Those who earned money arduously cutting cane were often the first to leave, while those who pursued their fortune in commerce stayed.[25] From the perspective of many pro-imperialist nationalists, the infusions of "whiter" races into Cuban society was supposed to jump-start the process of social and cultural "regeneration." In order for this to work, white immigrants had to come with the intention of staying and establishing families. Moreover, the goal of improving Cuba's racial stock through immigration went hand-in-hand with establishing a ready pool of cheap labor for plantations; one policy justified the other. Under Magoon, not only were such policy priorities reversed but also the possibilities of improving Cuba's "racial stock" were undermined altogether.

Magoon's Conservative advisers insisted that only immigrants of the "Caucasian" race who traveled with their families be admitted to Cuba.[26] However, to their horror, the period from 1906 to 1908 saw a dramatic rise in the number of people arriving from islands with overwhelmingly African-descended populations such as the British West Indies and Haiti. Even more worrisome, a large number of them—recruited as seasonal laborers—did not leave after their contracts expired but stayed to mix with the local population. Between 1906 and 1908, close to 9,000 people entered Cuba from the British Antilles, and for the first time nearly 1,400 Haitians entered. Only two-thirds of these appear to have returned to their home islands in the same period.[27] Given the desperation of U.S. sugar corporations for labor, especially in eastern Cuba where they were invading sparsely populated, virgin land, Magoon's commitment to meeting the labor needs of foreign capital apparently overrode any concerns he might have had with Cuba's "social progress."[28] But Magoon's failure to appreciate how Conservatives understood immigration as a method of social engineering extended beyond the racial identity of those immigrants his policies attracted.

In light of his greater commitment to promoting the interests of U.S. capital over those of local capital, Magoon paid little attention to the kind of priorities local politicians, whether Liberal or Conservative, set for him. This guiding principle in Magoon's policy is born out not only by the intensification in U.S. corporate expropriation of land and rapid expansion in eastern Cuba during this period but also by Magoon's more direct efforts to facilitate the activities of U.S. capital through government decrees. For example, in 1907 Magoon increased the possibilities that Cuban peasants would lose access to land by decreeing the division of *haciendas comuneras*. These were plots of land that peasants held communally, either because of grants made by the Spanish Crown or simply as a result of many years of "squatting" and mutual cultivation by more than one family.[29] By taking peasants (most of whom were illiterate) to court and demanding evidence of ownership that the majority could not provide, U.S. companies stood to gain not only land but also a ready pool of workers who would have to depend on wages derived from plantation work to survive. Those who had once retained titles from the Crown were especially vulnerable to such strategies in the first years after the war, since revolutionaries in the struggle for independence had destroyed the records of many municipalities.

Over time, Magoon's economic policies and their social implications proved equally frustrating to elite Liberals and Conservatives. One major bipartisan grievance was the legendary monopolization of government contracts for a massive number of public works projects that Magoon's administration granted to U.S. corporations. Independent journalist Enrique Barrabosa submitted a laundry list of bipartisan complaints concerning Magoon's expense decrees. These included a $12,000 budget per annum for palace banquets and private festivities; the maintenance of North American troops on Cuban soil at a cost of almost $1 million; and Magoon's refusal to make any of his government's accounts public—despite the fact that the money he spent belonged to Cubans—until the end of his administration in January 1909.[30] Especially symbolic of Magoon's decadence was his failure to enforce the same standards of public hygiene and cultural vigilance as his U.S. military predecessors had. According to Barrabosa, whereas General Wood had done away with stray dogs, gambling, and poor sanitation, Magoon turned a blind eye to all three with the result that crime, public "immorality," and disease proliferated.[31]

Yet, Cuba's popular classes did not necessarily perceive or experience Magoon's style of governing nor the effects of his expenditures in the same way nationalist elites did. For example, the impact of Magoon's economic policies was uneven, hitting the free peasants of Oriente especially hard but leaving areas with long-term histories of plantation agriculture less affected. Magoon's management of the Department of Public Works provides an even more dramatic case in point. Apparently, Magoon was unaware (or unconcerned) that the Estrada Palma administration's vast appropriations for phantom public works projects were only intended to buy votes for the national elections of 1905—they were never supposed to be carried out. Magoon took the implementation of these projects seriously and in three years nearly tripled the amount of money appropriated for their completion.[32] Importantly, Magoon justified recruiting the vast majority of highly paid technical advisers and engineers from the United States on the premise that there were hardly any qualified specialists in Cuba—a judgment that Cuban professionals both disputed and resented.

But while educated Cubans benefited little from Magoon's projects, the repair of island infrastructure provided much needed employment for the thousands of unemployed Cubans whom the plantation system left destitute for much of each year. As Magoon noted in his 1907 report to Roosevelt, "Practically all of the cane cutters [and 75 percent of agricultural workers] are without employment six months in the year, and by August are without money or means of support for themselves and families. . . . Under these conditions the proper course for the Government to pursue was plain, viz, to increase road construction and other public works during the dead season." But Magoon's lavish public works programs were meant to do more than employ the unemployed; they were also a pragmatic measure to "preserve public tranquility and substantially promote trade and commerce." Perhaps not coincidentally, Magoon launched initial projects in Pinar del Río province, point of origin for the defunct Revolution of 1906.[33] Later, Liberal president José Miguel Gómez would continue Magoon's policy of government-sponsored public works in order to alleviate mass unemployment and widespread rural poverty, a problem deeply rooted in Cuba's monocultural sugar economy and its domination by large-scale plantations rather than small-farming agriculturalists. The effect that Magoon's approach had on popular nationalists of the lower classes may have inspired Gómez to do so.

Indeed, similar techniques of awarding contracts to personal cronies, expanding bureaucracies, and increasing the availability of employment through public works later earned José Miguel Gómez the nickname of "Tiburón." He may have been a shark, Cubans said at the time, but when he bathes, at least he makes a splash (*"Es tiburón pero cuándo se baña, sarpica [sic]"*).[34] The fact that the beneficiaries of Gómez's policies of spreading the wealth around included rather than excluded a large portion of Cuba's Liberal-affiliated middle- and upper-class professionals explains their greater willingness to forgive Magoon's Cuban successor for excessive spending while not Magoon himself, the foreign originator of such policies.[35] But for those Cubans who had criticized the miserly ways of Estrada Palma and benefited from Magoon's extravagance in funding public works, the story may have been quite different.

Still, providing greater job opportunities and reducing authorities' vigilance over gambling and other parts of the informal sector constituted the least of Magoon's gestures of incorporation toward Cuba's popular classes. While Cubans of all social classes resented the condescension to which the U.S. military often subjected them, those most likely to draw the ire of listless, frequently bored army personnel were often the least capable of defending themselves. The social position of Cuban women and lower-class men simply did not allow them to contest U.S. soldiers' abuses with the same ease that politicians condemned Magoon's policies. In this regard, the benefits of Magoon's priority of social peace accrued to those who could not or would not count on political leaders to make their contempt for the wider U.S. military presence known.

While Magoon did his best to balance the forces of preexisting political disputes by playing the ambitions of local elites against each other, U.S. soldiers often jeopardized social peace by exacerbating tensions and creating conflict. For example, the arrival in port of the U.S. battleship *Michigan* unleashed a rampage of sailors on Remedios and Caibarién. The soldiers then occupied themselves with drinking excessively, refusing to pay for their alcohol, vandalizing taverns, and beating up the local policemen who tried to stop them. At one point, a U.S. soldier outfitted himself in the full dress uniform of a Spanish army officer. Locals interpreted this action as an affront to both Spanish citizens for having lost the independence war and "to the Cubans who could not look with pleasure upon a man dressed in the attire that represented their extermination." Meanwhile, another group of U.S. soldiers invaded the family home of respectable unmarried women in Remedios, apparently "mistaking them for being bad women [prostitutes]." With the help of local native police, the women managed to escape the grasp of the lascivious soldiers unharmed. In an act of similar imperialist caprice, U.S. soldiers who were stationed in Matanzas lowered the Cuban flag—an action expressly forbidden by the Magoon administration. In reporting these events to Liberal leaders, the Cuban agent ended his notes with the sarcastic assessment: "What intervention more for the sake of humanity [could we possibly expect]?"[36]

As these cases show, U.S. soldiers often acted as if they owned whatever establishment they entered and treated whomever they encountered as if they were objects of diversion rather than social equals endowed with rights. In this way, U.S. soldiers sent the message that Cuba was their private playground; that Cubans themselves were highly expendable; and that contrary to their government's stated policy, the U.S. military was there in spite of Cuban independence, not because of it. These were messages that Magoon's administration could not allow to stand. Accordingly, when news of such incidents reached Magoon's office, Magoon ordered U.S. commanders to control their subordinates and punish them summarily if they disobeyed the mandate of social peace. When, for instance, a violent row occurred between inebriated, off-duty soldiers and Cuban citizens on the streets of the city of Pinar del Río, military commanders were quick to excuse the soldiers' actions and blame the Cubans for provoking them. After all, one officer claimed, U.S. soldiers had no other role than to stand around on the streets looking tough. With Cubans constantly shouting insults such as "*Puto* [pimp]" at them, most soldiers felt the need to prove their valor. Yet, this officer's sympathy notwithstanding, the governor's office issued strict military orders to all units: "If United States troops cannot abstain from fighting the natives, their usefulness on this island is ended. . . . Disorders will deprive all soldiers [involved], innocent and guilty, of their liberty." From then on, any soldiers subjected to public insult were to concede authority over such matters to local Cuban police and were given cards printed in Spanish with the "demand for police assistance" to that end.[37]

Still more impressive was Magoon's willingness to stand his ground against U.S. Army abuses on his own. By far the most extreme case of conflict between native citizens and U.S. soldiers occurred in March 1908 when a U.S. corporal and two privates stationed in Pinar del Río hired and then killed two Cuban fishermen from Coloma with revolvers. After dumping their bodies overboard, the soldiers abandoned the vessel. Judged by a jury of U.S. officers and tried in a special court established for precisely such cases in the early days of the intervention, the soldiers were eventually acquitted and released. So convincing was the evidence against them that Governor Magoon himself publicly dissented from the findings and argued that the prosecution had established "a crime of homicide." Nonetheless, the three soldiers' only punishment for murdering the Cubans was their dishonorable discharge from the U.S. Army.[38]

Such actions gave Magoon a measure of credibility that previous administrators of the Estrada Palma government entirely lacked. While Magoon was himself personally responsible for every action taken by U.S. forces on the island, he also managed to act in ways that made his professed commitment to securing Cubans' civil rights and equality before the law appear sincere—even when that of the United States did not. Thus, Magoon may have inadvertently fulfilled the role of the good patriarch that popular nationalists had assigned former leaders of the 1895 War. In this regard, the most significant of Magoon's policies lay in the realm of race and class.

For the Sake of Social Peace: U.S. Imperialism and the Cigarmakers' Strike, 1906–1907

Only a few months after Magoon's installation as governor, cigarmakers who had battled the large U.S.-owned Havana Trust Company in the brutally repressed

General Strike of 1902 staged another strike against a related U.S. company. Under the leadership of Emilio Sánchez, a longtime labor activist and veteran of the 1902 strike, the strike of 1907 lasted over five months and affected the majority of tobacco factories in the western part of the island. Since battling police forces and the Rural Guard in 1902, cigarmakers had reconsidered the tactics of direct confrontation on which they once relied to paralyze the economy and raise the consciousness of other workers. In 1907, the strike's Central Committee softened its strategies of worker recruitment and settled in for a long, drawn-out conflict. In this way, strikers devised their demands in line with the official U.S. policy of political neutrality and its stated goal of social pacification. They also strove to articulate their message within a popular nationalist paradigm that appealed to the frustrations of politically and socially marginalized Cubans across race and class lines. While *La Lucha* and its English-language edition, *The Lucha*, did provide increasing coverage as the strike came to a head in the summer of 1907, labor newspapers like *La Voz Obrera* and *¡Tierra!* that normally covered all strikes (and had reported on the cigarmakers' strike of 1902 with great interest) largely ignored this one—ostensibly under orders from Governor Magoon's office. Still, despite the dearth of press coverage on the strike, cigarmakers' efforts to garner mass support for the key principles of the movement eventually succeeded. These principles were the right to strike and the primacy of national interests before those of foreign investors.

Known as "La Huelga de la Moneda" (The Currency Strike), the cigarmakers' movement stated from its outset in February 1907 that the strike's goal was payment of all cigarmakers' wages in U.S. gold and not the lower-valued Spanish currency. At the time, Cuba still had no national currency: both Spanish silver and U.S. dollars governed the island economy. Since foodstuffs and manufactured goods flooding the Cuban market were all priced in U.S. dollars, workers felt that payment in dollars was only fair. Significantly, strikers deepened the nationalist underpinnings of their demands by excluding locally owned independent cigar factories from the strike because they were already struggling to compete with the capital-rich, foreign-owned companies. For their part, foreign owners of tobacco factories and processing facilities opposed the change because implementing it would constitute an automatic wage hike of 10 percent per worker at all levels of the plant. Strikers countered that the hypocrisy of U.S. businesses in paying Cuban workers in Spanish currency at a time of U.S. intervention was indisputable.

In time, the popular nationalist implications of the strikers' arguments were equally hard to dispute. Despite the willingness of workers in independent factories to continue working and the strikers' support of this, the local owners of these factories decided to reject their workers' offer to continue working and declared a lockout. That many of the factories were owned by Spaniards is significant: independent factory owners preferred to lose money and cast their lot with foreign capitalists rather than appear complicit with the viewpoint of Cuban workers and endorse their popular nationalist call for state protection of local businesses. As late as the last week of the strike, the strike's Central Committee continued to insist that it had no gripe with independent factories.[39]

The implications that the renewal of the cigarmakers' strike movement held was not lost on political elites. At the start of the strike and at its height, *La Discusión* reflected on the meaning of current events and circumstances through the image of José Martí. Significantly, commentaries no longer focused on the meaning of Martí's death or his self-sacrifice. Rather, writers seemed bent on blaming Martí and condemning him for the model of rebellion that he had represented and inculcated in those who would become the sons of the Republic. Underneath a photograph of Martí's Central Park statue and surrounded by supplemental images of Martí, Antonio Maceo, and Máximo Gómez, one writer lamented, "The precursors of independence managed to filter the feeling of rebellion among the people, but they did not bother to form . . . a national soul."[40] Another article declared that February 24, the anniversary of Martí's Grito de Baire, was now a day of "atonement."[41] Three months later, on the anniversary of Martí's death, Cosme de la Torriente, a prominent Liberal, published his own view in the Conservatives' traditional newspaper, *La Discusión*. Appearing to question the intelligence of Martí's tragic decision to go to war, de la Torriente quoted the initial reaction to the news of Martí's death of a Spanish military officer: "But, Sir! Why was Martí in combat? How is it possible that a future President of the Cuban Republic would wage battle as if he were a guerrilla fighter?"[42]

Previously as reluctant to discuss the memory of Martí's life as Liberal and Moderate leaders were, editors of *La Discusión* suddenly reversed course, analyzing the memory of Martí's life rather than his death for the first time and attacking Martí for the mistaken views he had held. Specifically, *La Discusión* charged that Martí had not only acted naively when he forged "too many illusions among his compatriots" concerning the future of Cuba, but he had also been gravely mistaken in his belief that "the salvation of Cuba would not come from the North but from the South of America."[43] Thanks to the aid of the U.S. Army, Cubans had achieved their independence. Unfortunately, the "specific benefits, as much moral as material," of the first U.S. intervention have still not been fully realized in Cuba, the article concluded, because "specific elements [in the country] of little patriotism" have not known or wanted or take advantage of them.[44] Apparently, in the face of obvious displays of social unity by popular nationalist workers long associated with Martí, political elites seemed suddenly to have rejected both the ideal as they had respectively embodied it in the image of Martí as well as workers' performance of a popular nationalist meaning.

An extremely expensive undertaking, the strike lasted until mid-July at a cost of thousands of dollars per week in worker rations. Yet, at no time during the strike did the Central Committee appear desperate for funds. Weekly collections, even by July, still hovered around $3,000. Donations for the strike came from fellow cigarmakers in Tampa and Key West, U.S.-based labor organizations, and progressive Cuban merchants, including one man who donated $5,000 worth of foodstuffs. Providing an impressive idea of the cost of the strike, this donation was estimated as only enough to provision the thousands of strikers for a period of six days.[45]

Gender divisions in the labor movement and the traditional tobacco industry as a whole meant that women suffered indiscriminately the effects of the strike—especially if their jobs were not included under the strike's umbrella of goals. Confined to the most poorly paid tasks (such as the leaf stripping process), which did not necessarily take place on factory grounds, women workers had fewer resources on which to rely in times of hardship. One female worker whom the strike left with no work and therefore no wages went so far as to write an open letter to the editors of *La Lucha*. Using a discourse that appealed to the revolutionary nationalist sensibilities of Cuba's middle-class women, the letter asked such women to press for a quick and successful end to the strike in order to ensure her ability to fulfill her role as an honorable citizen. She signed the letter, "The one who begs this of you is a tobacco stripper [*despalilladora*] who is a mother and is in misery."[46] When labor activists finally visited the workplaces of *despalilladoras*, the strike of factory workers had already ended. Incognizant of the difficulties these women workers had suffered in the meantime, the former strike leaders paternalistically urged the *despalilladoras* to strike for their wages to be paid in U.S. dollars as they had done.[47]

However, cigarmakers suffered equally the effects of police harassment and political surveillance that inevitably accompanied the strike, despite its emphasis on private methods of protest over public tactics of rebellion. For example, one worker was quick to point out that the municipal police and lieutenant mayor of San Antonio de los Baños had violated Article 28 of the Cuban Constitution by entering the union local with "a revolver and club in hand." For doing nothing more than jumping to their feet and proclaiming "*¡Viva la huelga!* [Long live the strike!]," he reported, fourteen workers were arrested and taken to jail where they were charged with insulting and disobeying officers of the law. In response, the workers merely continued the meeting in jail, only ending it when its leader (the writer of the article) was released.[48] These workers' hard-line attitude toward police scare tactics indicates the extent to which they had committed themselves to demanding the unconditional surrender of their employers. By then, six months into the strike, Governor Magoon himself was fed up.

Perhaps conscious of this and perhaps a bit embarrassed by the U.S. businessmen whose hypocrisy was making him look bad, Governor Magoon took actions that proved instrumental in the resolution of the strike to the advantage —amazingly—of workers. Undoubtedly believing that the U.S. government would support U.S. capital as consistently as it had in other instances, the factory owners' association invited Magoon to serve as arbiter of the dispute on their behalf.[49] Magoon refused, citing as his primary reason the fact that only management and not labor had asked him to do so.[50] A few days later, Magoon wrote the owners' association to explain more fully his views on the strike. His decision to do so would have lasting repercussions for the nationalist consciousness of workers, their views of U.S. imperialism, and their strategies for contesting the power of foreign capital as well as of political elites. Magoon's letter to management read:

> The strikers decline to work unless paid the prices fixed by them for their labor. This is a right which every freeman possesses. They offer no obstacles to the manufacturers employing others; and they have not resorted to violence or other unlawful means of coercing the manufacturers into compliance with their requirements. Their refusal to work may be ill advised, or based upon imperfect understanding, or misinformation, but so long as they conduct themselves in an orderly manner as peaceable, law-abiding citizens, I can not interfere officially, for the occasion for the exercise of official powers is not presented.[51]

Whether by accident or deliberate action, Magoon's letter was hand-delivered not only to the owners' association but also to Emilio Sánchez, the president of the strike's Central Committee!

Magoon later denied that he had meant to make the letter's contents known to the strikers, chalking up the delivery to individual oversight in a "busy office."[52] But among the strikers, Magoon's excuses were unimportant: the effect of his letter could not have been more electric. Suddenly, the door swung open for popular nationalists and their radical allies to perceive Magoon's imperialism in a populist light. Making the most of Magoon's example, workers cast Magoon in the role of a fair and impartial *caudillo* who put his subordinates' interests first and recognized that their quiescence depended on his recognition of their dignity and the justness of their demands. Undoubtedly, the hyperbole that often accompanied these reactions implied a clear and mindful critique of the limited alternatives that Cuba's political elites had offered workers in similar circumstances four years earlier.

Shocked and offended by Magoon's explicit endorsement of workers' rights, U.S. capitalists were even more incensed when strikers printed the letter and leaked its contents to the international press.[53] Workers, on the other hand, were jubilant. In an open response to Governor Magoon, one striker expressed feelings of pride, joy, and exhilaration over the fact that the Cuban state—albeit an imperialist one—had for the first time since the 1895 Revolution's Government of the Republic-in-Arms finally declared itself in solidarity with the human dignity of Cuba's popular classes. Recalling the bloody sacrifice of so many workers in the 1902 General Strike, the writer accused the Estrada Palma government and its cowardly Liberal opponents of not recognizing workers as equal citizens in the Republic. In doing so, he pointed out the common nationalist thread linking the two strikes: the cigarmakers led the General Strike in 1902 to protest the preferential hiring of Spanish apprentices in U.S.-owned factories over young Cubans; in 1907, they protested the payment in Spanish currency to all workers in U.S.-owned factories. Such policies placed in doubt the historical enterprise of Cuban independence and the rights of Cubans before foreigners in their own country. However, he also articulated an understanding of liberation that fully engaged Magoon's populist role and the U.S. imperial presence as a welcome alternative to political stagnancy and the constitutional hypocrisy of the republican government that had repressed the earlier strike:

I believe it a debt, not of gratitude but yes, of sympathy, to the governor who knows how to live up to all laws declared before the civilized world, [and] by means of a reasonable document, confirms the right of the worker to ask for the improvement of his class, always condemned by those who live off of him. . . . Those moments [of protest] which arise daily in this world of exploited and exploiters, have been drowned out in this unfortunate country many times over. Sometimes in blood, such as occurred on the 24th of November in 1902, when [Cuban] workers asked for the free apprenticeship of their sons. And other times, overlooking all the laws that had been created, we were treated as subversives of the social order. . . . I congratulate myself as well, for having found . . . a leader (perhaps the only one there is) who declares the right pertaining to the humble to claim an additional piece of bread for his children, and a little better standard of living for his family.

Signing the letter Domingo Aragón, the writer ended by comparing French workers' veneration of Emile Zola's manifesto "I Accuse" to the regard with which he predicted Cuban workers would one day feel toward Magoon's letter to the factory owners.[54]

As early as the next day, rumors that the strike would end soon surfaced in the Havana press.[55] Faced with an impossible situation, management for the U.S.-owned Havana Trust consented to the strikers' demands, that is, a 10 percent raise for all workers, payable in U.S. dollars. As expected, the independent factories that had chosen to lock out their workers did not initially offer any changes and promised to continue paying wages in Spanish currency.[56] However, it was soon clear that the political momentum built by the strike would not be easily overcome.

Although they clarified Magoon's official justification that a Cuban economy based on U.S. currency favored U.S. interests, factory owners also conceded that their surrender to strikers' demands rested heavily on Magoon's disposition toward the workers. Their explanation only fueled strikers' enthusiasm for making the most of their victory over foreign capital and increased local politicians' fears of what the workers' successful engagement of an imperialist state could mean for their own power and authority. The more astute among them broke the silence of their counterparts to endorse Magoon's actions. Thus, Juan Gualberto Gómez, the black Liberal who had figured prominently in veteran leaders' attempts to mediate Havana's General Strike of 1902, stepped forward. Acting in accord with "modern principles" and "liberty," he said, Magoon had been a "faithful interpreter of the Honorable President Roosevelt" who "in contrast to other leaders that utilize power for harmful ends, worries about the situation of the disinherited classes."[57]

Despite the fact that Gómez clearly meant to capitalize on the strike victory for his own ends, his statement held an implicit critique of the lack of social priorities shown by all local politicians in recent times. It also reiterated the kind of revolutionary nationalist sentiment to which popular nationalists had once responded and trusted during the 1895 War.

Indeed, Magoon's populist gesture toward striking workers had the ironic effect of revitalizing public support of social democratic principles among Liberal leaders of the recent 1906 struggle, including Pino Guerra. Moreover, when the strike's Central Committee met with representatives of the Havana Trust Company to finalize an end to the strike, Generoso Campos Marquetti and Evaristo Estenoz, popular nationalists with long-established reputations of solidarity with both strikers and black veterans, joined them.[58] As a result of these Liberals' poststrike endorsements, two more victories were scored: not only did the independent factories consent to raising wages through payment in U.S. currency, but even the *despalilladoras* were included in the deal negotiated by the strike's Central Committee.[59]

Still, reactions among mainstream politicians seemed mixed: *La Lucha*, a Liberal Party newspaper, printed a cartoon under the heading "The Patron of American Gold." The cartoon featured Liborio, a peasant character who represented the Cuban people, kneeling before a Catholic monstrance in which a U.S. gold coin had replaced the Holy Eucharist. Nonetheless, the enthusiasm of workers could not be tempered.[60] Within days, it had extended well beyond the confines of former strikers to affect thousands of workers in multiple sectors of the economy from Havana to the provinces.

On July 22, 1907, 20,000 Cuban workers and labor delegations from as far away as Santiago de Cuba, Santa Clara, Matanzas, Tampa, and Key West converged on the capital for a mass demonstration celebrating the strike victory. Organized as a parade that explicitly honored Governor Magoon, celebrations began early that morning and ended at midnight. *The Lucha*, Havana's main English-language newspaper, declared that the parade rally "was the largest and most enthusiastic one ever given in the city since the Americans first landed in Cuba." Not even the departure of General Wood and the installation of the Republic had drawn such crowds. Notably, marchers organized themselves into 300 identifiable labor committees, representing the widest diversity of ages, genders, and ethnicities. Particularly conspicuous was a group of bakers who carried a giant loaf of bread to which they had attached an equally mammoth replica of the U.S. dollar. Rather anxiously, reporters also noted the preponderance of red flags and prominent markers that invoked the bloodied memory of the last strike cigarmakers had organized in 1902. English-language press accounts of the parade worked hard to dismiss the symbols of labor militancy that marchers displayed. Thus, *The Lucha* insisted that the red banners "did not bear the significance which is always attached to the red flag in European countries, of socialism, revolt and anti-government."[61]

But regardless of the interpretation that nervous U.S. investors, and perhaps even Magoon himself, struggled to impose on the event, there could have been little doubt of what the strikers' unprecedented victory meant. With the historic flag of the repressed strike under Estrada Palma raised high, workers carried posters honoring its "martyrs" and a banner that read "1907 is not 1902." Placards reading "Long Live Commerce" and "Long Live Magoon" were carried alongside those reading "Long Live the Labor Federation," a recently formed national union whose membership was no doubt bolstered by the strike.[62] With these demonstrations, Cuban workers announced to the world that it *was* possible

EL PATRON ORO AMERICANO

EL PUEBLO:—Hágase tu voluntad así en la Tierra como en el Cielo.

Published at the height of the 1907 cigarmakers' strike, which sought payment
for workers in U.S. currency, this cartoon depicts Liborio, a peasant representing the Cuban people. Bowing before a sanctified image of U.S. coinage portrayed as the "body of Christ," Liborio says, "May your will be done on
earth as it is in heaven." (From *La Lucha*, July 17, 1907, 1)

to get the attention of the state through struggle and press it to live up to the
constitutional mandates of past revolutions. The fact that at the time, foreigners were in charge of the state only seemed to add force and legitimacy to their
argument. By recognizing the justice of popular-class Cubans' demands, the U.S.
provisional government seemed to guarantee that in the future, Cuban politicians would no longer be able to do the opposite.

Exploiting the Precedent of Populist Imperialism, Preparing for a Restored Republic

Among those who first recognized the significance of the 1907 strike were Havana's stevedores, a sector of the Cuban workforce that was traditionally comprised of a majority of blacks and utterly fettered to the interests of foreign capital. As dockworkers employed by the national government, stevedores made

possible the importation of manufactured goods (largely from the U.S.) and the exportation of raw materials, especially sugar, for refinement abroad (again, mainly in the U.S.). Although Havana's stevedores, and subsequently those of other ports, had struck for and enjoyed guarantees of an eight-hour day during the first U.S. intervention, they had since lost that right under the Estrada Palma administration of the Republic. In September 1908, as they prepared to launch a renewed strike for the same demand, a group of popular nationalist stevedores wrote to Magoon on behalf of the city's union. From their perspective, the recent strike owed its victory as much to Magoon's appreciation of the principles of democracy and social justice as to the armed revolutionary movement of 1906 that preceded it. For them, the political landscape of possibilities open to workers was completely transformed: "And, in effect, the armed protest of August, the little war as they have wanted to call it, has rendered a great universal lesson. The face of the country has changed completely. Now Cuba shall enter into the company of free peoples in accordance with modern civilization; and as a logical consequence, the social order shall form part of that evolution." With this view in mind, the stevedores proposed that they elect a "respectable candidate" to represent them as an adviser to the provisional governor.[63] In subsequent correspondence with Magoon, the stevedores guild celebrated the fact that the cigarmakers' strike had succeeded in assigning the role of mediator between labor and capital to the state. This was its highest achievement. If the state agreed to continue serving as a mediator and not automatically take the side of capital, the stevedores union offered, such a reconciliation would benefit all of Cuban society.[64]

Importantly, Magoon did not intercede on behalf of the stevedores in their strike or in any of the hundreds of other strikes that railroad workers, masons, carpenters, and other workers unleashed on industry over the next several months. Moreover, he showed no patience for strikers who resorted to intimidation as a means of forcing other workers to strike and ordered civil authorities to make this known to strike committees on pain of arrest. However, while Magoon's sympathy for striking workers was increasingly replaced with ambivalence, he continued to fulfill as no national leader had done before him the paternalistic role that popular nationalist agendas imposed on him. Magoon's administration did not waver in its pragmatic refusal to repress workers and its corresponding endorsement of workers' right to negotiate a fair price for their labor and, if all else failed, to strike.[65] Whenever possible, Magoon's administration attempted to claim that the decision of local capitalists and politicians to endorse or reject workers' rights was up to them. After all, the United States was only serving as temporary caretaker of Cuba, not its permanent guardian.

Still, it was clear to many activists that organized cigarmakers had forced the Magoon administration into trading the appearance of social peace for recognition of their right to strike and of the legitimacy of local interests over foreign profits. The unprecedented nature of the previous year's events seemed to galvanize popular nationalists of all sectors into public commemorations of their own, independent of the political party establishment and the imperial state. For example, on May 20, 1908, the anniversary of the now-fallen Cuban Republic, Havana's Junta Patriótica, an anti-Plattist organization of veterans led by Salvador Cisneros Betancourt, invited the children of public schools and their teachers to join them in the late afternoon at the Malecón, the capital's sea wall. From there, they would parade as a group to lay flowers at the monument of José Martí in Central Park. The Junta announced the event in the local papers, inviting all to attend.[66]

More precise evidence of how popular nationalists sought to exploit the precedent that Magoon had set in his dealings with the 1907 strikers also emerged. Other popular-class Cubans, particularly black veteran activists, increasingly perceived the triangular nature of Cuba's political situation as potentially conducive to their interests. The fact that in 1907, almost half of all Cuban cigarmakers, both male and female, were "colored" may have done much to cement links between organized labor and an emerging group of black veteran activists who would later found the Partido Independiente de Color (Independent Party of Color [PIC]) in 1908.[67]

Importantly, the key figure in this process was Evaristo Estenoz. Since denouncing the laissez-faire policies of the Estrada Palma government in 1902, Estenoz had championed both the cause of striking workers and that of black veterans in related terms. Based on his experiences alongside Quintín Banderas's regiment as a general in the Constitutional Army of 1906, Estenoz was doubtful that Liberal politicians would ever live up to the expectations for change that many of them had helped to fuel among black subordinates during the 1895 War. As Aline Helg has shown, black veteran activists like Estenoz sought to chart an autonomous, third course away from the traditional lines of ideological deference and personal patronage that established national parties required of them.[68] That the cigarmakers' strike and Magoon's populist approach to ending it influenced the strategies and perspective of these black activists seems likely. Of four members of the first commission Estenoz organized to gather political support for a racial platform in the provinces in September of 1907, two were cigarmakers from Havana.[69]

Moreover, certain veteran activists who worked on behalf of black mobilization, such as Ricardo Batrell Oviedo, measured their resentment of the betrayals of which they accused white Cubans in terms of white politicians' efforts to blame the United States for a lack of social progress. In a manifesto that he inscribed and forwarded to President Roosevelt and Secretary of War Taft, Batrell Oviedo ignored the role of U.S. officials now in control of the government in perpetuating discriminatory policies in Cuba. He also questioned the veracity of reports on lynchings of blacks in the United States that circulated in the island press. By pointing out U.S. racism, he contended, white politicians simply wanted to sow fear of the United States among Cuban blacks and cast themselves in the role of protectors of national sovereignty. All they really cared about, however, was monopolizing political power.[70]

In a letter to Taft that accompanied the manifesto, Batrell Oviedo also implied that the real enemies of black rights in Cuba were not U.S. Americans at all but white, racist Cubans. Cuban blacks, he wrote, "almost single-handedly made the independence of their country. . . . The injustice committed against them becomes all the more serious if one considers that it takes place at the very door of the United States, with the added offense of having their white brothers saying that it is the Americans who authorize such grave injustice." True freedom in Cuba, Batrell Oviedo insisted, had little to do with whether the United States was present or not. Rather, freedom implied the right to act, think, and speak independently of white Cubans' control. If whites and blacks in Cuba did not commit to such a change—one for which equal access to political power over the state proved vital—neither would ever be truly free or, in his opinion, truly "civilized."[71]

However much his indictment of Cuban whites appeared to absolve U.S. imperialism in the political development of the country, Batrell Oviedo's words did not necessarily mean that organizers of the PIC harbored illusions about the extent of U.S. racism. In fact, the accumulated evidence on the early views of PIC leaders neither implies a wholehearted endorsement of U.S. imperial rule as a solution to Cuba's political stagnancy nor even a definite stance against it. Rather like Batrell Oviedo's defrauding of white Cubans' descriptions of U.S. society, the expressions of PIC activists said more about their frustration with white political elites than it did about their confidence in an internal role for the United States in Cuba. On the contrary, U.S. agents, always enthusiastic to report claims of an armed black conspiracy, reported that Estenoz vilified the U.S. government and lumped the interventionists together with white Cubans who opposed black advancement. They accused Estenoz of saying that he "prefer[ed] to live killing off [blacks'] oppressors rather than by begging."[72] However, as their actions attest, the position of PIC organizers during the second U.S. intervention and beyond remained dynamic, pragmatic, and open to engaging U.S. imperialism—but only if doing so served the greater goal of securing racial equality for blacks from a reformed and independent Cuban state.

For their part, U.S. officials of the provisional government seemed ready and willing to grant their approval to black activists' plan for an autonomous party. Accustomed as they were to the forcible separation of blacks into their own organizations back home, U.S. officials shared only a dull sense of foreboding about the impact that the PIC's formation might have on white political elites. For example, the chief of U.S. military intelligence who cited the PIC's establishment as "the beginning of the race problem in Cuba" did not think that much would come of the situation other than the forced coalition of the PIC with a mainstream political party. Such a coalition, he predicted, would get the PIC what it wanted: election of its own racially conscious and politically critical members to national office.[73]

Thus, on the afternoon of September 30, 1908, one year after initiating the movement, a commission of seven PIC officers headed by Estenoz called on Governor Magoon to pay their respects. On the following day, they sent him a follow-up letter in which they outlined the objectives and methods of their organization in this way:

> The ends which inspire us are those of satisfying the necessities of *many thousands of Cubans* systematically excluded from all participation in the affairs of our country and who are victimized and are known by the name of the "colored race." The benefits which the Independent Association of Color may obtain will always be legal, the product of a legitimate right, emanating from suffrage and acquired through the same title of citizens which all Cubans have. On exercising our rights freely and separately from all other political parties, we do so complying with a duty and out of respect for this class, ridiculed on all occasions in its aspirations against every right, marginalized from all participation, and like a dogma, denied all [possibility] of shared, fraternal life.[74]

The writers ended the letter by pledging to work for their cause through electoral political channels, at least "while Cuba remains a *unitary* Republic." This final phrase carried many deliberate, if as yet undefined, implications for the future of the restored Republic. With it, PIC organizers announced their contribution to the series of efforts launched by the popular classes since 1902 to claim the validity of their nation from the margins of their society. Like the cigarmakers union, the popular nationalist coalition that the PIC represented proposed a concerted, autonomous course of action. They aimed to see a restored Cuban state implement an alternative nation to the one the former, pro-imperialist nationalist administration had tried to impose as well as to that which revolutionary nationalist Liberals proposed in its stead. By articulating their own agenda to an imperialist state, cigarmakers and black veterans hoped to set a political precedent that would ensure the reform of the restored national state yet to come.

Conclusion

From the start, Governor Magoon's approach to what he considered "volatile" sectors of Cuban society hinged on an odd set of imperial principles: symbolic inclusion and strategic negotiation of radical activists' demands. Thus, between 1906 and 1909, Magoon shocked the leaders of both mainstream political parties by tolerating and even courting the activism of key sectors of the popular classes. Between 1906 and 1909, the activism of organized cigarmakers and formerly Liberal black veterans and Magoon's tolerance of it outraged political elites. Reasons for their outrage stemmed from political elites' interpretations of popular-class autonomy as a subversion of their authority and, by extension, a danger to the restoration of the Republic under their rule.

For organized workers and black veteran activists, on the other hand, Magoon's pragmatic populism paradoxically legitimated their interpretation of the 1895 War as a revolution for social change. It also brought the distrustful attitudes and authoritarian policies that the Revolution's former leaders-turned-politicians had practiced over the last four years of republican rule into sharp relief. Combined with popular perceptions of the provisional government's policies, the postrevolutionary context in which Magoon operated rendered a lethal dose of political dependency to all three forms of Cuban nationalisms.

Under Magoon, Cuban workers and black activists gave clear testimony of their willingness to bypass local political elites not only in pursuit of their own interests but also in pursuit of a popular nationalist image of nation that built upon them. The fact that the role of the United States in Cuba's internal affairs had facilitated the actions of popular nationalists signaled their emerging dependence on that role. However, the relative success of cigarmakers, other organized workers, and black veterans also signaled their independence from the vertical channels of authority and discourses of historical memory on which the power of political elites relied. Events from the start of the Republic through the Constitutional Revolution of 1906 had demonstrated the growing willingness of politicians to use the Plattist threat and U.S. imperialism to repress other sectors' needs and preserve their political advantage vis-à-vis one another. This was not a problem for the Liberal and Conservative leaders themselves as long as popular nationalists did not attempt the same thing. The Magoon years proved that they could.

In this sense, the events of the second U.S. intervention marked a watershed in the evolving relationship between U.S. imperialism and conflicting visions of nation in Cuba. They also marked a radical shift in revolutionary and pro-imperialist nationalists' official commemorations of José Martí as the embodiment of the myth of social unity achieved during the 1895 War. Indeed, the period from 1906 to 1909 witnessed the demise and revision of that construction. If pro-imperialist nationalists during the Estrada Palma regime had at one point advanced the notion that most Cubans would never achieve Martí's dream of social unity and blamed popular nationalists' rebelliousness for its demise, Liberal voices now increasingly echoed this view.

After almost three years of U.S. military occupation and administration by Charles Magoon, Cuba celebrated the restoration of the Republic to local control in 1909. Instead of inaugurating the Republic on the day following the anniversary of Martí's death as they had in 1902, however, Liberals, who won an overwhelming majority of seats in Congress and the presidency, decided to reclaim Cuba's independence on the anniversary of Martí's birth, January 28, 1909. Holding the inauguration on Martí's birthday had been the brainchild of Enrique Loynaz del Castillo, commanding general of the 1906 Constitutional Army and the only Liberal leader who had subsequently refused to cooperate with Magoon. It was the first time in the history of the Republic that Martí's birthday would be honored with the same reverence as the day marking his death. By co-opting his idea, other Liberals augmented their own legitimacy as guardians of Cuba's sovereignty, although they obfuscated the terms under which they would define it as well as the social conditions they deemed necessary for defending it.

Indeed, symbols of liberation and markers of memory, at least as the Liberal leadership constructed it, abounded. With his service as personal assistant to Governor Magoon ended, José Martí y Zayas Bazán now accompanied José Miguel Gómez, president-elect of the Republic, to his inauguration as Gómez's personal assistant. For the new presidential office, a local benefactress had ordered Havana's Versailles jewelers to design a special chair for Gómez to replace the Spanish throne on which colonial governors and former president Estrada Palma had sat. For the new president's official use, a twelve-pound silver desk set had also been designed. Crowned with a silver plated visage of Cuba Libre caught in the act of breaking her chains, the desk set also featured an inkwell made of solid 18-karat gold.[75] Inspired by similar themes, *El Fígaro*'s cover featured a sun-dappled brook carrying a flood of gold coins.[76]

Through such images, Liberal leaders claimed not only authority over the fate of Cuba's riches as heads of state but also paternal rights to set the terms under which the historic memory and ideal of social unity might again be achieved. Not surprisingly, the incarnation of this interpretation of social unity in the young, indeed, infantilized José Martí bespoke the power that revolutionary nationalists now felt they had and would need to exercise over the Cuban people to achieve their nation. In his inaugural address on January 28, 1909, Vice President Alfredo Zayas spoke to this idea when he declared that the viability of "'a cordial Republic with all and for all'" depended on whether or not the government would find "sincere support and a fervent desire to help it in all of the inhabitants of Cuba."[77] Like pro-imperialist nationalists had done before them, revolutionary nationalists already appeared to expect that the success of social unity depended not on their own policies or form of rule but on the willingness of popular nationalists to conform to the criteria for judging social unity set by the state.

SEVEN

· ·

Dependent Nationalisms, the Stillbirth
of the Republic, and Struggles over
the Myth of Martí, 1909–1921

WITH THE DEPARTURE OF U.S. military forces and the return of the island to local control in January 1909, the newly dominant Liberals worked hard to distinguish themselves symbolically from the Conservatives. Having gained a majority of seats in both houses of Congress, the Liberals selected Martín Morúa Delgado, the black senator whom Tomás Estrada Palma had once publicly rebuffed, as majority leader of the Senate.[1] President José Miguel Gómez also chose to break with Estrada Palma's earlier example by taking his oath of office publicly, on the balcony of the Presidential Palace, rather than behind closed doors in the former throne room of the Spanish government.[2] Such actions reflected how conscious Liberals were of popular nationalists' need to feel included. However, Liberals ominously coupled each one of these actions with messages about the limits and conditions of political inclusion that they aimed directly at popular nationalist constituents. For example, when Gómez delivered his inaugural address before huge crowds with José Martí Jr. at his side, he stressed the top-down means by which he and other Liberals intended to rule: "[with] the high spirit of justice and the vivid desire to decide for the good of all."[3] Echoing contentions in Vice President Alfredo Zayas's inaugural speech, Gómez made clear that the government and not the people would "decide" how to serve "the good of all."

However, with the precedent of Charles Magoon's concessions to workers and black veteran activists now set, popular nationalists' demands for profound social change emerged stronger than ever. During Gómez's Liberal administration (1909–13), followed by Mario Menocal's Conservative government (1913–21), many popular nationalists proved themselves willing to walk the tightrope between the threat of another U.S. intervention and the probability of state repression for the sake of a socially just and democratic vision of nation. The Veterans' Movement of 1910–11, Evaristo Estenoz's armed protest of the PIC in 1912, and the Liberals' failed "February Revolution" of 1917 all responded to the refusal of the Cuban state to negotiate and share power in the same way. Finding channels for engaging the state increasingly clogged by the state itself, many popular national-ists attempted to use the threat of a U.S. military intervention as the vehicle for commanding the attention of political elites and eliciting political concessions to their demands.

In dealing with these demands, political leaders of both the revolutionary and imperialist nationalist currents recalled the hard lessons of the aborted Con-stitutional Revolution of 1906. As Magoon's populist policies had proven, the United States could not be trusted; it sided with whoever best served its immedi-ate foreign policy needs, not the long-term political interests of Cuba. From the perspective of political elites, then, the stakes for the retention of state authority in locally responsible hands were higher than ever. For both groups of leaders, sovereignty was coming to mean the retention of internal stability rather than any particular program for change from which all sectors of society might ben-efit. Revolutionary nationalist Liberals like Juan Gualberto Gómez and Mario García Kohly who had once denounced the Platt Amendment and U.S. capital as principal enemies of Cuban sovereignty now focused their anger on the internal threat that protestors and activists represented. The only way to keep the U.S. military off Cuban soil was to keep popular nationalist protest and political ac-tion at bay.

In this period, direct U.S. intervention or individual agents of U.S. intelligence (especially the infamous military officer Enoch Crowder) attempted to impose the objectives of the U.S. State Department onto successive Liberal and Conser-vative administrations through formal and informal channels.[4] Yet, it was not until the collapse of sugar prices and the consequent banking crisis (known as "*el crac*") in 1921 that the financial fortunes of political elites and the day-to-day economic survival of the state came to depend on the whims of Washington officials as never before.[5] At the same time, Cuba's burgeoning labor movement increasingly rejected the political system as a vehicle for change. Rather than trust the empty promises of politicians, workers, including popular nationalist cigarmakers, mobilized through strike action and organization outside of the state. Coupled with the U.S. government's increasingly utilitarian approach to protecting the interests of U.S. capital abroad, Menocal's repressive measures (which came to include selective assassination of labor leaders) and deportations of Spanish activists only strengthened workers' resolve.[6]

Thus, the United States' neocolonization of Cuba strengthened from without the process of internal political decay taking place from within. Left with little legitimacy and few achievements to defend other than their own monopoly on power, political elites came to see the nation as both defined by and confined to themselves. Distinctions between them did not hinge on different approaches to policy but boiled down to little more than rivalries for power. Rivalry among politicians over power often crystallized in struggles to control collective historical memory about state-initiated massacres of black Cubans in 1912 and the meaning of the 1895 War for independence that the repression of blacks sought to protect. Yet, both revolutionary and pro-imperialist nationalisms became equally dependent on the United States in this period. Eventually, by 1921, the consensus among political elites on the need for social control and the danger that popular-class mobilization represented was coming to surpass any remaining ideological distinctions between them. This process found its analogue in national leaders' mutual efforts to muffle and control José Martí. From 1909 to 1921, state officials came to construct an increasingly mute Martí through which they asserted their own social unity before Cuba's critical and divisive masses. Over time, political elites sought to centralize the content of the myth of Martí as the embodiment of a definition of social unity that they no longer felt most citizens could fulfill and increasingly ascribed only to themselves.

Clashing Memories, Conflicting Nations, 1909–1913

Led by men who had defined their political legitimacy in opposition to the Republic's first administration, the state under General Gómez should have harbored no reservations about the needs of popular-class constituents. Only two weeks before Magoon's departure, the U.S. consul in Cienfuegos had taken the dramatic step of pressing local Liberal officials to use their influence with the masses to help U.S. businessmen complete a municipal aqueduct. Apparently, mobs of over 100 jobless Cubans had repeatedly halted progress on the project to demand the replacement of hundreds of Antillean contract laborers whom the U.S. company had hired with Cubans like themselves.[7] The event proved portentous in more ways than one. From the start of the Gómez administration, heady fusions of xenophobia and conflicted attitudes toward U.S. imperialism energized popular nationalists to challenge the authority of former revolutionary and pro-imperialist nationalist leaders in unprecedented ways.

During the Gómez administration, the Veterans' Movement of 1910–11 and the PIC campaign of political defiance of 1909–12, led by former Liberal Evaristo Estenoz, were the two most prominent movements to emerge. Broadly defined, their goals were about opening up the republican political system to more radical, popular nationalist politicians who would include and represent the needs of socially marginalized and dispossessed Cubans. The fact that the majority of the participants in these movements had been soldiers of the Liberating Army in the 1895 War may explain their continuing commitment to the idea that gaining political power in the state was the best means for implementing a popular nationalist nation. Other popular nationalists had already given up their faith in the political system. Shortly before the restoration of the Republic, the same cigarmakers who had celebrated Magoon's mediation in the 1907 strike declared that the greatest chance for successful social change lay in labor actions and strict autonomy from the political mainstream. In a published manifesto, the Federative Committee of the Society of Cigarmakers explained why: "The very leaders of the wars of Independence have been those who have been, and are, most disposed to tyrannize over the laboring classes and to prevent their economic progress." Repeated successes under Magoon occurred despite, not because of, the attitudes of local elites. What more evidence of the futility of the political system did they need?[8]

But unlike the cigarmakers, black and veterans' rights activists had played a combative rather than a supportive role in the 1895 War. As they increasingly reminded political leaders, their right of access to the state was not only constitutionally guaranteed but had been forged in their own blood. Memories of the independence struggle and the images of its martyrs formed the core discursive strategy through which participants of both movements, the PIC and the Veterans' Movement, launched their attacks on the republican state.

Since the time of its initial organization under Magoon, the PIC's persistent campaign to heighten awareness of the role of race in shaping the historical patterns and defining the rhythms of everyday life in Cuba had incensed political and social elites. Although race issues remained foremost in the pages of *Previsión*, the PIC organ, PIC leaders committed themselves to a political platform that prioritized a social agenda of state-sponsored programs. It drew most of its support from the popular-class constituencies of the Liberal Party, both white and black, urban and rural. PIC goals included the eight-hour day for all workers, preference for Cubans over foreign immigrants in all employment, state distribution of national lands to Cubans over sale to foreign companies, racial equity in government jobs, and an end to racial discrimination in immigration policy. Additionally, the PIC proclaimed its opposition to the Platt Amendment and demanded the revision of all legislation passed during the U.S. occupations.[9]

In contrast to the nostalgic discourse on Cuba's revolutionary past that dominated the way that white politicians and the mainstream media chose to remember it, the PIC adamantly rejected traditional images of fraternity among *mambises.*[10] Some of the PIC's grassroots activists went as far as to accuse all former revolutionaries-turned-politicians of violating the tenets of social unity achieved in the 1895 War to the point that they no longer remembered any part of Cuban history correctly. For that reason, they were doomed to repeat it. In a manifesto titled "Blacks, Now Is the Time," PIC member Porfirio Morgado wrote, "Never again [will blacks willingly] serve as a stepladder to either blacks or whites who forget the black in his rights as a free man and believe him to be incapable of thinking or of loving the good in peace as much as danger in war." Black politicians in the mainstream parties (like Martín Morúa Delgado and Juan Gualberto Gómez), he continued, were nothing but contemporary *contra-mayorales*, that is, the black or mulatto assistants to the white overseers of slavery times.[11]

What mainstream politicians had forgotten was the key lesson of the 1895 War: that social unity could not be achieved without creating and enforcing the conditions for blacks to achieve equality with whites through the institutions and governing bodies of the Revolution. Now in the Republic, politicians like Liberal Nicolás Valverde contended that black advancement would be more effective if it came about not through state policy or legislation but through individual self-improvement and the cultural education that black mutual aid societies offered, just as it had under the Spanish. Not surprisingly, such declarations sparked an avalanche of manifestos from the PIC. Collectively, they charged that politicians in the Republic were no more accountable to black citizens than colonial officials had been and they knew it. One writer went so far as to charge Valverde himself with sinning against God, since Antonio Maceo and José Martí had echoed the precepts of Jesus Christ, God's son on earth.[12] In other words, for the PIC, Cuba's ex-revolutionary leadership betrayed not only the authentic nation that black soldiers had battled to found but also both the Christian and the Cuban messiahs.

Creating a Republic for all meant discussing, not hiding, the factors that had prevented social unity under the Spanish and now, after the Spanish were gone, had emerged to impede it once again: "The Partido Independiente comes to reclaim for you and for all Cubans, what those who joined Spanish bayonets tried to destroy: Liberty, Equality and Fraternity. . . . This is what the [PIC] has come to do . . . , not to plant hatred between whites and blacks, since blacks and whites are already scourged enough by the whip of the *double* aristocracy [of race and class] that you [the politicians] defend."[13]

Of course, Cuba's political elite accused the PIC of the very same crime: of betraying the tenets of social unity, defying memories of the past that had sanctified its meaning, and violating the nation as they understood it. For this reason, what began as a condemnation of the PIC's political platform as "racist" quickly spiraled into a concerted political assault on the PIC's legal right to exist. With the sole dissent of Salvador Cisneros Betancourt, the Cuban Senate passed a bill in January 1910, known as the Ley Morúa in honor of the famous black Liberal, that criminalized the PIC's activities. President Gómez quickly signed the Ley Morúa into law.[14]

Subsequently, leaders of both parties pressed the Gómez administration to suppress the PIC on constitutional grounds and in the name of preventing a third U.S. intervention. Some PIC leaders were appalled at the degree of unanimity that political elites, once so dramatically divided, quickly mustered to defend against the threat of their popular nationalist enemies. For example, General Pedro Ivonnet, a veteran of the 1895 War and ex-Rural Guardsman, appealed to President Gómez's memories of benevolent exchange and mutual suffering with poor black soldiers, apparently aware that he viewed PIC activism as tantamount to military insubordination: "We all know that you are General Gómez who ate the *boniato* [sweet potato] with us, and that you have nothing to fear from the *mambises orientales*. They are the comrades of the President of the Republic of Cuba."[15] When personal entreaties to Gómez did not work, the PIC then turned to U.S. imperial agents as leverage in their struggle to regain their party's legality. In April 1910, party president and founder Evaristo Estenoz reminded the U.S. foreign minister in Havana that his party had been recognized by Magoon's administration and that in all other cases, the U.S. military had demanded that decrees and policies passed under its rule be maintained. Meanwhile, the PIC leadership in Cienfuegos wrote directly to the president of the United States.[16]

However, only other popular nationalist Cubans appeared to agree with the PIC's contention that in a pluralist democracy, every political party should have the right to exist, regardless of (or perhaps in this case, because of) the nature of its critiques. Despite its inability to campaign freely and the fact that the party had only existed for a few months before the passage of the Morúa Law, 10,000 Cubans voted for the PIC in the fall elections of 1910 in Havana, the only province where the party was allowed to register.[17] So popular was the PIC platform outside of Havana that in the town of Placetas, Santa Clara, Liberal candidates attempted to garner more votes by claiming a former affiliation with the PIC.[18]

In the end, the PIC found its paths to political participation and influence over public discourse deeply circumscribed by the combination of political elites' intransigence and the media's broad efforts to sensationalize racial fears. Whipped up by rumor and political strategizing, these fears approached a kind of paranoia that made all discussion of the legitimate concerns raised by the PIC taboo—even those extending beyond the bounds of race into questions of economic and social policy. PIC calls for a thorough revolutionizing of the Republic were roundly interpreted as a menace to the Republic's stability and, worse, as a call to establish another "Haiti" or black Republic.[19] Ironically, the claim that the state had to rely on political force in order to prevent another Haiti—Spain's discursive strategy of last resort in the 1880s—now became for many Cuban revolutionary and pro-imperialist nationalist officials an ideological weapon of choice.

As Aline Helg and others have shown, the results of this process were disastrous. On May 20, 1912, the tenth anniversary of Cuban independence, Evaristo Estenoz, known among PIC supporters as "the Redeemer of blacks,"[20] declared himself and several hundred followers in rebellion against the national state. They did so from the mountains of Oriente province, the historical point of origin for all three independence wars. Unleashing a wave of reprisals against blacks—armed or unarmed—the Liberal state responded to the PIC's rebellion by advocating a war of attrition against PIC supporters in town and field. Public justification of its repression came not only from large sectors of the white population but also from the Cuban media, which depicted the uprising as an unabashed campaign of black-on-white violence inspired by nothing more than racial hatred. One eyewitness, a dark mulatto intellectual, summed up subsequent events in this way:

> All the bitterness, all the hatred, all the ancestral prejudices of the white race against the black, were let loose. While the machine guns of the government troops were mowing down thousands of colored men, not alone those in arms, but the peaceful inhabitants of towns and villages in the Eastern Province of Cuba, in the larger cities and even in the Capital of the Republic, white men armed to the teeth went about ordering any and every black man to withdraw from the streets and public places on pain of death, and the mere color of his skin was sufficient reason to send a man to prison on the charge of rebellion.[21]

Yet, the rebels themselves—who probably numbered only a few hundred—defied all press accounts by refraining from launching direct attacks on people; rather, they confined what few revolutionary activities they carried out early in the war to assaults on property mainly owned by Spaniards. To the surprise of U.S. officials and U.S. citizens who demanded and received boatloads of U.S. marines for their protection, no U.S. property was ever damaged, or apparently even threatened.

In fact, their racial prejudice notwithstanding, most U.S. observers expressed horror rather than approval of the atrocities Cuban forces and white vigilantes openly committed. Thus, the U.S. legation's military attaché reported that under pressure to tally a high body count, officers of a Rural Guard unit had "shot down . . . in cold blood" a large number of peaceful black Cubans, including many women and children.[22] On June 14, G. C. Peterson, general manager of the Guantánamo & Western Railroad Co., reported seeing the corpses of two men "with their heads shot off, lying along side the track so that the people of the passenger train could see them." The main roads were also littered with bodies. Crews dispatched from Guantánamo to bury the dead did not do so if they turned out not to be white, and so "they were left until the buzzards finished them."[23]

Calling himself the "General in Chief of the Vindicating Army," Estenoz responded to the atrocities government forces perpetrated against black civilians with repeated attempts to contact the U.S. State Department. In the first of these, a letter dated June 6, 1912, Estenoz made clear that the source of conflict lay with other Cubans who did not share (nor cared to consider) racial equality and state enforcement of racial equality as the basis of the nation:

> Under present conditions, the black man has no chance in Cuba and we are carrying on this warfare in order to secure for him the civic rights to which he is entitled in common with other Cubans. . . . This war is not directed against foreigners and we hope that they will refrain from taking sides. . . . The Cuban government has tried to make people think that this is a race war but it is not, so as is indicated by the fact that there are many white men in our ranks and besides, a race war would be impossible in Cuba, because with the exception of the foreigners, all would be on one side. . . . All that we ask is our rights as citizens and we hope our position will be understood by the American people and that they will study the condition carefully before considering intervention.[24]

Importantly, Estenoz's insistence that a race war was not possible in Cuba because "all would be on one side" invoked Martí's discourse of denying the existence of race among Cubans. Yet, unlike Martí, Estenoz took this logic one step further. Condemning the fact that racial discrimination continued to exist in Cuba, Estenoz denounced white racism and the structural legacies of generations of white privilege and its resulting political and economic inequalities as responsible for it.

As vigilante violence rose, there seemed no end in sight to the Liberal state's toleration of abuses. Hoping to end the horrors as deftly as Liberal leaders had aborted the Revolution of 1906 and still salvage his goals of political reform, Estenoz wrote two more letters to U.S. officials. He asked for U.S. military intervention to stop the state's brutal repression and to "protect the interests of the

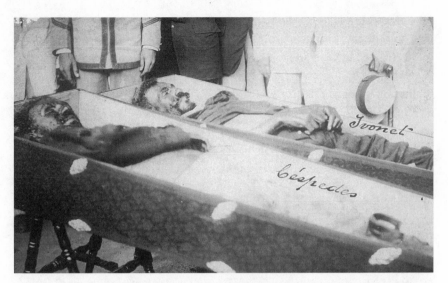

Postcard showing the bodies of Pedro Ivonnet and another PIC leader, killed by government forces in August 1912. The commanding officers of the Oriente campaign, General José de Jesús Monteagudo and Captain José Martí y Zayas Bazán, are standing in the background. The full image was widely published in Cuban newspapers. (Private collection of author)

subjects of this country."[25] Thus, Estenoz looked to the United States to save his popular nationalist vision of nation from extinction.

Evaristo Estenoz died on the evening of June 27, shot in the head from behind during an encounter in which 150 blacks were slaughtered.[26] Killed instantly, his body was transported to Santiago for a public viewing.[27] Postcards of his corpse, photographed with commanding officers José de Jesús Monteagudo and José Martí y Zayas Bazán standing in the background, were subsequently sold as souvenirs. That same day, President Gómez announced imminent troop withdrawal from Oriente.[28] On July 1, the small number of U.S. military forces that had invaded Oriente to protect U.S. plantations followed suit.[29] Pedro Ivonnet, although severely wounded, managed to elude capture until July 18, when he too was shot by government forces.[30] Shortly afterward, the nascent Cuban film industry released a government-issued propaganda film that featured staged scenes of captured rebels and of *reconcentrados* purported to have been forced from their rural homes by the rebels rather than by government troops. The opposite was probably true.[31] By early August when the last rebels and "conspirators" had been rounded up or executed, the Liberal-directed armed forces, volunteer militias, and a complicit white population had succeeded in killing between 4,000 and 6,000 black citizens, the vast majority of them civilians. Defying the plethora of official reports and justifications, the Cuban military reported the number of its own forces killed during the "race war" as only sixteen, eight of whom were black soldiers killed by their own white comrades on suspicion of conspiring with the revolutionaries.[32] But white racism alone cannot explain the course of these events nor the degree of overwhelming complicity that revolutionary nationalist leaders, once so critical of Estrada Palma's "anti-black" policies, displayed in making them possible.

In fact, the PIC's emergence and organization into a political party crystallized sentiments of opposition and anger that the activities of a parallel movement of veterans from 1910 to 1911 brought to the fore. The power of this movement lay in its contention that elected officials did not discriminate just against black Cubans in their policies but against all poor and working-class Cubans by sponsoring foreign immigration to the country and granting foreigners greater privileges than Cubans. In the press and on the streets, a coalition of veterans associations around the island organized a campaign that accused the Gómez administration and Congress of emulating the Spanish by bringing in Spanish immigrants and maintaining the class-race privileges that had characterized life under the colonial government.

Signed "The Nationalists, or better said, the thousands of Cubans who sign this protest without distinction of party or color," one manifesto explained:

> The same ones who yesterday insulted us on the streets, in cafés and plazas, protected by Weyler's bayonets, are the same ones who today . . . pretend to monopolize the public destinies of the Republic that they once so brutally combated. . . . Among the pariahs [who flood our shores] — without a fatherland and without a home — come an infinite number of artisans and servants who steal the sustenance of our female and male Cuban workers. And then, after exploiting the country, . . . they return to their lands saying that we are *cafres* and tumultuous Indians.[33]

Although veteran activists condemned all Spanish immigration, leaders of the movement had more specific goals in mind. They demanded that the government ban any Spanish resident or native Cuban who had born arms against rebel forces during the independence wars from holding national or local public office.

Originating from among thousands of rank-and-file members of the National Council of Veterans, manifestos like this one defied the credibility of the state and questioned the reliability of their own organization's leaders. At first, revolutionary nationalist generals Enrique Loynaz del Castillo and Enrique Collazo sympathized with popular-class veterans' sense of frustration over how little had

DEPENDENT NATIONALISMS

changed. Still, they couched their complaints in a carefully worded discourse that blamed the Spanish rather than men like themselves, revolutionary leaders-turned-politicians, for continuing social discrimination. For example, a 1911 manifesto signed by Loynaz del Castillo, Manuel Sanguily, and other luminaries, including the son of José Martí, demanded that Spanish *guerrilleros* (guerrillas) and Cuban *traidores* (traitors) be forcibly removed from any posts they currently held. The decision of Cuban veterans to forgive loyalists rather than deport them, as prescribed by José Martí in his Manifesto of Montecristi, had proven naïve. Spanish loyalists had gone so far as to move to other towns in order to hide their identity and had joined mainstream political parties in order to "climb up the ladder of posts that should be reserved for those who lack stains on their name."[34] In short, veteran leaders of the campaign, most of them Liberals in their own right, pressed the Liberal-dominated state for change. Yet, they deliberately avoided mentioning the two issues that most indicted the preferential treatment and opportunities for social advancement that Spaniards enjoyed over the majority of popular nationalist veterans that the campaign represented: race and class. Social unity had always defined *cubanidad*, these leaders implied, just as it continued to define it. Any problems in the Republic were not the result of the revolutionary leadership's complicity or inactivity on such issues but rather their deception at the hands of Cuba's traditional enemy: Spain.

Moreover, official publications of the Veterans' Movement clearly rejected Estenoz and his followers for betraying the past and jeopardizing Cuba's political present. In an article whose title echoed the theme of Martí's famous essay "Mi Raza" — "Neither Whites, Nor Blacks: Only Cubans" — the National Veterans Association condemned as "damned those who rip out the soul of the *Patria*, converting into enemies those who should live as brothers in the home built by the Revolution."[35] Veteran leaders appropriated the figures of revolutionary heroes, as did the PIC, in order to draw out the discrepancies between the imagined nations that the Revolution promised and the fragmented, dependent ones that the Republic had created. However, in contrast to the PIC, they deflected blame for the failure of the Republic by denying any conflict between Cuba's political elites and popular nationalists and diverted attention from the deep ideological sources of conflict in the areas of race and class.[36] Apparently, they meant to legitimate popular nationalists' frustration while providing an antidote to the PIC.

Not surprisingly, the Veterans' Movement soon became the victim of the very divisions and conflicted interests that its leaders tried so hard to deny in its analysis of the Revolution and critique of the Republic. In fact, rank-and-file veterans went as far as to propose the establishment of their own political party with a pro-veteran platform, just as PIC leaders had done on behalf of blacks.

Veteran leaders rejected this option for similar reasons: not only was the idea politically narrow, they argued, but it divided Cubans and defied the tenet of social unity on which the nation had been founded. Instead, they promised to press the two existing parties into passing legislation that restricted public office to candidates who had favored Cuban independence.[37] As the movement reached a head, however, the autonomous radicalism of its popular nationalist supporters convinced veteran leaders and many national officials of the severity of the threat that activists posed.

By November 14, 1911, thousands of veterans representing all five provinces took to the streets of Havana, voicing their collective outrage over Cuba's new and surviving aristocracy and the political stagnation of the Republic. The massive demonstration quickly prompted Manuel Sanguily, Gómez's secretary of state, and Senator Salvador Cisneros Betancourt, president of the National Veterans' Council, once the champions of the movement condemning the privilege of Spaniards, to turn against their popular nationalist constituents.[38] Veteran protestors, meanwhile, remained oblivious to Sanguily's constant harangues "on the necessity for orderly procedure" and the horrors of a "possible civil war or another American intervention." Rather than capitulate, the veterans issued the Liberal administration an ultimatum. Unless all the *guerrilleros* were dismissed from office by November 27, they would "take the law into their own hands." In response, President Gómez retreated from his original rebuke of the veterans' demands and appointed a committee of arbitration. But given the committee's political composition and Gómez's top-down method of appointment, the veterans would not agree to participate. Gómez, in turn, refused to make any more concessions.[39] Soon afterward, the defection of highly influential leaders such as Cisneros Betancourt doomed any prospects for legislative action in the Senate.

Although the depth of his feelings was never relayed to the public, the defiant attitude of the veterans had privately enraged Cisneros Betancourt. Much as Liberals and Conservatives had regarded PIC demands, he viewed the movement's open subversion of leaders' orders to cease and desist their activities in racialized terms. In a condemnatory manifesto that he later decided not to publish, Cisneros Betancourt went so far as to compare veteran protestors of 1911 to the "barbaric" royalist militias of black volunteers who had assaulted the Palacio Aldama in 1868 in order to intimidate civilized, aristocratic white supporters of Cuban independence.[40] One can only imagine the kind of reaction that black veterans might have had if the manifesto had been published: after all, revolutionary leaders of Cisneros Betancourt's generation had once contrasted Cuba's virtuous black *mambises* with the same pro-Spanish black militias whom they had earlier described as automatons of a colonial slave master. Veteran *mambises* must have felt the weight of Cisneros Betancourt's reversal heavily. During the Ten Years' War, Cisneros Betancourt had taken the symbolic step of burying his white daughter in the same grave as a black rebel, a testament to his belief in the docility and selflessness of Cuba's black insurgents. Martí had made a legend of the act by retelling the story in 1894.[41]

Clearly, by 1911, even the most radical revolutionary nationalist leaders like Cisneros Betancourt were more wedded than ever to the notion of a nation built from the top down. For them, social unity depended on the willingness of popular nationalists to follow orders and remain patient. Any violation of such fundamental principles of nation as leaders like Cisneros Betancourt perceived it earned popular nationalists rebuke and condemnation. Consequently, Liberals and Conservatives closed ranks against making concessions to the ungrateful and volatile masses. No changes to the civil service law were made, and the ex-loyalist "enemies" of Cuban independence remained where they stood, their social and political privileges protected from the demands of Cuba's poor and largely black veterans by the men who had once been their leaders in war.[42] Given Estenoz's long history of activism in veterans' circles, the shutting down of any chances of state redress for the veterans' plight might have been the last straw.

Seen in this light, the PIC's challenge to the state and the political establishment did not just elicit racial fears; it also elicited emotional terror over the possibility that the political elites' historical authenticity was in imminent danger of collapse. The frustration of popular nationalists had reached the point of social explosion, and Cuba's political elites knew it. When the PIC burst into armed protest in May 1912, Cuba's leaders put the full weight of the state behind efforts to crush popular nationalist defiance wherever they saw it. That Cuba's armed forces and allied militias chose to see it in the bodies of blacks, whether or not they affiliated with the PIC and whether or not they were even Cuban, revealed the depth of their desperation. In places as diverse as San Antonio, Oriente, and Sagua la Grande, Santa Clara, Rural Guardsmen proudly claimed responsibility for atrocities against non-PIC-affiliated blacks.[43] In San Antonio, officials reported that when Haitian workers shouted their identity to Guardsmen, the latter prefaced a hail of bullets by shouting back: "Haitian blacks or Cuban blacks, it's the same thing."[44] Of course, the notion that Cuban blacks were innately different from Haitians had been a key tenet of Martí's discourse during the 1895 War. By eradicating any claims of belonging to, let alone founding, the nation that blacks might make, revolutionary and pro-imperialist nationalists responsible for the 1912 massacre convinced themselves that only they were the authentic founders of the nation and that only they were its true guardians. In this way, Liberals came to confine the nation to the state, much as pro-imperialist nationalists had once done.

Certainly, PIC intentions to provoke or seriously threaten a U.S. intervention for the sake of electoral reform were critical in defining the objectives and responses of both sides. Despite the fact that Gómez and other Liberals had utilized the same tactic against Estrada Palma's government in 1906, they saw the PIC's armed rebellion as an intolerable form of political blackmail.[45] In short, for Gómez and other Liberal officials, the sanctity of vertical lines of authority and the subordination of popular nationalists to them came first and foremost in their vision of nation. Gómez realized that defending such a nation in a neocolonial setting had come to mean taking a hard line against not only popular-class rebellion but also those who sought to profit from its results: agents of U.S. imperialism. This included the many U.S. citizens who offered to help the Cuban government "persecute niggers."[46] Of course, Cuban Conservatives had always taken the view from the inception of the Republic that popular nationalist activism was dangerous and antipatriotic.

The mutual complicity and participation of both groups in the black massacre of 1912 set the stage for the decline and eventual disappearance of distinctive ideological differences and approaches to the nation among political elites. As the following section shows, popular nationalist sympathy for and interpretation of the meaning behind the PIC protest far exceeded the PIC's goals. Indeed, the meaning of the black massacre in 1912 and implications that it held for the political development of the Republic lay in the battles over memory and the myth of Martí that the Veterans' Movement revived and the PIC deepened. With more fervor and greater unanimity than ever before, Cuba's national political elites sought to neutralize, extinguish, and eclipse these memories.

Combating Popular Nationalist Memories
before and after the Repression of 1912

The Gómez administration augured the end of the "race war" not with gestures of compassion but with spectacles of self-congratulation. On July 27, 1912, the government hosted a mass banquet in honor of the "heroic" armed forces who had risked their lives for the sake of the "nation." The banquet was accompanied by music that included a newly commissioned military march named after the commander of the armed forces, General Monteagudo, and such favorites as "Paz Universal" (Universal Peace). Monteagudo himself and José Martí Jr. joined the entire officer corps for a sumptuous, open-air feast featuring roast pork, ham, arroz con pollo, wines, desserts, and cigars. Among the nonactive military officials in attendance were prominent Liberals who had led and later condemned the Veterans' Movement of 1910–11 such as Enrique Collazo and Manuel Sanguily and Conservatives like Mario Menocal as well the entire Gómez administration. The only black Cubans in attendance were General Jesús Rabí and the journalist Nicolás Guillén, father of the Cuban poet of the same name who later became a literary icon of negritude. Despite his vociferous support for the government, Juan Gualberto Gómez was conspicuously absent: although he was not a blood relative, his wife's family ties to Evaristo Estenoz may have prompted him to remain at home.[47]

Most significant of all, though, was not the bipartisan nature of the event or its lavish quality; it was the fact that the whole celebration took place around the statue of José Martí in Havana's Central Park. As the seating chart for the event shows, the figure of José Martí stood at the epicenter of eight long banquet tables that radiated out like a star from his pedestal.[48] Topping off the celebration, the keynote speaker, Mario García Kohly, asked guests to rise and make "a sincere pledge before the statue of the supreme one . . . who is the emblem of the Cuban ideal, that this may be the first and the last party with which we may be honored, and because never in Cuba should Cuban blood again be shed." Great applause followed this pledge.[49]

In unprecedented ways, revolutionary and pro-imperialist nationalists put their partisan differences aside and signaled the merging together of their respective political and social visions for a nation directed by and for political elites. In rationalizing the "justice" of violating black Cubans' civil and human rights in the name of preserving the Constitution and protecting a Republic "with all and for all," most officials seemed oblivious to the irony of their actions. During the course of the repression of blacks that consumed the summer of 1912, many statesmen remembered the tactical strategies on which they themselves had relied in their struggle against Spain in order to prevent the supposed black rebels from doing the same.

For example, Secretary of Justice Juan Menocal ordered the arrest and imprisonment of civilians in Oriente on the mere suspicion that they might sympathize with the PIC. Doing so would prevent the possible emergence of secret "revolutionary clubs" linked to a grassroots espionage network modeled on Martí's PRC.[50] Such paradoxes of logic among the Revolution's former leadership paralleled developments among Cuban citizens. For example, a mulatto social club in Sagua la Grande condemned the "suicidal movement" that endangered "our beloved Cuba . . . in which never have existed, nor exist, nor can exist, . . . differences and privileges [of any kind]."[51] Similarly, fifty "Cuban mothers" re-

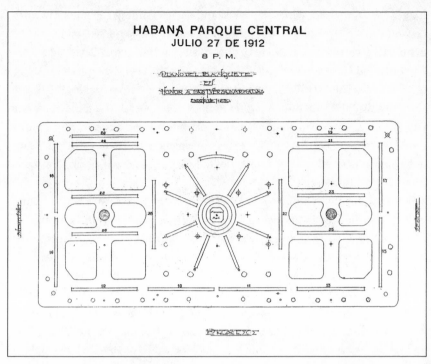

HABANA PARQUE CENTRAL
JULIO 27 DE 1912
8 P. M.

Staged in the midst of the government-backed repression of blacks in the summer of 1912, Liberal and Conservative leaders organized a celebratory banquet after the murder of PIC founder Evaristo Estenoz and held it in Havana's Central Park around the monument to José Martí. (From "Dos impresos del Plano del Parque Central, con motivo del banquete dado al Ejército Nacional después de la Campaña Racista," in ANC, Fondo Academia de Historia, Caja 106, Signatura 235)

fashioned the moralizing discourse of female support for the suffering *mambises* of the 1895 War into an indictment of political leaders' masculinity if they consented to support a general amnesty bill presented by General Campos Marquetti to the House of Representatives. Cuban men, they urged, should give no quarter to the "African barbarians [*cafres africanos*]" who, they imagined, were pillaging and raping all of Oriente.[52] Ironically, the women took advantage of the opportunity that the repression of blacks represented to launch an argument for their own political enfranchisement: they, not blacks, had always fought on behalf of civilization. A short time later, 287 young men of the same town endorsed the women's argument. The youths warned against any future intermingling of the two races as detrimental to the well-being of civilization and demanded politicians provide strict legislation to prevent it.[53]

Importantly, however few and far between, voices of protest to the massacre posed their arguments on the same basis as its perpetrators and supporters: the sanctity of the Constitution and the ideal of social unity. Although his instructions must have seemed laughable by summer's end, the chief prosecutor for the provincial supreme court of Oriente originally reminded all municipal mayors of Oriente that the right of free association had been guaranteed by the 1901 Constitution; only armed rebels could be arrested.[54] The mayor of Matanzas and a judge in Las Villas declared themselves personally responsible for the safety of black citizens and invited them to seek their protection immediately in case of threat.[55] In such a context of violence and intimidation, such acts often proved costly, provoking death threats and the like.[56] But if whites were too scared to dissent, one can only imagine how much more terrified blacks were.

Even after the massacre and mass imprisonment of blacks had ended and the state declared a "victory," blacks continued to be prosecuted for sedition because they defied rules of deference in dealing with whites or simply discussed the news coverage in public.[57] Openly "insulting and offending the white race" also became a crime.[58] Especially targeted were blacks who challenged white women's displays of greater respectability with verbal statements of rebellious contempt. In one case on the Merceditas plantation near Cabañas, Pinar del Río, simple possession of a letter written to a woman suspected of being white opened a black worker up to prosecution.[59] Political elites remained solidly committed to their policy of eliminating and extinguishing a political role for the blacks who had been arrested. Despite hundreds of letters written by prisoners and their spouses pleading for a general amnesty, President Gómez turned a deaf ear. Even the entreaties of Liberal mulatto society club "Morúa Delgado" and the brother of Martín Morúa Delgado—the author of the Ley Morúa that the PIC had been protesting—did not move Gómez.[60] In fact, full amnesty did not come from either Gómez or his Conservative successor to the presidency, Mario Menocal. Not until March 1915 when the Cuban Congress overrode Menocal's veto did the thousands of black Cubans imprisoned without charge, and mostly without trial, finally regain their freedom.[61]

Political elites' stone wall of opposition to granting amnesty for those blacks who were arrested may have resulted from the fact that, despite the absence of much violence on the part of PIC rebels, the rebellion itself had catalyzed a great deal of spontaneous support. In other words, the threat to the state and political elites' developing equation of the state with the nation was not just symbolic or perceived, but real. Like the 1906 call to arms, support came from unexpected places, especially Pinar del Río, focal point for Estenoz's 1905 failed uprising and the Liberals' 1906 Revolution. For example, in the provincial capital of Pinar del Río, a group of black women founded a revolutionary club with the name

"Missionaries of Progress" to help supply rebels in the field. Because of the secret nature of the organization, the women themselves do not appear to have been arrested. However, male prisoners were found with printed proclamations issued by the women. One of these stated, "I invite you [in the name of General Estenoz] never again to feel weak in order to pursue the grand and noble labor he has begun, for his is seconded by many blacks with dignity and *vergüenza* [humility] . . . because they understand that [the PIC] has been born in a brilliant hour for every black who, with reason, believes himself equal to the white."[62] In contrast to the white women of Sagua la Grande, these black women did not emphasize "innate" feminine weakness. Rather, they asserted that any weakness they might have as women derived from society's oppression of them, not from any law of nature. Helping Estenoz's men in the field would free them forever of this weakness and confirm their strength in a new popular nationalist "nation."

Inspired by the justness of PIC demands but apparently unaffiliated with the party, some black *pinareños* took to the field in revolutionary solidarity with the basic cause of black liberation. Others declared their solidarity publicly. Both strategies, of revolt and resistance, often met with dire consequences. For instance, Félix Oceguera from Puerta de Golpe, Pinar del Río, was arrested with an incriminating letter on his person. Angrily, its writer chided him, "What is the matter with you that you have not complied with your promise[? The men on whom you can count] are all men who have no fear and are ready when you give them the signal[.]" Saying that over a thousand men under Armentero awaited additional reinforcements, the writer noted that the men who had already joined him were veterans of previous wars. "*This one is ours*," he declared meaningfully.[63] Representing the other end of the spectrum, Vicente Crespo exhibited solidarity with the PIC by reading newspaper accounts to illiterate blacks in cafés and making numerous public threats to white supremacy in San Antonio de los Baños. Not only did he say on various occasions, "We have to get rid of the whites," but, as two Rural Guardsmen passed through a train station, he loudly remarked, "That is meat for Estenoz."[64] His words, like Oceguera's possession of an enticing letter, were enough to ensure a long and difficult stay in jail.

Other *habaneros* went even further. Perhaps most illustrative of this was the interpretation of the PIC uprising that the *centro espiritista* (spiritualist center) of San Antonio de los Baños gave its members. According to believers at the center, "Estenoz is directed by the spirit of General Maceo and this Republic ought to be for blacks, being the instruments through which this may be achieved, Estenoz and Yvonet [*sic*]."[65] Expressing similar sentiments, Seberiano Soliz, a self-described *guajiro* from Manicaragua, a small town in the province of Havana, wrote a *décima* in grammatically crude but lyrically beautiful Spanish:

Cuba I freed you and my blood I have spilled
Little concern do I receive in return
The plantation grounds were waiting again. You know
The reason why I feel so abused
For the blacks with great will
Fought much in the field
Now you only love the whites
And you despise Maceo.

Good it would be if the Spanish lion
Returned to the Country once again
Because in Cuba no
Unity among Cubans may be found
I, since I am a veteran,
Take the opportunity to say
They got the front and I got the flank
From the treasure
The whites got the star of gold
The blacks the star of lead.[66]

Both Soliz and the *espiritistas* chose to appropriate Maceo as the symbol of the popular nationalism that they believed the PIC expressed and that they claimed to share. In choosing the figure of Maceo, these popular nationalists distinguished themselves from PIC leaders who endorsed a martyred pantheon of war heroes headed by Martí. The distinction spoke to the more radical end that these rebels apparently sought: revolution, and not mere electoral participation in a morally and ideologically corrupted republican state.

Once they were left to languish in prison, black popular nationalists articulated precisely this view of the Cuban state, marking their appeals for amnesty with statements of what they believed political elites needed and wanted to hear. Repeatedly, writers declared their submission to political elites' authority and deference to their higher knowledge of what was good for Cuba as the only means for promoting social change.[67] In return for their freedom, 1,000 prisoners even promised to vote for Gómez and all Liberal Party candidates in the upcoming presidential elections.[68] In Santa Clara, Rafael Surí Guerra appropriated the figure of Martí as a means of claiming his innocence of the charges that he presumed had been made against him.[69] Reminding Gómez of the role of blacks in the "glorious adventure of 1895" in a second letter written one week after his first, Surí Guerra declared that blacks deserved justice "because we as well are *subjects* of this Republic."[70] The fact that Surí Guerra, a veteran, would use "subject," the language of the colony, rather than "citizen," the term of address among participants in the independence movement, is stunning. The most he could expect from the nation espoused by political elites was the same treatment afforded to blacks by the Spanish Crown. Still, not all prisoners surrendered to the merged authority and vision of political elites in their letters. Unwilling to apologize for wrongs they did not commit or did not consider criminal, six prisoners insisted, "[This is a]ll because we are blacks, sad, sad end . . . but the verdict of the Heavens on behalf of the poor man and above all, for the Cuban peasant in its judgment shall be terrible."[71] But regardless of the form their protest took, black prisoners clearly understood the grounds for their ideological excommunication and consciously resisted it from inside their jail cells.

Looking back on the movement and the massacre ten years later, mulatto scholar Bernardo Ruíz Suárez characterized the PIC-led uprising as a "revolution," not as a "*guerrita*" (little war) or "protest," as most historians have been wont to see it. Thoroughly disgusted with the lack of alternatives he faced in Cuba, Ruíz Suárez staged his own protest to events in Cuba and the horrors he had witnessed firsthand by going into exile in Harlem, where, he claimed, at least blacks had the right to organize for their rights independently of whites.[72]

Obviously, the ironic wrenching and paradoxical twisting of memory that the process of 1912 evoked among all Cuban nationalists is indisputable. Until then, discourses on the past and strategies of political action had hinged on engaging the state. Over time, however, revolutionary and pro-imperialist nationalists had reconfigured the channels that the 1895 Revolution had opened up for engaging the state into truncated passageways that differed little from those that Spanish colonialism had offered. By breaking with raceless discourses of *cubanidad*, the PIC had provided the popular classes an alternative path to liberation that was autonomous of the vertical channels offered by ex-caudillos. In so doing, the PIC opened doors in the consciousness of many Cubans, not just blacks and mulattoes. In the coming years, these doors would remain open despite the efforts of both Liberals and Conservatives to shut them. Indeed, the state's repression of the PIC and attending massacre of 1912 may have accomplished more than the PIC did in convincing popular nationalist Cubans that traditional party politics represented nothing more than a dead end on the road to greater liberation.

Rivalries for power replaced rifts over their purposes in exercising power. As both Liberals and Conservatives further confirmed the dependency of their nationalisms, first on one another's fears of popular protest and then on a role for the United States, popular nationalists increasingly began to reject both the state and the neocolonial hegemony that it entailed.

In the months following the war of 1912, Conservative and Liberal leaders entered a well-publicized honeymoon of peaceful national elections and cordial political relations.[73] Apparently, the opportunity to come together against the forces of popular-class rebellion and the PIC's armed defiance of their supreme authority over the nation had served them well.[74] By the time Mario Menocal's election victory over Alfredo Zayas was secured, both Menocal's Conservative supporters and Zayas's Liberal detractors claimed that with their vote, the Cuban people had decided that no civilian like Zayas could ever merit the president's chair: only the "revolutionary generals" of the independence wars were capable of keeping the social peace in Cuba, they contended.[75] Historians and observers alike later agreed, however, that if most Cubans had viewed the election as a referendum on the use of force, they chose Menocal precisely because they disapproved of the overtly brutal tactics to which Liberals had resorted only weeks before. In any case, relations between Liberals and Conservatives did not remain rosy for long.

By 1917, the history of the Republic came full circle. Only two years into Menocal's term, Conservatives began to plot his return to office using the same means that many of the same men had used during their former political incarnation as Moderates. Once again, Conservatives relied on fraud to win national elections, and Liberals, this time led by Zayas, attempted to galvanize popular nationalists in an armed protest meant to restore the sanctity of constitutional elections. And once again, both currents of nationalism depended on the U.S. to back their claims and justify their greater right to rule.[76] Yet, 1917 was not 1906: not only had conditions and the scope of Cuban nationalisms changed, but imperialism had as well. Most importantly, perhaps, all that seemed left fighting for and over was the fairness of elections. In the Constitutional Revolution of 1906, tens of thousands of Cubans, most of them popular nationalist veterans and former *pacíficos*, had mobilized to defend the promise of a democratically elected government. By comparison, the February Revolution of 1917 seemed to show how few popular nationalists believed that a democratically elected government held *any* promise for change. For many, the cause of free elections was no longer worth fighting for.

Only days before Menocal conceded to holding new partial elections (which Conservative henchmen assured would also be rigged), Liberal chiefs under the supreme command of José Miguel Gómez rose in arms in the three provinces whose election results were in dispute, Oriente, Camagüey, and Santa Clara. As in 1906, Liberal commanders named their forces the "Constitutional Army," and once again, Alfredo Zayas remained in Havana as the Liberals' principal civilian representative. Adamantly denying that their goal was to topple the Menocal administration, the revolutionary leadership declared that its sole purpose was to force the state into holding new, free elections—preferably under the supervision, not through the intervention, of the United States. Likewise, Menocal did everything he could to cajole the U.S. Minister in Havana into pleading his case before the White House by telegram. But in sharp contrast to Estrada Palma, what Menocal asked for was not a military intervention to save his administration. In fact, he meant to crush the Liberals' "lawlessness" outright: in addition to mobilizing the armed forces under Chief of Staff José Martí y Zayas Bazán, Menocal ordered the secret police to arrest scores of civilians, including such prominent men as Orestes Ferrara, Speaker of the House of Representatives, simply for being Liberals.[77]

After a brief inspection of Santa Clara's militarized polling stations, Alfredo Zayas went into hiding.[78] The fact that Menocal neither needed nor wanted direct U.S. intervention made the situation of 1917 inherently different from that of 1906. Yet, the very conditions that made it different reveal not only how committed the state had become to the use of force but also how little difference any changes in the political elites' control over the state really meant.

When the Liberal Revolution originally began in February 1917, Liberal leaders counted on the fact that the national army that they themselves had founded under Gómez's administration would desert the Conservative state and join them in the field. Alfredo Zayas even boasted to U.S. officials that "75% of the army would come to him when called."[79] The U.S. minister later reminded Zayas of this statement when Zayas proposed that he be allowed to flee to Washington.[80] But in fact, only two full battalions ever defected to the Liberal side.[81] Moreover, the general uprising of tens of thousands of popular-class Cubans on which Liberal leaders counted to repeat the successful taking of the state in 1906 never materialized.

In the three eastern provinces where the revolution was declared, support was strongest in Camagüey, Cuba's "whitest" province, where rebel leaders rallied up to 4,000 troops.[82] Significantly, Camagüey was the home province of such legendary figures as Salvador Cisneros Betancourt (recently deceased) and Enrique Loynaz del Castillo, undoubtedly the most consistently and overtly radical of the Liberal Party leadership. Moreover, Camagüey had been the site of the least PIC activity since its founding and, during the summer of 1912, had experienced little if any government repression. By contrast, only 126 individuals rebelled in Matanzas, and according to U.S. officials, both Havana and Pinar del Río—

former hotbeds of support for Liberals in 1906 — were "clear" of all rebel support from the start of the war.[83]

Perhaps most disconcerting to the Liberals was the case of Santa Clara, site of intense military intimidation by Menocal's forces and home province of José Miguel Gómez, the 1917 Revolution's supreme commander. Yet, there Gómez only mustered a few hundred troops, most of them deserters from the national army. Defeated almost immediately by 2,000 national troops, Gómez was arrested along with 229 of his men. Significantly, analysis of the professions listed for 192 of the prisoners indicates a striking preponderance of middle-class professionals, former government officials, and ex-policemen (probably dismissed in 1912 with the surrender of the spoils system to Conservative control). Of the 192 rebels arrested with Gómez for sedition, only 10 were landless peasants and 33 were skilled workers. By contrast, 125 were small businessmen, lawyers, property owners, politicians, and the like.[84] More complete prisoners' lists for Camagüey reveal a similarly high number of middle- and upper-class participants, many of whom are mentioned as belonging to high-placed families ("*de muy buena familia*").[85]

Given the generally small and middle- to upper-class character of the resurrected Constitutional Army, it is not surprising that it was defeated. Although there was some popular nationalist participation in the movement, it seems to have been a highly localized effort in which personal loyalties and the possibility for personal reward among soldiers may have trumped a popular nationalist agenda. In many ways, the Liberal uprising appears to have amounted to an army of patrons with a few well-chosen clients. Although sporadic armed encounters continued for several months, government troops garnered control over the national territory by early March 1917, scarcely a month after the "revolution" had started. Unlike 1906, when Liberal revolutionaries marched from town to town, rapidly taking over municipal governments, the revolutionaries of 1917 only succeeded in executing a coup d'état in the provincial capital of Oriente, Santiago de Cuba. Because Oriente had been the site of the bloodiest repression engineered by Gómez's Liberal administration in 1912, reasons for the rebels' success in Santiago remain unclear. Initial research appears to indicate that rebels in the countryside may simply have taken advantage of the revolutionary opportunity that Liberal leaders in the city had opened up. Rather than taking over local seats of government, these rebels sought revenge on the oppressors of 1912 — including Menocal himself.

While Liberals in Santiago attempted to persuade U.S. officials to land troops and commit to the supervision of new elections, rebels in the countryside reportedly acted like "destructive bandits," eventually burning down 35 million arrobas of sugar at one of President Menocal's personal estates.[86] The estate rebels chose to burn was located at Palma Soriano, only a few miles away from the death site of José Martí. Meanwhile, Liberals in the city of Santiago simply forced Conservatives out of civil service posts and took elected positions for themselves.[87] A combined force of U.S. Marines and government troops finally forced the rebels' surrender on March 30, 1917. Rafael Manduley, the governor-elect of the province, signed the surrender.[88] Manduley had been a principle engineer of Liberal state repression of PIC supporters in Oriente during the summer of 1912.[89]

Despite President Menocal's characterization of the 1917 revolutionaries as "the most ignorant, lawless and depraved classes of our people,"[90] the Revolution of 1917 was on the whole a patrician-led movement that inspired a limited number of the Liberal Party's traditional constituents to rebel on their behalf. Most of Cuba's popular-class, popular nationalists proved unwilling to ally their vision of nation to a large body of corrupt, self-interested leaders who differed little in their attitudes toward popular nationalists' needs and interests than their opponents. Indeed, the fact that Liberals would resort to the same tactic that the PIC had used in order to seek justice at the polls only five years before was nothing short of hypocrisy. Armed rebellion, like that of the PIC, served an equally sectoral end. But if the irony of the situation was lost on Liberals, it remained plain to Conservatives. In explaining his reasons for refusing Liberal leaders a general amnesty, Mario Menocal accused Liberals of the same betrayal of nation with which Liberals had charged the PIC. "In proceeding thus," he declared, "these men have seriously impaired the prestige of Cuba and have attempted to bring into disrepute the capacity of our people for self-government."[91]

Indeed, however dramatic the rivalry and even enmity between Liberals and Conservatives grew, their increasing adherence to the common principle of social unity *against* popular nationalist dissent showed how shallow the ideological differences between them actually were. Since the first years of his administration, Menocal had merely continued policies that his Liberal predecessors had begun. Encouraging foreign investment as the foundation of an economy based on sugar, he expanded Gómez's policy of allowing U.S. corporations to hire hundreds of Antillean contract laborers in order to brake the rapid advances of organized Cuban labor.[92] Like Gómez, he attempted to position himself as a friend to black Cubans, even inviting a small number of surviving PIC activists in Oriente to reorganize into a political appendage of the Conservative Party in return for his protection. But like the Liberals, whose leader Juan Gualberto Gómez had campaigned tirelessly to bring black voters back to the Liberal flag, few blacks found Menocal (who had personally led a force of 3,000 in the repression of 1912) either believable or appealing.[93]

Yet, the actions of Alfredo Zayas, chief of the Liberal Party whose fraudulent loss to Menocal had instigated the 1917 revolt in the first place, best exemplifies the replacement of ideological proclivities with strict, self-serving standards of political pragmatism. When José Miguel Gómez refused to cede the presidential candidacy on the Liberal ticket to Zayas in the elections of 1920, Zayas quickly sought a pact with the very political enemies who had stolen his presidential victory from him in 1916: Menocal's Conservatives. Breaking with Gómez, Zayas founded a new party, the "National League," from Conservatives loyal to Menocal and his own *zayista* Liberals. Now in command of a new political organization that could ensure his victory, Zayas then used exactly the same technique that Conservatives had used against Liberals in the partial elections to determine the presidency in 1916. Relying on Menocal's administration to issue the orders to Cuba's armed forces, Zayas counted on military "supervisors" whom the national state appointed to oversee polling stations and thereby ensure his election.[94] Moreover, while *miguelista* Liberals maintained the cock, the plow, and the busts of revolutionary heroes as symbols of their populist leadership during the 1895 War, Zayas's party resurrected the Cuban version of the Statue of Liberty that had presided over festivities in 1902 for the inauguration of the Republic as its emblem.[95] Apparently, Zayas believed that Cuba's popular nationalists were as convinced of the need to cooperate with the United States' wishes as he. Thus, he openly campaigned for votes on the premise that U.S. officials disapproved of his Liberal opponent, José Miguel Gómez.[96] In this effort to put power before ideals, Zayas quickly found that he was not alone.

Perhaps for this reason, politicians turned to replacing the evidence of any mass support for either political party with publicly funded monuments that would subvert symbolically the reality of what the state lacked: an engaged and trusting citizenry. Thus, Menocal courted and received bipartisan backing for such contradictory projects as a monument to the U.S. victims of the *Maine* and a monument to Antonio Maceo.[97] Like Estrada Palma had done with the monument to Martí in 1905, Menocal attended the unveiling of Maceo's statue only months before initiating his own wave of political repression meant to ensure his reelection in 1916.[98] Responding to the public's alleged call for "machetes," not brains, at the head of government, Menocal also sponsored a plan to build a $220,000 monument to the military figure Máximo Gómez.[99]

In many ways, Menocal's frenzied obsession with monument building exemplified the fragility of the state's historic legitimacy. Never before had Cuba's political elites, former leaders of the 1895 Revolution, been so resolved to draw the authenticity of its martyrs' selfless sacrifice to themselves. However, in light of all that had happened since 1902, it is no wonder that they resorted to marbling memories of historic heroes and forcing the celebration of their sacrifice into the service of the state. What other evidence was there that the Republic had lived up to the promise of the Revolution than the existence of the state and the success of its leaders themselves? At the pinnacle of the Republic's disillusion, the fact that official appropriations of the 1895 War's heroes took the form of marbled statues is no coincidence. Controlling the voice, meaning, and memory of Cuba's dead, especially Martí, was more critical by 1921 than ever before.

The Dilution of Political Elites' Dependent Nationalisms and the Muting of Martí

By the time the Veterans' Movement and the PIC burst onto the scene from 1911 through 1912, both Liberals and Conservatives were already forging a common myth of Martí that embodied the ideal of social unity as they defined it and subsequently attempted to police it. Roque Garrigó provides a case in point. Although his first book indicted Estrada Palma for subverting Cuba's sovereignty by refusing to consider the interests of popular nationalists, his second book, *América. José Martí,* for which Liberal president José Miguel Gómez awarded him a prize in 1911, essentially celebrated the Liberals for doing the same. Simply maintaining order and overseeing the modernization of the economy "cast greater glory" on Martí's "martyrdom" than any tears or hymns might have done.[100]

This image paralleled the view that Conservative politician and longtime pro-imperialist nationalist Gonzalo de Quesada had been constructing for years. From 1898 to 1902, de Quesada had served as an adviser to the U.S. military in Washington and later became Cuba's ambassador to the United States under both Estrada Palma's and Gómez's administration. During this time, but especially after the U.S. intervention of 1906, de Quesada published volume after volume of Martí's "complete" works. However, these volumes did not include any of Martí's socially critical essays such as "Mi raza," "Pobres y ricos," "Los cubanos de Jamaica y los revolucionarios de Haití," or even "Nuestra América." Such essays were not published in any volume of the first edition of Martí's complete works until the early 1920s when de Quesada's widow published them. Indeed, de Quesada's volumes, published between 1901 and 1915, focused almost exclusively on Martí's minor works (such as the draft of an unfinished play) and laudatory works discussing art or the domestic policies of the United States. During the second U.S. intervention, de Quesda published two volumes of Martí's essays on the United States and dedicated a third to Martí's translation of Helen Hunt Jackson's novel about the forced integration of a mixed-blood Indian woman to

U.S. society, *Ramona*.[101] Clearly, the Martí who emerged from these volumes was a scattered, eclectic, and idealistic intellectual whose concerns seemed to clash rather than resonate with the internal turmoil and external pressures enveloping Cuban society.

Between 1909 and 1921, political elites began to overlap images of Martí and thereby initiated the process of ideologically consolidating their visions of nation through repeated political acts of repression and the discourse of "social unity" that accompanied them. Through annual commemorations of the anniversary of Martí's death in the Cuban Congress, political leaders of both nationalist currents ritualized the articulation of their respective images toward each other as the only legitimate participants within the state.

Curiously, the speakers chosen for the Cuban Congress's *sesiones solemnes* to honor Martí on the anniversary of his death after 1909 were largely former Autonomists who had opposed independence and for pragmatic reasons joined the two major political parties. Apparently, it seemed appropriate to former revolutionaries that they rely on former enemies of independence to speak for them in commemorating the memory of Martí before Congress. Unity through the metaphor of the repentant Spaniard was more convincing than anything that former revolutionaries, now rivals for power, were willing to work up for public effect. After the second U.S. intervention marked a three-year hiatus from congressional commemorations of Martí's death, commemorations allowed political elites to rehearse the fusion of the images of their Martís and weigh the advantages or disadvantages of allying their own political forces against direct threats to their power from below.

The insular nature of the themes in these speeches indicate political elites' increasing self-absorption and proposed solution to the national question of how to maintain Cuban sovereignty by limiting access to state power to themselves. At the solemn session of 1911, for example, a Conservative congressman's speech showed signs of anxiety. He could not deny the reality that increasing demonstrations by organized workers, the Veterans' Movement of that year, and the apparent political resiliency of black civil rights activists called into question the political system's legitimacy. Demanding that all Cubans recognize the liberty they enjoyed as the 1895 Revolution's "prize," the speaker not only scolded dissatisfied Cubans for expecting "happiness" as well but literally erased the participation of tens of thousands of poor Cubans from the struggle: "Let us live perfectly convinced that the generation which preceeded us was much more disgraced, much more sacrificed than ours. It fought much longer than we. . . . They were ruined completely, *being rich*, they suffered indescribably, having been born happy . . . and they did not have the compensation that we have managed of seeing the flag of our illusions . . . [unfurled]. Why ask for more?"[102]

Similarly, in 1911, Estrada Palma's former coordinator of terror in the Gabinete de Combate, Fernando Freyre de Andrade, predicted that if Martí had had to suffer the kind of unwarranted criticism from the public that politicians had, he would have died of sorrow. If a bullet had not killed Martí, he said, "perhaps the deception of reality might have killed him anyway." Dead and buried, Martí was better off since, according to Freyre de Andrade, "Martí was not a man, he was a symbol."[103] The notion that Martí's greatest utility to the Republic had derived from his death in the Revolution continued the pattern that pro-imperialist nationalists had established earlier. However, their insistence on Martí's death no longer emphasized his martyrdom but rather his good fortune: death had protected Martí from Cuba's current reality.

Because the PIC rebelled between the anniversary of Martí's death on May 19, 1912, and the anniversary of the inauguration of the Republic on May 20, 1912, the commemoration led by Freyre de Andrade in 1911 marked the last time that top political leaders collectively interpreted the image of Martí in Congress. In 1913 and 1914, congressmen simply voted to go home. On May 19, 1915, a metaphoric decision on the future of such commemorations was taken. Convinced that the best way to honor Martí was to do so "mutely," as one Conservative representative put it, congressmen proposed that no session be held that day or on any future May 19 at all. The sole voice of dissent came from a Liberal who supported the emerging labor movement and was well known among repatriated Florida emigrés and veterans for espousing progressive positions on issues of social change. Ironically, it was this same Liberal, Saturnino Escoto Garrión, who would have given the address that day.

When Escoto Garrión protested both his own silencing and that of any future discussions of the memory of Martí in Congress, his dissent prompted a furious debate. In response, supporters of "mute" acts of commemoration claimed that for lesser reasons, the work of Congress was often suspended. Indeed, one representative charged, just recently a congressional session had been canceled merely to commemorate the anniversary of the death of Jesus. Martí, he argued, was much more important. In the end, however, it was the reaction of Juan Gualberto Gómez, well known to have been a personal friend of Martí, that forced a unanimous vote for a "mute" commemoration. "And when in the Cuban House [of Representatives] the memory of José Martí is invoked, . . . everyone, those of the Right and those of the Left, ought to bow down in reverence," he chastised. To shouts of "Well said!," Gómez continued:

In the end, we are all living through . . . a truly critical period in the history of the fatherland. The memory of the great deeds of our history is being abandoned to some extent, [a fact] that is to blame for this situation. We are losing the religion of memory, we are turning our backs a bit on our past. . . . Let us, then, . . . ask that the House accord the suspension of this debate as nothing less than an act of homage . . . to the old ideals of our patriotism and as a kind of oath that we should like to continue the work of the founders of the Republic, and in this sense, the Right and the Left, Conservatives and Liberals, must show that we all agree.[104]

And so, Gómez, who inaugurated the Republic by championing the image of an alternative, anti-imperialist Martí who was firmly rooted in the specific events of the past, stepped into a new phase of political struggle in the Republic by advocating for the opposite: an inaudible Martí who would rather forget the past than discuss it, no matter how many lessons it held for the present. In this way, Gómez convinced Liberals and Conservatives alike that they could commit to a singular image of Martí who justified the ideal conditions under which they might share power and consolidate the increasingly waning power of the state: that is, without open debate and without conflict.

After the pivotal year of 1916, no further congressional acts commemorating the death of Martí took place. Between 1917 and the early 1920s, during the same years in which Liberals and Conservatives began to fuse their nations for the sake of retaining power over the state, political elites also collectively sought to codify the image of the muted Martí and his silent memory with a new law.

In 1921, officials proscribed the means for commemorating Martí and codified the meaning behind such commemorations. Political elites hoped to control interpretations of the past that contested the fulfillment of its promises in the present. They also mediated displays of loyalty to Martí by glossing them as demonstrations of public loyalty to the state. Thus, arising from the fusion of political interests among Conservatives and Liberals emerged a Martí that was as equally self-satisfied and triumphalist about the past as he was philosophically reticent about the present. This Martí embodied perfectly the neocolonial, *veteranista* nation fully accommodated to the ties of cultural and economic intimacy with the United States that both Liberal and Conservative administrations had helped to cement.

Unlike the 1903 law requiring commemorative public action from political elites, the 1921 "Law That Glorifies the Apostle" placed the burden of commemoration squarely on the shoulders of average citizens. No longer fixated on the day of Martí's death, the law recognized January 28, the day of Martí's birth, as a national holiday. Appropriating the date Martí was born over the date of his death signaled the first of a series of state attempts to co-opt and neutralize the emergent image of a resurrected Martí that had been constructed by popular nationalist intellectual and activist critics since the earliest years of the Republic. The law of 1921 also regulated the terms for referring to Martí and dictated the means by which the younger generation of Cubans, especially schoolchildren, should honor him.[105]

In short, the timing of the law and its contents augured a culmination in the discursive evolution of political elites' image of Martí from a muffled and then muted symbol into an official, silent, and silencing Martí. By commemorating him on the day of his birth, political elites effectively reduced the role of citizen-participants to that of children in a national family in which the state got to play the role of the father.

"The Law That Glorifies the Apostle" required that all municipalities dedicate not only a principle street in every town to Martí but also "a statue, bust, obelisk, commemorative column, bronze plaque or stone tablet" in whatever public space was deemed most appropriate. Further, the law ordered that annually, at exactly eight o'clock in the morning on the day of Martí's birth, all schoolchildren in Cuba "with a flower on their breast . . . offer an affectionate tribute to José Martí" at this commemorative site. Accompanied by local citizens, the children were then to recite verses, sing hymns, and listen to the "panegyrics" of one or more speakers. The preamble of the law gave many reasons for these rites. Most interesting, however, were not the reasons given but the language used in giving them. "All parts of the civilized world" had already recognized Martí as "one of the continental glories" of America. Yet, despite the fact

> that all the people of Cuba bless his name and adore his memory; that they invoke him with exalted tenderness: "Maestro" and with devoted sincerity: "Apostle," because those two sacred vocables are an eternal consecration and an eternal poem of affection; that they repeat like a psalm his venerating sermons; that they hold in each of their consciences as a Cuban, a votive lamp and an altar of devotion; . . . despite . . . this undeniable idolatry that is felt for Martí . . . *he has never been rendered a true national homage;* a homage in the *unanimous sense,* . . . of positive moral, social and intellectual transcendence equal to his infinite greatness and his multiple, singular glories.[106]

The text of this law incorporated what had become by the time of its writing a codified discourse with regard to Martí, that is, a set of labels and epithets used so repeatedly over time that most of them, if applied to any other figure, would have caused confusion.[107] To avoid this confusion on the question of who Martí was and what he meant, the law stated that the terms "*Apóstol*" and "Maestro" could no longer apply to any other figure in public discourse. Indeed, as political elites had consistently demonstrated over the course of the past decade, the standard of submission to their authority by which they measured the worthiness of the masses for inclusion in their nation had changed. No longer did they expect to achieve social unity with them; instead, they demanded and legally mandated unanimity.

However, even as the law attempted to standardize references to Martí and homogenize Cubans' understanding of him as an official representative of the Cuban state, it also confirmed that Martí was, in death as in life, many things to many people. Among these, the law recognized "[Martí's] most original condition of poet, orator, sociologist, psychologist, teacher, publicist, newspaperman, politician, revolutionary and any other of his most high manifestations."[108]

In other words, "The Law That Glorifies the Apostle" prescribed a solution to the very problem inscribed in its text. That is, the Cuban state hoped to keep its citizens from holding alternative interpretations of Martí, conflicting images of nation, and contrary memories of the social unity that had been forged in the 1895 War by appropriating the image of a Martí that could be annually reborn. Symbolically, the law attempted to subvert the reality of the stillbirth of the Cuban Republic by claiming the rebirth of the public's loyalty to the state on an annual basis. Architects of the law hoped to erect a Martí that citizens would perceive as eternally optimistic about the future rather than deeply embittered about the past.

However, as the tumultuous history of twentieth-century Cuban proves, such efforts failed miserably. Cultural duels between "Martís" cut to the heart of an ideological struggle over the definition of the nation and the character of the state that continued to envelope Cuban society for generations to come.

Conclusion

Whether they were veteran protestors, PIC activists, or Liberal and Conservative caudillos, nationalists of all ideological positions legitimated a political role for the United States through their actions and discourse. Inevitably, therefore, they deepened the relationship between their own political consciousness and the cultural, ideological dimensions of U.S. imperialism. More broadly, they ensured the development of neocolonialism in Cuba by making the state's implementation of their imagined nations depend on the threat of a U.S. intervention. In the end, the efforts of popular nationalists to bypass political elites for their own sectoral gain confirmed the course that political elites were already taking. Since 1909, this steered the state away from the possibility of popular-class political participation and the taking up of any activist social agenda altogether. By 1921, pro-imperialist nationalist Conservatives and revolutionary nationalist Liberals would reach the same conclusion that they had achieved in 1912: namely, that they had far greater interests in common than they had apart.

CONCLUSION

· ·

Lessons of the Early Republic
and the Transcendence of
the Myth of Martí

IN THE OPENING SCENE of director Tomás Gutiérrez Alea's 1966 Cuban film, *Death of a Bureaucrat*, mourners stand at the grave of Franciso J. Pérez, an "exemplary worker" whose death serves to parody the life of Cuba's working class in the twentieth century. Standing under a blazing sun in Havana's Cemetery of Columbus, once the burial site of presidents, sugar barons, and socialites, his eulogizer narrates scenes from Pérez's life. "Paco," as his friends called him, had been a longtime supporter of labor rights and the cause of national liberation since the 1920s. The owner of a marble-working shop prior to the triumph of the 1959 Revolution led by Fidel Castro, Paco became the principal sculptor of busts of José Martí when, after 1959, these busts (both in reality and in the movie) suddenly proliferated all over the island. Working tirelessly to surpass state-ordered production goals, Paco sculpted bust after bust with his own hands so as to fill shrine after shrine. Eventually, he became "obsessed with the idea that for the next year, the production goals should allow every Cuban family to have a patriotic shrine in their own house." And so Paco invented what would become his greatest work: a machine that could mass-produce busts of José Martí with "great speed."

Sadly, however, just as Paco's machine was rapidly producing busts of Martí, it got stuck. Hoping to fix it, Paco climbed to the top of the machine's mixing vat of mortar. Reaching inside with a tool in his hand, Paco suddenly fell helplessly into the machine. Within seconds, the machine had transformed Paco from a vibrant and "exemplary worker" into nothing more than a mortar bust of himself. His fellow workers used the bust of Paco-Martí to crown his grave.

This scene from *Death of a Bureaucrat* brilliantly reveals a great deal about how far the cycles of violent revolution and debates over the meaning of Martí had come since the early Cuban Republic. As in the past, the new revolutionary state that took power in 1959 appropriated the image of Martí. Immediately, a new revolutionary nationalist elite set Martí to work as the supreme authenticator of the legitimacy of its leaders, of which none was greater than Fidel Castro himself. Yet, as *Death of a Bureaucrat* allegorically illustrates, the revolutionary state, as Cuba's popular class experienced it in the early 1960s, differed fundamentally from any that had come before. On one hand, its leaders recognized that all Cubans possessed the right to a private Martí of their own. On the other hand, they desperately wanted to centralize the process by which Cubans arrived at that right as well as to monitor its results. Rapidly firing off policy after policy, guerrilla leaders of the 26th of July Movement that had brought the Revolution to power attempted to equalize the lives of Cubans through rations, state-directed production, and a vast, regulated school system open to all Cubans. Simultaneously, however, the state also sought to homogenize the consciousness of its citizens in ways that guaranteed stability, social harmony, trust in their own revolutionary leadership, and a belief in a fatherland with all and for the good of all.

From the early 1960s to the 1970s, the Revolution brought the voice of Martí to the Cuban public through multiple new editions of the most complete works of Martí ever published. At the same time, Fidel Castro declared the state's actions a historical fulfillment of the 1895 project of Martí. The Revolution's leading intellectuals fostered the idea that Martí's spirit had reincarnated first in the life and then in the death of the Revolution's most famous martyr, Ernesto "Che" Guevara. Thus, through the eyes of writers Roberto Fernández Retamar and Leonardo Acosta, Martí traded his silk bow tie and black wool suit for the olive green fatigues, black beret, and submachine gun of El Che. Just as Martí had traveled widely to spread the good news of hemispheric solidarity against U.S. imperialism and total independence for Cuba, so El Che renewed Martí's efforts by leaving Cuba to spread the gospel of guerrilla warfare for social change to Bolivia and beyond.[1] Ironically, it was from Simón Bolívar, the South American independence hero whose name Bolivia bears, that José Martí had drawn much of his original ideological inspiration. For the moment, at least, it seemed that on one level, the historical circle of Cuba's mission in the world was finally complete.

And yet, perhaps some historical circles can never really be fully closed. This work suggests many lessons for how to understand the course of Cuban history in the twentieth century as well as the direction that it is taking today. One of the greatest and self-constructed legacies of Cuba's past has been the state's reliance on a paternalistic form of authoritarianism, ostensibly as a bulwark against U.S. imperialism but also as a means for justifying and enforcing its own monopoly on political power. Since the 1895 War, the desire of revolutionary leaders to implement social change from the top down and the demands of popular-class Cubans to influence the terms of change from the bottom up have always been at odds with one another. At the center of these struggles, the figure of Martí has remained the central image through which political elites and activist groups have fought over the direction of the nation and the means by which to achieve and protect national sovereignty through the nature and policies of the state.

Beginning with Tomás Estrada Palma, successive Cuban governments of the early Republic justified their turn toward authoritarianism under the threat of a U.S. intervention or military invasion. And yet, over time, their justifications came to sound more and more like hollow excuses, especially as political elites hypocritically revealed that they could manipulate U.S. imperialism to further their own goals of constructing and retaining a monopoly on state power. The pivotal decision of Liberals and Moderates to invite and not contest U.S. military intervention in 1906 provided the first example of this. Fearful that popular-class veterans' and workers' demands on the state jeopardized the hierarchies of power that held the pace of social change in check, political elites preferred to invite the United States to step in. In doing so, political elites wanted the United States to do its dirty work for them: foreign intervention, they thought, would cut off the process of applying direct pressure to the state and neutralize the credibility of those who supported such a process by displacing the national state with a foreign one.

And yet, under the rule of Provisional Governor Charles Magoon, veterans of color and an organized working class proved that they could also manipulate the objectives of U.S. imperialists to their advantage as well. Between 1906 and 1909, workers gained recognition of their right to strike and activists of color gained the right to organize politically in ways that foregrounded race and the legacies of slavery. Based on this experience, political elites would never view their situation in quite the same way again. From 1909 to 1921, the question increasingly became one of how to dominate groups that contested state authority rather than how to include, negotiate, or compromise with them. In the process, political elites exchanged political and social accountability to their citizens for diplomatic and economic accountability to foreigners. The result was that a hegemonic U.S. neocolony came to displace what might otherwise have become a hegemonic nation-state.

Originally meant to prevent the usurpation of government control by U.S. interventionist forces, the evolving Liberal-Conservative alliance against dissent from below had nonetheless come to undermine the distinctive forms of logic that had once given their nationalisms meaning in the 1890s. By marginalizing and repressing alternative popular nationalist agendas that prioritized policies of social change and political inclusion, revolutionary and pro-imperialist nationalists made their own fears of permanent external manipulation a self-fulfilling prophecy. In 1921, the end of the sugar boom and the collapse of the state's financial autonomy from foreign lenders and their backers in Washington sealed Cuba's status as a U.S. neocolony. This study has shown that the links between Cuba's economically dependent development and the formation of a politically authoritarian state were not forged by U.S. capital or U.S. imperialists alone. These links were shaped, honed, and cast by the decisions of revolutionary and pro-imperialist nationalists who chose to exclude rather than to include, to repress rather than to respect, and to distrust rather than to compromise. In making these decisions, political elites confined the formation of the state to their own imagined blueprints for a "nation" and rejected the opening up of state structures and policies to the visions, ideas, and agendas of others. In retaining an agenda of social change and fighting for its recognition by state leaders, even under U.S. imperial occupation, popular nationalists both contributed to neocolonialism and ultimately served to undermine it. The memory of their actions and the resistance of a popular nationalist Martí formed the basis for the new forms of nationalism that a younger generation of workers, students, and progressive sectors of the bourgeoisie would soon take up.

During the 1920s, a consensus emerged among a generation born after the 1895 War that political authoritarianism, state-sponsored violence, and extreme social disparities doomed prospects for the progress of society as a whole. Moreover, the unwillingess of former leaders of the 1895 War to broaden the structures of power into arenas for debate and dissent rendered their codified memories of Cuba's past personal rather than national, insignificant rather than relevant.

Over the course of the early Republic, the more authoritarian political elites became, the more muffled and muted their Martís became. Recovering the historical Martí's critiques of imperialist capitalism and applying them to political elites' rampant collaborationism, students, intellectuals, and workers eventually formed an anti-imperialist movement that resurrected a historically rooted and ideologically relevant Martí. Their purpose was to create a new state, a new society, and a new vision of nation in which social change and popular participation was not only possible but guaranteed. In liberating Martí, a younger breed of anti-imperialist revolutionary nationalists joined socialist and anarchist inter-nationalists to liberate Cuba. Widening sectors of society understood themselves and the nations for which they struggled in ways that political elites not only seemed to have ignored but actively betrayed. Eventually, the gap between the historical promise of the 1895 War and the ideological decrepitude of Cuba's present would grow into a chasm, prompting the subsequent collapse of the state under Gerardo Machado in 1933 and the repetition of a cycle similar to that of the early Republic until the triumph of the radically nationalist and ultimately socialist Revolution of 1959.

Arguably, the stability and signs of support that the Cuban people have given Cuba's government since 1959 derives in large measure from its recognition of the failures of political elites in the early republican past. Rather than shed the burden of their connections to Cuba's popular and working classes or deny the primacy of popular interests to nation-state hegemony, as most revolutionary nationalists had done in 1898, 1906, 1912, 1917, and beyond, the new revolutionary cadre led by Fidel embraced these very groups in the first years of the Revolution and continued to do so, both discursively and practically, for decades to come. Looking back on the first three decades in which the Revolution survived despite the hostility of the United States and the hemispheric community at large, it is clear that Cuba achieved what had eluded it for so long after independence from Spain: national sovereignty, the hegemony of the nation-state, and an appreciable degree of social, if not electoral or pluralistic, democracy.

In some ways, the future stability of the Cuban state may depend, as it did in the early Republic, on its leaders' ability to live up to the promises and expec-tations that popular nationalists associated with their Martí: a self-sacrificing messiah who embraced rather than punished, who loved rather than policed, who trusted rather than alienated, Cuba's poor. Leaving history as well as Martí open to inspection, interpretation, and appropriation to all Cubans, not just the state, may determine today the degree to which Cuba retains its sovereignty and the state maintains its hegemony as it did in the past. The humorous scene of a worker's fatal fall into a Martí-making machine of his own invention in *Death of a Bureaucrat* illustrates the cost of enforcing ideological uniformity. Whether those doing the enforcing are the state, its citizens, or the machines that glorify symbols of a past that they themselves create, that cost is always great.

In fact, if the past is any indication, alternative Martís have always remained hidden in the shadow of official images, only to step forward when we least expect them. Indeed, the creation myth of social unity in which all Cuban na-tionalists staked their future in the Revolution of 1895 was predicated, at the time, on the idea of radical and transformative change that embraced everyone. In the course of the early Republic, revolutionary and pro-imperialist nationalists seemed to have forgotten that point. Remembering a Martí who stood for change remains now, as it did then, the means for recovering the ideal of a social unity not predicated on continuity with the past but on developing a consensus for change in the present and future.

NOTES

Abbreviations

AIHC	Archivo del Instituto de Historia de Cuba (Archive of the Institute of History of Cuba), Havana
AMCH	Archivo del Museo de la Ciudad de la Habana (Archive of the Museum of the City of Havana)
ANC	Archivo Nacional de Cuba (National Archive of Cuba), Havana
APC	Archivo Provincial de Cienfuegos (Provincial Archive of Cienfuegos)
CRJOF	Caso Referente a Juan O'Farrill (Court Records for Juan O'Farrill)
HSSCT	Harvard Summer School for Cuban Teachers
HUA	Harvard University Archives
OC	*Obras completas* (Complete Works)
PRC	Partido Revolucionario Cubano (Cuban Revolutionary Party)
RG	Record Group
USNA	United States National Archives, Washington, D.C.

Introduction

1. "Del Presidente de la República," *El Fígaro*, February 26, 1905, 103.

2. Santí, "Thinking through Martí," 67–68; Ronda Varona, "On How to Read Martí's Thought," 85–86; Saumell-Muñoz, "Castro," 97–109; Ripoll, *José Martí* and "Falsification of José Martí"; Kirk, *José Martí*.

3. Estrade, *José Martí*, 19–20.

4. Faber, "Beautiful"; Helg, "La Mejorana Revisited"; Ferrer, *Insurgent Cuba*, 112–16, 122–38; Ramos, *Divergent Modernities*, 187–212, 251–64; Rotker, *American Chronicles*, 1–30.

5. Saumell-Muñoz, "Castro," 105.

6. del Río et al., *Texto de la Ley que Glorifica el Apóstol . . .* , June 15, 1921.

7. Martí to Manuel Mercado, May 18, 1895, in Martí, *OC*, 4:169–70.

8. See Pérez, *Cuba between Empires*; Hidalgo de Paz, *Cuba*; and Barcia Zequeira, *Élites y grupos de presión*.

9. Doty, *Mythography*, 7–8.

10. Ibid., 25.

11. Ibid., 26.

12. Ibid., 14.

13. Ibid., 25.

14. See Knight, *Slave Society in Cuba*; Paquette, *Sugar Is Made with Blood*; and Martínez Alier, *Marriage, Class and Colour.*

15. See Chaffin, *Fatal Glory.*

16. Ferrer, "Esclavitud, ciudadanía y los límites"; Scott, *Slave Emancipation in Cuba*, esp. 45–62 and 111–24; Abad, Barcia, and Loyola, *Historia de Cuba II*; Cepero Bonilla, *Raúl Cepero Bonilla*, 80–171.

17. Ferrer, "Social Aspects of Cuban Nationalism" and *Insurgent Cuba*, 15–89.

18. Hevia Lanier, *El Directorio Central*; Howard, *Changing History*, esp. 122–209.

19. Casanovas, *Bread or Bullets!*, 127–221.

20. See Healy, *United States in Cuba*; LeRiverend, *La república*; Pérez, *Cuba under the Platt Amendment*, *Cuba: Between Reform and Revolution*, and *Cuba between Empires*; and Ibarra, *Cuba.*

21. Pérez, *On Becoming Cuban*, esp. 7–13, 345–53.

22. See Zanetti, *Cautivos de la reciprocidad*; Ibarra, *Prologue to Revolution*; and Pérez de la Riva et al., eds., *La república neocolonial.*

23. Helg, *Our Rightful Share*; Ferrer, *Insurgent Cuba*; de la Fuente, *Nation for All*; Iglesias, *Las metáforas del cambio.*

24. Renan, "What Is a Nation?," 19.

25. Chatterjee, "Whose Imagined Community?," 214–15.

26. Gellner, *Nations and Nationalism*; Hobsbawm, *Nations and Nationalism since 1870.*

27. Anderson, *Imagined Communities.*

28. Mallon, *Peasant and Nation*, 5.

29. Ibid., 4–20.

30. "De Haiti. La visita del Delegado," "La Sociedad Literaria," "El Delegado en New York," *Patria*, November 1, 1892, 2.

31. Gertrudis Van Cortlandt Hamilton's three-part series "Las Damas Norte-Americanas" in *Patria*, February 3, 6, and 10, 1897, page 3 of each edition. See also the following articles in *Patria*: "Acuerdos del Senado del Estado de Nueva York" and "Acuerdos de la Legislatura de Nebraska," February 6, 1897, 2; "El señor Pierra en Ohio," February 13, 1897, 2–3; "El banquete del Lincoln Club," February 24, 1897, 2; and "George Washington y Cuba," February 27, 1987, 1.

32. "24 de Febrero de 1897," *Patria*, February 24, 1897, 1; "Segundo aniversario," ibid., February 27, 1897, 2; the commemorative edition of *Patria* on the second anniversary of Martí's death, May 19, 1897, 1–3.

33. "Efemerides del Cuartel General del Ejército Libertador de Cuba. Biografía y Diario de la Guerra del Brigadier de Estado Mayor Vicente Pujals Puente," in ANC, Fondo Donativos y Remisiones, Caja 612, Signatura 20, 43–44. The manuscript is typed and was edited by the author's son, Santiago Pujals Cancino, in Santiago de Cuba, 1917. It was apparently never published. See also Valdés Domínguez's *Diario de Soldado*, 2:84–87; and Enrique Collazo's letter to his wife in Tampa cited in "De Cuba Libre," *La República Cubana*, October 8, 1896, 10.

34. Wenceslao Galvez, "EL," *Cuba y América*, May 15, 1897, 16. Emphasis added.

35. For examples, see "Homenaje de gratitud. A los cuatro caudillos de la Revolución cubana," and "A los mártires cubanos. Credo," in *La nueva lira criolla*, 53, 163.

36. See Foner, *Spanish-Cuban-American War*; and Pérez, *Cuba between Empires.*

37. Casanovas, *Bread or Bullets!*, 6.

Chapter One

1. Casanovas, *Bread or Bullets!*, 10–11.

2. Bonilla to Juan Gualberto Gómez, June 8, 1899, in ANC, Fondo Adquisiciones, Caja 13, Signatura 575, 5–7.

3. Fernández Retamar, *Calibán*, 3–45; Ette, *José Martí.*

4. Ferrer, *Insurgent Cuba*, 121–24.

5. Ibid., 4, 122–28.

6. Ibid., 1–12, 112–69.

7. See A. Guerra, *Martí y los negros*; Ortiz, *Martí y las razas*; Stabb, "Martí and the Racists"; Fornet Betancourt, "José Martí"; Fernández Retamar, *Calibán*, 27; and Pérez, "Approaching Martí."

8. Carbonell to Tomás Estrada Palma, July 30, 1896, in ANC, Fondo PRC, Caja C-3, No. 733, 1–2.

9. Hevia Lanier, *El Directorio Central*, 39–53.

10. Zacharie de Baralt, *El Martí que yo conocí*, 51–52.

11. Delgado, "Martí en Cayo Hueso," 73.

12. Poyo, *"With All and for the Good of All,"* 96–97.

13. For example, see Tampa's weekly labor newspaper, *El Esclavo*, 1891–94.

14. Poyo, *"With All and for the Good of All,"* 70–94.

15. Martí to Trujillo, July 6, 1885, in Martí, *OC*, 1:181–83.

16. One exception is Faber, "Beautiful," 175. For more traditional critiques, see Ramos, *Divergent Modernities*, 254–64, and Savala, *Colonialism and Culture*, 6–9, 35–38, 57.

17. Martí, "Nuestra América," in *OC*, 6:20.

18. Ibid., 17.

19. Rotker, *American Chronicles*, 6.

20. Ibid., 6–30.

21. Ibid., 5.

22. Ibid., 84–85.

23. Martí, "La guerra de razas" and "Una orden secreta de africanos," *Patria*, April 1, 1893, and Martí, *OC*, 5:323–25.

24. Martí, "En La Liga," *Patria*, November 1, 1892, 2.

25. Knight, *Slave Society in Cuba*, 85–120; Paquette, *Sugar Is Made with Blood*, 29–50, 104–28.

26. Helg, *Our Rightful Share*, 27–40; Hevia Lanier, *El Directorio Central*, 42–46.

27. Ferrer, *Insurgent Cuba*, 8, 48–49, 54, 77–89, 94; Knight, *Slave Society in Cuba*, 23, 68, 113; Knight, "Haitian Revolution," 113–15.

28. Martí, "¡Basta!," in *OC*, 1:338–39.

29. Ibid., 338.

30. Martí, "El plato de lentejas," in *OC*, 3:26–30.

31. See Martí to Enrique Trujillo, July 6, 1885; Martí to Ricardo Rodríguez Otero, May

16, 1886; and Martí to Máximo Gómez, December 16, 1887, all in Martí, *OC*, 1:182–83, 192, 220–21; Martí, "Discurso en el Liceo Cubano, Tampa," November 26, 1891, ibid., 4:270–73, 275; and Ferrer, *Insurgent Cuba*, 114–15.

32. Martí, "La Campaña española" and "Los cubanos de afuera y los cubanos de aden-tro," in *OC*, 1:465–72, 475–81.

33. Martí, "Sobre negros y blancos," ibid., 3:82.

34. Martí, "Resoluciones tomadas por la emigración cubana de Tampa el día 28 de noviem-bre de 1891" and "Bases del Partido Revolucionario Cubano," ibid., 1:271–72, 279–84.

35. Martí, "Pobres y ricos," ibid., 2:251.

36. Mayner y Ros, *Cuba y sus partidos políticos*, 78, 139–41.

37. Ibid., 131–38; see also Bellido de Luna, *La anexión de Cuba*.

38. Poyo, *"With All and for the Good of All,"* 86.

39. Martí to Bonilla, August 8, 1890, in Martí, *OC*, 1:261.

40. See Martí, "Los Lunes de 'La Liga,'" "La Liga Antillana," and "Una orden secreta de africanos," ibid., 5:252–53, 323–25.

41. Martí to Serra, September 22, 1888, ibid., 1:226.

42. Abad, *De la Guerra Grande*, 202–9.

43. Martí to Serra, September 1893, in Martí, *OC*, 2:393. Emphasis added.

44. Martí to Nuñez, September 26, 1888, ibid., 1:227.

45. Martí, "Para las escenas."

46. Martí, "Antonio Maceo," in *OC*, 4:451–55.

47. Martí, "Rafael Serra," ibid., 4:379–80.

48. Martí, "Juan Gualberto Gómez en la Sociedad Económica de Amigos del País," ibid., 4:4, 417; see also Ferrer, *Insurgent Cuba*, 128–32.

49. Tejera, *Diego Vicente Tejera*, 239.

50. Ibid., 242.

51. Ibid., 240. See also Moore, *Nationalizing Blackness*, 23–26, 42–53.

52. Martí, "Pobres y ricos," in *OC*, 2:252.

53. Rafael Serra y Montalvo, "Filantropía," *La Doctrina de Martí*, September 2, 1896, 1.

54. Martí to Ricardo Rodríguez Otero, May 16, 1886, in Martí, *OC*, 1:196.

55. Martí, "Mi raza," "Pobreza y Patria," and "El obrero cubano," ibid., 2:298–300, 370–72, 51–53.

56. Martí, "La estatua de Bolívar," "El Centenario de Bolívar," "San Martín," "Discurso pronunciado en la velada de la Sociedad Literaria Hispanoamericana en honor de Simón Bolívar el 28 de Octubre de 1893," and "La fiesta de Bolívar en la Sociedad Literaria His-panoamericana," ibid., 8:175–84, 225–36, 241–53. See also Martí's didactic stories for chil-dren, "Tres héroes" and "El Padre Las Casas," ibid., 18:304–8, 440–48.

57. Martí, "A los Cubanos," in *OC*, 1:262, and "Hora suprema," in *OC*, 2:249–51.

58. Martí, "El Presidio político en Cuba," ibid., 1:61.

59. Martí, "El viaje del delegado a la Florida," ibid., 2:472.

60. Pérez Carbó, "José Martí—Enrique Trujillo"; Trujillo, *Apuntes históricos*, 60–61; Oviedo, *La niña de New York*; Zacharie de Baralt, *El Martí que yo conocí*, 82–83.

61. Martí to Serafín Bello, January 1892, in Martí, *OC*, 1:300. Martí also lamented the loss of the secure livelihood he had earned as consul to Argentina and Paraguay in his open letter to rival and critic Enrique Collazo. See Martí to Collazo, January 12, 1892, ibid., 1:293.

For a complete synopsis of Martí's life, see "Tabla cronológica de la vida de Martí," ibid., 27:189–209.

62. Quoted in Cabrera Alvarez, "Doña Leonor," 3.

63. See Martí to José Dolores Poyo, December 5, 1891, in Martí, *OC*, 1:275–76.

64. See, for example, Martí to Emilio Nuñez, February 12, 1888, and September 26, 1888, ibid., 1:225, 227.

65. Collazo, *Cuba independiente*, 26–27.

66. Martí to Gonzalo de Quesada, October 29, 1889, in Martí, *OC*, 1:251–52.

67. Poyo, "José Martí," 26–28.

68. Martí, "Los sucesos de Tampa," in *OC*, 2:143–46; "Conflicto en el Cayo," "A Cuba," and "To Cuba," ibid., 3:31–32, 47–62. See also Poyo, *"With All and for the Good of All,"* 107–10.

69. Ramón de Armas is generally responsible for popularizing such a view in his highly influential essay, *La Revolución pospuesta*; see also Pérez, *Cuba under the Platt Amendment*, 23–27, and *Cuba between Empires*, 90–99.

Chapter Two

1. Gómez to Benjamín Guerra, August 29, 1895, in Primelles, *La Revolución del 95*, 1:71.

2. "Informe del Académico de Número Dr. Emeterio S. Santovenia," August 16, 1938, in ANC, Fondo Academia de la Historia de Cuba, Caja 12, Signatura 52; "Declaración del Coronel Enrique Céspedes y Romagosa," Asociación de los Hijos y Nietos de los Veteranos de la Independencia, June 18, 1953, Fondo Donativos y Remisiones, in ANC, Caja 358, Signatura 31; López Rodríguez and Morales Tejeda, *Piedras imperecederas*, 15–35.

3. Gómez to Estrada Palma, August 22, 1895, in Primelles, *La Revolución del 95*, 1:67.

4. Gómez to Benjamín Guerra, ibid., 1:70–71.

5. *Suplemento al Diario de la Marina*, Havana, May 21, 1895, in ANC, Fondo Asuntos Políticos, Legajo 84, Signatura 23.

6. Emilio to Francisco Gómez y Toro, May 23, 1895, in ANC, Fondo Máximo Gómez, Legajo 39, Expediente 4858.

7. S. J. Massenel to Francisco Gómez y Toro, June 8, 1895, ibid.

8. Aguirre to Juan Gualberto Gómez, May 25, 1895, in ANC, Fondo Adquisiciones, Caja 9, Signatura 207.

9. Ferrer, *Insurgent Cuba*, 109–10.

10. Ibid., 150–51.

11. Pérez, *Lords of the Mountain*, 45–47; *Historia de Manuel García*; Gutiérrez Fernández, *Los héroes del 24 de febrero*; de Paz Sánchez et al., *El bandolerismo en Cuba*, 206–24.

12. *La nueva lira criolla*, 106–8.

13. Sánchez to Cisneros Betancourt, January 20, 1896, in Primelles, *La Revolución del 95*, 1:11–12.

14. Ibid., 13.

15. Ibid., 15.

16. "Diario de la Guerra del Doctor Eugenio Sánchez de Agramonte," in AIHC, Fondo Eugenio Sánchez de Agramonte, Signatura 21/1.1/1–81, 18; see also "Historia del Cuerpo de Sanidad Militar del Ejército Libertador de Cuba. Campaña de 1895–1898. Trabalo [*sic*]

Encomendado por la Sección XIV del VI Congreso Medico-Latino Americano. Leído por su Autor el Día 24 de Noviembre de 1922," in AIHC, Fondo Eugenio Sánchez de Agramonte, 2–4.

17. "Diario de la Guerra del Doctor Eugenio Sánchez de Agramonte," 28–29; 37.

18. "Historia del Cuerpo de Sanidad Militar," 6.

19. "Diario de la Guerra del Doctor Eugenio Sánchez de Agramonte," 44.

20. Ibid., 34.

21. Batrell Oviedo, *Para la historia*, 32–37.

22. *Ley Penal de la República de Cuba*, "Capítulo X. Delitos Contra la Propiedad," Articles 129–34, 37.

23. *Ley Penal de la República de Cuba*, "Capítulo IX. Delitos Contra La Honestidad," Articles 120–25, 35–36.

24. Helg, *Our Rightful Share*, 66.

25. Ferrer, "Rustic Men, Civilized Nation."

26. Helg, *Our Rightful Share*, 59–60.

27. Valdés Domínguez, *Diario de Soldado*, 1:158–59.

28. Helg, *Our Rightful Share*, 60–65.

29. Stoner, *From the House to the Streets*, 28. In recognizing Magdalena Peñarredonda y Doley with the rank of general, Stoner cites Caballero, *La mujer en la 95*. However, Peñarredonda never achieved such a rank, although she appears to have done so in the popular imagination.

30. García Galán, *Magdalena Peñarredonda*, 12–13.

31. Ibid., 14–16.

32. Ibid., 17–27.

33. Stoner, *From the House to the Streets*, 29–30; García Galán, *Magdalena Peñarredonda*, 25–29. Stoner reports the date of Peñarredonda's imprisonment as falling in 1896. However, García Galán indicates that her role as an operative was not cut short until at least December 1897 or the beginning of 1898. See also Peñarredonda to Estrada Palma, May 17, 1897, in ANC, Fondo PRC, Caja 74, No. 13016.

34. Peñarredonda to Estrada Palma, May 15, 1896, in ANC, Fondo PRC, Caja 74, No. 13009.

35. Quoted in García Galán, *Magdalena Peñarredonda*, 20.

36. Ibid., 21. Emphasis added.

37. Ibid., 29.

38. Ibid., 30–31.

39. Interview with Luisa Rodríguez Rosado, youngest daughter of Captain Rafael Rodríguez Santos and Teresa Rosado Santos (his wife and first cousin), Cienfuegos, Cuba, August 18, 1997. The author retains a copy of the affidavit signed in 1939.

40. Teresa de Jesús a Estrada Palma, November 5, 1897, in ANC, Fondo PRC, Caja 22T, No. 3362-A. Original Spanish text:

> Te recomiendo a mis hijos
> que hoy la patria me los quita
> porque de ellos necesita
> para hacer su libertad . . .

Tu que eres madre también,
la voz de una madre escucha,
también tu pena fue mucha en la pasión de Jesús
en cada revolución
hay mártires de una idea
como el que murió en Judea
en una afrentosa cruz;
por la memoria sagrada de los mártires de Cuba
mi voz hasta el cielo suba
en fervorosa oración;
en paz sus almas reposen
en el ceno de la gloria,
mientras tu nombre la historia
guarde con veneración.

41. Aguirre to Juan Gualberto Gómez, May 25, 1895, in ANC, Fondo Adquisiciones, Caja 9, Signatura 207, 1–2.

42. Captain Martín to Francisco Gómez y Toro, July 6, 1895; Cristino Zeno to Gómez y Toro, July 9, 1895; both in ANC, Fondo Máximo Gómez, Legajo 39, Expediente 4858.

43. Manuel de la Cruz, "José Martí," *La Nación*, September 26, 1895, 3.

44. de Zayas, "La Apoteosis de Martí."

45. Aristides Martínez to Estrada Palma, undated, in ANC, Fondo Correspondencia de la Secretaría de la Presidencia, Serie Felicitaciones y Muestras de Apoyo.

46. Estrada Palma to Olney, secretary of state, December 7, 1895, in *Report of the Committee on Foreign Relations*, 12.

47. Ibid., 15.

48. Ibid., 15–16.

49. Estrada Palma, *Address*, 3.

50. Poyo, *"With All and for the Good of All,"* esp. 57–61; Ibarra, *Cuba*, 224–29; Soto, *La Revolución del 33*, 1:47; Acosta de Arriba, *El pensamiento político*, 30–34.

51. Estrada Palma, *Desde el Castillo de Figuera*, 72–75.

52. See Viotti da Costa, *Brazilian Empire*, xix–xxi, 5–8, 53–60, 69–75; Mallon, *Peasant and Nation*, 319–23; Berquist, *Coffee and Conflict*, 8–12; R. Woodward, "Changes in the Nineteenth-Century Guatemalan State," 59–61; and Smith, "Origins of the National Question in Guatemala," 83–90.

53. Poyo, *"With All and for the Good of All,"* 114–18.

54. For example, see "Tampa y West Tampa," *Cuba y América*, July 1, 1897, 2–4.

55. Rafael Serra, "Filantropía," *La Doctrina de Martí*, September 2, 1896, 1.

56. Serra, "Con nuestros heroes reales," *La Doctrina de Martí*, March 30, 1897, 1.

57. Serra to Estrada Palma, January 19, February 13, March 20, and July 26, 1902, in ANC, Fondo Correspondencia de la Secretaría de la Presidencia, Serie Felicitaciones y Muestras de Apoyo.

58. Yero to Domingo Figuerola Caneda, January 22, 1897, in ANC, Fondo Academia de la Historia de Cuba, Caja 168, Signatura 468; "Vientos de Fronda," *La Doctrina de Martí*, January 15, 1897, 1.

59. Agreement between Eduardo Yero and Manuel Sanguily, July 9, 1897, in ANC, Fondo Academia de la Historia de Cuba, Caja 61, Signatura 66.

60. de Saavedra to Figuerola Caneda, October 20, 1896, ibid., Caja 167, Signatura 457.

61. Yero to Figuerola Caneda, January 22, 1897, ibid., Caja 168, Signatura 468.

62. de Saavedra to Figuerola Caneda, February 9, 1897, ibid., Caja 167, Signatura 457.

63. Foner, *Spanish-Cuban-American War*, 1:168–70, 189–90.

64. Eligio Carbonell to Gonzalo de Quesada, March 1, 1896, and de Quesada to Carbonell, March 6, 1896, in Primelles, *La Revolución del 95*, 3:238–40.

65. Poyo, *"With All and for the Good of All,"* 119–20.

66. Ibid., 100.

67. Carbonell to Estrada Palma, July 30, 1896, in ANC, Fondo PRC, Caja C-3, No. 733, 1–2.

68. Poyo, *"With All and for the Good of All,"* 87–94; Appel, "The Unionization of Florida Cigarmakers," 45–49.

69. Poyo, *"With All and for the Good of All,"* 104–5.

70. Tejera, *Conferencias sociales y políticas* and *Diego Vicente Tejera*, 169–92, 205–26, 235–46, 257–79.

71. Los Tabaqueros de Ibor City to Estrada Palma, October 26, 1895, in ANC, Fondo PRC, Caja 22T, No. 3375.

72. Ramón Rivero to Estrada Palma, September 25, 1897, ibid., Caja 20R, No. 2953.

73. Los Tabaqueros de Ibor City to Estrada Palma.

74. Rivero to Estrada Palma, November 9, 1896, in ANC, Fondo PRC, Caja 20R, No. 2944, and December 14, 1896, Caja 20R, No. 2945.

75. Rivero to Estrada Palma, April 10, 1897, ibid., Caja 20R, No. 2949.

76. Yero to Rivero, New York, June 19, 1897, in ANC, Fondo Academia de la Historia de Cuba, Caja 61, Signatura 41, 2–6.

77. Auxier, "Propaganda Activities," 294.

78. Pierra to Figuerola Caneda, October 3, 1898, in ANC, Fondo Academia de la Historia de Cuba, Caja 166, Signatura 444.

79. Pierra to Estrada Palma, November 25, 1895, in Primelles, *La Revolución del 95*, 2:258–64.

80. Reno, "Operating an 'Underground' Route to Cuba."

81. See Matthews, *Cuban Patriots' Cause Is Just*.

82. Pierra and J. A. Gutiérrez to Estrada Palma, December 22, 1895, in Primelles, *La Revolución del 95*, 2:339.

83. Both of these works were published separately and as one edition, *Free Cuba*, in 1897.

84. Rubens, *Liberty*, 107–8.

85. *Speech delivered by Mr. Fidel G. Pierra at Washington, D.C. on October 31, 1895*, 1; also *Speech delivered by Mr. Fidel G. Pierra, at Chickering Hall, New York, on the night of October 10th, 1895*.

86. Auxier, "Propaganda Activities," 295.

87. Pierra to Estrada Palma, June 26, 1896, in Primelles, *La Revolución del 95*, 4:435–36.

88. Tejera, "Capacidad cubana," in *Diego Vicente Tejera*, 190–91.

89. Estrada Palma to Juan Guiteras, October 21, 1895, in Primelles, *La Revolución del 95*, 2:75.

90. Estrade, "Los clubes femeninos," 178–79.

91. Fernando Figueredo to Estrada Palma, April 28, 1896, in Primelles, *La Revolución del 95*, 4:30–31.

92. "Reglamento Interior del Club Discípulas de Martí," in ANC, Fondo Donativos y Remisiones, Caja 295, Expediente 4.

93. Adelina Sánchez and María Rodríguez Delgado to Rosario Sigarroa, March 19, 1897, ibid., Caja 308, Expediente 53.

94. *Cuba y América*, September 15, 1897, no pages.

95. Mantilla to Francisco Gómez y Toro, Central Valley, April 20, 1895, in ANC, Fondo Máximo Gómez, Legajo 39, Expediente 4858, 5–6.

96. Mario [pseudonym] to Rosario Sigarroa, Havana, December 21, 1897, in ANC, Fondo Donativos y Remisiones, Caja 308, Signatura 46, 4–6.

97. "Expediente que contiene comprobantes de los efectivos enviados por el Club Cubanita a los distintos componentes insurrectos," in APC, Fondo Rita Suárez del Villar y Suárez del Villar, Legajo 2, Expediente 48, 1–2.

98. Ibid., 1–40.

99. Ibid., 33.

100. Adelante [pseud. of Joaquín Fortún] to Estrada Palma, October 8, 1895, in Primelles, *La Revolución del 95*, 2:221–22.

101. F. Woodward, *With Maceo in Cuba*, 14–15.

102. José Dolores Poyo to Estrada Palma, April 1, 1896, in Primelles, *La Revolución del 95*, 4:78.

103. Ch. [Francisco Chenard] to Estrada Palma, October 24, 1895, ibid., 2:226.

104. Pierra to del Castillo, March 5, 1896, ibid., 3:236–37; Pierra to Figuerola Caneda, October 3, 1898, in ANC, Fondo Academia de la Historia de Cuba, Caja 166, Signatura 444.

105. Estrada Palma to Miguel Betancourt, September 26, 1896, in Primelles, *La Revolución del 95*, 5:368–71; personal communication with Marial Iglesias, Havana, Cuba, August 1998.

106. Gómez to Estrada Palma, August 28, 1895, in Primelles, *La Revolución del 95*, 1:69.

107. See Primelles, *La Revolución del 95*, 2:6–10, 3:5–8, 4:5–9, 5:6–9.

108. "Manifesto de Montecristi," in Martí, *OC*, 5:93–103.

109. Gómez to Estrada Palma, August 11, 1896, in Primelles, *La Revolución del 95*, 5:47–48.

110. Gómez to Estrada Palma, April 29, 1896, ibid., 55–56.

111. Maceo to Estrada Palma, November 21, 1895, ibid., 2:314–15.

112. Maceo to Estrada Palma, April 14, 1896, ibid., 4:62–63.

113. Cisneros Betancourt to Estrada Palma, August 22, 1895, ibid., 1:57–58.

114. Estrada Palma to Secretario de Relaciones Exteriores de Cuba, November 11, 1897, in ANC, Fondo Gobierno de la Revolución de 1895, Caja 44, Signatura 6332.

115. Estrada Palma to T. E. Culmel[l], December 7, 1895, in Primelles, *La Revolución del 95*, 2:288–89.

116. Informe General al Gobierno de la República de Tomás Estrada Palma, May 30, 1896, and Estrada Palma to Máximo Gómez, July 29, 1896, ibid., 2:14–25, 37–39.

117. Gómez to Estrada Palma, September 26, 1896, ibid., 5:267.

118. Ibid.

119. "Mario" to Sigarroa, March 8, 1898, in ANC, Fondo Donativos y Remisiones, Caja 308, Signatura 46, 5–6.

120. Estrada Palma to Cisneros Betancourt, July 22, 1896, in Primelles, *La Revolución del 95*, 5:33.

121. "Memorandum of Agreement made this Eleventh Day of May 1897, between Tomás Estrada Palma, Delegate Plenipotentiary of the Republic of Cuba of the first part and John R. Dos Passos, of the City of New York, of the second part," in ANC, Fondo Gobierno de la Revolución de 1895, Caja 44, Signatura 6306, 1.

122. Estrada Palma, "Informe de la Delegación de la República de Cuba al Gobierno," October 15, 1897, ibid., Signatura 6329, 9.

123. "Copia redactada por J. Zayas de la nota de Tomás Estrada Palma to Samuel L. Janney Esq.," June 5, 1897, ibid., 1–2.

124. "Agreement made this fifth day of August, A.D. 1897, between Señor Don Tomás Estrada Palma . . . ," ibid., 1.

125. Ibid., 5–6.

126. Estrada Palma, "Informe de la Delegación," 12.

127. Ibid., 4–5.

128. Ibid., 11.

129. Ibid., 13.

130. For accounts of this process, see Foner, *Spanish-Cuban-American War*, 1:230–80; and Pérez, *Cuba between Empires*, 139–93.

Chapter Three

1. Pérez, *War of 1898*, 81–107; *Cuba between Empires*, 197–227.

2. Pérez, *Cuba between Empires*, 233–67.

3. Foner, *Spanish-Cuban-American War*, 1:115.

4. Ibid., 2:379–87.

5. Pérez, *Cuba between Empires*, 257–58.

6. *La nueva lira criolla*, 114, 130, 133–36, 139–41, 146–50, 172–76, 259, 277–78.

7. Peñarredonda to Tomás Estrada Palma, May 15, 1896, in ANC, Fondo PRC, Caja 74, No. 13 009.

8. Peñarredonda to Estrada Palma, April 21, 1897, and May 17, 1898, ibid., Nos. 13 010 and 13 016. All letters are signed "La Delegada."

9. Statement of Stephen Bonsal, June 11, 1897, and C. F. Koop, February 21, 1898, in *Report of the Committee on Foreign Relations*, 404–5, 458–68.

10. Peñarredonda to Estrada Palma, May 5, 1897, in ANC, Fondo PRC, Caja 74, No. 13 013.

11. Foner, *Spanish-Cuban-American War*, 2:382.

12. Ibid., 383; see also Hobbs, *Leonard Wood*, 57–59; and Hagedorn, *That Human Being*, 42–44.

13. Hagedorn, *That Human Being*, 45–48.

14. Foner, *Spanish-Cuban-American War*, 2:457–58; Estrada Palma to U.S. Secretary of State William R. Day, August 11, 1898, in ANC, Fondo Gobierno de la Revolución de 1895, Caja 44, Signatura 6354, 1.

15. Lockmiller, "Church Property Question."

16. Foner, *Spanish-Cuban-American War*, 2:456–57.

17. "Al pueblo cubano y a nuestros compañeros de trabajo," in ANC, Fondo Academia de la Historia de Cuba, Caja 106, Signatura 221; "Supplemento a *Bandera Socialista*: Al pueblo cubano," ibid., Signatura 225; "Cosas de la semana," *Democracia: Seminario político. Defensor de la absoluta independencia de Cuba*, November 26, 1899, 2.

18. González del Valle, "El clero en la revolución cubana."

19. See "Comité popular de propaganda y acción. Manifesto al pueblo de Cuba," January 1, 1900, in ANC, Fondo Adquisiciones, Legajo 86, Signatura 4390; and "Conmemoración del 24 de Febrero al pueblo cubano," February 21, 1900, in ANC, Fondo Academia de la Historia de Cuba, Caja 498, Signatura 538.

20. Leopardino, "Cosas de la Semana," *Democracia: Seminario político. Defensor de la absoluta independencia de Cuba*, December 8, 1899, 2.

21. "El 24 de Febrero," *Democracia: Periodico Político Inspirado por Estudiantes de la Universidad*, February 27, 1900, 1.

22. See, for example, "Reglamento de la Asociación Patriótica de Damas," in ANC, Fondo Donativos y Remisiones, Caja 662, Signatura 13.

23. *Mujeres que contribuyeron a Libertar [sic] a Cuba*, 3–5.

24. Personal communication with Rita Suárez del Villar, January 11, 1998, Miami, Fla. The informant was the niece and namesake of Ritica, who also raised her until her death in 1961.

25. Ibid.

26. Personal communication with Rita Suárez del Villar, and various correspondence on claims for pension increases, in APC, Fondo Rita Suárez del Villar y Suárez del Villar, Legajo 2, Expediente 37.

27. "La Cubanita," *La Mariposa: Semanario Dedicado a las Bellas*, January 14, 1900, 2.

28. "Al pueblo de Cuba," September 10, 1898, reprinted in Varona, *De la colonia a la república*, 197–205.

29. *Mujeres que contribuyeron a Libertar [sic] a Cuba*, 10.

30. Ibid.

31. M. Gómez, *Cartas desconocidas de Máximo Gómez a Rita Suárez del Villar*, Anexo 10.

32. *Mujeres que contribuyeron a Libertar [sic] a Cuba*, 10. See also Suárez del Villar, *Mis memorias*, pamphlet published posthumously in 1961.

33. "La Cubanita," 2.

34. "Modelo 4. Form 4. Para todos los distritos escolares. For All School Districts. Informe mensual de los maestros a los secretarios. Teachers' Monthly (or Yearly) Report to the Clerk. De las juntas de educación. of the Board of Education," in APC, Fondo Rita Suárez del Villar y Suárez del Villar, Legajo 2, Expediente 35.

35. Section 12, "De la Historia," in Frye, *Manual para maestros*, 134–36.

36. "Elogio de la Educadora Cubana Señora Rita Flores de Campos Marquetti (1931)" and "Elogio de la Sra. Erundina Fernandez de Borges," among a group of documents titled

"Tres Expedientes del Dr. Carlos Genova Zayas," in ANC, Fondo Donativos y Remisiones, Fuera de Caja 147, Signatura 1. For evidence of the youth of many of Cuba's female teachers, see the photograph captioned "Un grupo de maestras cubanas, de trece a diez y seis años con su chaperone" in *Album de la expedición de los maestros cubanos* (1900) in HUA, HSSCT, HUE 83.100.9F (A, B) Oversize.

37. Guerra y Sánchez, *Fundación del sistema de escuelas públicas en Cuba*, 30–31.

38. "Alexis Everett Frye," *La Escuela Cubana*, November 25, 1899, 57–59, 42, 66; "Who's Who in America," *Redlands Daily Facts*, January 5, 1935, and "Life Brought to Close," *Redlands Daily Facts*, July 2, 1936.

39. Guerra y Sánchez, *Fundación del sistema de escuelas públicas en Cuba*, 45.

40. Ibid., 44–45; "Crónica," *La Escuela Moderna*, November 15, 1899, 23, and December 15, 1899, 15.

41. Frye, *Manual para maestros*, 150–51; *La Gaceta Oficial*, December 6, 1899.

42. Guerra y Sánchez, *Fundación del sistema de escuelas públicas en Cuba*, 15, 44.

43. Ibid., 27, 46.

44. Ibid., 24, 59.

45. Ibid., 17.

46. Ibid., 155, 188–92.

47. Ibid., 25.

48. See "La actual escuela cubana," *Revista Pedagógica Cubana*, November 15, 1900, 122.

49. Guerra y Sánchez, *Fundación del sistema de escuelas públicas en Cuba*, 31–32.

50. *Revista de Instrucción Pública*, January 10, 1901, 158–60.

51. "La Raza de Color. Juicio de una distinguida profesora sobre la educabilidad de las niñas de color en Cuba," *La Escuela Cubana*, November 25, 1899, 59–60.

52. Frye, *Manual para maestros*, 131. Frye cites pages 34–54 of his own *Geografía elemental*.

53. Frye, *Manual para maestros*, 148–49.

54. See advertisement for La Modern Poesía in *La Escuela Moderna*, May 30, 1900, 85.

55. See full-page advertisement that begins "¡¡¡Somos Irresistibles!!!" in the 1900 editions of *Revista Pedagógica Cubana*.

56. Frye, *Manual para maestros*, 131.

57. "Un excepcional," *El Vigilante*, no. 91, December 20, 1900.

58. Wood to Elihu Root, December 30, 1899, Leonard Wood Papers, General Correspondence, Manuscripts Division, U.S. Library of Congress.

59. "Crónica," *La Escuela Moderna*, November 15, 1899, 23–24.

60. *El Vigilante*, no. 92, December 23, 1900.

61. "Crónica," *La Escuela Moderna*, October 30, 1899, 11.

62. *Almanaque del Maestro*, 1–2.

63. A complete list of donors may be found in the last pages of *Album de la expedición de los maestros cubanos*, in HUA, HSSCT, HUE 83.100.9F. For the list of participants, see "Isla de Cuba. Superintendencia de Escuelas. Escuela de Verano de Harvard. 1900," ibid., HUE 83.100.1; *Harvard Graduates' Magazine*, September 1900, 37; and Guerra y Sánchez, *Fundación del sistema de escuelas públicas en Cuba*, 66–70.

64. Frye and Ernest L. Conant to Eliot, February 6, 1900, quoted in an unattributed

press clipping titled "Expedition of Cuban Teachers" in the scrapbook collection *Cubans in Cambridge: Accounts* in HUA, HSSCT, HUE 83.100.6, 36–37.

65. Guerra y Sánchez, *Fundación del sistema de escuelas públicas en Cuba*, 70.

66. See the manuscript "Autographs and Testimonials of Students" in HUA, HSSCT, HUE 83.100.16 (unpaginated).

67. Autograph of Carlos Valdés Posas, director of the Escuela "Martí" of Hoyo Colorado, and Eduardo D. Roque, in "Autographs and Testimonials of Students."

68. Ibid.

69. "Carta de Harvard. 29 de Julio de 1900," *Revista Pedagógica Cubana*, August 24, 1900, 15.

70. Autograph of Francisco Rodríguez of Gibara, Cuba, in "Autographs and Testimonials of Students."

71. "Correspondencia," *El Telégrafo: Periódico Político*, July 31, 1900, 2.

72. Guerra y Sánchez, *Fundación del sistema de escuelas públicas en Cuba*, 71.

73. Joseph Roger Williams, "Boston's Cuban Guests: Their Summer School in Cambridge," *Donahue's Magazine* (August 1900), in *Cubans in Cambridge: Accounts*, 142.

74. "Autographs and Testimonials of Students."

75. "Mr. Frye: Pugilista," *El Telégrafo: Periódico Político*, July 18, 1900, 2.

76. "Declaraciones de Mr. Frye," ibid., September 13, 1900, 2.

77. Wood to Root, January 8, 1901, in Leonard Wood Papers, General Correspondence, Manuscripts Division, U.S. Library of Congress.

78. "Mrs. Alexis E. Frye dies," *Redlands Daily Facts*, April 27, 1973.

79. Alexis Everett Frye, "Himno de Bayamo," *Revista Pedagógica Cubana*, December 31, 1900, 173–74; see also "Crónica," *El Fígaro*, January 6, 1901, 10.

80. Foner, *Spanish-Cuban-American War*, 2:4887–89.

81. Antonio Díaz y Arrasco et al. to Gómez, February 24, 1899, in ANC, Fondo Máximo Gómez, Legajo 20, Expediente 2883.

82. Manifesto "A los cubanos," January 28, 1899, in ANC, Fondo Academia de la Historia de Cuba, Caja 105, Signatura 205.

83. Foner, *Spanish-Cuban-American War*, 2:488.

84. See ibid., 2:491–503, for a full account of the strike. Fernández Robaina confirms Estenoz's leadership in *El negro en Cuba*, 36.

85. Díaz y Arrasco et al. to Gómez, February 24, 1899.

86. See Foner, *Spanish-Cuban-American War*, 2:499–500.

87. Ibid., 502.

88. Helg, *Our Rightful Share*, 91–116.

89. Francisco Piñeiro to Leonard Wood, May 22, 1901, in USNA, RG 140, File 2499.

90. See Javier Medina Escalona to Wood, February 18 and April 16, 1901, ibid., File 1186.

91. See series of telegrams sent from Matanzas and Santa Clara provinces, dated May 6 and May 9, 1900, ibid., File 2651. See also Commanding Officer Captain W. J. Turner, Captain 2nd Infantry, to Adjutant General, May 3, 1900, ibid.

92. Rabí and Lara to Miró, June 21, 1900, in ANC, Fondo Máximo Gómez, Legajo 21, Expediente 2825.

93. Rodríguez to Adjutant General, January 31, 1901, in USNA, RG 140, File 640.

94. Emmanuel to Elihu Root, February 15, 1901, and Emmanuel to William McKinley, February 15, 1901, ibid., RG 350, File 2499.

95. Emmanuel to Wood, January 11, 1902, ibid., RG 140, File 180. See also "Mr. William Geo. Enmanuel [*sic*]" and "A los señores dignísimos e ilustradísimos de la convención cubana," *Diario de la Marina*, January 26, 1901.

96. Newspaper clipping titled "Ex-Slaves in Cuba Fear U.S. American Rule. Petition Signed by 18,000 asks Belgium the Right to Settle in Congo Free State. Brussels. March 20." See Samuel Fox to Juan Gualberto Gómez, April 11, 1901, in ANC, Fondo Adquisiciones, Caja 21, Signatura 1423.

97. Foner, *Spanish-Cuban-American War*, 2:534–46; Pérez, *Cuba between Empires*, 304–14.

98. *Diario de las sesiones de la Convención Constituyente*, 52–53, 92–93, 107–15, 129–31, 134, 192–93, 279.

99. Ibid., 95.

100. Ibid., 272–86.

101. Ibid., 284.

102. Ibid., 232–37, 289–91.

103. Ibid., 12, 428; Foner, *Spanish-Cuban-American War*, 2:569.

104. *Diario de las sesiones de la Convención Constituyente*, 207–8, 462.

105. "Documentos relacionados con el incidente Cisneros Betancourt–Giberga," in ANC, Fondo Academia de la Historia de Cuba, Caja 496, Signatura 514.

106. "En honor de Martí," *El Fígaro*, August 11, 1901, 351; "La Fiesta de Martí," ibid., August 18, 1901, 359; Enrique H. Moreno Plá, "Doña Leonor en la emigración."

107. Cisneros Betancourt et al. to Méndez Capote, August 31, 1901; Enrique Loynaz del Castillo et al. to Cisneros Betancourt, undated; minutes of a meeting held in the Sala de Sesiones del Centro de Veteranos de los Veteranos de la Independencia in Havana, August 4, 1901, in "Documentos relacionados con el incidente Cisneros Betancourt–Giberga."

108. "Manifiesto al Pueblo Cubano del Consejo Supremo de la Institución 'Veteranos de la Independencia,'" August 8, 1901, ibid.

109. See receipt signed by Doña Leonor's granddaughter, Carmen Radillo Martí, in ANC, Fondo Donativos y Remisiones, Caja 308, Expediente 27.

110. Foner, *Spanish-Cuban-American War*, 2:571–77, 593–627; Pérez, *Cuba between Empires*, 316–27.

Chapter Four

1. Foner, *Spanish-Cuban-American War*, 2:657–63.

2. de la Fuente, *Nation for All*, 60–61.

3. "Manifiesto del Mayor General Bartolomé Masó al Pueblo de Cuba," October 31, 1901, in ANC, Fondo Adquisiciones, Legajo 86, Signatura 4390.

4. "Comité Central de Propaganda y Acción por Bartolomé Massó [*sic*]," September 20, 1901, ibid.

5. Cisneros Betancourt to President McKinley, undated, in ANC, Fondo Donativos y Remisiones, Caja 308, Signatura 15, 6; Cisneros Betancourt to Masó, July 3, 1901, ibid., Signatura 12.

6. "Plan de Gobierno: Acta del 23 de Agosto de 1901, Sala de Gobierno Civil de la Provincia de la Habana," in AIHC, Fondo Eugenio Sánchez de Agramonte, Signatura 21/16.1/1–7.

7. Miró to Máximo Gómez, July 30, 1901, and November 5, 1901, in ANC, Fondo Máximo Gómez, Legajo 21, Expediente 2944 and 2954 respectively.

8. Untitled enclosure in Enrique Messonier to Estrada Palma, November 23, 1901, in ANC, Fondo Correspondencia de la Secretaría de la Presidencia, Serie Felicitaciones y Muestras de Apoyo.

9. Ramón Rivero y Rivero to Estrada Palma, January 4, 1902, ibid.

10. Estrada Palma to José A. González Lanuza, October 8, 1898, in ANC, Fondo Gobierno de la Revolución de 1895, Caja 44, Signatura 6357.

11. Lincoln de Zayas, "El solitario de Central Valley"; Alfredo Martin Morales, "Tomás Estrada Palma"; Ricardo E. Manrique, "La prueba de un carácter"; "El Fígaro en Central Valley"; Eulogio Horta, "Estrada Palma en Nueva York," all in El Fígaro, May 4, 1902, 86, 88–91.

12. Helg, Our Rightful Share, 98.

13. "¡19 y 20 de mayo," La Discusión, May 19, 1902, 1.

14. "Biografía del Dr. Luis Estévez y Romero," and M. Márquez Sterling, "Luis Estévez y Romero," El Fígaro, May 4, 1902, 91–93.

15. Pérez, Cuba under the Platt Amendment, 58–77; Zanetti, Cautivos de la reciprocidad, 53–69.

16. "Por la madre de Martí," La Lucha, May 6, 1902; "Las Ultimas Visperas" and "Crónica (Martí)," ibid., May 19, 1902, 2; "El aniversario del Apóstol. Velada en el Círculo National. La Preside General Gómez," ibid., May 21, 1902, 4.

17. "Las Visperas Republicanas. Dichos y Hechos," La Lucha, April 17, 1902, 2.

18. "La Excursión del Presidente," ibid., April 23, 1902, 2; see also "Estrada Palma in the East," The Lucha, April 23, 1902, 1.

19. "Señor Estrada Palma. Visited by a Committee from the Spanish Club," The Lucha, May 15, 1902, 1. For Martí's view of the casino, see "Los cubanos de Jamaica y los revolucionarios de Haití" and "¡Basta!" in OC, 3:103–8 and 1:338–39.

20. "Estrada Palma and the Marquis of Santa Lucía," The Lucha, May 15, 1902, 1.

21. See the most complete collection of El Proletario in the library of Havana's Instituto de Historia de Cuba.

22. Schaffer, "Cuban? Spaniard? Anarchist?," 28–35.

23. "Es nuestra obra," El Proletario, June 23, 1903, 3.

24. "El caciquísmo," ibid., 2.

25. "A dónde vamos," ibid., 2.

26. Helg, "Afro-Cuban Protest", 105–6; Aguirre, "El cincuentenario de un gran crimen," 39.

27. Orum, "Politics of Color," 96.

28. Pérez, Cuba between Empires, 383.

29. For example, see Estrada Palma to T. E. Culmel[l], December 7, 1895, in Primelles, La Revolución del 95, 2:288–89.

30. Póveda de Ferrer to Estrada Palma, May 29, 1903, in ANC, Fondo Correspondencia de la Secretaría de la Presidencia, Serie Felicitaciones y Muestras de Apoyo.

31. Foner, Spanish-Cuban-American War, 2:464.

32. Orum, "Politics of Color," 95.

33. Helg, *Our Rightful Share*, 103.

34. Orum, "Politics of Color," 96.

35. Fernández Robaina, *El negro en Cuba*, 41.

36. Pérez, "Politics, Peasants, and People of Color," 528.

37. *La Lucha*, June 9, 1902, 2. For a quite different interpretation of this same article, see Orum, "Politics of Color," 97.

38. Juan Gualberto Gómez, "La Revolución del 95," *El Fígaro*, May 20, 1902, 242.

39. "Discurso de Mario García Kohly en el Teatro Nacional, el 24 de febrero de 1902," *La Discusión*, February 24, 1904, 11.

40. Banderas to Estrada Palma, undated, in ANC, Fondo Correspondencia de la Secretaría de la Presidencia, Serie Felicitaciones y Muestras de Apoyo. The letter includes a copy of Banderas's business card.

41. "Habla el bravo general Quintín," *La Lucha*, November 22, 1902, 2.

42. Helg, *Our Rightful Share*, 150, 156, 170, 186, 246.

43. Estuch Horrego, *Martín Morúa Delgado*, 195–96.

44. Howard, *Changing History*, 190–205.

45. Orum, "Politics of Color," 98.

46. Fernández Robaina, *El negro en Cuba*, 43–44.

47. Howard, *Changing History*, 139–40, 145–46, 196–202; Helg, *Our Rightful Share*, 38–40.

48. Howard, *Changing History*, 138–39, 165–167, 169.

49. Helg, *Our Rightful Share*, 39–41.

50. Orum, "Politics of Color," 99–100, 107.

51. Helg, *Our Rightful Share*, 126–27.

52. Ibid.; Orum, "Politics of Color," 108.

53. R. Sartorio B. to Máximo Gómez, 5 December 1902, in ANC, Fondo Máximo Gómez, Caja 36, Expediente 4476.

54. "Cock Fighting," *The Lucha*, November 10, 1902, 1.

55. "The Bootblacks. The Mayor Forbids Those Which Have No Chairs," ibid., November 14, 1902, 1. The article cites issuance of the decree on November 11, 1902.

56. "Nothing Has Happened," ibid., November 27, 1902, 1. The piece reprints in full an article from Juan Gualberto Gómez's newspaper *La República*.

57. "Nothing Has Happened," ibid., November 26, 1902, 1.

58. Ibid.

59. "¡Dios mío, qué solos se quedan los muertos!" *La Lucha*, November 14, 1902, 2.

60. Personal communication with Joseph Hall, January 22, 1999.

61. "La huelga general: La asamblea magna de anoche en el teatro cuba," *La Lucha*, November 13, 1902, 2.

62. Native white cigarmakers numbered 14,922 while "colored" cigarmakers numbered 10,485. Spaniards, preferentially treated, were a minority of only 2,096. See *Cuba: Population, History and Resources*, 220.

63. de la Fuente, "Two Dangers, One Solution," 39.

64. "La huelga general toma cada vez mayores proporciones . . . ," *La Lucha*, November 19, 1902, 2.

65. See the following in *La Lucha*: "La huelga general: La liga general de trabajadores cubanos. Importante asamblea en marte y belona," November 14, 1902, 2; "La huelga general: Numerosas fábricas secundan el movimiento y abandonan trabajo ayer por la tarde," November 18, 1902, 2; "La huelga general: El comité central pide a sus compañeros los trabajadores de la Habana que abandonen sus trabajos el lunes," November 16, 1902, 2; and "La huelga general: Su terminación definitiva," December 1, 1902, 1.

66. "El banquete a Mérchan en el Casino Español," ibid., November 16, 1902, 2.

67. CRJOF, Primer Escrito, December 8, 1902, in ANC, Fondo Audiencia de la Habana, Caja 468, Expediente 8.

68. "La huelga general: Sus proporciones alarmantes. Motines en las calles," *La Lucha*, November 20, 1902, 2.

69. "La Cámara de Representantes. See acuerda la elección de la mesa. Caída de los repúblicanos," ibid., November 17, 1902, 1.

70. CRJOF, Primer Escrito.

71. "La huelga general: Sus proporciones alarmantes. Motines en las calles," *La Lucha*, November 20, 1902, 2.

72. For parallels in Florida, see Greenbaum, "Marketing Ybor City," 61–64.

73. "To the Cuban Congress. The Mayor of Havana on the Strike," *The Lucha*, November 21, 1902, 1.

74. Orum, "Politics of Color," 103.

75. "La huelga general: Sesenta fábricas en huelga," *La Lucha*, November 21, 1902, 2.

76. "La huelga general: Toma cada vez mayor incremento," ibid., November 22, 1902, 2.

77. "Bandera negra. La huelga. ¡Guerra sin cuartel! ¡A sangre y fuego!," *El Reconcentrado*, November 20, 1902, 1; "Bandera negra. La huelga," ibid., November 22, 1902, 1.

78. Ibid. See CRJOF, "Declaración de O'Farrill," Tercero Escrito.

79. "La huelga y el 'Diario,'" *Diario de la Marina*, November 22, 1902, 2; "Incidente con los tipografos," *La Lucha*, December 1, 1902, 1.

80. "La huelga general: Importancia y gravedad del movimiento obrero," *La Lucha*, November 26, 1902, 2, 4.

81. Ibid., 2; CROJF, "Declaración de José Ugarte y Graelly, Capitán de Policía," Cuarto Escrito.

82. "La huelga general: Importancia y gravedad del movimiento obrero," *La Lucha*, November 26, 1902, 2.

83. Ibid.

84. "Terminación de la huelga: Patriótica y oportuna intervención de los veteranos," *La Lucha*, November 26, 1902, 4. See also the defense of O'Farrill and Tamayo reprinted from *El Mundo*, a pro–National Convention paper, in "La nota del día," *Diario de la Marina: Edición de la Tarde*, November 26, 1902, 1.

85. See court records from the case against O'Farrill for usurpation of functions and dereliction of duty, titled "Primer Escrito," dated December 8, 1902, in ANC, Fondo Audiencia de la Habana, Caja 468, Expediente 8. See also Expediente 9 for surviving documents of the defense.

86. See CROJF, "Declaración de José Ugarte y Graelly, Capitán de Policía."

87. "Terminación de la huelga: Patriótica y oportuna intervención de los veteranos," *La Lucha*, November 26, 1902, 4.

88. "La huelga general: No ha terminado todavia. Nuevas complicaciones," ibid., November 28, 1902, 2; "La huelga general: Patriótica actitud de los obreros," ibid., November 29, 1902, 2.

89. "La Cámara de Representantes," ibid., November 27, 1902, 1.

90. "La Cámara de Representantes. Debate sobre la huelga," ibid., December 3, 1902, 2.

91. Helg, *Our Rightful Share*, 106–16.

92. Juan Santos Fernández, "La inmigración," *Anales de la Academia de Ciencias Médicas, Físicas y Naturales de la Habana*, 43 (1907): 7, 13, 24–25. Santos delivered the address on May 19, 1906, the anniversary of the founding of the academy in Cuba.

93. Ibid., 6–8.

94. Ibid., 10–11, 17–21.

95. See for example, Esteban N. Robert to Estrada Palma, June 10, 1902, in ANC, Fondo Correspondencia de la Secretaría de la Presidencia, Serie Felicitaciones y Muestras de Apoyo.

96. Riera, *Cuba política*, 91–101.

97. "Proyecto de Ley de Inmigración y el Fomento Nacional. Capítulo II. De los inmigrantes," *El Economista: Revista Financiera y Comercial. El Hacendado y el Agricultor Cubanos. Gaceta Industrial de Ferrocarriles de Cuba*, 5, no. 7 (February 18, 1906): 134–35.

98. "Proyecto de Ley de Inmigración y Fomento Nacional," ibid., 5, no. 6 (February 11, 1906): 109–11. Emphasis added.

99. *La Gaceta Oficial de la República*, July 11, 1906, in ANC, Fondo Secretaría de la Presidencia, Caja 121, Signatura 82.

Chapter Five

1. "Proyecto de Ley propuesto por Juan M. Galdos, Francisco Carrillo, José Antonio Frías, F. Méndez Capote," *Senado. Diarios de sesiones*, 9th Legislature, 8th sess., May 9, 1906.

2. Quoted in Beals, *Crime of Cuba*, 199.

3. Riera, *Cuba política*, 67–69.

4. "Partido Nacional Cubano," January 28, 1903, in ANC, Fondo Adquisiciones, Legajo 86, Signatura 4390.

5. According to the 1907 census, 6,923 of all bricklayers in Cuba were "of color" while 2,645 were white foreigners and 2,595 were white natives. *Anuario estadístico de la República de Cuba*, 28, 74.

6. Guerra y Sánchez, *Fundación del sistema de escuelas públicas en Cuba*, 187–88.

7. Evaristo Estenoz, Arturo R. Díaz, Eduardo Portela, Nazario de Puzo, Felipe Alloga, and José Sánchez, "Al Pueblo de Cuba," January 17, 1904, in ANC, Fondo Adquisiciones, Legajo 86, Signatura 4390.

8. See "¿Qué opina usted del sufragio universal . . . ?" and "El sufragio," *El Fígaro*, May 15, 1905, 263–69, 251.

9. Riera, *Cuba política*, 75–76.

10. Ibid., 77–81.

11. Ibid., 70–73.

12. Ibid., 74–75, 77. For full election results, see 77–81.

13. E. Estanillo, H. Portuondo, et al., "Partido Liberal Nacional. Comité del Cerro a los afiliados y vecinos del barrio," November 18, 1904, in ANC, Fondo Academia de la Historia de Cuba, Caja 498, Signatura 542.

14. Riera, *Cuba política*, 76–77. Roosevelt subsequently refused the gift. Personal communication with Marial Iglesias, July 18, 1997.

15. Magoon, *Annual Report of the Provisional Governor of Cuba, from October 13, 1906 to December 1, 1907*, 48.

16. "¡La 'avaricia' de Don Tomás!," originally published in *La Discusión*, February 11, 1911, and reprinted as "Apéndice B" in de Velasco, *Estrada Palma*, 77–79. See also Barrabosa, *El proceso de la República*, 77–78, and Trelles, *El progreso*, 9.

17. Vicente Cagigal to the Provisional Governor of Cuba, October 23, 1906, in ANC, Fondo Secretaría de la Presidencia, Caja 37, Signatura 6.

18. Leonard Brown to Estrada Palma, August 12, 1902, in ANC, Fondo Correspondencia de la Secretaría de la Presidencia, Serie Felicitaciones y Muestras de Apoyo.

19. "El Destino manifiesto," *La Lucha*, August 15, 1906, 1.

20. Lockmiller, *Magoon in Cuba*, 134.

21. Tomás Estrada Palma, "Nuestro programa (del mensaje presidencial)," *La Instrucción Primaria*, August 10, 1902, 1.

22. Guerra y Sánchez, *Fundación del sistema de escuelas públicas en Cuba*, 190–191.

23. Ibid., 190–95.

24. *Anuario estadístico de la República de Cuba*, 18.

25. "Carta abierta," dated "Campos de Cuba, 23 de Octubre de 1902," and "Notas escolares" in *La Instrucción Primaria*, November 10, 1902, 312–14.

26. Taft and Bacon, *Cuban Pacification*, 321.

27. Lockmiller, *Magoon in Cuba*, 134 n. 39. Today, *pedir botella*, or "to ask for a bottle," is synonymous with hitchhiking.

28. "La Cámara de Representantes. Debate sobre la huelga," *La Lucha*, December 3, 1902, 2.

29. Frye to Xiqués Arango, reprinted in *La Instrucción Primaria*, January 10, 1904, 22–26.

30. Ezequiel García, "Día cubano," *El Fígaro*, May 22, 1904, 253.

31. "Nostalgia colonial," *La Escuela Moderna: Periódico de Educación y de Enseñanza*, February 15, 1906, 53.

32. "Fecha de gloria," *La Discusión*, May 20, 1904, 1.

33. "Martí," ibid., May 18, 1903,1.

34. "La página más hermosa sobre José Martí," ibid., May 19, 1905, 4.

35. "A Martí," ibid., May 20, 1903, 7.

36. "Editoriales. Martí, 19 de mayo de 1895," ibid., May 19, 1905, 2.

37. "Editoriales. Fecha de luto," ibid.,, May 19, 1904, 1–2.

38. "En cumplimento de un acuerdo de la Cámara el 17 de mayo de 1905, el Presidente de ella, Santiago García Cañizares hace 'El elogio a Martí en esta ocasión,'" *Diario de las sesiones del Congreso. Cámara de Representantes*, 7th Legislature, 3rd sess., May 19, 1905.

39. "El partido obrero. Señora Leonor Pérez, madre de Martí," *La Discusión*, May 21, 1904, 5.

40. "Buena seña," *El Proletario*, August 27, 1903, 2. See also Carlos Baliño, "El divino descontento," ibid., November 23, 1903. 1.

41. See César Lombroso, "Impotencia de la caridad"; C. Elizburu, "Espíritu de asociación"; and the article "Un anarquista" by "Un Socialista" in *El Proletario*, October 16, 1903, 1, 3.

42. *Martí: Novela histórica*; Lizaso, *José Martí*, 1, 50; personal communication with Renio Díaz Triana, Centro de Estudios Martianos, Havana, June 18, 1996.

43. *Martí: Novela histórica*, 148–49.

44. Ibid., 96.

45. Ibid., 48.

46. Ibid., 121.

47. Ibid., 158.

48. Ibid., 161.

49. Riera, *Cuba política*, 86–90.

50. "Cuestionario," November 14, 1899, in AMCH, Fondo Personalidades de la Guerra de la Independencia, Caja 68, Expediente 20: #5.

51. "Manifiesto del Partido Republicano Liberal al Pueblo Espiritiano," May 28, 1905, in ANC, Fondo Adquisiciones, Caja 86, Expediente 4390.

52. R. Armentos to Gómez, May 1, 1905, in AMCH, Fondo Personalidades de la Guerra de Independencia, Caja 68, Expediente 20: #10.

53. Iznaga, *Por Cuba*, 15–16, 26.

54. See Garrigó, *La convulsión cubana*.

55. "Liberal Contention Regarding the Ayuntamiento of Cruces: Case #4," in ANC, Fondo Secretaría de la Presidencia, Caja 86, Signatura 55.

56. "Liberal Contention Regarding Different Ayuntamientos in the Province of Pinar del Río: Case #5," ibid.

57. Exhibit 4, manifesto translated from *El Liberal*, written by the Executive Committee of the National Convention of the Liberal Party, September 27, 1905, in Taft and Bacon, *Cuban Pacification*, 496–98.

58. "Liberal Contention Regarding the Town of Santa Isabel de las Lajas: Case #19," in ANC, Fondo Secretaría de la Presidencia, Caja 86, Signatura 55.

59. "Liberal Contention Regarding the Town of Rodas: Case #17," ibid.

60. Cisneros Betancourt to Francisco Carrillo, Pedro Betancourt, Pedro Díaz, et al., September 1905, in ANC, Fondo Donativos y Remisiones, Caja 308, Signatura 16, 9.

61. "Liberal Contention Regarding the Town of Caibarién: Case #2," in ANC, Fondo Secretaría de la Presidencia, Caja 86, Signatura 55.

62. Exhibit 4, Taft and Bacon, *Cuban Pacification*, 495.

63. J. García González, "Manifiesto. Consideraciones a las clases de color," September 1905, in ANC, Fondo Especial, Caja 15, Expediente Antiguo 43, Nuevo 2811.

64. Castillo, Rojas, Vale[z], and Vazquez y Sánchez to Varela, May 18, 1906, ibid., Legajo 7, Signatura 114.

65. Juan Jiménez to William H. Taft, September 29, 1906, in ANC, Fondo Secretaría de la Presidencia, Caja 116, Signatura 116; "Liberal Contention Regarding Different Ayuntamientos in the Province of Pinar del Río: Case #5," ibid., Caja 86, Signatura 55.

66. "Liberal Contention Regarding the Town of Sagua la Grande: Case #18" and "Liberal Contention Regarding the Town of Camajuaní: Case #12," ibid., Caja 86, Signatura 55.

67. Riera, *Cuba política*, 90.

68. "Liberal Contention Regarding the Town of Güinez [*sic*]: Case #16," and Otto Schoenrich to Provisional Governor's Office, October 28, 1906, both in ANC, Fondo Secretaría de la Presidencia, Caja 86, Signatura 55.

69. Exhibit 5, "Painful Figures," translation of an article from *La Discusión*, November 11, 1905, in Taft and Bacon, *Cuban Pacification*, 500.

70. Taft and Bacon, *Cuban Pacification*, 454–55.

71. Riera, *Cuba política*, 94; "Liberal Contention Regarding the Ayuntamiento of Ranchuelo: Case #13," in ANC, Fondo Secretaría de la Presidencia, Caja 86, Signatura 55.

72. Giddens, *Nation-State and Violence*, 18–22, 154–55, 171–86.

73. "Más amor," *El Fígaro*, May 20, 1906, 251.

74. See the photograph of José Castellanos, head of New York *junta*, in *El Fígaro*, September 2, 1906, 443.

75. Cisneros Betancourt to Francisco Carrillo, Pedro Betancourt, Pedro Díaz, et al., September 1905, in ANC, Fondo Donativos y Remisiones, Caja 308, Signatura 16.

76. *Joint Resolution Inviting the Republic of Cuba to Become a State of the American Union*, November 23 and 25, 1903. See also Lockmiller, *Magoon in Cuba*, 21–22.

77. Collazo, *Los sucesos de Cienfuegos*; Riera, *Cuba política*, 92–93.

78. Lockmiller, *Magoon in Cuba*, 31.

79. "Instantáneas del camino," *El Fígaro*, April 15, 1906, 191–95 (see especially the photograph and caption on 194); "El General José Miguel Gómez," ibid., May 21, 1905, 250–55.

80. Liberal manifesto of September 27, 1905, quoted as Exhibit 4, Taft and Bacon, *Cuban Pacification*, 498.

81. "El nuevo ayuntamiento," *La Lucha*, August 2, 1906, 1.

82. See the telegram from Alquízar to Brigadier Chief of the Rural Guard, November 27, 1905; and the list of charges brought by the prosecution, November 30, 1905; both in ANC, Fondo Audiencia de la Habana, Legajo 231, Expediente 1, Séptima Pieza, Quinta Pieza, respectively.

83. Lockmiller makes vague reference to these uprisings in *Magoon in Cuba*, 33.

84. "Negociado de orden público," Emilio Presal to Guillermo Valdés Fauli, November 20, 1905, in ANC, Fondo Audiencia de la Habana, Legajo 231, Expediente 1, Primera Pieza; "Romam" [pseud.] to E. Taracena, November 27, 1905, ibid., Tercera Pieza.

85. Captain José Perdonde Martínez to Chief of the F Squadron, Regiment #1, Rural Guard, November 23, 1905, ibid., Segunda Pieza.

86. Report of Secret Police lieutenant Rafael Muñoz y Ayala et al., November 18, 1905, ibid., Primera Pieza.

87. "Declaración de D. Antonio Cueto y Peña," November 30, 1905, ibid., Tercera Pieza.

88. This information comes from the *Yndice* of 74,000 surviving veterans of the Liberating Army compiled by Carlos Roloff. The following names appear in both the list of prisoners and Roloff's *Yndice*: Manuel Piedra Martell, page 701, case #49004; Antonio Quesada Borrero, page 737, case #51353; Evaristo Estenoz Colomina, page 273, case #19551; Rafael Sánchez Macías, page 889, case #63120; Aurelio Vidal Rodríguez, page 975, case #68761;

Modesto Cruz Alarcón, page 162, case #12177; Germán Domínguez y Domínguez, page 251, #18216; Ramón Díaz y Díaz, page 250, case #18139; Modesto Estrada Contreras, page 275, case #19627. The author gratefully acknowledges the aid of María Alvarez de Quintana and Orlando García, director of the Archivo Provincial de Cienfuegos, in this endeavor.

89. See Jefatura del Presidio de la República de Cuba to Jerónimo [sic] Valdés Fauli, December 12, 1905, and Valdés Fauli to Juez de Instrucción de San Antonio de los Baños, November 28, 1905, in ANC, Fondo de la Audiencia de la Habana, Legajo 231, Expediente 1, Septima Pieza and Sexta Pieza, respectively.

90. "Declaración del Guardia 670, Octavio Díaz y Rubio," November 30, 1905, ibid., Tercera Pieza.

91. See, for example, the certification of Ldo. Gustavo Pino y Quintana, May 19, 1905, ibid., Sexta Pieza.

92. "Casa presidencial," La Lucha, August 15, 1906, 1; "Levantamientos armados," ibid., August 19, 1906, 2.

93. "Situación difícil" and "Movimiento Armado. Se generaliza en Pinar del Río," ibid., August 20, 1906, 1, 2.

94. "Movimiento armado," ibid., August 20, 1906, 4.

95. See the cover and opening of El Fígaro, August 26, 1906, 429–30.

96. "Sorpresa de campamento. Confidencia segura," La Lucha, August 23, 1906, 2.

97. "Carta del General Quintín Banderas," ibid., August 25, 1906, 2.

98. Taft and Bacon, Cuban Pacification, 457.

99. Ibid., 456–57; "Movimientos armados," La Lucha, August 23, 1906; Magoon, Annual Report of the Provisional Governor of Cuba, from October 13, 1906 to December 1, 1907, 72.

100. "Contra los alzados," La Lucha, August 25, 1906, 1.

101. Taft and Bacon, Cuban Pacification, 457, 465, 468, 487.

102. Exhibit 8, "Manifesto of the Revolution," July 28, 1906, ibid., 505–6.

103. "Al gobierno actual de Cuba y al pueblo cubano," September 1, 1906, quoted in Collazo, La Revolución de Agosto de 1906, 18–21.

104. R. Gaytan de Ayala to Provisional Governor, October 2, 1906, in ANC, Fondo Secretaría de la Presidencia, Caja 37, Signatura 6.

105. "Causes of the Cuban Insurrection."

106. See the following in La Lucha: "Mirando el peligro," August 23, 1906, 1; "Dos fechas. 1895 = 1906," August 28, 1906, 1; and "Movimiento armado. Se generaliza en Pinar del Río," August 20, 1906, 2.

107. "Pino Guerra al reporter de The Havana Daily Telegraph," ibid., August 23, 1906, 2.

108. "Carta del Padre Miret," ibid., August 25, 1906, 2.

109. "De Pinar del Río" and "Los campesinos trabajan," ibid., 2.

110. "Interview con el Senador Cabello," ibid., September 4, 1906, 2; "La entrevista con el Senador Cabello. Erratas," ibid., September 5, 1906, 1.

111. "En la junta de veteranos," ibid., September 9, 1906, 2.

112. Exhibit 6, "A Brief Description of the Steps Taken by the Veterans of the War of Independence in Favor of Peace," in Taft and Bacon, Cuban Pacification, 501.

113. Ibid., 502.

114. Ibid., 444–45.

115. Ibid., 445.

116. Ibid., 472.

117. Ibid., 473.

118. Ibid., 479–81.

119. *Mensaje al Congreso de la República por el Presidente Tomás Estrada Palma con motivo de la rebelión armada que se ha producido en todo el país, a fin de se acuerden las disposiciones convenientes*, September 14, 1906, in ANC, Fondo Secretaría de la Presidencia, Caja 107, No. 49.

120. Taft and Bacon, *Cuban Pacification*, 476.

121. Ibid., 477.

122. Enrique José Varona, "El abismo," *El Fígaro*, September 2, 1906, 442.

123. Taft and Bacon, *Cuban Pacification*, 482–83, 515–16.

124. Lockmiller, *Magoon in Cuba*, 56–57.

Chapter Six

1. Major W. Walker, Captain 15th Cavalry, Commanding Troop 'A,' to the Adjutant, June 7, 1907, in USNA, RG 199, File 014/34.

2. Affidavit of Sergeant Harry W. Frenyere [*sic?*], Corporal 15th Cavalry, Troop 'A,' signed June 8, 1907, before Sergeant Van Lear Jr., ibid.

3. Ibid.

4. Mayor Domingo Urquiola to the Military Commander, June 7, 1907, in USNA, RG 199, File 014/34.

5. Colonel E. H. Crowder, General Staff, on duty with the Department of State and Justice, June 20, 1907, ibid.

6. See "Españoles y Cubanos toman parte en las fiestas," *La Lucha*, July 4, 1907, 1; "An Interesting Fourth. Exercises at Camp Columbia Tomorrow will Attract Large Number of Americans," "Questions of the Day" [lamentation on the absence of baseball], and "To Celebrate Fourth" [report from Sancti Spíritus], *The Lucha*, July 3, 1907, 1; "The Glorious Fourth. Patriotically Celebrated by Americans Throughout the Island. Day of Field Sports," *The Lucha*, July 5, 1907; and "El cuatro de Julio. Los cubanos fraternizan con los americanos en la celebración del glorioso aniversario," *La Lucha*, July 5, 1907, 2.

7. See the cover of *El Fígaro*, February 24, 1907.

8. Taft and Bacon, *Cuban Pacification*, 463.

9. J. de A., "El gobernador de Cuba," *El Fígaro* November 14, 1906, 515. See also Lincoln de Zayas, "Teodoro Roosevelt," ibid., September 30, 1906, 492–94, 494–95.

10. See Taft and Bacon, *Cuban Pacification*, 463–64, 467, 471, 476–79, 487–88.

11. Captain John W. Furlong to Chief of Staff, March 28, 1907, in USNA, RG 199, File 096/4.

12. Lockmiller, *Magoon in Cuba*, 73–76.

13. For a photograph depicting the inner circle of the U.S. Provisional Administration, see "La actualidad política," *El Fígaro*, April 14, 1907, 174. In the picture, "Capitán José Martí" is standing directly behind and on the right side of Secretary of War William Howard Taft (on a return inspection tour of the island).

14. Magoon, *Annual Report of the Provisional Governor of Cuba, from October 13, 1906*

to December 1, 1907, 16–17. See also Memorandum from Provisional Governor's Office to Colonel Enoch H. Crowder, U.S. Army, General Staff, on duty in Department of State, October 31, 1906, in ANC, Fondo Secretaría de la Presidencia, Caja 86, Signatura 55.

15. "Preliminary Report upon Removed Ayuntamientos," undated, in ANC, Fondo Secretaría de la Presidencia, Caja 86, Signatura 55.

16. Lockmiller, *Magoon in Cuba,* 83–84.

17. Ibid., 145.

18. Ibid., 146–73.

19. Loynaz del Castillo to Magoon, October 22, 1906, in ANC, Fondo Secretaría de la Presidencia, Caja 71, Signatura 41.

20. "El componente en las Lomas. Un liberal ahorcado. ¿Vivimos entre cafres? A Mr. Magoon," Supplement to *La Realidad,* November 23, 1906, ibid., Caja 116, Signatura 9. The word *cafre* is a common Cuban expression, probably of African linguistic derivation, which means "savage" or "barbaric."

21. "Expediente que contiene una expedición de mandamiento judicial solicitada por Bernabe Martínez y Díaz, miembro de la Guardia Rural de San Antonio de los Baños, para efectuar un registro en la finca 'Carmen' por confidencias de la existencia de Armas. Incluye telegrama del alcalde municipal a Alfredo Zayas solicitando garantías para él y vecinos de ese termino, por los atropellos de la Guardia Rural," ibid., Caja 112, Signatura 48. See especially telegram from Alcalde Municipal de Alquizar, Rodulfo del Castillo to Dr. Alfredo Zayas, October 5, 1907, and Captain Powell Clayton to Major Herbert J. Slocum, October 11, 1907.

22. Inglis, "Future in Cuba," 1039.

23. See Exhibit 26 in Taft and Bacon, *Cuban Pacification,* 541–42.

24. Anonymous letter signed by "X" to Magoon, October 16, 1906, in ANC, Fondo Secretaría de la Presidencia, Caja 115, Signatura 80.

25. Juan Bances Conde to Magoon, April 1, 1908, ibid., Signatura 95.

26. Gabriel García Ruíz to Magoon, undated, and Francisco Y. de Vildósola to Magoon, October 25, 1906, ibid., Signaturas 101 and 99.

27. *Anuario estadístico de la República de Cuba,* 24–25.

28. See Carr, "'Omnipotent and Omnipresent'?"

29. Pérez, "Politics, Peasants, and People of Color"; Magoon, "Decree Facilitating the Division of 'Haciendas Comuneras,'" in *Report of Cuba,* Decrees 566 and 1080 of 1907.

30. Barrabosa, *El proceso de la República,* 77–87. See also the following in *La Lucha:* "Los presupuestos," July 6, 1907, 1, and "Los diez mil," July 12, 1907, 2.

31. Barrabosa, *El proceso de la República,* 71–75. For Magoon's justifications, see Magoon, *Annual Report of the Provisional Governor of Cuba, from October 13, 1906 to December 1, 1907,* 40–42.

32. Magoon, *Annual Report of the Provisional Governor of Cuba, from December 1, 1907 to December 1, 1908,* 86–87; Magoon, *Annual Report of the Provisional Governor of Cuba, from October 13, 1906 to December 1, 1907,* 87–88.

33. Magoon, *Annual Report of the Provisional Governor of Cuba, from October 13, 1906 to December 1, 1907,* 44–46.

34. Thomas, *Cuba,* 483–85, 504–7.

35. See the section titled "Secretaría de obras públicas" in *Memoria de la administración del Presidente de la República de Cuba Mayor General José Miguel Gómez*, 241–84.

36. Anonymous document filed together with various correspondence of prominent Liberals titled "Abusos americanos" in AMCH, Fondo Personalidades de la Guerra de la Independencia, Caja 333, Expediente 1.

37. See telegram received from Colonel James Parker, Commanding Officer of the 11th Cavalry, to Adjutant General, November 17, 1907; General Orders, No. 51, November 17, 1907; Parker to Lieutenant Colonel Waltz, Chief of Staff, November 19, 1907; and Parker to Chief of Police through Municipal Mayor, November 18, 1907; all in USNA, RG 199, File 096/30.

38. Magoon, *Annual Report of the Provisional Governor of Cuba, from December 1, 1907 to December 1, 1908*, 75–76.

39. "Strike in Cuba. President of the American Federation of Labor Is Greatly Interested in Cigarmakers' Strike," *The Lucha*, July 2, 1907, 1; "Strike Is Not Settled. Negotiations Are Progressing . . . ," ibid., July 12, 1907, 1.

40. "Fecha del hierro," *La Discusión*, February 24, 1907, 1 and 16.

41. "La fecha de ayer," ibid., February 26, 1907, 2.

42. Untitled comments by Cosme de la Torriente, ibid., May 19, 1907, 1.

43. "El recuerdo de Martí," ibid., May 19, 1907, 2.

44. "In memoriam," ibid., May 19, 1907, 12.

45. See the sections in *La Lucha* titled "Auxilios" and "Raciones" under "La huelga de tabaqueros," July 6, 1907, 2; and "La recolecta," "Giros," and "Viveres" under "La huelga de tabaqueros," July 2, 1907, 2. See also Cabrera, *Los que viven por sus manos*, 97.

46. "La huelga de tabaqueros. Las damas," *La Lucha*, July 4, 1907, 4.

47. "La huelga de tabaqueros. El acuerdo de anoche," ibid., July 17, 1907, 2.

48. "La huelga de tabaqueros. Lo de San Antonio de los Baños. Habla un obrero," ibid., July 6, 1907, 4.

49. See the section titled "La huelga de tabaqueros" under "El gobierno provisional. Noticias de ayer," ibid., July 4, 1907, 2.

50. "La huelga de los tabaqueros," ibid., July 7, 1907, 2.

51. Quoted in Magoon, *Annual Report of the Provisional Governor of Cuba, from October 13, 1906 to December 1, 1907*, 57.

52. "Messenger Made Mistake in Delivering Letter of Governor Magoon to Manufacturers. Mistake of a Clerk," *The Lucha*, July 9, 1907, 1.

53. See ibid. and "La huelga de tabaqueros. Los obreros publican un manifesto dando a conocer la contestación de Mister Magoon a los fabricantes," *La Lucha*, July 8, 1907, 2.

54. "La huelga de tabaqueros. Al Honorable Charles E. Magoon. Gobernador provisional de Cuba," ibid., July 9, 1907, 3. The letter was dated July 8, 1907.

55. "La huelga de tabaqueros. El cielo se despeja — la huelga toca a su fin," ibid., July 10, 1907, 3.

56. "La huelga de tabaqueros. El 'Trust' abre sus fábricas el martes, pagando en moneda americana," ibid., July 14, 1907, 2.

57. "Entrevista con el Sr. Juan Gualberto Gómez," ibid., July 15, 1907, 2.

58. "Strike Formally Settled. Trust Will Open Its Factories Tomorrow — Day Being Spent in Jollification Meetings," *The Lucha*, July 15, 1907, 1.

59. See sections titled "Las fábricas independientes pagarán en oro americano" and "Las despalilladoras" under the heading "La huelga de tabaqueros," *La Lucha*, July 16, 1907, 2.

60. Ibid., 3.

61. "Cigarmakers Celebrate. Make a Monstrous Parade and Present Governor Magoon with Evidence of Appreciation," *The Lucha*, July 23, 1907, 1.

62. "La gran manifestación obrera. Estarán representados todos los obreros de la isla," *La Lucha*, July 21, 1907, 2; "La gran manifestación obrera. Como veinte mil trabajadores en marcha," ibid., July 22, 1907, 2.

63. "Moción presentada en Asamblea Extraordinaria del Gremio de Estibadores [*sic*] de la Bahía de la Habana," September 13, 1908, in ANC, Fondo Adquisiciones, Caja 75, Signatura 4309.

64. Gremio de Estibadores [*sic*] to Provisional Governor, September 1908, ibid.

65. Magoon, *Annual Report of the Provisional Governor of Cuba, from October 13, 1906 to December 1, 1907*, 57–59.

66. "Conmemoración patriótica," *La Discusión*, May 20, 1908, 2.

67. *Cuba: Population, History and Resources*, 220.

68. Helg, *Our Rightful Share*, 141–91.

69. "Confidential Report No. 15," Major W. D. Beach, 15th Cavalry, to the Chief of Staff, Army of Cuban Pacification, September 16, 1907, in USNA, RG 199, File 014. See also "Las razas cubanas," *La Lucha*, July 15, 1907, 1.

70. Ricardo Batrell Oviedo, "Al Pueblo de Cuba y a la raza de color," July 3, 1907, in USNA, RG 350, File 2499. Different aspects of the same manifesto are analyzed in Helg, *Our Rightful Share*, 142–44.

71. Ricardo Batrell Oviedo to Secretary of War, July 16, 1907, in USNA, RG 350, File 2499.

72. "Translation of a letter referring to meeting of August 4 at San Juan y Martínez, Pinar del Río Province," enclosed in "Memorandum for the Chief of Staff" submitted by Captain John W. Furlong, Chief of the Military Information Division, August 11, 1907, in USNA, RG 199, File 159/1.

73. "Memorandum for the Chief of Staff. Subject: Organization and object of the Independent negro party," Captain John W. Furlong, September 23, 1908, ibid., File 246/7602.

74. Agrupación Independiente de la llamada 'raza de color' to Charles Magoon, October 1, 1908, in ANC, Fondo Secretaría de la Presidencia, Caja 22, Signatura 33. See also the copy furnished by Magoon to the Chief of the Bureau of Insular Affairs, in USNA, RG 350, File 2499.

75. Montero, "Cuarenta años de la restauración de la República."

76. See cover for *El Fígaro*, January 28, 1909.

77. *Duodécima legislatura*.

Chapter Seven

1. See photographs and captions of newly elected congressmen in *El Fígaro*, January 28, 1909, 41.

2. Montero, "Cuarenta años de la restauración de la República," 13.

3. Ibid., 12, 92–94.

4. Thomas, *Cuba*, 534–35, 547–56, 584, 586; Primelles, *Crónica cubana, 1919–1922*, 10–18, 28–36, 338–45.

5. Jenks, *Our Cuban Colony*; Primelles, *Crónica cubana, 1919–1922*, 375–82; Thomas, *Cuba*, 544–63; Pérez, *Cuba under the Platt Amendment*; Zanetti, *Cautivos de la reciprocidad*.

6. Primelles, *Crónica cubana, 1919–1922*, 77–81, 193–94; Dumoulin, *Azúcar y lucha de clases, 1917*, esp. 57–58, 64–67, 71, 95–96; LaFeber, *American Age*, 256–58, 260–65, 269–74, 281–84.

7. See telegrams between Frank Steinhart and Leopoldo Figueroa, Municipal Mayor of Cienfuegos, especially those dated January 15 and 18, 1909, in ANC, Fondo Secretaría de la Presidencia, Caja 71, Signatura 39.

8. See English synopsis of the "Manifesto of the Federative Committee of the Society of Cigar-makers of the Island of Cuba to the People at Large," ibid.

9. Helg, *Our Rightful Share*, 146–48.

10. Ibid., 149–53.

11. Porfirio Morgado, "Negros, ya es hora," November 15, 1909, in ANC, Fondo Especial, Caja 4, Expediente 123 (antiguo), 715 (nuevo).

12. Juan de Dios Duany, "Mal presago. El microbio moral en nuestra sociedad," ibid., Expediente 63 (antiguo), 720 (nuevo).

13. J. A. C., "Para blancos y negros. Via veritas et vita," ibid., Expediente 134 (antiguo), 726 (nuevo).

14. Helg, *Our Rightful Share*, 165–67.

15. Ivonnet to Gómez, February 3, 1910, in AMCH, Fondo Personalidades de la Guerra de la Independencia, Caja 68, Expediente 39. For confirmation of Ivonnet's military antecedents, see Secretaría de Justicia to Minister of France de Clercq, June 26, 1912, in ANC, Fondo Secretaría de la Presidencia, Caja 110, Signatura 2.

16. Helg, *Our Rightful Share*, 168–69.

17. Ibid., 167–68, 172–86.

18. Manifesto "Partido Independiente de Color. Comité de placetas. A nuestros correligionarios," March 28, 1910, in ANC, Fondo Especial, Caja 4, Expediente 131 (antiguo), 723 (nuevo).

19. Helg, *Our Rightful Share*, 164–65, 175.

20. "Grandes fiestas del Partido Independiente de Color. El Domingo 24 de Abril de 1910," in ANC, Fondo Especial, Caja 4, Expediente 132 (antiguo), 724 (nuevo).

21. Ruíz Suárez, *Color Question in the Two Americas*, 42–43.

22. Quoted in A. M. Beaupré to Philander Knox, June 4, 1912, USNA, RG 59, File 837.00/711. Another U.S. officer testified, "Several collisions between the so-called whites and blacks have taken place in the city and its vicinity. Several negroes have been killed; in fact, in the various reports of those conflicts, I find, as a rule, that the negro is always killed." See Commander in Chief to Secretary of the Navy, June 13, 1912, ibid., File 837.00/799.

23. Peterson to M. H. Lewis, June 14, 1912, ibid., File 837.00/834.

24. Estenoz to the U.S. Department of State, June 6, 1912, ibid., File 837.00/697. Official translation.

25. Estenoz to U.S. Secretary of State, June 15, 1912, ibid., File 837.00/865. See also Helg, *Our Rightful Share*, 204–5; 210–11.

26. Telegram from A. M. Beaupré to Philander Knox, June 27, 1912, USNA, RG 59, File 837.00/843; *Cuba Magazine*, July 1912, 648; R. E. Holaday to Beaupré, June 28, 1912, USNA, RG 59, File 837.00/877.

27. *La Lucha*, July 29, 1912, 1.

28. *New York Times*, June 27, 1912, 5.

29. A. M. Beaupré to Philander Knox, July 1, 1912, USNA, RG 59, File 837.00/876.

30. *New York Times*, July 18, 1912, 1.

31. The film *Salida de tropas para Santiago de Cuba durante la guerra racista o la campaña*, directed by Enrique Díaz Quesada, does not survive in Cuban film archives at the Instituto Cubano de Artes e Industrias Cinematográficas. Cited in Rodríguez, *El cine silente en Cuba*, 158.

32. Helg, *Our Rightful Share*, 194–96, 200–201, 224–25.

33. "A los Cubanos," October 1908, in ANC, Fondo Academia de la Historia de Cuba, Caja 498, Signatura 560.

34. "Los veteranos de la Independencia al pueblo de Cuba," October 28, 1911, ibid., Caja 105, Signatura 208.

35. "Ni blancos, ni negros: Solo cubanos," published in *El Veterano: Revista Cívico Militar de Intereses Generales, Suplemento*, April 23, 1910.

36. Manuel Arando, "Pro-Patria," *El Veterano* 2, no. 1 (January 9, 1910): 6.

37. "¡Alto, compañeros!," *El Veterano* 2, no. 3 (January 23, 1910): 1.

38. "A los veteranos," August 8, 1910, in ANC, Fondo Academia de la Historia de Cuba, Caja 498, Signatura 564.

39. See documents under the heading "Veteranista Agitation—Attitude of the United States" in *Papers Relating to the Foreign Relations of the United States with the Annual Message of the President Transmitted to Congress December 3, 1912*, 236–42.

40. Typed manuscript written on letterhead of the Cuban Senate and held in documents donated by the estate of Cisneros Betancourt, titled "Manifesto con motivo de la campaña de los Veteranos (no llegó a publicarse) (Lo trajo V. Villar)" in ANC, Fondo Academia de la Historia de Cuba, Caja 498, Signatura 555.

41. Ferrer, *Insurgent Cuba*, 121.

42. *Papers Relating to the Foreign Relations of the United States with the Annual Message of the President Transmitted to Congress December 3, 1912*, 241–42.

43. "Francisco Estrada Aguila, Guardia Rural, Escuadrón D, Regimento 2 y Jefe de la milicia del Pueblo de Viana," June 15, 1912, and Robau to Camay, May 31, 1912, in ANC, Fondo Secretaría de la Presidencia, Caja 110, Signatura 2, Primera Pieza.

44. C. V. Carvalho to Rafael Manduley, May 27, 1912, and José Fernández Alvarez to Juan Menocal, June 27, 1912, ibid., Segunda Pieza.

45. See A. M. Beaupré to U.S. secretary of state Philander Knox, July 19, 1912, in *Papers Relating to the Foreign Relations of the United States with the Annual Message of the President Transmitted to Congress December 3, 1912*, 309–11.

46. See telegrams from Mier to Gómez and Gómez to Mier, May 26, 1912, in ANC, Fondo Audiencia de la Habana, Caja 113, Signatura 16.

47. For a nearly complete list of attendees and account of the event, see Conte and Capmany, *Guerra de Razas*, 173–93.

48. "Dos impresos del Plano del Parque Central, con motivo del banquete dado al Ejér-

cito Nacional después de la Campaña Racista," in ANC, Fondo Academia de la Historia de Cuba, Caja 106, Signatura 235.

49. Conte and Capmany, *Guerra de Razas*, 178.

50. Menocal to José Fernández Alvarez, June 1, 1912, in ANC, Fondo Secretaría de la Presidencia, Caja 110, Signatura 2, Primera Pieza.

51. Carlos Rodríguez, Serafín Peerez, Martín Iglesias, José Mesa, Salvador Marín Alfredo Lara, Fernando Dorticó, et al., "Manifiesto de la Unión Saguera Al Pueblo," ibid.

52. Manifesto "Reproducido por varias Damas Sagiieras [*sic*]. Hablan las mujeres cubanas," June 18, 1912, ibid.

53. Manifesto "Nuestra Actitud," signed "Jovenes de Sagua. Suscripto hasta la fecha por 287 firmas," ibid.

54. Fiscal de la Audiencia de Oriente to Alcaldes Municipales, May 30, 1912, ibid.

55. Manifesto of José García Díaz, municipal judge of Caibarién, "A los hombres de color, residentes de Este Término Municipal," June 2, 1912; Manifesto of Alfredro Carnot, "Alcalde municipal de Matanzas. Orden público y policía. A los vecinos del término municipal de Matanzas," June 9, 1912; Wenceslao Galvez, Fiscal de la Audiencia de Matanzas, June 9, 1912; ibid.

56. See M. Aróstegui, Fiscal de la Audiencia de Pinar del Río, to Juan M. Menocal, Secretario de Justicia, June 12, 1912, ibid.

57. "Auto de Enrique Rodríguez Nin," June 7, 1912, and June 12, 1912, respectively, ibid.

58. "Auto del Juez Eduardo Potts y Castellanos," June 8, 1912, ibid.

59. See the case of Feliz Izquierdo y Vistores quoted June 11, 1912, in "Auto de Enrique Rodríguez Nin," ibid.

60. León Morúa Delgado to Gómez, July 30, 1912, ibid.

61. Helg, *Our Rightful Share*, 240.

62. Quoted in "Auto del Juez Dr. Pedro C. Salcedo y Cuevas," June 11, 1912, in ANC, Fondo Secretaría de la Presidencia, Caja 110, Signatura 2, Primera Pieza.

63. Alfredo P. to Oceguera, May 27, 1912, quoted in "Auto del Juez Enrique Rodríguez Nin," ibid.

64. "Auto del Juez Gonzalo del Cristo y Del Corral," June 14, 1912, ibid. The events apparently took place in the region of San Antonio de los Baños.

65. Ibid.

66. The *décima* was signed "Del guajido Seberiano Soliz pertenece al comité de Manicaragua natural de Esperanza al Sñr Esfaristo Esenos [*sic*]," undated. See "Poesía manuscrita firmada por Siteriano Solíz, dedicada a Evaristo Estenoz," in ANC, Fondo Especial, Caja 4, Expediente 137 (antiguo), 729 (nuevo). Original Spanish text:

> Cuba yo te liberté y mi sangre [h]e derramado
> Sé mé dá poco cuidado
> el baté[y] esberaba otra vez. Sabes la razón
> Cual es porqué siento el estropeo
> Los negros con gran deceo [*sic*]
> Pelearon mucho en el campo
> ahora quieres a los blancos
> y aborreces a Maceo.

Bueno es que el leon ispano [*sic*]
Buelba [*sic*] al Paíz otra vez
Porqué en Cuba no se bé [*sic*]
Unión dentro los cubanos
Yó como soy beterano [*sic*]
esta inspiración me tomo
ellos la Puerta yo el lomo
Alcanzarón del tesoro
Los blancos la estrella de oro
Los negros estrella de plomo.

67. José Santamaría et al. to José Miguel Gómez and Alfredo Zayas, August 13, 1912, in ANC, Fondo Secretaría de la Presidencia, Caja 110, Signatura 2, Segunda Pieza; José Ascencio, Ysidoro Santos Carrero, Juan Duany, Julio Antomarchi, and B. Parada to Gómez, undated, in ANC, Fondo Adquisiciones, Caja 11, Signatura 400.

68. Juan Bell to Gómez, July 29, 1912, in ANC, Fondo Secretaría de la Presidencia, Caja 110, Signatura 2, Segunda Pieza.

69. Surí Guerra to Gómez, July 30, 1912, ibid. Surí Guerra was being held in Santa Clara prison.

70. Surí Guerra, Luis Pérez Gromasa, and Francisco González to Secretario de Justicia, August 7, 1912, ibid.

71. Manuel G. González et al. to Gómez, ibid.

72. Ruíz Suárez, *Color Question in the Two Americas*, 42, *passim*.

73. Primelles, *Crónica cubana, 1915–1918*, 9–10.

74. Ibid., 33.

75. Ibid., 33–34.

76. Zayas, *Statement by Alfredo Zayas*, 8–21; Primelles, *Crónica cubana, 1915–1918*, 12–13, 147–48, 151–56, 235–36.

77. See various telegrams submitted by U.S. minister William E. Gonzales to Secretary of State Philander Knox, January 22, 1917, to February 14, 1917, in *Papers Relating to the Foreign Relations of the United States with the Address of the President to Congress, December 4, 1917*, 350–58. For the official statement of rebel intentions, see Gómez to Gonzales, undated, 370–71.

78. See correspondence between Zayas and Gonzales, March 29, 1917, through April 2, 1917, in *Papers Relating to the Foreign Relations of the United States. With the Address of the President to Congress, December 4, 1917*, 397–400.

79. Gonzales to Knox, February 15, 1917, ibid., 359.

80. Ibid., 400.

81. Gonzales to Knox, February 12, February 25, 1917, ibid., 354–55, 367.

82. Consul General Rodgers to Knox, February 13, 1917, ibid., 355–56. These numbers correspond to lists of rebels captured in Camagüey, cited below.

83. Gonzales to Knox, February 16, 1917, *Papers Relating to the Foreign Relations of the United States. With the Address of the President to Congress, December 4, 1917*, 361.

84. "Relación de las personas descartadas del jurio número 177 de 1917 Juzgado . . . por rebelión y sedición. Personas que guardan prisión y personas en libertad bajo fianza con

expresión de su significación política y social," in ANC, Fondo Secretaría de la Presidencia, Caja 115, Signatura 2. The majority of these prisoners (142) were released almost immediately.

85. Lists from Camagüey report that by November 17, 1917, when amnesty bills were being considered, 3,600 people had been processed in all, but most of them had already been released, ostensibly because of their families' connections. See lists for Camagüey dated November 1917 in "Expediente referente a los procesados de Matanzas, Camagüey y Oriente por los delitos de rebelión y sedición," in ANC, Fondo Secretaría de la Presidencia, Caja 115, Signatura 1.

86. See U.S. officials' reports to Knox, in *Papers Relating to the Foreign Relations of the United States. With the Address of the President to Congress, December 4, 1917*, 365, 369, 373–74, 376–77, 380–81.

87. See lists of prisoners for Santiago de Cuba dated October 1917 in "Expediente referente a los procesados de Matanzas, Camagüey y Oriente por los delitos de rebelión y sedición," in ANC, Fondo Secretaría de la Presidencia, Caja 115, Signatura 1.

88. Gonzales to Knox, March 30, 1917, in *Papers Relating to the Foreign Relations of the United States. With the Address of the President to Congress, December 4, 1917*, 392–93.

89. See Manduley's orders, dated June 6, 1912, in ANC, Fondo Secretaría de la Presidencia, Caja 110, Signatura 2, Primera Pieza.

90. "President Menocal's Manifesto of March 26, 1917," in *Papers Relating to the Foreign Relations of the United States. With the Address of the President to Congress, December 4, 1917*, 391.

91. Ibid., 392.

92. Ibid., 62–72.

93. Primelles, *Crónica cubana, 1915–1918*, 14–15, 146.

94. Primelles, *Crónica cubana, 1919–1922*, 153–202, 307–31.

95. Ibid., 153.

96. Ibid., 176.

97. *Papers Relating to the Foreign Relations of the United States. With the Address of the President to Congress, December 4, 1917*, 200.

98. Ibid., 131.

99. Ibid., 85, 200.

100. See Garrigó, *América*.

101. First edition sets are very rare, although available for viewing at the Centro de Estudios Martianos in Havana. See a complete listing of their contents in Trelles, *Bibliografía cubana del siglo XX*, and Peraza, *Bibliografía martiana*. For a contemporary critique and de Quesada's response, see M. Márquez Sterling, "La obra del maestro," *El Fígaro*, August 4, 1901, 334.

102. González Lanuza, *Discursos y trabajos del Doctor en la Cámara de Representantes*, 35–37; emphasis added. See also the speech of Miguel Viondi y Vera, "Cuarto período congresional, segunda legislatura, sesión extraordinaria solemne a José Martí, 19 de mayo de 1909," *Diario de las sesiones del Congreso. Cámara de Representantes*, unpaginated.

103. "Quinto período congresional, primera legislatura, 16 sesión extraordinaria solemne en honor de Martí celebrada en la noche del 19 de mayo de 1911," *Diario de las sesiones del Congreso. Cámara de Representantes*, unpaginated.

104. "Séptimo período congresional, primera legislatura, sesión extraordinaria: 19 de mayo de 1915," ibid.; emphasis added.

105. del Río et al., *Texto de la Ley que Glorifica el Apóstol* . . . ; and "Proyecto de ley declarando fiesta nacional el día 28 de enero y otorgando otros honores a Martí" in *Revista Martiniana* 1, no. 1 (October 10, 1921): 12–15.

106. del Río et al., *Texto de la Ley que Glorifica el Apóstol* . . . ; and "Proyecto de ley declarando fiesta nacional el día 28 de enero y otorgando otros honores a Martí" in *Revista Martiniana* 1, no. 1 (October 10, 1921): 12–15.

107. An example of just such a situation involved a song titled "Himno a Luz y Caballero" written by Guillermo M. Tomás and Oscar Ugarte and dated February 24, 1913. See the editor's note attached to the original printed version of the hymn, in ANC, Fondo Academia de la Historia de Cuba, Caja 500, Signatura 573.

108. See the preamble in del Río et al., *Texto de la Ley que Glorifica el Apóstol* . . .

Conclusion

1. Acosta, "La concepción histórica de Martí"; Fernández Retamar, "Martí en su tercer mundo."

BIBLIOGRAPHY

Archives—Cuba

Archivo del Instituto de Historia
    Fondo Eugenio Sánchez de Agramonte
    Fondo Ofelia Domínguez Navarro
    Fondo Rubén Martínez Villena
Archivo del Museo de la Ciudad de la Habana
    Colección Archivo Histórico Municipal de la Habana
    Fondo Personalidades de la Guerra de la Independencia
Archivo Nacional de Cuba, Havana
    Fondo Academia de la Historia de Cuba
    Fondo Adquisiciones
    Fondo Asuntos Políticos
    Fondo Audiencia de la Habana
    Fondo Correspondencia de la Secretaría de la Presidencia
    Fondo Donativos y Remisiones
    Fondo Especial
    Fondo Gobierno de la Revolución de 1895
    Fondo Máximo Gómez
    Fondo Partido Revolucionario Cubano
    Fondo Secretaría de la Presidencia
Archivo Provincial de Cienfuegos "Ritica Suárez del Villar y Suárez del Villar"
    Fondo Rita Suárez del Villar y Suárez del Villar
    Fondo Veteranos

Archives—United States

U.S. Library of Congress, Manuscripts Division, Washington, D.C.
    Leonard Wood Papers
U.S. National Archives, Washington, D.C.
    General Records of the Department of State. Record Group 59.
    Records of the Bureau of Insular Affairs. Record Group 350.
    Records of the Military Government of Cuba. Record Group 140.
    Records of the Provisional Governor of Cuba. Record Group 199.
Harvard University Archives, Cambridge, Mass.
    Harvard Summer School for Cuban Teachers

Government Documents—Cuba

Anuario estadístico de la República de Cuba formado principalmente con datos facilitados por las oficinas del gobierno o contenidos en publicaciones oficiales. Edited by Orestes Ferrara et al. Havana: Imprenta El Siglo XX, 1915.

Diario de las sesiones de la Convención Constituyente. 1901.

Diario de las sesiones del Congreso. Cámara de Representantes. 1900–1915.

Senado. Diarios de sesiones. 1906.

Ley Penal de la República de Cuba. Camagüey: Imprenta del Gobierno, ca. 1896.

Government Documents—United States

Cuba: Population, History and Resources. 1907. Washington, D.C.: United States Bureau of the Census, 1909.

Joint Resolution Inviting the Republic of Cuba to Become a State of the American Union. Remarks of Hon. Francis G. Newlands of Nevada in the Senate of the United States. Washington, 1903. Pamphlet.

Magoon, Charles. *Annual Report of the Provisional Governor of Cuba, from October 13, 1906 to December 1, 1907.* Havana: Rambla y Bouza, 1908.

————. *Annual Report of the Provisional Governor of Cuba, from December 1, 1907 to December 1, 1908.* Havana: Rambla y Bouza, 1908.

————. *Report of Cuba, Under the Provisional Government of the United States, Decrees, 1906–1909.* Havana: Rambla y Bouza, 1911.

Papers Relating to the Foreign Relations of the United States (1917–1918). Washington, D.C.: Government Printing Office, 1930.

Papers Relating to the Foreign Relations of the United States with the Address of the President to Congress, December 4, 1917. Washington, D.C: Government Printing Office, 1926.

Papers Relating to the Foreign Relations of the United States with the Annual Message of the President Transmitted to Congress December 3, 1912. Washington, D.C.: Government Printing Office, n.d.

Report of the Committee on Foreign Relations, United States Senate, Relative to Affairs in Cuba. 55th Cong., 2nd sess., Doc. 885. Washington, D.C.: Government Printing Office, 1898.

Taft, William Howard, and Robert Bacon. *Cuban Pacification: Excerpt from the Report of the Secretary of War, 1906.* Washington, D.C.: Government Printing Office, 1907.

Newspapers and Periodicals

Anales de la Academia de Ciencias Médicas, Físicas y Naturales de la Habana, 1904–7.

Cuba y América. New York, 1896–99.

Democracia. Havana, 1899–1901.

Diario de la Marina. Havana, 1901–2.

La Discusión. Havana, 1902–11.

La Doctrina de Martí. New York, 1896–98.

El Economista: Revista Financiera y Comercial. Havana, 1906.

El Esclavo. Tampa, 1891–94.

La Escuela Cubana. Havana, 1899–1901.

La Escuela Moderna. Havana, 1899–1901.

El Fígaro. Havana, 1898–1912.

Harvard Graduates' Magazine. Cambridge, Mass., 1900.

La Instrucción Primaria. Havana, 1902.

La Lucha. Havana, 1898–1911.

The Lucha. Havana, 1906–9.

La Mariposa. Trinidad, 1900.

La Nación. Buenos Aires, 1895.

The New York Times. New York, 1912.

El Nuevo Criollo. Havana, 1904–6.

Patria. New York, 1892–98.

El Proletario. Havana, 1902–3.

El Reconcentrado. Havana, 1902.

Redlands Daily Facts. Redland, Calif., 1935–36; 1973.

Reforma Social, 1915–25.

La República Cubana. Paris, 1895–98.

Revista de Instrucción Publica. 1900–1.

Revista Martiniana. Havana, 1921–22.

Revista Pedagógica Cubana. Havana, 1900–1910.

El Telégrafo: Periódico Político. Trinidad de Cuba, 1900.

El Veterano. Havana, 1910–11.

El Vigilante. Guanajay, Pinar del Río, 1900.

Other Primary Sources

Academia de Historia. *Colección de documentos. Actas de las Asambleas de Representantes y del Consejo de Gobierno durante la Guerra de la Independencia. Tomo V. (1898–1899).* Edited by Joaquín Llaverías y Emeterio S. Santovenia. Havana: Imprenta El Siglo XX, 1932.

Almanaque del maestro. 1901. Havana: Librería e Imprenta "La Propagandista," 1901.

Barbarrosa, Enrique. *El Proceso de la República, análisis de la situación política y económica de Cuba bajo el gobierno presidencial de Tomás Estrada Palma y José Miguel Gómez.* Havana: Imprenta Militar, 1911.

Batrell Oviedo, Ricardo. *Para la historia: Apuntes autobiográficos.* Havana: Seoane y Alvarez, 1912.

Beals, Carlton. *The Crime of Cuba.* Philadelphia, Pa.: J. B. Lippincott Co., 1933.

Bellido de Luna, Juan. *La anexión de Cuba a los Estados Unidos.* New York: El Porvenir, 1892.

Bullard, R. L. "The Cuban Negro." *North American Review* 184 (March 15, 1907): 623–30.

"Causes of the Cuban Insurrection. By General Faustino Guerra Puente, Leader of the Insurrectionists." *North American Review* 183 (September 21, 1906): 540.

Cisneros Betancourt, Salvador. *Appeal to the American People on Behalf of Cuba*. August 24, 1900. Pamphlet.

Collazo, Enrique. *Cuba independiente*. Havana: Imprenta y Librería "La Moderna Poesía," 1900.

——— . *La Revolución de Agosto de 1906*. Havana: Imprenta C. Martínez y Ca., 1907.

——— . *Los sucesos de Cienfuegos*. Havana: Imprenta C. Martínez y Ca., 1905.

Conte, Rafael, and José M. Capmany. *Guerra de Razas: Negros contra blancos en Cuba*. Havana: Imprenta Militar, 1912.

Delgado, Manuel Patricio. "Martí en Cayo Hueso." *Revista Cubana. Homenaje a José Martí en el Centenario de Su Nacimiento: "Los que Conocieron a Martí"* (July 1951–December 1952): 73–77.

del Río, Pastor, Joaquín Panadés, Manuel Villalón, Justo Carrillo Rubio, G. Wolter del Río, Manuel Montes de Oca, and R. Pardo. *Texto de la Ley que Glorifica el Apóstol, presentada a la Cámara de Representantes por el Dr. Pastor Del Río*. June 15, 1921. Pamphlet.

de Quesada, Gonzalo. *Free Cuba: Her Oppression, Struggle for Liberty, History and Present Condition with the Causes and Justifications of the Present War for Independence*. Edited by John Guiteras. New York: Publishers' Union, 1897.

de Velasco, Carlos. *Estrada Palma: Contribución histórica*. 2d ed. Havana: Imprenta y Papelería "La Universal," 1911.

de Zayas, Lincoln. "La apoteosis de Martí." *Revista Cubana Homenaje a José Martí* (n.d.): 143–50.

Duodécima legislatura. Segunda sesión conjunta, efectuada en el Senado, Enero 28 de 1909. Tome de posesión del Vicepresidente de la República, Señor Alfredo Zayas. Pamphlet.

Duque, Matías. *Nuestra patria: Lectura para niños*. 2d ed. Havana: Imprenta Militar, 1925.

Estrada Palma, Tomás. *Address of Tomás Estrada Palma to the American Public*. N.p., 1896.

——— . *Desde el Castillo de Figuera: Cartas de Tomás Estrada Palma*. Edited by Carlos de Velasco. Havana: Sociedad Editorial de Cuba Contemporánea, 1918.

Frye, Alexis Everett. *Manual para maestros*. Havana: n.p., 1900.

Garrigó, Roque E. *América. José Martí*. Havana: Rambla y Bouza, 1911.

——— . *La convulsión cubana*. Havana: Imprenta "La Razón," 1906.

Gómez, Juan Gualberto. "Martí y yo." In *Revista Cubana. Homenaje a José Martí en el Centenario de su Nacimiento: "Los que conocieron a Martí."* (July 1951–December 1952): 64–71.

Gómez, Máximo. *Cartas desconocidas de Máximo Gómez a Rita Suárez del Villar*. Edited by Doris Eva González and José Díaz Roque. Cienfuegos: Ediciones Mecenas, 1992.

——— . *Papeles dominicanos de Máximo Gómez*. Edited by Emilio Rodríguez Demorizi. Ciudad Trujillo, D.R.: Editora Montalvo, 1954.

González Lanuza, José. *Discursos y trabajos del Doctor en la Cámara de Representantes procedidos por su biografía*. Havana: Imprenta y Papelería de Rambla, Bouza y Ca., 1921.

Guerra y Sánchez, Ramiro. *Nociones de historia de Cuba para uso de las escuelas primarias elementales*. 2d ed. Havana: Cultural, S.A., 1931.

Historia de Manuel García. Rey de los Campos de Cuba (Desde la cuna hasta el sepulcro), por uno que lo sabe todo. Havana: Imprenta y Librería Moderna Poesía, 1898.

Inglis, William. "The Future in Cuba." *North American Review* 18 (November 16, 1906): 1038–40.

Iznaga, J. M. *Por Cuba: El Mayor General José Miguel Gómez, la política de Estrada Palma y los ideales revolucionarios. Programa de Gobierno del Ilustre General José Miguel Gómez.* Havana: Imprenta y Papelería Rambla y Bouza, 1907.

Kennedy, W. M. "The Revolution in Cuba." *Living Age* 276 (February 22, 1913): 465–67.

Martí, José. *Obras completas.* 27 vols. Havana: Editorial de Ciencias Sociales, 1991.

———. "Para las escenas." *Anuario del centro de estudios martianos* 1 (1974): 31–40.

Martí: Novela histórica por un patriota. Havana: Cultural, S.A., 1905.

Martínez Villena, Rubén. *Poesía y prosa.* Vol. 2. Havana: Editorial Letras Cubanas, 1978.

Matthews, Claude. *The Cuban Patriots' Cause Is Just, the Right Shall Prevail and in God's Own Time Cuba Shall Be Free.* Philadelphia: Charles F. Simmons, 1895.

Mayner y Ros, José. *Cuba y sus partidos políticos.* Kingston, Jamaica: Mortimer C. De-Souza, 1890.

Memoria de la administración del Presidente de la República de Cuba Mayor General José Miguel Gómez, durante el periodo comprendido entre el 1o. de enero y el 31 de diciembre de 1910. Havana: Rambla y Bouza, 1911.

Montejo, Estebán. *The Autobiography of a Runaway Slave.* Edited by Miguel Barnet. Translated by Jocasta Innes. New York: Random House, 1968.

Montero, Tomás M. "Cuarenta años de la restauración de la República." *Bohemia* (February 6, 1949): 12–14.

Mujeres que contribuyeron a Libertar [sic] a Cuba. Datos Biográficos de "La Cubanita" por Ricardo Valdés Izaguirre. Homenaje de la Asociación Nacional. Hijas de Libertadores. Delegación de Cienfuegos. A La Insigne Patriota Srta. Rita Suárez del Villar, "La Cubanita," de Julio de 1956. Pamphlet.

La nueva lira criolla. Guarachas, canciones, décimas, canciones de la guerra por un vueltarribero. 5th ed. Havana: Moderna Poesía, 1903. First published in 1897.

Primelles, León. *La Revolución del 95 según la correspondencia de la delegación cubana en Nueva York.* 2 vols. Havana: Editorial Habanera, 1932.

Reno, George. "Operating an 'Underground' Route to Cuba." *Cosmopolitan Magazine,* August 1899, 429–32.

Rubens, Horatio S. *Liberty: The Story of Cuba.* New York: Brewer, Warren & Putnam, Inc., 1932.

Ruíz Suárez, Bernardo. *The Color Question in the Two Americas.* Translated by John Crosby Gordon. New York: Hunt Publishing Co., 1922.

Salazar, Salvador. *José Martí. Conferencia leída en el Ateneo de la Habana el 10 de marzo de 1918.* Havana: Imprenta Siglo XX, 1918.

Speech delivered by Mr. Fidel G. Pierra, at Chickering Hall, New York, on the night of October 10th, 1895. Pamphlet.

Speech delivered by Mr. Fidel G. Pierra at Washington, D.C. on October 31, 1895. Pamphlet.

Suárez del Villar, Rita. *Mis memorias.* Cienfuegos: n.p., 1961.

Tejera, Diego Vicente. *Conferencias sociales y políticas dadas en Cayo Hueso.* Havana: Imprenta "El Fígaro," 1899.

———. *Diego Vicente Tejera, 1848–1903. Patriota, poeta y pensador cubano. Ensayo biográfico partical de su obra poética y política.* Edited by Eduardo J. Tejera. Madrid: n.p., 1981.

Trelles, Carlos M. *El Progreso (1902 a 1905) y el retroceso (1906 a 1922) de la república de Cuba.* Havana: Imprenta el Score, 1923.

Trujillo, Enrique. *Apuntes históricos. Propaganda y movimientos revolucionarios cubanos en los Estados Unidos desde enero de 1880 hasta febrero de 1895.* New York: Tipografía "El Porvenir," 1896.

Valdés Domínguez, Fermín. *Diario de Soldado.* 4 vols. Edited by Hiram Dupotney Fideaux. Havana: Universidad de la Habana, Centro de Información Científica y Técnica, 1972.

Varona, Enrique José. *De la colonia a la república.* Havana: Cuba Contemporánea, 1919.

Williams, Herbert Pelham. "The Outlook in Cuba." *Atlantic Monthly* 83 (June 1899): 826–38.

Woodward, Franc R. E. *With Maceo in Cuba: Adventures of a Minnesota Boy.* Minneapolis, Minn.: Scarlett Printing Company, 1896.

Zacharie de Baralt, Blanche. *El Martí que yo conocí.* Havana: Centro de Estudios Martianos, 1990.

Zayas, Alfredo. *A Statement by Alfredo Zayas on the Elections Held in Cuba, November 1, 1916.* N.p.: 1917.

Secondary Sources

Abad, Diana. *De la Guerra Grande al Partido Revolucionario Cubano.* Havana: Editorial de Ciencias Sociales, 1995.

Abad, Diana, María del Carmen Barcia, and Oscar Loyola. *Historia de Cuba II: La guerra de los Diez Años. La tregua fecunda.* Havana: ENPES, 1989.

Acosta, Leonardo. "La Concepción histórica de Martí." *Casa de las Américas* 67 (July–August 1971): 36–42.

Acosta de Arriba, Rafael. *El pensamiento político de Carlos Manuel de Céspedes.* Havana: Editorial de Ciencias Sociales, 1996.

Aguirre, Sergio. "El cincuentenario de un gran crimen." *Cuba Socialista* 2 (December 1962): 33–51.

Allen, Thomas B. "Remember the *Maine*?" *National Geographic* 193, no. 2 (February 1998): 102–7.

Anderson, Benedict. *Imagined Communities.* London: Verso, 1983.

Appel, John C. "The Unionization of Florida Cigarmakers and the Coming of the War with Spain." *Hispanic American Historical Review* 36, no. 1 (February 1956): 38–49.

Auxier, George. "Propaganda Activities of the Cuban *Junta* in Precipitating the Spanish-American War." *Hispanic American Historical Review* 19, no. 3 (August 1939): 286–305.

Barcia Zequeira, María del Carmen. *Élites y grupos de presión: Cuba, 1868–1898.* Havana: Ciencias Sociales, 1998.

Bengelsdorf, Carolee. *The Problem of Democracy in Cuba.* New York: Oxford University Press, 1994.

Berquist, Charles. *Coffee and Conflict in Colombia, 1886–1910*. Durham, N.C.: Duke University Press, 1978.

Caballero, Armando O. *La mujer en la 95*. Havana: Editorial Gente Nueva, 1982.

Cabrera, Olga. *Los que viven por sus manos*. Havana: Editorial de Ciencias Sociales, 1985.

Cabrera Alvarez, Guillermo. "Doña Leonor: La tierna opositora de José Martí." *Granma*, May 13, 1995, 3.

Carr, Barry. "'Omnipotent and Omnipresent'? Labor Shortages, Worker Mobility and Employer Control in the Cuban Sugar Industry, 1910–1934." In *Identity and Struggle at the Margins of the Nation-State: The Laboring Peoples of Central América and the Hispanic Caribbean*, edited by Aviva Chomsky and Aldo Lauria-Santiago, 260–91. Durham, N.C.: Duke University Press, 1998.

Casanovas, Joan. *Bread or Bullets! Urban Labor and Spanish Colonialism in Cuba, 1850–1898*. Pittsburgh: University of Pittsburgh Press, 2000.

Cepero Bonilla, Raúl. *Raúl Cepero Bonilla: Escritos históricos*. Havana: Editorial de Ciencias Sociales, 1989.

Chaffin, Tom. *Fatal Glory: Narciso López and the First Clandestine U.S. War against Cuba*. Richmond: University of Virginia Press, 1996.

Chatterjee, Partha. "Whose Imagined Community?" In *Mapping the Nation*, edited by Gopal Balakrishnan, 214–25. London: Verso, 1996.

de Armas, Ramón. *La Revolución pospuesta: Contenido y alcance de la revolución martiana por la independencia*. Havana: Ediciones Políticas, 1975.

Deere, Carmen Diana. "Here Come the Yankees! The Rise and Decline of United States Colonies in Cuba, 1898–1930." *Hispanic American Historical Review* 78, no. 4 (November 1998): 729–65.

de la Fuente, Alejandro. "Cuban Myths of Racial Democracy: Cuba, 1900–1912." *Latin American Research Review* 34, no. 3 (1999): 39–74.

———. *A Nation for All: Race, Inequality and Politics in Twentieth-Century Cuba*. Chapel Hill: University of North Carolina Press, 2001.

———. "Two Dangers, One Solution: Immigration, Race, and Labor in Cuba, 1900–1930." *International Labor and Working-Class History* 51 (Spring 1997): 30–49.

de Paz Sánchez, Manuel, et al. *El bandolerismo en Cuba (1800–1933): Presencia canaria y protesta rural*. Vol. 1. Santa Cruz de Tenerife: Centro de la Cultura Popular Canaria, 1993.

Diacon, Todd. *Millenarian Vision, Capitalist Reality: Brazil's Contestado Rebellion, 1912–1916*. Durham, N.C.: Duke University Press, 1991.

Díaz Quiñones, Arcadio. "Martí: Las guerras del alma." *Apuntes postmodernos* 5, no. 2 (1995): 201–27.

Doty, William. *Mythography: The Study of Myths and Rituals*. 2d ed. Tuscaloosa: University of Alabama Press, 2000.

Duara, Prasenjit. *Rescuing History from the Nation: Questioning Narratives of Modern China*. Chicago: University of Chicago Press, 1995.

Dumoulin, John. *Azúcar y lucha de clases, 1917*. Havana: Editorial de Ciencias Sociales, 1980.

Estrade, Paul. "Los clubes femeninos en el Partido Revolucionario Cubano." *Anuario de Estudios Martianos* 10 (1987): 175–92.

———. *José Martí 1853–1895 ou des fondements de la democratie en Amerique Latine.* Paris: Editions Caribeennes, 1995.

Estuch Horrego, Leopoldo. *Martín Morúa Delgado: Vida y mensaje.* Havana: Editorial Sánchez, S.A., 1957.

Ette, Ottmar. *José Martí. Apóstol, poeta revolucionario: Una historia de su recepción.* México: Universidad Nacional Autónoma de México, 1995.

Faber, Sebastiaan. "The Beautiful, the Good, and the Natural: Martí and the Ills of Modernity." *Journal of Latin American Cultural Studies* 11, no. 2 (2002): 173–93.

Fernández Retamar, Roberto. *Calibán and Other Essays.* Translated by Edward Baker. Minneapolis: University of Minnesota Press, 1989.

———. "Martí en su tercer mundo." *Cuba Socialista* 41 (January 1965): 44–49.

Fernández Robaina, Tomás. *El negro en Cuba: 1902–1958, apuntes para la historia de la lucha contra la discriminación racial.* Havana: Editorial de Ciencias Sociales, 1990.

Ferrer, Ada. "Esclavitud, ciudadanía y los límites de la nacionalidad cubana: La Guerra de los Diez Años, 1868–1878." *Historia Social* 22 (1995): 101–25.

———. *Insurgent Cuba: Race, Nation and Revolution, 1868–1898.* Chapel Hill: University of North Carolina Press, 1999.

———. "Rustic Men, Civilized Nation: Race, Culture and Contention on the Eve of Cuban Independence." *Hispanic American Historical Review* 78, no. 4 (November 1998): 663–86.

———. "The Silence of Patriots." In *José Martí's "Our America": From National to Hemispheric Cultural Studies,* edited by Jeffrey Belnap and Raúl Fernández, 228–49. Durham, N.C.: Duke University Press, 1998.

———. "Social Aspects of Cuban Nationalism: Race, Slavery and the Guerra Chiquita, 1879–1880." *Cuban Studies* 21 (1991): 37–56.

———. "To Make a Free Nation." Ph.D. diss., University of Michigan, 1995.

Foner, Philip. *The Spanish-Cuban-American War and the Birth of American Imperialism.* 2 vols. New York: Monthly Review Press, 1972.

Fornet Betancourt, Raúl. "José Martí y el problema de la raza negra en Cuba." *Cuadernos americanos: Nueva época* 2, no. 1 (January–February 1988): 124–39.

Frederickson, George M. *The Black Image in the White Mind: The Debate on Afro-American Character and Destiny, 1817–1914.* Middletown, Conn.: Wesleyan University Press, 1971.

García Galán, Gabriel. *Magdalena Peñarredonda: La Delegada. Trabajo leído por el Académico Correspondiente en Guanabacoa Dr. Gabriel García Galán en sesión pública, el día 14 de diciembre de 1951.* Havana: Academia de Historia de Cuba, 1951.

Gellner, Ernest. *Nations and Nationalism.* Ithaca, N.Y.: Cornell University Press, 1983.

Giddens, Anthony. *The Nation-State and Violence.* Vol. 2 of *A Contemporary Critique of Historical Materialism.* Berkeley: University of California Press, 1987.

González del Valle, Francisco. "El clero en la Revolución cubana." *Cuba Contemporánea* 18, no. 2 (October 1918): 140–205.

Gould, Lewis. *The Presidency of William McKinley.* Manhattan: University of Kansas Press, 1980.

Greenbaum, Susan. "Marketing Ybor City: Race, Ethnicity, and Historic Preservation in the Sunbelt." *City and Society* 4, no. 1 (June 1990): 58–76.

Guerra, Armando. *Martí y los negros*. Havana: Editorial Lex, 1947.

Guerra, Lillian. *Popular Expression and National Identity in Puerto Rico: The Struggle for Self, Community and Nation*. Gainesville: University of Florida Press, 1998.

Guerra y Sánchez, Ramiro. *Fundación del sistema de escuelas públicas en Cuba, 1900–1901*. Havana: Editorial Lex, 1954.

Gutiérrez Fernández, Rafael. *Los héroes del 24 de febrero*. Havana: Carasa y Cía., 1932.

Hagedorn, Herman. *That Human Being, Leonard Wood*. New York: Harcourt, Brace and Howe, 1920.

Healy, David. *The United States in Cuba, 1898–1902: Generals, Politicians and the Search for Policy*. Madison: University of Wisconsin Press, 1963.

Helg, Aline. "Afro-Cuban Protest: The Partido Independiente de Color, 1908–1912." *Cuban Studies* 21 (1991): 101–21.

———. "La Mejorana Revisited: The Unresolved Debate between Antonio Maceo and José Martí." *Colonial Latin American Historical Review* (Winter 2001): 61–89.

———. *Our Rightful Share: The Afro-Cuban Struggle for Equality, 1886–1912*. Chapel Hill: University of North Carolina Press, 1995.

Hevia Lanier, Oilda. *El Directorio Central de las sociedades negras de Cuba, 1886–1894*. Havana: Editorial de Ciencias Sociales, 1996.

Hidalgo de Paz, Ibrahim. *Cuba, 1895–1898: Contradicciones y disoluciones*. Havana: Centro de Estudios Martianos, 1999.

Hobbs, William Herbert. *Leonard Wood: Administrator, Soldier, and Citizen*. New York: G. P. Putnam's Sons, 1920.

Hobsbawm, Eric J. *Bandits*. London: Weidenfeld and Nicolson, 1969.

———. *Nations and Nationalism since 1870: Programme, Myth and Reality*. New York: Cambridge University Press, 1990.

Howard, Philip. *Changing History: Afro-Cuban Cabildos and Societies of Color in the Nineteenth Century*. Baton Rouge: Louisiana State University Press, 1998.

Ibarra, Jorge. *Cuba: 1898–1921. Partidos políticos y clases sociales*. Havana: Editorial de Ciencias Sociales, 1992.

———. *Prologue to Revolution: Cuba, 1898–1958*. Boulder, Colo.: Lynne Rienner Publishers, 1998.

Iglesias, Marial. "José Martí: Mito, legitimación y símbolo. La génesis del mito martiano y la emergencia del nacionalismo republicano (1895–1920)." Paper presented at the Conference of the Latin American Studies Association, Washington, D.C., March 1996.

———. "Las metáforas del cambio: Transformaciones simbólicas en el tránsito del 'entre imperios' (1898–1902)." Ph.D. diss., University of Havana, in progress.

Jameson, Elizabeth, and Susan Armitage, eds. *Writing the Range: Race, Class and Culture in the Women's West*. Norman: University of Oklahoma Press, 1997.

Jenks, Leland. *Our Cuban Colony: A Study in Sugar*. New York: Vanguard Press, 1928.

Joseph, Gilbert. "On the Trail of Latin American Bandits: A Re-examination of Peasant Resistance." *Latin American Research Review* 25 (1990): 8–52.

Kirk, John. *José Martí: Mentor of the Cuban Nation*. Tampa: University Press of Florida, 1983.

Knight, Franklin. "The Haitian Revolution." *American Historical Review* 105, no. 1 (February 2000): 103–15.

———. *Slave Society in Cuba during the Nineteenth Century.* Madison: University of Wisconsin Press, 1970.

LaFeber, Walter. *The American Age: U.S. Foreign Policy at Home and Abroad, 1750 to the Present.* 2d ed. New York: W. W. Norton & Co., 1994.

LeRiverend, Julio. *La república: Dependencia y revolución.* Havana: Instituto Cubano del Libro, 1975.

Levine, Robert M. *Secret Missions to Cuba: Fidel Castro, Bernardo Benes, and Cuban Miami.* New York: Palgrave, 2001.

Lizaso, Felix. *José Martí: Recuentro de Centenario.* Vol. 1. Havana: n.p., 1953.

Lockmiller, David. *Magoon in Cuba: A History of the Second Intervention, 1906–1909.* Chapel Hill: University of North Carolina Press, 1938.

———. "The Settlement of the Church Property Question in Cuba." *Hispanic American Historical Review* 17 (November 1937): 488–98.

López Rodríguez, Omar, and Aida Morales Tejeda. *Piedras imperecederas: La ruta funeraria de José Martí.* Santiago de Cuba: Editorial Oriente, 1999.

López Segrera, Francisco. "Imperialismo y caudillismo (1902–1933)." In *La república neocolonial: Anuario de estudios cubanos*, vol. 1, edited by Juan Pérez de la Riva et al., 130–44. Havana: Editorial de Ciencias Sociales, 1973.

Mallon, Florencia E. *Peasant and Nation: The Making of Postcolonial Mexico and Peru.* Berkeley: University of California Press, 1995.

Martínez, Juan A. *Cuban Art and National Identity: The Vanguardia Painters, 1927–1950.* Gainesville: University Press of Florida, 1994.

Martínez Alier, Verena. *Marriage, Class and Colour in Nineteenth-Century Cuba: A Study of Racial Attitudes and Sexual Values in a Slave Society.* Ann Arbor: University of Michigan Press, 1974.

Maza Miguel, Manuel P. *El clero cubano y la independencia: Las investigaciones de Francisco González del Valle (1881–1942).* Madrid: Compañia de Jesús en las Antillas, 1996.

Moore, Robin. *Nationalizing Blackness: Afrocubanismo and Artistic Revolution in Havana, 1920–1940.* Pittsburgh: University of Pittsburgh Press, 1997.

Moreno Plá, Enrique H. "Doña Leonor en la emigración." *Anuario Martiano* 1 (1969): 229–37.

Ortiz, Fernando. *Martí y las razas.* Havana: n.p., 1953.

Orum, Thomas Tondee. "Politics of Color: The Racial Dimension of Cuban Politics during the Early Republican Years, 1900–1912." Ph.D. diss., New York University, 1975.

Oviedo, José Miguel. *La niña de New York: Una revisión de la vida erótica de José Martí.* Mexico, D.F.: Fondo de Cultura Económica, 1992.

Padilla, Heberto. *Fuera del juego. Premio Julián del Casal, 1968. Edición conmemorativa, 1868–1998.* Miami: Ediciones Universal, 1998.

Paquette, Robert. *Sugar Is Made with Blood: The Conspiracy of La Escalera and the Conflict between Empires over Slavery in Cuba.* Middletown, Conn.: Wesleyan University Press, 1988.

Peraza, Fermín. *Bibliografía martiana: 1853–1953.* Havana: Comisión Nacional Organizadora de los Actos y Ediciones del Centenario y del Monumento de Martí, 1954.

Pérez, Louis A., Jr. "Approaching Martí: Text and Context." In *Imagining a Free Cuba:*

Carlos Manuel Céspedes and José Martí, edited by José Amor y Vázquez, 13–23. Providence, R.I.: Thomas J. Watson Jr. Institute for International Studies, 1996.

———. *Cuba between Empires, 1878–1902*. Pittsburgh: University of Pittsburgh Press, 1983.

———. *Cuba: Between Reform and Revolution*. 2d ed. New York: Oxford University Press, 1995.

———. *Cuba under the Platt Amendment, 1902–1934*. Pittsburgh: University of Pittsburgh Press, 1986.

———. *Lords of the Mountain: Social Banditry and Peasant Protest in Cuba, 1878–1918*. Pittsburgh: University of Pittsburgh Press, 1989.

———. *On Becoming Cuban: Identity, Nationality and Culture*. Chapel Hill: University of North Carolina Press, 1999.

———. "Politics, Peasants, and People of Color: The 1912 'Race War' in Cuba Reconsidered." *Hispanic American Historical Review* 66, no. 3 (August 1986): 509–39.

———. *The War of 1898: The United States and Cuba in History and Historiography*. Chapel Hill: University of North Carolina Press, 1998.

Pérez Carbó, Federico. "José Martí— Enrique Trujillo." In *El Archivo Nacional en la conmemoración del centenario del natalicio de José Martí y Pérez, 1853–1953*, 673–76. Havana: Archivo Nacional de Cuba, 1953.

Pérez de la Riva, Juan, et al., eds. *La república neocolonial: Anuario de estudios cubanos*. Vol. 1. Havana: Editorial de Ciencias Sociales, 1973.

Pérez-Stable, Marifeli. *The Cuban Revolution: Origins, Course and Legacy*. New York: Oxford University Press, 1993.

Portuondo Linares, Serafín. *Historia del Partido Independiente de Color*. Havana: Editorial Librería Selecta, 1950.

Poyo, Gerald A. "José Martí: Architect of Social Unity in the Emigré Communities of the United States." In *José Martí: Revolutionary Democrat*, edited by Christopher Abel and Nissa Torrents, 16–31. Durham, N.C.: Duke University Press, 1986.

———. *"With All and for the Good of All": The Emergence of Popular Nationalism in the Cuban Communities of the United States, 1848–1898*. Durham, N.C.: Duke University Press, 1989.

Primelles, León. *Crónica cubana, 1915–1918: La Reelección de Menocal y la Revolución de 1917. La Danza de los Millones. La Primera Guerra Mundial*. Havana: Editorial Lex, 1955.

———. *Crónica cubana, 1919–1922: Menocal y la Liga Nacional. Zayas y Crowder. Fin de la Danza de los Millones*. Havana: Editorial Lex, 1955.

Ramos, Julio. *Divergent Modernities: Culture and Politics in Nineteenth-Century Latin America*. Translated by John D. Blanco. Durham, N.C.: Duke University Press, 2000.

Renan, Ernest. "What Is a Nation?" In *Nation and Narration*, edited by Homi K. Bhabha, 8–22. New York: Routledge, 1990.

Riera, Mario. *Cuba política: 1899–1955*. Havana: Impresora Modelo, 1955.

Ripoll, Carlos. "The Falsification of José Martí in Cuba." *Cuban Studies* 24 (1983): 3–56.

———. *José Martí, the United States and the Marxist Interpretation of Cuban History*. New Brunswick, N.J.: Transaction Books, 1984.

Rodríguez, Raúl. *El cine silente en Cuba*. Havana: Editorial Letras Cubanas, 1992.

Romero Alfau, Fermín. *Traer a Martí. De su monumento en el Parque Central.* Edited by Pablo de la Torriente Brau. Havana: n.p., 1995.

Ronda Varona, Adalberto. "On How to Read Martí's Thought." In *Re-reading José Martí: One Hundred Years Later,* edited by Julio Rodríguez-Luis, 85–96. Albany: State University of New York, 1999.

Rotker, Susana. *The American Chronicles of José Martí: Journalism and Modernity in Spanish America.* Translated by Jennifer French and Katherine Semler. Hanover, N.H.: University Press of New England, 2000.

Santí, Enrico Mario. "Thinking through Martí." In *Re-reading José Martí: One Hundred Years Later,* edited by Julio Rodríguez-Luis, 67–84. Albany: State University of New York, 1999.

Saumell-Muñoz, Rafael. "Castro as Martí's Reader in Chief." In *Re-reading José Martí: One Hundred Years Later,* edited by Julio Rodríguez-Luis, 97–114. Albany: State University of New York, 1999.

Savala, Iris. *Colonialism and Culture: Hispanic Modernisms and the Social Imaginary.* Bloomington: Indiana University Press, 1992.

Schaffer, Kirk. "Cuban? Spaniard? Anarchist? Anarchist Internationalism Confronts the Beast of Cuban Nationalism, 1898–1925." Paper presented at the Conference of the American Historical Association, Seattle, Wash., December 1997.

Schwartz, Rosalie. *Lawless Liberators: Political Banditry and Cuban Independence.* Durham, N.C.: Duke University Press, 1989.

Scott, Rebecca. *Slave Emancipation in Cuba: The Transition to Free Labor, 1860–1899.* Princeton, N.J.: Princeton University Press, 1985.

Smith, Carol A. "Origins of the National Question in Guatemala: A Hypothesis." In *Guatemalan Indians and the State, 1540–1988,* edited by Carol A. Smith with Marilyn A. Moors, 83–90. Austin: University of Texas Press, 1990.

Soto, Lionel. *La Revolución del 33.* 3 vols. Havana: Editorial Pueblo y Educación, 1985.

Stabb, Martin S. "Martí and the Racists." *Hispania* 40 (1957): 434–39.

Stoner, Lynn. *From the House to the Streets: The Cuban Women's Movement for Legal Reform, 1898–1940.* Durham, N.C.: Duke University Press, 1997.

Thomas, Hugh. *Cuba: The Pursuit of Freedom.* 3d ed. New York: Da Capo Press, 1998.

Trelles, Carlos M. *Bibliografía cubana del siglo XX. Tomo Primero (1900–1916).* Matanzas: Imprenta de la Vda. de Quirós y Estrada, 1916.

Utset, Marial Iglesias. *Las metáforas del cambio en la vida cotidiana: Cuba, 1898–1902.* Havana: Ediciones Union, 2003.

Viotti da Costa, Emilia. *The Brazilian Empire: Myths and Histories.* Chicago: University of Chicago Press, 1985.

Wolf, Eric R. *Envisioning Power: Ideologies of Dominance and Crisis.* Berkeley: University of California Press, 1999.

Woodward, Ralph Lee. "Changes in the Nineteenth-Century Guatemalan State and Its Indian Policies." In *Guatemalan Indians and the State, 1540–1988,* edited by Carol A. Smith with Marilyn A. Moors, 59–61. Austin: University of Texas Press, 1990.

Zanetti, Oscar. *Cautivos de la reciprocidad: La burguesía cubana y la dependencia comercial.* Havana: Ministerio de Educación Superior, 1989.

INDEX

Guevara, Ernesto, 256
Guillén, Nicolás, 237
Gutiérrez Alea, Tomás, 255
Guzmán, Eduardo, 184

Haiti and Haitians, 9, 16, 56, 129, 201, 229, 235, 248
Harvard University, 99, 103; Summer School for Cuban Teachers, 95, 103–8
Havana, 1–2, 5, 59, 94, 109–10, 124–25, 130, 133, 139, 142–45, 154, 157, 159, 167, 190, 199, 213–17, 221, 228, 233, 240, 244
Havana Commercial Company, 138; Havana Trust Company (after 1906), 207, 213. *See also* Strikes
Helg, Aline, 11
Hidalgo Santana, María, 60
Hobsbawm, Eric, 13
Hugo, Victor, 53

Iglesias, Marial, 11
Immigration and immigrants, 226; Spanish, 2, 10, 38, 128, 146–50, 202–3, 232; Antillean, 203
Ivonnet, Pedro, 228, 231, 240

Jamaica, 37–38
Janney, Samuel M., 85
Jesus Christ, 42, 61, 96, 164, 166, 215, 227

Keil, Marie, 99
Key West, 5, 30, 34, 44, 50, 52, 71, 85, 210, 213
Knights of Labor, 30

La Liga Antillana (Antillean League), 16, 23, 28, 34, 38–39, 43
Lara, Saturnino, 111
Ley Morúa (Morúa Law), 228, 239
Liberalism: as movement in Latin America, 65
Liberals and Liberal Party, 140, 143, 146, 148, 150, 153–54, 157–61, 163–64, 168–91, 193, 196, 198–203, 205, 209, 213, 217, 220–21, 223-30, 234–39, 241–54, 257

Liberating Army, 49–53, 60, 83, 86, 89, 93, 103, 128, 174, 180, 226; rebel soldiers of (*mambises*), 49, 63, 83, 87, 92, 234; supporting forces of (*impedimenta*), 58; female rebel soldiers of (*mambisas*), 60–62
Loynaz del Castillo, Enrique, 145, 182, 199–200, 221, 231–32, 244

Maceo, Antonio, 5, 17, 25, 30, 39, 49, 52–53, 57, 59, 81, 83; memory of, 96–97, 111, 120, 163, 209, 227, 240–41, 247
Maceo, José, 23
Machado, Gerardo, 259
Magoon, Charles, 193–208, 211–14, 216–21, 223–24, 228, 257
Mallon, Florencia, 13
Mambises and *mambisas. See* Liberating Army; Women: as revolutionaries
Manifesto of Montecristi, 83, 133, 233
Manigua (liberated zones), 49–50, 56–58, 62, 78, 94
Mantilla, Carmen, 78–79
Martí, José: commemorations of, 1, 2, 17, 77, 94, 96–97, 115, 123, 154–55, 163, 181, 194, 221–22, 237, 241, 247–53; death of, 1, 45, 47–48, 87, 209, 246; mythification of, 3, 4, 7, 21, 24–25, 91, 113–18, 164, 167, 185, 191, 194, 225, 255–56, 258–60; social unity as ideal of, 4, 6, 7, 25–29, 37, 42, 44–45, 101–2; as Cuban messiah or apostle, 4, 18, 23–24, 36, 42–43, 63, 116–17, 121, 132, 165, 187, 191, 227, 252–53; political activities of, 10, 16, 27, 30, 37–41, 62, 66–68, 70–71, 76; social unity as embodied by, 14, 25, 47–48, 57, 88, 115, 119, 123–27, 131, 133–34, 137, 150–51, 154, 156, 168–69, 221, 225, 259; and workers, 31, 43–44, 59, 166; racial attitudes and views of, 31–36, 38–41, 230, 233, 235; views on class struggle of, 42
Martí y Zayas Bazán, José, 198–99, 221, 223, 231, 236, 244
Masó, Bartolomé, 119, 124, 132, 163
Matanzas, 53, 60, 104, 206, 213, 239, 244

Matthews, Claude, 76
McKinley, William: U.S. presidential administration of, 69, 85, 87, 92, 97, 110, 198
Méndez Capote, Domingo, 114–15, 174, 199
Méndez Capote, Fernando, 174
Menocal, Juan, 237
Menocal, Mario, 109, 187–88, 223–24, 237, 239, 243–47
Messonier, Enrique, 110, 120–21, 138
Miret, Agustín, 186
Miró, José, 111, 120–21
Moderates and Moderate Party, 136, 146, 148–49, 156, 164, 168, 169–91, 193, 257
Montalvo, Rafael, 169, 174
Monteagudo, José de Jesús, 111, 182, 231, 236
Morgado, Porfirio, 227
Morúa Delgado, Martín, 133–35, 137, 141, 148, 157, 223, 227, 239
Mutual aid societies, 35, 112, 130

Nation: and nationalism as category of analysis, 12–14, 90; definition of, 14–15, 18; and pro-imperialist nationalist actors, 15, 19, 24, 41, 72, 87, 115, 118, 121, 128–30, 132, 136–38, 145–46, 148, 150, 154, 156, 163–65, 168–70, 176, 190, 196, 221, 224, 228, 235, 254, 258; pro-imperialist nationalism, 15, 50; and revolutionary nationalist actors, 16, 19, 24, 41, 51, 60, 87–88, 98, 114–15, 121–22, 132, 135–38, 140, 142, 145–46, 148, 150, 153, 160, 176, 181, 191, 196, 210, 220, 224, 235, 254, 258; revolutionary nationalism, 16, 30, 49–50; popular nationalism, 17, 19, 24, 49, 52; and popular nationalist actors, 41, 49–51, 77, 80, 87–88, 90, 92, 94, 101, 109, 113, 118, 121–23, 127, 131–32, 134, 137, 139, 144–46, 148, 150, 153, 160, 162, 166, 181, 185, 190–91, 193, 196, 202, 207–10, 221–22, 224, 228, 235, 242, 253, 258; within context of 1895 War, 51–66, 74, 77, 83; after 1895 War, 103, 112, 125, 134, 140, 154, 160, 162, 169, 202
National Convention Party, 140, 157

National University of Havana, 139, 141, 202
New York, 18, 28–29, 37–38, 44, 48, 50, 59, 62–64, 68–69, 75, 84, 89, 99, 123–24, 169, 177, 178
Nuñez, Emilio, 39, 120, 183

Oceguera, Félix, 240
O'Farrill, Juan, 125, 136, 140–44, 157, 175
Olney, Richard, 64
Oriente, 92, 104, 120, 124, 136, 159, 167, 235, 238, 243, 245

Pact of Zanjón, 9, 23
Palomino, José de C., 104
Panama and Panama Canal, 197–98
Paredes Gómez, José, 125
Parrilla, Justo P., 102
Partido Independiente de Color (PIC), 217–19, 226–29, 233, 236, 240–42, 244, 246, 249
Partido Revolucionario Cubano (PRC), 16, 23, 27–28, 36–39, 43–45, 52, 59, 61–62, 66, 69, 72, 76–87, 89–90, 92, 119, 123, 125, 129, 139; *Patria* as newspaper of, 16, 28, 33, 35, 42, 47, 68, 82; revolutionary clubs affiliated with, 16, 37, 48, 52, 70–71, 73, 77–80, 94–95
Peasants, 20, 51, 59, 204, 245; as noncombatants (*pacíficos*), 49, 53–54, 91–92, 120, 136
Peñarredonda y Doley, Magdalena, 59–62, 92–93, 112, 144, 182
Pérez, Leonor, 42, 115, 166
Pérez, Louis A., 11–12
Perna, Luis, 96
Philadelphia, 75
Pierra, Fidel, 44, 75–77, 81
Pinar del Río, 59, 100, 159, 171, 174, 184, 186, 197, 207, 239–40, 244
Platt Amendment, 1, 118, 120, 143, 188, 190, 224, 226
Póveda de Ferrer, Antonio, 128–29
Public schools. *See* Education: public system of

161, 190, 195; military of, 170, 197, 204, 209, 223, 228; and abuses of U.S. soldiers, 193–94, 206–7

Valdés Domínguez, Fermín, 17, 57, 125, 139
Valdéz, Ramón, 158
Valverde, Nicolás, 227
Varela, José, 174
Varona, Enrique José, 68, 96
Vatican, 94
Veterans: of Cuban independence wars, 14–15, 20, 159, 226, 232–34; black veterans, 56, 111, 122, 127–33, 135–36, 142, 144, 148, 150, 159, 174, 196, 217, 220, 235, 257
Veterans' Movement of 1910–11, 225, 233–34, 236, 249
Virgin of Charity, 61

War of 1895, 1–8, 10, 12, 14, 15–18, 20, 25, 27, 35–36, 38, 44–45, 48, 50, 52, 57–59, 64–88, 119, 132, 159, 164, 168, 175, 177, 190, 198, 225–26, 228, 247, 257; memories of, 94–96, 153–54, 191
Weyler, Valeriano, 59, 60, 81, 91

Whitening: as cultural ideal, 34–35; as racial mixing, 147
Women, 18, 37; as revolutionaries, 58–62, 77–78; as political activists, 92–94, 210, 239–40
Wood, Leonard, 92–94, 96, 107, 110–13, 119, 129, 204, 214
Woodard, Franc R. E., 81
Workers, 10–11, 16, 20, 28, 49, 59, 63, 90, 108–10, 112, 122, 125–27, 143–44, 172, 180, 196, 208–11, 214, 216, 220, 224, 226, 257–58. *See also* Strikes

Ximénez de Sandoval, José, 47
Xiqués Arango, Juan R., 145, 163

Yero, Eduardo, 68–69, 74, 162
Yero Miniet, Luis, 97

Zacharie de Baralt, Blanche, 29
Zayas, Alfredo, 179, 188, 199–200, 222–23, 243–45, 247
Zayas, José, 85
Zola, Emile, 213